W9-BZB-222

The Greenwood Encyclopedia of Homes through World History

The Greenwood Encyclopedia of Homes through World History

Volume 3

The Industrial Revolution to Today,
1751 to the Present

James Steele

With research by Olivia Graf

Greenwood Press
Westport, Connecticut · London

Library of Congress Cataloging-in-Publication Data

Steele, James, 1943–
   The Greenwood encyclopedia of homes through world history / James Steele ;
   with research by Olivia Graf.
     p. cm.
   Includes bibliographical references and index.
   ISBN 978–0–313–33788–8 (set : alk. paper) — ISBN 978–0–313–33789–5 (vol. 1 : alk.
   paper) — ISBN 978–0–313–33790–1 (vol. 2 : alk. paper) — ISBN 978–0–313–33791–8
   (vol. 3 : alk. paper)
1. Architecture, Domestic—History—Encyclopedias. 2. Dwellings—History—
Encyclopedias. I. Greenwood Press (Westport, Conn.) II. Title. III. Title: Encyclopedia of
homes through world history.
NA7105.S74   2009
728—dc22   2008018310

British Library Cataloguing in Publication Data is available.

Library of Congress Catalog Card Number: 2008018310
ISBN: 978–0–313–33788–8 (set)
        978–0–313–33789–5 (vol. 1)
        978–0–313–33790–1 (vol. 2)
        978–0–313–33791–8 (vol. 3)

First published in 2009

Greenwood Press, 88 Post Road West, Westport, CT 06881
An imprint of Greenwood Publishing Group, Inc.
www.greenwood.com

Printed in the United States of America

The paper used in this book complies with the
Permanent Paper Standard issued by the National
Information Standards Organization (Z39.48–1984).

10 9 8 7 6 5 4 3 2 1

Contents

Contents

Contents

Acknowledgments

The author would like to thank the following people for their special contribution to this series: Debra Adams, Tadao Ando, Rasem Badran, Shigeru Ban, Ken Breisch, Soo K. Chan, Hannah Choi, Balkrishna Doshi, Frank Gehry, Olivia Graf, Joan Jacard, The Aga Khan Award for Architecture, Gloria Koenig, Kengo Kuma, Jimmy Lim, Laurence and Lillian Loh, Thom Mayne, Richard Meier, Alex Mosely, Eric Moss, Abdul Harris Othman, Yatin Pandya, Stefauor Polyzoides, Dimitre Porphyrios, Richard Rogers, Maria Romanach, Rockwell and Marua Schnabel, Julius Shulman, Christopher Steele, Robert Venturi and Denise Scott Brown, Abdel Wahed El-Wakil, Zhang Xiu and Pan Shiyi, and Ken Yeang.

Introduction

AN AGE OF GLOBAL CHANGE

The historical period covered by this volume is tumultuous and diverse due to the rapid growth of the importance of science and technology. This resulted in the Industrial Revolution in one part of the world at its start and the continuation of other traditions that were unaffected by this cataclysm elsewhere. Vast social and economic changes occurred in the countries where this revolution started, and these expanded, like the ripples caused by throwing a stone into a pond, until they affected all other cultures throughout the world. These effects are perfectly reflected in the domestic architecture in both the developed and the developing world today.

The most obvious legacy of the Industrial Revolution has been the explosion of manufactured consumer goods that are now available to everyone and the growth of the advertising profession needed to sell them, in both electronic and print forms. In his treatise *The English House*, written in 1856, Hermann Muthesius argued that the entirety of industrial production is evident in the individual house and the way that people of different income levels fit it out. He also said that if Germany wanted to excel in manufacturing it would be beneficial for educators to study both the design and contents of the typical Arts and Crafts home in England at that time. His theory finally resulted in the establishment of modern design principles taught at the Bauhaus Universität in Weimar and Dessau.

The Industrial Revolution made possible the mass production of traditional construction materials such as brick and lumber, as well as the manufacture of new products, such as float glass, steel, and reinforced concrete. This revolutionized house design because conventional solid bearing walls could be replaced with steel or reinforced concrete columns and glass walls, allowing more flexible floor plans and light.

Introduction

The need for resources to feed the Industrial Revolution led to Colonial enterprise, which imposed foreign styles on indigenous societies. Independence movements after World War II resulted in a retranslation of vernacular traditions.

The progress of domestic architecture throughout the world then, during the period covered here, can be tied directly to the trajectory of the growth of consumerism, initiated by the Industrial Revolution at its start. A theoretical challenge to the Modern Movement, which itself was based on the idea of progress, first took place in the 1960s, just before the advent of the Information Age. While postmodernism ostensibly reflected a general social trend toward diversity, and a return to tradition, it was really just an amplification of those forces, as was the equally short-lived trend labeled "Deconstructivism," which concentrated even more heavily on the notion of human values being overwhelmed by the growing technological imperative launched at the end of the eighteenth century.

Marshall Berman, in his landmark book *All That Is Solid Melts into Air*, captured the essence of this historical period when he said, in part, that

> The maelstrom of modern life has been fed from many sources: great discoveries in the physical sciences, changing our images of the universe and our place in it; the industrialization of production, which transforms scientific knowledge into technology, creates new human environments and destroys old ones (and) speeds up the whole tempo of life. . . .

The impact that these dramatic changes had upon the domestic architecture on the countries that were most directly affected by them is difficult enough to measure, but what of those areas, in Africa, Asia, and elsewhere that were initially bypassed by them entirely? It has too often been assumed that the discoveries that Berman refers to were uniformly distributed, but consider that there is one fact that could be mentioned to show otherwise. When Newcomer's Engine, which was a steam-powered pump used to drain water from tin and coal mines and is one reliable marker of the beginning of the Industrial Revolution, was unveiled in 1717, the Tokugawa Shogunate was only about halfway through its more than two century run. During that time, Japan was almost completely isolated from the outside world, until a military flotilla led by American Commodore Matthew C. Perry forced it to open up to trade with the West in 1861. It was not the only international instance of a country that industrialized only under duress, but it is certainly the most graphic example of the political and social upheavals that occurred throughout the
world from the eighteenth century onward. These weakened the leadership of established power bases as social diversity started to increase. This shift was evident by new forms of government that started to emerge, ranging from democratic to socialistic.

The change that Berman describes was accelerated by new or improved communication systems, as the media, fueled by commodification, made information available to everyone in the developed world, raising awareness of changing styles, including those of residential architecture. Once these styles were linked to commercial cycles, they became shorter in duration and subject to a decreasing span of consumer interest. The need for more resources to support rapid industrialization in the developed world also fed a growing network of colonial exploitation. Throughout the British Empire, for example, which extended into countries as diverse as Egypt, India, Malaysia, and Singapore, this meant the importation of a foreign western culture, as well as its residential conventions into a number of different traditional societies, with hybridity being the result. British colonial societies typically have a tripartite organization being deliberately divided into a military zone, where soldiers lived, the civil lines, which were set aside for bureaucrats, administrators, and their families, and the preexisting city, where the indigenous population lived. Many of the homes described here come from one of these sectors, or, like the Straits Shophouse, are a result of the cultural fusion that resulted from their inevitable interaction.

Colonization, which affected much of Africa, Asia, and South America, depended on trade, which became a worldwide industry as a result, increasing social interaction, and domestic styles and trends along with it. This, in turn, provided support for international banking systems, which then became powerful autonomous institutions.

The progressive improvement of manufacturing techniques extended to building materials and systems as other residential examples described here indicate. Fordism, or the use of interchangeable parts that were mass produced using strict quality control regulations and then put together using industrial methods also had direct application to the construction trades, even though this did not happen as quickly as some architects, like those involved in the Case Study House Program in post–World War II Los Angeles, would have liked. A process for the commercial production of steel was invented by Henry Bessemer in 1850, and Josef Monier realized that the tensile qualities of steel would be a perfect marriage to the compressive strengths of cement, combining them into reinforced concrete in 1867.

These new manufacturing techniques also provided architects with larger sheets of float glass, milled timber, Portland stone, and many more new materials to select from, increasing putting traditional crafts and building methods at risk, in the process. In one sense, the delayed industrialization of the developing world has meant that many of these crafts have been preserved there, adjusting for local cultural traditions.

THE CONSEQUENCES OF INDUSTRIALIZATION

In the first stages of the first Industrial Revolution in what is now the developed world, just as we are seeing in its equivalent in the developing sector today, communally based cottage economies were replaced by factory production centered in the urban areas to take best advantage of the potential of scale and proximity to transport. Transportation, including steamships, trains, streetcars, and automobiles, and the canals, railroad tracks, and highways that they travel on, increased exponentially over the three centuries covered here. As factories were built in cities, such as London, Birmingham, Manchester, and Glasgow in the United Kingdom, or Lowell, Massachusetts, in the United States, the demographics of such countries were radically altered. Rural urban migration and the dislocation of entire community populations resulted in the disintegration of old social ties and values. Only a few visionary architects, such as Adolf Loos fully realized the implications that this shift had on residential design, and his insights changed the direction of modern architecture.

As more people moved from the countryside to the cities in search of work that was then denied them in their existing towns and villages, slums with extremely high population densities sprawled almost overnight, with a concomitant rise in social problems such as homelessness, drug use, crime, prostitution, and disease. Long work hours in poor conditions for low wages, predominantly carried out by women and children, as well as huge discrepancies in the lifestyles and life expectancy of those who actually did the labor and those who benefited from its proceeds, in combination with the social problems mentioned earlier, resulted in a backlash. In Britain this took the form of child labor laws. The first, in 1819, prohibited employers from hiring children under nine years old and limited workers to ten and a half hours a day. Trade unions were established in England in 1871. At the same time that the Child Labor Law was being signed, the British public was enthralled by *Ivanhoe*, by Sir Walter Scott, showing their eagerness to escape to an earlier, less complicated time. In 1848, John Ruskin wrote his *Seven Lamps of Architecture*, followed in 1851 by *The Stones of Venice*, with its famous chapter "On the Nature of the Gothic." In that chapter, which contains the seeds of what would happen in modern architecture over the next century, Ruskin set out to correct what he believed to be the misrepresentation that the Gothic style is derived from natural forms. In it, he connects architecture to moral, rather than simply technical, issues. He maintained that human imagination is necessary to prevent design from becoming a purely scientific exercise, which is relevant today, in a time of ready-made "flat pack" homes and computer-aided design as it was when he wrote it more than a century and a half ago.

Ruskin was at the leading edge, following Augustus Welby Northmore Pugin, of what would later become the Arts and Crafts Movement, which spread rapidly from Britain throughout the rest of Europe and America by the end of the twentieth century. He and William Morris, who followed him, became the social conscious of a nation that had become inured to the shocking discrepancies associated with Britain's and, by extension, the rest of the developed world's industrial miracle. While he finally came to understand that it was impossible to return to the world that Sir Walter Scott described in his novels or that the Pre-Raphaelite leader Dante Gabriel Rossetti fictionalized in his paintings, Morris did concur with Ruskin's conclusion that Gothic architecture was a perfect antidote to the soul killing and backbreaking routine of assembly line production because it had a moral rather a technical basis, and sprang from an altruistic, collective, and deliberately anonymous social intention rather than an egoistic, profit-oriented, individualistic one.

Each of the houses included here, including a majority of the most contemporary examples, responds in either an active or a reflexive way, to the industrial phenomenon that dominates the period at hand. The unwilling departure of millions of people from their rural paradise, and their attempt, supported by architects and planners, to recover it, led some designers to try to ameliorate the harsh lives of those who did leave the countryside for the city. The surge of colonialism caused by a rush for the natural resources needed to support industrial growth and the ultimate failure of such enterprise, due to exploitation. The cultural interaction that industrialization and the colonial initiatives that fled it ultimately led to, as a precursor, globalization. These are as legible in the Salinger House designed by Malaysian architect Jimmy Lim near Kuala Lumpur in the 1990s as they are in the houses built for mill workers in Lowell, Massachusetts, in 1831, or the Robie house in Chicago, built for a factory owner in 1909 by Frank Lloyd Wright, who started his career as an Arts and Crafts advocate and remained one for the rest of his life, trying to reconcile "Art" with the "Machine."

1

The Americas

NORTH AMERICA: THE EAST COAST

H. H. Richardson: The Ames Gate Lodge

For all of his famous contributions to the history of American architecture such as Trinity Church in Boston or the Marshall Field warehouse store and the Glessner House in Chicago, or even his contribution of a prototypical library design that became ubiquitous along the East Coast at the end of the nineteenth century, Henry Hobson Richardson is best known to many admirers as the architect of the Ames Gate Lodge in North Easton, Massachusetts.

A Precursor of an American Icon This rather diminutive house, which was commissioned in the early spring of 1880 and finished about a year later, has a following that far exceeds its size for several important reasons. The first of these is that it established a precedent for a more casual American domestic lifestyle. The second, which derives from the first, is that this precedent eventually evolved into the bungalow typology, which was one of the most popular house styles in the history of the United States, primarily between the First and Second World Wars.

The gate lodge was expected to play only a minor role as a guesthouse and refuge for the male members of the Ames household when it was commissioned, but has now eclipsed the main parts of the estate, designed by Snell and Gregerson in 1859 and John A. Mitchell in 1876. Richardson was a close friend of F. L. Ames, and they, along with the famous American sculptor Saint-Gaudens, had visited Sherman, Wyoming, in 1879. They were inspired by the rough-hewn ranches and hunting lodges that they saw there, but Richardson emphasized the use of boulders to an unexpected extent in his reinterpretation of the lodge he had seen in the West.

In his rendition in Massachusetts, which intentionally straddles a road entering the north side of the Ames estate as if protecting the inner sanctum of the family, Richardson has used boulders on every external surface, except for the Longmeadow brownstone used as trim around the windows, the glass of the windows themselves, the wood used to support the roof of an entry porch and the railings around it, and the reddish orange clay tiles used on the roof.[1] The boulders are graded in size, so that the biggest are at the foundation and get smaller moving up the walls to the roof.

The exclusive use of boulders for the walls, and their decreasing size from the bottom of the exterior walls to the top, give the gatehouse a compact, massive, primitive, and elemental appearance, as if rocks that had been found in a field had been piled up and a thin roof had been hastily built over the rudimentary structure for temporary occupation. Very low eyebrow dormers on the roof, along with a thin eave line and minimal projection of a chimney, also combine to put the emphasis on the unfettered rustication below.

The interior of the lodge, which is divided into a sitting or living room and servants' quarters on the ground floor of the main house and four bedrooms and a "bachelor's hall" on the first, as well as a two-story orangery in an extended wing across the road, has intentionally been treated with a bit more sensitivity by the architect than the exterior. It is predominantly fitted out with wood paneling painted bluish green to complement the color of the stone.

There are several especially innovative features in some of the rooms. One of these is a turret-like window, with its own steeply pitched roof leaning against the formidable tapering stone tower that encloses the main stair, to provide light to the lower reaches of the run. The second is a covered corner porch connected to the upstairs "Bachelor's Hall," which has a secondary projection over a well below. This has been designed to allow water to be drawn up in a bucket to this large room. The "Hall" also has a corner fireplace, which conforms to the asymmetrical approach that Richardson has taken throughout the rest of the house.

It is the casual, almost random, layout of rooms that provides the most prescient indication of good things to come in the domestic architecture of America. As he did in this case, Richardson generally designed for wealthy clients, but the less formal, nonsymmetrical room arrangement he used in the Ames Gate Lodge was soon to become more widely accepted across the social spectrum only three short decades after this house was finished. In its own time, the Ames Gate Lodge also established a trend toward rustic getaways on a private or even public scale, while it is built of dressed ashlar rather than natural boulders. The country retreat called Wyntoon that Bernard Maybeck designed for Phoebe Hearst in 1902 is of the same genre as the Ames Gate Lodge, since, in addition to its chiseled lava rock walls, it also has a fair amount of rubble stone and local timber in sight, as well as a glazed green tile roof.

In the public realm, the Ahwahnee Lodge, in Yosemite National Park, which was built in 1927, is a monumental testimony to the enduring allure of Richardson's fantasy, which seemed to evoke rugged American individualism and pioneer spirit. There are other parallels, such as Parc Guell in Barcelona by Antoni Gaudi, completed in 1900.

Frederick Law Olmstead, who also contributed invaluable advice and planning to the Vanderbilt mansion called Biltmore, in North Carolina, described elsewhere here, provided a landscape plan for the Ames estate as well, which was carried out between 1886 and 1887.

Richard Morris Hunt and Frederick Law Olmstead: Biltmore

There are few instances in the history of architecture in which a visionary client has collaborated with a talented architect and landscape architect to good effect, without the ego of one of them getting in the way. Nero claimed to have designed the Golden House and its vast landscaped grounds in the middle of Rome, as did Cardinal Woolsey at Hampton Court. Versailles also comes to mind with a historical collaboration between King Louis XIV and Le Brun, Mansart, and Le Notre, as do various projects such as Deanery Garden by Sir Edwin Lutyens and Gertrude Jekyll, but there are few others. Biltmore, which was designed and built for George Vanderbilt by architect Richard Morris Hunt and the legendary landscape architect Frederick Law Olmstead, is one of them. Thanks to Olmstead's vision, which his client shared, Biltmore is much more than a house; it became the model for forest conservancy at a critical juncture in American history.

The Vanderbilts George Washington Vanderbilt was one of eight children of William Henry Vanderbilt. William Henry was the oldest son and heir to the fortune of Cornelius Vanderbilt, who had established it by building up a fleet of steamships. He expanded these into holdings of small railroad lines connecting New York City to his shipping lanes on the Great Lakes, and finally consolidated

The Biltmore House   *Source:* AP / Wide World Photos

all of this into the New York Central railroad system. When he died in 1877, he left an estate worth more than $100 million. William Henry was very conservative and when he died, only eight years after his father, he had doubled the estate. His two eldest sons, Cornelius II, and William K., received the bulk of this because they were directly involved in the management of the family's railroad interest, but George Vanderbilt received $10 million, which was even more substantial at that time than it is now.

George visited Asheville, North Carolina, with his mother soon after his father's death because it was well established as a resort for the wealthy. While riding outside of town, on a ridge above where the Swannanoa and French Broad Rivers meet, he decided he would like to have a house there because of the beautiful view.[2] He bought a few acres at first, incrementally increasing his property until it reached 125,000 acres. He had worked with architect Richard Morris Hunt on several projects before this, such as a library that he had sponsored on West 13th Street in New York City and on the family estate at New Dorp on Staten Island as well as on several remodeling projects. He asked Hunt to design a modest country retreat for him on this site. He then commissioned Frederick Law Olmstead, who had designed the landscape around the family mausoleum, to consult on the grounds. Olmstead had previously designed Central Park in New York City and had been the landscape architect for the Capitol Building in Washington, D.C. He had also produced a visionary plan including a series of open spaces for Los Angeles, California, which, unfortunately, was never implemented. As a consequence, that city is one of the most impoverished in terms of public parks in the United States. Because of his training and aesthetic preferences, Hunt was in favor of a formal, French garden in the immediate area of the house, whereas Olmstead preferred a more organic approach in the English tradition, similar to the loosely structured language he had used in the Central Park design. In the end, Hunt and Olmstead reached a happy compromise, in which a more naturalistic method of organization was used along the three-mile approach from the front gate to the main house, slowly giving way to a more formal one, so that the garden directly in front of the house matches its chateau-like style.

By 1891, when the design phase began, these grounds had reached 6,000 acres, and Olmstead wisely advised that Vanderbilt begin a thorough survey of the property including an inventory of plants and trees.[3] Hunt, in the meantime, had convinced Vanderbilt to expand his expectations for the house itself, convincing him that a large property should have a residence big enough to balance it. Olmstead was on site for some time before Hunt arrived for his first visit and had determined the best location and orientation for the new house, based on wind direction, view, and the best line of approach. He also determined that, because of the relatively poor quality of the soil and the number of trees in the valleys, the majority of the property should be planted as forest, as a viable commercial enterprise that would also allow the land to be preserved. Olmstead presented his idea to George Vanderbilt in terms of a self-sustaining estate that would provide a public service and be a benefit to the nation as well. Both Vanderbilt and Hunt were swayed by Olmstead's ideas. The plans that followed, which were staked out in 1889, dealt with the cold winter wind from the northwest by having a large courtyard, containing all of the service functions in it, on that side. This made it possible to focus on the view from the southeast that had attracted George Vanderbilt to this site in the first place by placing a broad terrace there at the edge of the steep slope and the valley below. The house was subsequently moved slightly to the east because of foundation considerations, but these general conditions remained the same.

Biltmore Vanderbilt named the estate Biltmore, after the town of Bildt, in Holland, where his family had originated, along with "more," which is an old English word meaning rolling hills.[4] Hunt did not actually visit the site until 1890, and by that time work on the grounds was already well underway. Hunt's background was rooted in the *Ecole des Beaux-Arts* in Paris, and he was one of the first American students to be admitted there. He was a Francophile and had designed a townhouse on Fifth Avenue in New York City for George's older brother, William K. Vanderbilt, based on the style of Loire Valley chateaux. This house, with its white limestone façade and fine detailing, stood in sharp contrast to the rather drab brownstones next to it and started a trend for similar "chateauesque" houses among the rich. Including Biltmore, Hunt designed another six houses in this French Renaissance style, but the one in Asheville, with 255 rooms, is certainly the largest of these.

While Hunt used the country houses along the Loire River in France as an inspiration, he interpreted elements from them rather than literally copying them, so that his own personality is evident in each design. Following the eclectic tendency of the time, in which historical periods were seen as stylistic phases that could be freely adopted from, Hunt also used other styles throughout the house, such as Italian Baroque and Spanish Mission.

The Chateau of Blois is the most obvious direct influence on the design of the Biltmore, and the reason is clearly the similarity of their siting. Biltmore, like Blois, has been placed at the edge of a prominent ridge, seeming to continue its vertical face, as the human-made crest of a natural precipice. The west façade of Biltmore, which overlooks the river valley, is very reminiscent of the approach elevation of its French equivalent. Blois was the favorite of Francois I, and it is here that he hosted Leonardo da Vinci, where the Italian Renaissance architect and artist actually died. Blois has a famous winding stair, which Hunt copied in mirror image on the eastern entrance elevation of Biltmore, placing it just to the left of the front door leading into a long, narrow entrance hall. This establishes a pattern throughout the remainder of the main façade of asymmetrical parts added to a basically symmetrical elevation, which enlivens it enormously. An English style conservatory, called the Winter Garden, has been placed on the opposite side of the entry, balancing the Blois-like stair to the left.

In spite of its size, Biltmore actually has only four main rooms on the ground floor of the main house. In addition to the Winter Garden, which is a square in plan with its corners clipped off to accommodate stairs up into it at each of those points and has a glass ceiling that culminates in a dome, these are a gallery that is perpendicular to the entrance hall and the library at its far, southern end, to which it connects. The fourth main room is the Banqueting Hall on the other side of the Winter Garden, to the north. There are also less grand spaces, such as a music room and a smaller dining room, which the family preferred when they were alone because it was more intimate and provided a clear view to the mountains.

The library held more than 10,000 books and reflects George Vanderbilt's inquiring intellect. He studied architecture and art, and spent a great deal of time in this room. It is rectangular, with a huge fireplace on the long wall next to the entrance from the gallery, as the north-south axis, and has two large windows overlooking the terrace and the view in that direction to the south. Bookshelves full of leather-bound treasures run up the entire height of the wall to the ceiling soaring high above. The extensive use of wood on these walls, as well as the fireplace mantle and windows, combined with oriental carpets and tapestries on the sections of wall not covered by shelves, makes this a dignified and inviting scholar's retreat, in spite of its scale.

The Banqueting Hall at the other end of the longitudinal axis that Hunt has used to organize these large spaces opens directly into the Winter Garden, which obviously served as an area to receive guests before dinner was served. It is also rectangular and is slightly larger than the library opposite to it. Unlike the library, however, the Banqueting Hall is a cavernous space, which, in spite of its wood parquet floors and fireplace, seems inhumanly large at 42 feet wide and 72 feet long, with a 70 feet high ceiling.

George Vanderbilt married Edith Stuyvesant Dresser, who was related to Peter Stuyvesant, the last Dutch governor of New York.[5] They had a child, Cornelia, who was born at Biltmore in 1900. George died unexpectedly after surgery for a minor ailment in 1914, and his wife subsequently sold off 100,000 acres of the property. It was then made part of the public forest system of the United States, forming the center of the Pisgah National Forest. Through the foresight of Frederick Law Olmstead and the generosity of George and Edith Vanderbilt, their home in Asheville served more than just a private role, becoming a model of environmental stewardship that others may now follow.

Gwathmey Siegel Architects: The De Menil House

Francois De Menil is a member of the De Menil family, based in Houston, Texas, which is well known for its philanthropy and support of the arts. The De Menil Gallery in Houston, designed by Renzo Piano and sponsored by family matriarch Dominique De Menil, is eloquent testimony to this support. In 1978, Francois De Menil approached Gwathmey Siegel Architects and asked them to design a house for him on a site near the beach in the South Fork district of Long Island. At that point, he lived in Manhattan and wanted a house he could escape to on weekends. The house, which took four years to design and build, ended up as a three-story high, four-bedroom retreat that is 11,000 square feet in size. Mr. De Menil spent only about six years in the house, which was put up for sale in 1988 for $12 million. He was a bachelor when he commissioned it, but subsequently married, and the couple had their first child in 1986. His intense involvement in the process of realizing the house was also instrumental in turning his interest toward architecture and, when he was 36 years old, he entered Cooper Union in New York City to get a professional degree. He then joined the firm of Kohn Pedersen Fox. Architects typically do not want to live in houses designed by other architects, no matter how special the house is, and want to design their own. That was the case with Francois De Menil and one of the reasons behind his decision to sell the Gwathmey Siegel–designed house. It certainly was not because of a lack of space.[6]

Toad Hall In discussing his impressions of the house, which he inexplicably named Toad Hall during the relatively short time that he, and then he and his wife and son, had lived there, Mr. De Menil offered the insightful observation that a great work of architecture transcends a specific time or inhabitant. This characteristic may also be applied to each of the houses in the later historical periods that have been included in Volumes I and II of this set. This also presents the apparent paradox of a house being specifically designed for one person or family in a way that is directly related to their personal habits and lifestyle, then being sold several times over the lifetime of the dwelling to people who do not share those patterns. The number of examples that may be used to illustrate this discontinuity are legion and include Fallingwater, the Tugendhat House, and the Villa Savoye. In these cases, however, each of the houses has now been taken into trust by some organization or other and opened to the public as a museum, or three-dimensional time capsule of the cultural values that prevailed when the house was built. Assuming that to be the case with the De Menil house, it is relevant to ask: what are the values that it presents and preserves, in addition to its obvious allegiance to the excesses that seemed to identify the decade in which it was built in America?

A Regional Take on the Five Points Before he entered into partnership with Robert Siegel, Charles Gwathmey was included, along with Richard Meier, Peter Eisenman, Michael Graves, and John Hejduk, in a definitive book entitled *Five Architects*, published in 1961. The premise of the book was simply that these five designers, who did not work together, shared a recognizable affinity with the principles put forward by Le Corbusier, as specifically defined by his "Five Points of a New Architecture." These five points, which Le Corbusier intended as a shorthand way of remembering the larger issues being addressed by the Modern Movement when he published them in the early 1920s, started with the grid, which was the most important one of the five, and generated, or determined, the rest of them. The grid was a code word for the much larger structural transformation that had taken place as a result of the new construction materials, such as steel and concrete that had been made available to architects and engineers because of the Industrial Revolution, making it possible for them to explore point loaded systems instead of the uniformly loaded bearing wall that they had been restricted to in the past. This transformation was not really all that new, since the builders of the Gothic cathedrals had done the same thing in their invention of the rib vault in the thirteenth century, which made it possible to bring structural loads from the roof and the walls down to the ground in clusters of vertical piers, or columns. This allowed them to move on from using a single massive wall as the Romanesque builders who preceded them were forced to do. The limiting factor for the Gothic builder, however, was being forced to use stone, since reinforced concrete and high strength steel were not available to them. They pushed stone to the limit of its structural capacity, but they were still limited by the spans it was capable of providing. The curtain wall that the point load system makes possible is also evident in the Gothic cathedral, in dramatic contrast to its Romanesque counterpart, which has few openings in the massive walls that are typical of that style.

The Grid Provided Freedom Reinforced concrete or steel columns, and the beams they supported, provided the engineer or architect with the opportunity of achieving longer spans, and were most effective and efficient when placed on a module, or grid. This is the designation used by Le Corbusier as his first point. His second and third points, which are the "free plan" and "free elevation," follow on logically from the first in that, as with the example of the Gothic cathedral, both the interior space and the walls were allowed to be more open once the burden of carrying the roof was transferred to the columns and they were freed from that task. This meant, in the contemporary condition, that the interior walls of a building could be placed at will, without having to worry about their bearing capacity or structural role. They could, in fact, be treated as screens or partitions, as they are in the Tugendhat House by Ludwig Mies van der Rohe, without touching the ceiling at all.

The same freedom then applied to the use of exterior walls, which were delivered from their historical burden of having to carry the load of the roof and floors along with their own considerable weight. This led to the "free elevation" that Le Corbusier refers to. The fourth point, which is the strip window, relates to the free elevation, in that the possibility of substituting a long horizontal window that ran across the entire elevation then replaced the smaller opening used in the bearing wall, which had to be modestly sized because of the difficulty in transferring the structural load around it. The strip window as used by Le Corbusier in his design for the Villa Savoye became a proud declaration of the new opportunities offered by the structural grid. The last of the five points was the roof garden, which was representative of the possibility of using the grid, or point load system of reinforced concrete or steel columns, to lift a building off the ground entirely. This is extremely difficult to do with a bearing wall system. To celebrate this possibility, Le Corbusier recommended the replication of the ground plane that was freed up by suspending the building above it, by having a garden on the roof as well. This is less clear than the first four points, which seem to flow logically from each other.

The Five Points in South Park Charles Gwathmey and Robert Siegel differ from the other members of the so-called "New York Five" in adapting this Corbusian shorthand to the American, and specifically the East Coast, tradition of carpentry and timber construction. They have attempted to find parallels between the use of reinforced concrete and steel and this venerable heritage, in an effort to translate it into a regional language. They are not the first high profile Modernists to do so, since Walter Gropius did the same thing in the house he designed for himself and his wife, Ise, in Lincoln, Massachusetts, in 1938. In that instance, Gropius spent a considerable amount of time traveling around that region of New England and analyzing the vernacular architecture there before he conceptualized the design, and he was impressed with the ways in which earlier builders had adopted British construction techniques to local conditions.

A Processional Route Gwathmey and Siegel still used concrete and steel as well as wood in the De Menil house, but have adapted the tradition of a natural tongue and groove exterior skin to Corbusian principles. In the De Menil residence design, they have also adopted what Le Corbusier referred to as the "processional" route in his own use of that device at the Villa Savoye. In that instance, he deliberately placed the house in the middle of a large, slightly convex site ringed with trees, so that it could best be appreciated in three dimensions as a beautifully crafted architectural object as one approached it by car, and then closed in on it, in an ever-decreasing spiral along a driveway that finally ends up beneath the house, which is raised up on columns to receive the car.

A Processional Route The processional route that the architects have used in East Hampton is less lyrical and far more formal, due to the fact that the house had to be located near the ocean and was designed as two conjoined linear bar buildings running parallel to the beach to take maximum advantage of its privileged location. The arrival sequence begins in a wooded area proceeding into the property and starts in earnest after the driveway leads through a security gate, turns at a right angle to the west, and then makes another to the south, which then puts it, and those approaching the house, on a direct access with its elongated entrance elevation. The visual experience of moving along the route is heightened after passing through a wall that is deliberately placed across it, and passing by a large pond on its left-hand side with a long single file row of Linden trees planted along its entire length on its right. There is also a uniformly wide rank of outdoor sports facilities, including a tennis court and a swimming pool, leading up to the house on the left.

There seems to have been a deliberate intention on the part of the architects to use the first of the two long, narrow façades that are placed perpendicular to this formal processional path as a barrier, to finally stop it, and to heighten the contrast with the openness of the other side of the house, which faces the ocean. Except for a glass conservatory that takes up about one-quarter of the length of the three-story entry elevation, the general impression the house gives is solidity. This is predominantly conveyed by a large expanse of the narrow vertical tongue and grooved wooden strips that have been used to sheath the exterior walls. These are treated and exposed to weather to whiten naturally in the salt sea air. There is a gap at the far right-hand side of this bar, created by a first floor bridge leading to a stair up to the roof at that end of the house. This frames a fleeting glimpse of the ocean through the scrub on the dunes beyond, but the overall effect is otherwise one of imposing grandeur. Scale is mitigated somewhat by the gabled roof of the greenhouse, which subliminally conveys a traditional image of domesticity and shelter, but on balance the mood is somber, at best.

The entry side of the house faces north, so the architects have been fortunate in having the view to the ocean coincide with an advantageous solar angle as well. They took advantage of this by extending both the north and south elevations and shortening those to the east and west to make them solid to cut down on solar gain. There is a long, thin wooden canopy placed high above the south-facing ocean front elevation to regulate the glare caused by the sun on the water from that direction and to unify the disparate parts of an elevation that extends horizontally for more than 100 feet. It is on this elevation that the Corbusian lineage of this house is most evident, since the tall vertical supports that hold up this high canopy roof march along in a regular modular order as a reminder of the important role that the grid plays as a communicative device in this adopted language. The grid on this ocean front elevation also supports numerous balconies obviously intended to provide viewing platforms for looking out to the sea, on the first floor, above the dunes.

The greenhouse acts as both a spatial buffer between the driveway and parking lot on the entry side and the living areas of the house itself beyond, and a temperature regulator because of the plants and trees that thrive there. A fanciful, curvilinear balcony projecting out into it from the house side on the upper levels stitches it to the interior. The use of polished stone or wood on all of the interior floors, and the absence of carpets that might trap sand, as well as the generous use of glass block in the walls of the entry foyer, master bedroom, and elsewhere throughout the house give the interiors a brittle, formal, almost cold feeling that seems out of keeping with a day or weekend at the beach.

Richard Meier: The Smith House and Douglas House

Richard Meier is one of the most prominent architects in America. He came to international attention soon after he graduated from Columbia University in the mid-1960s. At that time, he made an alliance with four other architects and together they published a book called *Five Architects*. The direction they shared was the work of the French architect Le Corbusier. They each translated the work of this heroic modernist in a slightly different way, but they also had a deep respect for his groundbreaking ideas. The basic premise that they shared can be summarized in what Le Corbusier called his "Five Points." These five points amount to a shorthand diagram of the breakthroughs that Modernism was able to make possible. They are all predicated on the point, which is what Le Corbusier called the grid. What he meant by the grid was the use of the column as opposed to the bearing wall. The column, or point load system, of architecture that was introduced during the Modern Era was made possible by industrial materials such as concrete and steel. The column differs from the bearing wall in that it allows the complete structure to be held up by a series of vertical supports rather than a continuous wall. The difference between the grid and the bearing wall then is the basis for the next four points that Le Corbusier listed.

The second of these points is the possibility of making a floor plan more flexible because the bearing walls have been eliminated. Le Corbusier referred to this as the free plan, since it provided the architect with more options in locating various areas in the house. Walls used in the free plan only served as room dividers and did not carry any structural weight. So, they could be shaped differently than walls in the past. They could curve or be angular rather than be straight.

The third criteria of the five points was what Le Corbusier called the "free elevation." By this he meant that, because of the point load system provided by the grid of columns, the exterior wall no longer needed to support the floors or the roof of the house. And so simply because the exterior wall was like a curtain drawn across the columns and was not doing all of the structural work, this is referred to as a curtain wall.

This freedom from structural requirements led to the fourth point, which Le Corbusier referred to as the strip window because it allowed for long narrow openings to be drawn across the entire elevation of the house. In a bearing wall condition, openings must be treated carefully because the structural weight is transferred from the roof to the ground in a uniform way. In engineering terms, this kind of loading is called homogeneous and isotropic. This uniform loading means that a window cut into the wall disrupts the uniform flow of forces and these must be dealt with by putting a horizontal lintel across the top of the window to deal with them. This is not necessary with a curtain wall, which is basically much lighter than a bearing wall and in which the architect must only deal with the weight of the material of the wall itself, rather than the structural forces caused by the roof. Openings in the curtain wall can be much larger. In his own work, Le Corbusier used long narrow horizontal windows on purpose as a way of expressing the new freedom provided by the grid.

The fifth point that Le Corbusier added to his shorthand was the roof garden. This flows less logically from the starting point of the grid than the free plan, the free elevation, and the strip window, but does have a rationale of its own. Le Corbusier felt that the innovation of the point load system provided by the column made it possible to eliminate the basement that was usually necessary because of the bearing wall structure used in the traditional house prior to the industrial revolution. To emphasize that point, he felt that putting a patio or garden on a roof of a house would be symbolic of the area that was freed up by using the grid at ground level.

The Smith House The architects that shared Le Corbusier's idea of the five points and who were featured in the publication that included Richard Meier, called *Five Architects*, became known as "the New York Five." Richard Meier's particular take on the ideas of his Modernist mentor involves a consistent attempt to expand on these five points, to stretch the boundaries of the ways in which they can be expressed.

One of the first residential examples of his method of doing this is the Smith House, which was built in Darien, Connecticut, between 1965 and 1967. The Smith House is located on a dramatic one-half acre site on the shore of the Long Island Sound. This site slopes down to the water, dropping gently at first and then more sharply as it reaches the shoreline. Meier has established a formal line of progression from the parking lot and garage across the site toward the water and has placed the house perpendicular to this line of progression. He has then established a series of layers from the entrance at the back of the house toward the front, which overlooks the water. These mark a movement from an area of privacy in the back to the public areas in the front. This sets up a series of points of discovery for the visitor to the house that are carefully choreographed by the architect to provide a sense of surprise and delight when the final view across the water is revealed.

The first stage in this sequence of discovery is finding a pathway that connects to the entrance driveway. This pathway steps gently downward, ending at a bridge that crosses over a divide between the land and the main entry, which is at the upper level of the house. The doorway of this entry then leads into a small foyer and then to a balcony with a railing that provides a view down into a three-story high space and through a large glass window to a view of the Connecticut coast and beyond. In addition to his adherence to the ideas of Le Corbusier, Meier frequently shows references to the work of architect Frank Lloyd Wright in gestures like this. Meier, like Wright, uses the idea here of bringing a visitor into a situation of doubt by having the main entrance on a blank wall followed by a small entrance vestibule and then providing the final dramatic surprise of a spectacular view of the entire house and the water in the distance. This sequence is reminiscent of one that Frank Lloyd Wright orchestrated so carefully in the Hollyhock House described elsewhere in this volume. In that instance, Wright also begins the entry sequence at the parking lot and garage area, leading on to a thin pathway up through a long and narrow arcade to a heavy massive metal door. This door is easier to open than it looks because Wright took great care in detailing the hinges so that they would open easily, belying the appearance of weight that the door has. After negotiating the door, the person entering the house is also faced with a very small, constricted entrance vestibule and must also negotiate a sharp turn into a loggia, before being rewarded by a breathtaking view into a central courtyard and the vista of the mountains beyond. Meier magnifies that experience by placing the entrance on an upper level, thereby providing the visitor with both a view outward into the distance and downward into the house itself. This provides a clear sense of orientation into the entirety of the house. There is a stairway on the right side of the main doorway that is part of the private half of the house in the back. This is the main source of connection between all the floors. Other spaces in this private or service zone include a kitchen and master bedroom wing. This whole area is differentiated by the open, transparent volume of the living area in the front near the water by being surrounded by bearing walls. But the front elevation facing the view is the *pièce de résistance* of the residence and best describes Meier's intention, even at this early stage, to expand on Le Corbusier's five points.

The grid, which is the first point, is clearly expressed by the architect as a series of four equally spaced round columns that extend from the ground floor level all the way to the roof. The free plan, which is the second point of Le Corbusier's shorthand, is evident in the volumetric explosion of space on the inside. The strip window that was used by Le Corbusier, which is the third point, is expanded by Meier to become a series of large plate glass windows with no mullions or dividers of any kind to maximize the view outward as well as the amount of natural light coming in. Meier uses a series of horizontal bands that correspond to the floor lines of the levels behind them, which interlock to create an exciting visual counterpoint for those looking at the house from the water's edge. This counterpoint is extenuated further by the vertical element of the chimney, which balances the interlocking horizontals. Meier further utilizes this vertical element almost as a sculpture by pulling it away from the front elevation. This allows it to appear to be freestanding when it is seen by those entering the house by the back and looking at it from their high vantage point of the balcony above.

In addition to being a highly talented architect, Richard Meier is also an accomplished artist as was his mentor, Le Corbusier. He confines himself, however, to the rigorous discipline of small collages that are rarely larger than one foot square. He has continued to do collage during his long career and, like Le Corbusier, has used this medium as a way of exercising his compositional skills and testing his organizational ideas. The front elevation of the Smith House is a clear testimony to the efficacy of his collage exercises, since it is an elegant example of his ability to achieve compositional balance. In this instance, in one of his earliest works, he also shows his discipline in being able to achieve this balance within a very constrained framework in which each element is carefully placed to achieve a final goal. An additional element in this balance is a second stairway, which leads from the living room area in the front of the house out and down to the ground level and to an outside patio beside the water.

At this early point in his career Meier also established an element of his architectural language in that the Smith House is entirely white except for the use of natural wood for the floors. This choice of an entirely white palette, which Meier has strictly adhered to with few exceptions throughout his entire career, is not a spontaneous choice, but has deep ideological significance. By doing this he aligns himself with the Modernist principle that all references to historical style should be eliminated, because such references would underscore class differences as well as be a reminder of the problematic legacy of the past. In his most famous purist houses such as the Villa Savoye and the Villa Stein, Le Corbusier also adhered to this all-white palette for similar reasons, and because of these eliminated the gable roof as well. The neutral image of the flat roof and the all-white palette, then, was intended to support a more universal, egalitarian position. Meier has supported this image most uniformly with the notable exception of the Getty Museum in Los Angeles, which he designed in the late 1990s. In that case the client required that he use natural materials on the outside of the buildings. At first Meier reluctantly turned to the use of Carrara marble but mitigated its rough characteristics by having it cut and faced in a very mechanistic way. However, as the two houses described here indicate, he enthusiastically embraced the all-white image of the Villa Savoye and has even exceeded it. An additional reason for the selection of this image is that it makes the house stand in stark contrast to its natural surroundings, setting up a paradoxical relationship between the human-made structure and nature. This image of the machine in the garden has been a compelling fantasy throughout the Modern Movement, representing the unwritten intention of architecture in opposition to nature. This intention is expressed most clearly by the fact that the windows in the front elevation of the Smith House facing the water are fixed glass. Only the doorway leading to the stairs, which provides access to the water, is operable. This begins a pattern, which can be traced throughout Meier's work, of a separation of using glass as a means of dividing the interior of the house from the natural world. These large areas of glass, however, allow natural white light to flood into the interior, creating dramatic shadows, which are constantly changing during the day as the sun moves across the sky. This is especially true near the water where reflection augments these shadows. The result is a paradox of glass being used as a means of separation between the inside and outside as well as a transmitter of light into the interior. This paradox also leads to a magical sense of almost celestial light, which plays off the abstract white surfaces of the walls and ceilings of Meier's houses.

The Douglas House The second example of Meier's virtuosity in expanding on the Modernist vocabulary of Le Corbusier is the Douglas House, which he designed in 1973. This house is in Harbor Springs on a high bluff above the shore of Lake Michigan and shares many characteristics with the Smith House, which Meier designed a decade earlier. It is much larger than the Smith House but is also entered by crossing a bridge from the back of the house, which leads through a screen wall. In this instance it leads into a tight glass-enclosed vestibule that provides selected views out and down into a vertiginous three-story high living room space. The similarity between the Douglas House and the Smith House continues in the division of the rectangular profile placed perpendicular to the line of entry into a solid back portion, which is relegated to the private functions of the house. A glass-enclosed multistory open portion to the front is given over to the more public uses as in the Smith House, and there is also a stair to the right of the entrance connecting all of the floors of the house. In addition, there is a secondary stair leading to the waterline at the left of the public spaces in the front. The chimney here is also used as a sculptural element detached from the front wall of the house, but in this case it has a pair of circular flue stacks, which give it a more mechanistic appearance. These stacks underscore another similarity between Meier's houses and those of Le Corbusier in that they all convey the subliminal image of being an ocean liner. The story behind this image relates to Le Corbusier's love of modern means of transportation that were being developed during the early part of his career in the 1920s, such as airplanes, ocean liners, and railroad trains.

These breakthroughs at the beginning of the Modern Age fostered a cult of speed that culminated in several architectural movements such as the Futurists and the Constructivists that were dedicated to translating them into architectural form. In a book he wrote in the early 1920s called *Vers Une Architecture*, Le Corbusier cites the engineers who were then designing ocean liners, airplanes, railroads, trains, and automobiles as being more innovative than architects at that time, and of also being at the leading edge of a new age. He adopted some of the language of the ocean liner in his work, most notably in the pipe railings that he used along the ramp that leads up through the center of the Villa Savoye, the mechanical stacks that protrude from the roof, which look like the smokestacks on an ocean liner, and the thin parapet walls that are intentionally designed to look like gunwales. The use of the roof garden or deck on the top of the Villa Savoye also recalls similarities with the deck of a ship, so that the house finally has the appearance of sailing across the sea of grass, which is the site around it. Because of their sitting on fairly steep slopes near the water's edge, both the Smith and Douglas Houses do not have quite the same image as sailing off into the sunset, but the Douglas House does have the look of a ship coming through the trees toward the water. In addition to the two round vertical smokestacks at the top of the chimney, the metal railings and the exterior stairway leading down from the living room to the forest floor also help to contribute to a nautical image that recalls Le Corbusier as well.

As in the Smith House that preceded it, the Douglas House interiors are revealed to the visitor incrementally by a very carefully planned experience of procession. When approaching the house from the road at the top of the mountain on which it sits and through the woods behind it, guests first perceive it as a small one-story linear strip hidden behind the trees. They then cross a bridge and see the hillside sloping steeply away from them. Only then are they able to realize that there is a five-story structure below. The view toward Lake Michigan is still blocked at this point. The bridge leads into a screened deck, and then visitors enter into a glazed curved conservatory and are able to see the magnificent lake in the distance. When they move down the main stairway past the bedroom floor to a mezzanine level that overlooks a double high living room space, they have an even clearer view of Lake Michigan and the tops of the evergreen trees that cover the mountains below. Moving down another level brings guests to the main living room. Beneath this living room floor are the dining room and kitchen, which also have spectacular views toward the lake. The lowest level of the house is a podium base in which the mechanical room and the basement storage rooms are hidden.

Space is a Key Component The idea of procession, which is used in both the Smith and Douglas Houses as well as in all of Meier's other projects, is a key part of his Modernist heritage. The central part of that tradition is the character of interior space and the sequence in which a person is exposed to it. All of the other factors in the building such as structure, natural light, and materials are secondary players in a drama that revolves around the major actor, which is space. This is a key element in the Modernist belief that space as an almost tangible element in the architectural experience has the power to uplift, inspire, thrill, and transform a person who is exposed to it. And so the processional sequence in both the Smith and Douglas Houses is central to the entire idea of each design, to squeeze as much emotion out of the viewer as possible. Living in this house from day to day obviously increases exposure to the interior space and is intended by the architect to be an inspiring and transformative experience.

Expanding on the Five Points In the Douglas House, Meier experimented further with the five points of Le Corbusier that he introduced in the Smith House earlier. In this instance in Michigan, he uses a tartan grid rather than a regular spacing of columns. This tartan grid of wide bay and narrow bay, which marches across the front elevation of the house, is used to emphasize the view through the central axis and the wide bay that is located there. The narrow bay corresponds to the chimney and so emphasizes its verticality. The plan arrangements of each of the two houses are relatively similar, although the Douglas House is much larger and taller. The third point of the free elevation corresponds to the first point of the tartan grid as does the fourth point of the strip window. In the Douglas House, the notion of the strip window is transformed into a checkerboard of wide and narrow spaces in each direction. The roof garden in the Douglas House becomes a screened-in viewing platform designed to heighten the anticipation and delayed surprise of people entering into it before they are provided with the opportunity to see the spectacular view of the lake that is given to them once they are inside of the house.

In other residential projects, Richard Meier also favors the method of using a ramp as a main circulation system throughout a house as his mentor Le Corbusier did in Villa Savoye. And so the Smith and Douglas Houses are exceptions in this regard. The technique of using a ramp accentuates the idea of the exposure to interior space mentioned earlier because it slows the pace of the observer down and allows one to focus on the quality of the volumes of space that are being presented by the architect. A ramp takes up far more area inside a house, and so it is a major commitment by a client to accept it as an alternative to a stairway. But the advantage of a ramp as far as a modernist like Richard Meier is concerned is that it does not require the person using it to be concerned about looking down when they want to be sure of their step as a stairway does. The idea here is similar to one used by Japanese garden designers who use the spacing and roughness of the materials through the pathways in a garden to control when viewers look up and down. This was especially important during the Preindustrial Age in Japan when men wore long robes and women wore kimonos and stacked wooden shoes. When the garden designer wanted the people to look down and not be so aware of their surroundings, he would make the paving stones rough so they had to look carefully at the ground to negotiate them. When he wanted them to look up and be surprised by the view he created for them, he made the paving smooth so they would not have to worry about tripping or falling down. The ramp as a device in the processional ritual serves the same purpose, and Meier, like Le Corbusier, uses it to encourage people to look up and appreciate the spaces he created. The decision not to use the ramp in the Douglas House was obviously driven by the confined vertical volume of the house. In this case, he uses the stairs as a way of punctuating the progressive exposure to the view outside, allowing ample opportunity to stop at each landing to gradually introduce the progressive discovery of spaces that he is involved in creating.

Louis Kahn: The Esherick and Fisher Houses

While many of his contemporaries were caught up in the search to expand the structural possibilities inherent in lightweight industrial materials, such as steel, aluminum, and glass, architect Louis I. Kahn (1901–1974) wrestled with more substantial issues, such as historical continuity, basic human values, social relevance, and environmental appropriateness. Because he was initially unable to reconcile the basic premise of Modernism, defined by one of the movement's most prominent founders, Mies van der Rohe (1886–1969), as the expression of the technology of the times, with its poor performance and lack of popular appeal, Kahn sought a clearer mandate in a quality he described as timelessness.

A More International Background Kahn's father emigrated from Estonia, then part of Russia, to the United States in 1904, with his wife and three children, including Louis aged five, following a year later. Kahn's birth in Russia at the dawn of the new century and the dire economic circumstances his family endured during his childhood in Philadelphia have been described as both an unfortunate twist of fate and a blessing in disguise. He had just graduated from the University of Pennsylvania in the mid-1920s when Modernism was about to come to full flower in Europe. The Great Depression and subsequent onset of World War II were epic obstacles to the beginning of a promising career. However, the extreme poverty of his youth, which at one point forced his family to move 17 times in two years in the heavily industrialized Northern Liberties neighborhood in Philadelphia because they could not pay the rent, made him resilient and inventive. And his delayed rise to prominence meant that when major building commissions did finally materialize in the 1950s (when he was in his mature fifties), he was singularly qualified to redirect the antipopulist course of Modernism, write the final chapter of its heroic phase, and lay the groundwork for the diversity that he singularly helped to make possible. In sharp contrast to Frank Lloyd Wright, who was the only other American architect of sufficient intellectual stature at that time to have effected such momentous change, Kahn had a more immediate empathy with the European birthplace of the Modern Movement, as well as a common touch. Unlike Wright, the third generation of a Welsh family from the American heartland, who began his career as a society architect in the exclusive Chicago suburb of Oak Park and became the epitome of the upper class, white Anglo-Saxon Protestant establishment architect, Kahn was an outsider, the first generation of his working-class family to be educated in the United States, with a radical set of social sensibilities. These were quite unlike the exclusive notion of democracy that Frank Lloyd Wright tried to express in what he cryptically called a "usonian" architecture, his own code word for democracy. While Kahn was also exposed to American philosophers that extolled the virtues of independence even if at the expense of social norms and the common good, the exigencies of his background would not allow him to indulge in the same flamboyant behavior that Wright did. Wright seemed to relish scandal; Kahn managed to avoid it. Even while breaching similar social constraints, he kept up the appearance of a normal family life since marriage was among the institutions that he believed should be protected.

To an extent unsurpassed in their relatively short national history, Americans have experienced an unprecedented change in lifestyle in the three decades between 1920 and 1950. The Depression followed by World War II created a pent-up demand for housing exacerbated by the baby boom that followed. Significant legislation discouraged renovation of inner-city dwellings, encouraged the construction of new single-family houses in the suburbs, and facilitated the building of a highway system to reach them, giving a new breed of property developers the opportunity to supplant the architect as the arbiter of public taste. Architects in general failed to anticipate this change and reacted with disdain when it occurred, abdicating responsibility for mass housing, the domestic future of their country, and one of the major components of the Modernist agenda as a result. At the end of his career, Frank Lloyd Wright boasted of having built houses in every state in America, but they were all custom designed reserves for the rich. Aside from his admittedly visionary Broadacre City plan, which was a utopian proposal for organizing the suburbia that he then knew was inevitable, Wright led the retreat to the Ivory Tower that many architects of his generation were proud to emulate, to their cost. Half a century later, those who continue to adhere to that model are in real danger of being professionally marginalized, while for others Kahn's enlightened activism offers an inspiring alternative, leading the seemingly inexorable transmutation from high to popular culture, fueled by globalization. He showed the way.

An Early Concern for Housing In the 1950s, during the presidency of Dwight D. Eisenhower, the United States experienced an economic surfeit. Prosperity was accompanied by a desire for stability and a concern that his legacy be passed on to posterity. For the first time since the nation's early history, when Neoclassicism was chosen for many buildings in Washington, D.C., because of its associations with Ancient Greek democracy and the style reverberated across the United States, there was renewed speculation about the possibility of a national style, until a gathering storm ended this reverie. Throughout his early career, Kahn attempted to have the middle class rush to the suburbs include the economically disadvantaged as well. In housing projects such as Pine Ford Acres, Pennypack Woods,

Carver Court, Stanton Road, Lincoln Highway, Willow Run, Lilly Ponds, and Mill Creek, he demonstrated early in his career that he understood the threat the demographic shift to exurbia posed to the Modernist ideal of equal access to shelter as well as the architect's role of mediator in this process. His valiant attempt to redefine that ideal, so that it might more readily conform to an inexorable urban exodus, was recognized by his peers who were then able to accept him as the architectural mediator of sociological change.

Kahn dearly loved Philadelphia because it had given him so many life-changing opportunities, and by extension he revered the institutions it had historically fostered. He also understood that the organizations that had evolved from social interrelationships in the past would have to change to adapt to new conditions, but he believed that, in spite of such changes, certain elemental aspects present in the formation of each tacit social contract should remain immutable. During this period of redefinition of what an institution should be, he was fascinated by what he called "beginnings," thinking back when designing a school, for example, to the time when people "who did not know they were students" sat under a tree listening to someone who did not use the title of teacher. In this way he sought the essential nature of education, realizing that the details made necessary by curricular shifts or technological innovations did not alter this critical relationship.

A Volatile Time Consider that from the time when Kahn's major public building, the Yale University Art Gallery, appeared in 1953 until his death in 1974 the United States experienced John F. Kennedy's version of Camelot with his space program, the Lunar Landing, and his tragic assassination in Dallas in 1963. This was followed by Lyndon Johnson's Great Society, War on Poverty, the *Civil Rights Act of 1964*, the Job Corps, Project Head Start, and the Model Cities program of 1966, largely undone by racial riots in Harlem and Philadelphia in 1964, in the Watts neighborhood of Los Angeles in 1965, and in Detroit in 1967, determined by the Kerner Commission to have been caused by the existence of "Two societies in America, one white and one black." [7] More than anything, however, Johnson was defeated by the war in Vietnam, which had grown from an exotic incident during the Eisenhower and Kennedy administrations to an escalating quagmire that would claim more than 60,000 American lives. By this time President Richard Nixon was in office, elected in 1963 primarily on his promise to extract troops from Southeast Asia. But doing so proved more difficult than he had anticipated, and funding for the poor and the rapidly deteriorating inner cities declined accordingly. Eventually he was forced to resign because of the Watergate debacle. One important legacy of Vietnam, directly related to Kahn's contribution, was that it decisively proved that ideology is far more potent than technology; the United Stated with all its sophisticated weaponry and firepower could not defeat a far less "developed" nation, which essentially had a Third World economy. It has also allowed this message of the fallibility of progress to be delivered into the nation's living rooms, usually on the six o'clock news between commercial breaks, through the increasingly important medium of television. This dealt a decisive blow to what has been called the "grand narrative" of Western superiority, primarily obtained through industrial production, and to the idea that there is only one answer to any problem, as those promoting the scientific method had insisted.

The worldview that began to emerge as an alternative referred to as postmodernism is less optimistic and less certain. It stresses multivocality rather than a single Western voice, positing that there are many valid views and different perspectives in the world.

Kahn's major projects during this period of unprecedented upheaval demonstrate his anticipation of this multivocality, which has now become a global chorus, although as the last chapter on his legacy will show, his inclusion in or responsibility for the emergence of postmodernism in architecture is highly controversial.

Going It Alone The intense period of commitment to the Modernist agenda of finding a solution to the problem of housing the economically disadvantaged, which corresponded exactly with World War II, ended abruptly on March 4, 1947, when Kahn left his partnership with Oscar Stonorov and opened his own office. He and Stonorov had been unlikely partners with their diametrically opposite personalities and divergent approaches to design, but Stonorov's affable character, social skills, and political connections made it possible for Kahn to explore polemical tendencies and to express them in proposals for mass-produced shelter. The partnership with Stonorov, which had begun when Kahn's professional alliance with George Howe had been strained by Howe's consulting work in Washington, ended when Kahn felt that Stonorov unfairly took credit for a design that was not his. Anne Tyng began working at the office at this time. She was just the opposite of Louis Kahn in social status and family background. Of Boston Brahmin roots, she was born in Kuling, a small village in the Lushan Mountains of Kiangsi China in 1920, while her parents Ethel and Walworth Tyng were Episcopal missionaries there. As a result of the Communist takeover, her parents sent her to boarding school in the United States in 1933, but she returned to visit her parents in China before beginning architectural school at Harvard in 1943, after majoring in fine arts at Radcliffe. She recalls her surprise at seeing a portrait of distant relative and namesake Anne Tyng at the Boston Museum of Fine Arts by the favorite artist of high society, John Singleton Copley, which reminded her of "New England roots." [8] She was one of the first women to study architecture at Harvard at a time when the faculty were heavily influenced by the new director, Walter Gropius, who had organized the Bauhaus in Germany, before emigrating to the United States because of World War II. The war also ensured a high female to male ratio in her class, which changed only after troops returned. Philip Johnson, now the doyenne of critics and style maker extraordinaire in his nineties, followed the notoriety he had received by curating the International Style Exhibition at the Museum of Modern Art in New York City by enrolling as a "mature student" at Harvard at the same time Tyng was there. She often invited him to review her work. Other notable students such as William Wurster, who went on to become a Bay Area legend, and I. M. Pei, who is arguably one of the leading Modernists in the world at the end of the twentieth century, added dimension to Tyng's formative experience, as did faculty member Marcel Breuer, who was on staff at Gropius's Bauhaus and had followed him to Harvard.

Anne Tyng After graduation Tyng had a series of jobs in New York City, including the architectural furniture company Knoll Design, and soon realized that there was a real barrier against female architects. Her parents had relocated to Philadelphia and she decided to join them there. Anne Tyng first met Louis Kahn in 1945, when she visited a friend working in the office in the old Evening Bulletin Building across from City Hall that Kahn then shared with Oscar Stonorov and George Howe. Her friend, Betty Ware Carlhian, had to return to Harvard to complete her degree, and Tyng was offered her position. She was aware of the firm's reputation for designing progressive, low-cost housing projects and she readily accepted. She was pleased that, unlike her previous, restrictive experience in New York, she was involved in all aspects of office experience, but also recalls that Kahn and Stonorov seemed to be competing for her attention. She was attracted to Kahn because of a charisma that many others have mentioned, which seemed to grow as he matured, related to his physical strength, unusual facial characteristics of piercing blue eyes and scars, and his passionate belief in ideas. He was 44 and she 25 when they met, and she soon became aware that, "Louis' interest in me was unusually intense and included a powerful physical attraction that I immediately realized was mutual." She also found it "difficult to believe that he was a happily married, and at the same time, so intensely interested in another woman." [9]

When their affair began, Tyng was the slightly built, fair-haired, clear-eyed image of Main Line privilege, the area of Philadelphia suburbs that grew up along its premier railway route and took its name from it. She represented everything he was not: a long-established Anglo-Saxon lineage, from a wealthy Christian family that had provided her with the best education that money could buy. She described Kahn as being, "Extremely shy because of the scars on his face from his childhood burn," while Stonorov "was a great bluffer and quick to seize the opportunities . . . confident in this ability and charm." [10] She also noticed, "How unusually broad his lightly freckled shoulders were in proportion to his slim hips, when Kahn worked shirtless" [11] because of the stifling heat in the small office. Their passionate, personal, and professional relationship lasted 15 years and finally became platonic at her suggestion, "because I realized he was involved with someone else." [12] As with Tyng, however, he remained married and still lived at home even though more and more time was spent at the office. Kahn's theoretical maturity during this period is intricately bound up in this affair, making it essential to clarify Tyng's part in that evolution.

The Sky Is the Limit The years immediately following World War II were a time of unbounded optimism in the United States, which suffered none of the appalling damage that bombing had caused to cities in Europe and was not experiencing the material shortages and rationing that were enforced across the Atlantic for many years after the war ended until these were alleviated by the Marshall Plan. Nonetheless, the common sense of an ominous weight being lifted from the national consciousness was literally translated into urban opportunity in Philadelphia when the huge masonry viaduct supporting the elevated railroad tracks running north and west out of the old Suburban Station was finally torn down. In the late 1940s the massive bridge known as the "Chinese wall" because of its resemblance to the Great Wall of China effectively separated the eastern and western halves of the city, which, even though still connected by streets running through arches below it, were psychologically divided.

In addition to housing, or as a corollary to it, the second great agenda of modernism was urban design, contingent on a belief in the omnipotence of the individual designer and the possibility of one person accommodating the needs, aspirations, and secret desires of thousands in a single "master" plan. Consistent with his allegiance to the movement, Kahn not only agreed with that belief, but actively participated in proposing a plan for the area of Philadelphia left vacant by the fall of the wall. In 1946 Kahn and Stonorov were appointed by the Philadelphia Planning Commission to join a team of architects working on an area of the city called "the triangle," founded by the diagonal axis of the Benjamin Franklin Parkway connecting the Art Museum with Logan Circle as the northeast border, the Schuylkill River on the west, and Market Street on the south. The 200-acre area had badly deteriorated but the part of the "Chinese wall" that had been removed near the river was catalyst for development. The team proposal included a new civic center, an amusement park along the riverbank, new office towers, referred to as "Philadelphia's new business address," and a "New Town Living Center" of slab block housing complete with raised pedestrian walkways presented in drawings by Kahn in 1947 that were prescient of the Penn Center development west of City Hall realized in the early 1950s. While still with Stonorov and Howe, Tyng and Kahn had begun collaborating on their shared interest in urban design on the Triangle Area Redevelopment Plan.

Anne Tyng accompanied Kahn in the move to a new office at 1728 Spruce Street in March 1947, made possible, in part, by the confidence he derived from having a new commission for the Philadelphia Psychiatric Hospital. The hospital, part of the Federation of Jewish Charities, came to Kahn because of his long involvement with, and hard work on behalf of, the Federation and his association with Samuel Radbill, the president of the hospital board. During the design of the hospital between 1944 and 1946, realized in 1949, Kahn was also working on alterations to the Radbill company offices and a renovation of the Radbill House in Merion. Clad in slate, the hospital is T-shaped in plan, with patients' rooms in the cross bar and administration offices in the stem, which has a curved entry piece at its base, facing the street. A *porte cochère* under this curved façade provides convenient access to the ground floor of the facility.

The Houses From 1946 to 1950, Kahn and Tyng worked together on six houses, in addition to a renovation to the Hooper House in the suburbs of Baltimore, Maryland (1946). After his split with Oscar Stonorov, when he moved into his own office, Kahn initially relied heavily upon commissions for private houses to survive. He had some opportunities to explore this kind of highly detailed, customized design while working on low-cost housing schemes with Stonorov, but they were few. One of these was for friends Jesse and Ruth Oser for a site in Elkins Park, north of Philadelphia, in 1940. Strong formal similarities between the Oser House and a much larger residential project by his close friend George Howe for the Wasserman family in Whitemarsh Township eight years earlier are evident. Although the Osers had a restricted budget, Kahn attempted to replicate the muscular verticality of Howe's palatial project by clustering casement windows on both the first and second floors at one corner of a square, tower-like projection to allow a vertical band to occur at the opposite side. The Oser House is simple in plan, a rectangle with a straight stair leading up to a large bedroom with an en suite bath, and three smaller bedrooms sharing a second bath on the first floor, with a partition wall parallel to the long sides of the rectangle creating a corridor to a gallery kitchen and office clustered at one end. The thin horizontal tongue and groove wood siding used on the Oser House, which is inexpensive and paradoxically seems to increase scale because of the absence of any usual frames of references, shows up again in vertical application on the Baltimore house of Mr. and Mrs. Arthur Hooper in 1946. Unfortunately this, along with a one-story addition to the Ardmore House of Kahn's friends Lea and Arthur Finkelstein, had to be abandoned because of material shortages caused by the war.

The L-shaped plan of the Hooper addition to a two-story colonial farmhouse hints at more than just a passing familiarity with the Modernist adaptations then being attempted in Los Angeles, particularly in the Case Study House Program being sponsored by influential editor John Entenza in *Arts and Architecture* magazine. Aside from the L-shaped plan, which was favored by California architects because it served to capture outside garden space and make an external equivalent to internal rooms possible as a statement of loyalty to the modernist principle of a free flow of space interior to exterior, Kahn also replicated the structural frame and flat roof of the Western equivalent.

The Weiss House The Weiss House, completed in 1950, won a gold medal from the Philadelphia chapter of the American Institute of Architects as an indication of Kahn's rising professional visibility at the beginning of the decade. It begins to present what was soon to become his clarity of the articulation of individual spaces. Faced in rough stone, the house is arranged in two distinct blocks connected by the thin neck of a covered recessed entry passage. The block on the left of the entry, connected by a pathway to a garage behind it, contains a kitchen and dining room beside a massive stone fireplace and a living room with a "conversation pit" that was popular at the time in front with copious windows. A master bedroom with en suite bath and dressing room, as well as a maid's room and second bath, are located to the right of the main entry with deep recesses used to ensure privacy.

The Genel House Kahn's eagerness to challenge the orthodoxy of infinite space takes a second baby step forward in the Genel House in Wynnewood, in 1948 and 1951, which is even more compartmentalized than the Weiss House with a subtle hint of iconoclastic departures to come in a nonfunctional marble partition angled around a brick fireplace. Such a relatively small gesture may seem inconsequential in retrospect, and yet it is symptomatic of the restlessness that Kahn and many others were feeling about the structure that form must follow function. In Pacific Palisades near Los Angeles five years earlier, Charles and Ray Eames had fired the first visible shot across the bow of conformity in a house they designed for themselves, introducing the issue of personalizing spaces that Modernists had previously felt should be anonymous. Using the latest prefabricated steel technology as a frame, the Eames' personalized their house to express their individuality in the color schemes they chose and the personal collections they displayed in it, making it one of the first attempts at humanizing a sterile formula that literally seemed to be cast in concrete during the preceding decade. Kahn expanded on this idea and made it his own.

Anne Tyng provided Kahn with the mathematical and geometric weapons he needed to carry out his own personal campaign against Modernist sterility, which he also felt was the result of the loss of monumentality that had made historical architecture so powerful. Kahn's affinity toward public housing, as well as his rationalist bent and functionalist technique all place him squarely in the Modernist camp, yet he had a different viewpoint, based in humanism, and social awareness.

The Norman Fisher House Kahn designed a house for Norman Fisher for a site near Hatboro, close to Philadelphia. It took more than seven years to build, from 1959 until early 1967, an indication of his perfectionism, as well as his belief that architecture was a living thing and should keep evolving during the design and even the construction process. The house is on a gently sloping, heavily wooded hill that slants downward from the entrance driveway at the main road toward a small stream at the back of the property. The house demonstrates the early exploration of what are now seen in retrospect as Kahn's essential principles: the use of geometry, the manipulation of natural light in all exterior and interior spaces, and a love of natural materials, rather than the industrial palette preferred by a majority of Modernists. The house is composed of intersecting cubes hinged together at a 45 degree angle. These are placed between existing trees to form two interconnected outdoor spaces: an entrance court in front and a patio adjacent to the kitchen, which is open and overlooks the stream in the back. The cubes are distinctively different with the one on the south being private and the northern one being public. The one on the south contains the master bedroom and bath as well as two additional bedrooms and another bath on the second floor.

The cube on the north shares the entrance lobby and contains a soaring two-story living area with a fireplace as a focal point, which separates it from a dining room and kitchen beyond. Increased window size in this cube is used by Kahn as a means of introducing more natural light, making the double-height space seem even larger than it is. In this house and in the Esherick House that followed, Kahn plays with the height, depth, and location of windows as a musician plays with sound, carefully manipulating both their placement on each wall and their depth, which varies by inches in each case. For instance, the entrance hall ends at a large window, which allows a view out and through to the lush wooded lot in the distance, on the other side of the house. Other parts of the exterior wall, such as the south façade, only have narrow slit windows, to let a minimal amount of light in and to preserve the privacy of this area. Kahn firmly believed that every room in any building he designed should have light, and he approached the issue of natural light on a spiritual level. He even called material "spent light." There is also a basement under this more public part of the house, which is positioned in such a way as to take advantage of the sloping site to open up toward the view of the stream in the back. The two cubes are placed so that they read as one house from certain angles and two separate houses from others, and this dichotomy is obviously not coincidental.

The Esherick House The Esherick House, near Fairmount Park in Philadelphia, is also the result of a strict geometric order since its main public living area is square in plan, and the private area, with kitchen and a laundry on the ground floor, and the bedroom and bathroom above are attached to it in a rectangular piece that is half the width of the square. There is a mezzanine at the bedroom level that overlooks the double-height living space. Kahn used a three-feet six-inch module; the living area is nine modules square, but deviates by one module, and the staircase, which separates the square from the private rectangular portion running along its long side, is one module wide. There is a fireplace opposite the stair on the far side of the living room, which Kahn uses as a sculpture by detaching the tall vertical volume of the chimney, and showing it off as a tower that is visible through a long narrow window placed above the fireplace.

In the Esherick House, as in the Fisher House, windows are used very strategically, but in this instance he goes even further, by imbuing them with a pedagogical purpose. Kahn was a teacher as well as an architect, frequently using the designs as a way of pedantically making a point. And here, the point is to demonstrate that a window is more than an opening in a wall, to be used to let light into a room. In the Esherick House he stacks windows of fixed glass, which serve that purpose, over a custom-made counterpart that is a casement paired with a sliding screen, to be opened when it is necessary to have natural ventilation. Philadelphia has exaggerated seasons; that is, winters can be very cold and summers very hot and humid, so having windows that open is a good idea.

Kahn also made a point of differentiating between the front or formal and back or less formal elevations here, taking advantage of the proximity of the park behind the house by making the front very flat and almost anonymous, and the back of the living room square very open, by articulating it with these paired stacks of deep fenestration.

Mill Town Houses in Lowell, Massachusetts

The Industrial Revolution was not confined to Great Britain alone. It was launched by steam power in many other countries almost simultaneously, and America was not far behind. But the rush to industrialization was not completely driven by steam in the United States. Several entrepreneurs took advantage of the power provided by rivers and streams, which are especially abundant in New England, and located mills and factories there. If it can be argued that the Industrial Revolution started with the invention of Newcomer's Engine in 1717, which was a steam-driven pump used for removing water from coal and tin mines, it started a bit later in America, but was well underway by the mid-1800s. It was then that Francis Cabot Lowell established a town centered around his textile mills that now carries his name. It prospered for little more than 15 years, until the mills were closed because of the Civil War.[13]

An Industrial Utopia Lowell established his eponymous settlement in Massachusetts as an ideal industrial community rather than just a company town, but also as a social utopia intended to improve the lives of the workers. The majority of the laborers in these mills were young women from rural areas, and records show that a majority of them came from as far away as the neighboring states throughout New England.[14] The main attraction of Lowell for them, in addition to earning more money than would have been possible in domestic service, was the promise of personal improvement offered by its founder. Lowell was not alone in his idealistic quest, since other utopian communities, such as Port Sunlight, had already been established in England before Lowell was founded.

By necessity, the layout of the town was predicated on two givens, which were the need for the mills to be near the water and the need for the workers to live near the mills. Because the factories were powered by a long driveshaft running along the ceiling, connected to the individual machines by belts, factories had to be long and narrow. The women, who were predominantly of Irish, Scottish, German, and Polish descent, typically worked a 12-hour day, six days a week, with a break for lunch. They lived in boarding houses built by the management, which had to be located near the mills so the workers could walk back and forth from their rooms to work as quickly and easily as possible. The boarding houses, which were lined up along the main and side streets in neat rows, were each run by a landlady who acted as surrogate mother, chaperone, chief cook, and property manager. She provided her young guests with breakfast, lunch, and dinner, and they had prodigious appetites. This was not free. The women earned about $8 a week after they became proficient, but after expenses were deducted, this was reduced to only $2. But, this was still about twice the amount that they could make in many other jobs that were then available to them and was considered generous at the time.[15]

These laborers stayed in Lowell for an average of four years, and during that time actually managed to save enough money to send home to help their families. The "improvement" part of this harsh social contract, in which these women traded about 14,000 hours of their young lives in front of a machine in a textile mill in exchange for $400, was the opportunity to attend church and the social events connected to it in the little free time that they had left.

Lowell grew, and under Kirk Boott the Merrimack Manufacturing Company became more established. Boarding houses became even more regularized. One cluster of them in particular was patterned after a traditional New England village, with each house being recognizably part of that spare vernacular vocabulary. These were built of wood, as farmhouses in that region typically are, with the exception of four houses in the middle of the row, which were built of brick to emphasize a feeling of stability. This row was echoed by another on the opposite side of a canal running between them, which was used to run a mill at the far end.[16]

Competition between mills started and owners became more aware of the need to brand the architecture of both the factory and the housing of the employees who worked in it in order to differentiate their company from others. In the opinion of one historian who has studied these mill towns thoroughly, the popularity of the Greek Revival style between 1835 and 1845 in this part of New England was due to a retrospective urge and the desire to recognize past accomplishments.[17] To convey the impression of a well-established community based on democratic principles, builders in Lowell selected the style that the founders of the Republic had also chosen nearly a generation earlier for the same reasons, and it served both purposes well.

Michael Graves: The Benacerraf, Hanselman, and Snyderman Houses

It is fairly common to be able to follow the transformation of an individual architect's ideas through his or her work over an extended period of time. In fact, that evolution is one of the surest signs of greatness. What is not usual is to see that transition compressed into the design of only three houses that were completed over a five-year period and that subsequently resulted in a remarkable volte-face in a designer's entire career. This dramatic, soul-searching change of direction also contributed to a completely new trajectory in the history of architecture.

The New York Five The architect in this instance is Michael Graves, who, in the early 1960s, was included in a book entitled *Five Architects* along with Richard Meier, Charles Gwathmey, John Hedjuk, and Peter Eisenman because of their common allegiance to the Modernist principles of the Swiss-French architect Le Corbusier. These principles, related to machine production, were summarized by the protean architectural guru in his own shorthand as "the five points," made possible by industrial materials such as steel and concrete. They made it possible to move on from the traditional bearing wall, in which fewer openings for windows and doors are possible because of its structural homogeneity. So, Le Corbusier's five points begin with the "grid," which was his code word for a frame system, since it is typically laid out on a module. The second and third "points," which derive from the first, are a free plan and a free elevation, as in the free-skating sense of free. These are made possible by the point load frame system, as opposed to the uniformly loaded bearing wall. The fourth point is the strip window, which Le Corbusier felt was an especially descriptive symbol of the freedom that a structural frame provides because it expands the limited opening in a bearing wall to a horizontal slice in a curtain wall that can run across column lines at the designer's will, because it is the line of columns and not the exterior wall that is supporting the load. The fifth and final point is that the frame allows a building, or house, to be lifted up above the ground, suggesting that a garden can be planted on the roof, as well.

The Hanselman House Each of the members of the New York Five, as they began to be called after the book on their work appeared, differently approached the ideas of Le Corbusier, summarized in his five points. Perhaps because of his background in art as well as architecture, Michael Graves concentrated on his mentor's exploration of the Cubist's vision of comprehensive spatial perception, adding what Alan Colquhoun has described as "new metonymic and metaphoric interpretations of the spaces made possible by the freedom that the grid allowed." [18]

Although Michael Graves worked on several other projects between 1967 and 1972, he completed two houses and one addition during that time that seemed to him to exhaust the possibilities inherent in those interpretations, forcing him to reconsider his loyalty to the principles of Modernism as well. The first of these projects to be completed is the Hanselman House in Fort Wayne, Indiana, built in 1967. It was designed to accommodate a family of six, and it was located on a heavily wooded corner lot with a stream running diagonally across it. Graves positioned the house along the northernmost lot line with a driveway leading to a carport on the eastern end, beginning a linear progression toward the house to the west. The site plan is based on a 35-feet grid, perpendicular to this northern lot line, divided into five bays to establish a sense of progression toward the house, which is treated like a temple or sacred object. After the first two of these bays, used for the driveway and the carport, Graves uses the third for a step stair and screen, the fourth for a bridge to the house, and the fifth for the house itself. The house is a square in plan and a cube in volume, and it is elaborately introduced in this sequence by elements intended to provide a sense of spatial layering when approaching it from the carport. A screen at the third grid line, echoed by another that also acts as the first, outer skin of the house, punctuates a carefully choreographed ritual of penetration that Graves sets up before reaching the front door.

Graves treats this first floor inner sanctum, which is the final goal of this procession, as a *piano nobile* in a way that is reminiscent of those found in the Italian palazzos and villas described elsewhere here, but then contradicts that simile by putting the three bedrooms for the children and the bathroom they would all share on the ground floor level, along with a playroom in their midst. Although this was obviously done for privacy and better acoustics, it contradicts the golden rule of palazzo and villa design in the past, which was to confine all service functions, such as commercial uses, servants' quarters, kitchen-related spaces, and storage to the ground floor level. This confirms, rather than denies, a Corbusian connection, however, because Le Corbusier also exploited the compromises that modern life forced an architect to make to a pure system. In his classic essay "The Mathematics of the Ideal Villa," Colin Rowe was the first to establish clear geometric parallels between the Palladian system of proportion, including the use of a podium base and *piano nobile* and the early houses of Le Corbusier, such as the Villa Stein at Garches.[19] The Hanselman House, then, is intentionally a part of this tradition of the compromised Italian villa typology.

The second and third levels of the Hanselman House are consistent with this analogy, as a series of zones, rather than rooms, in an open plan. In outward appearance, they seem to pay homage in every way to their Modernist heritage down to details such as the pipe column railing, thin slatted wooden floors, and Corbusian furniture. What clearly establishes this house, and those that would soon follow it, as a radical departure from that dogma, however, is Graves's attempt to extend his commentary on Cubism by focusing on architectonic parts, such as columns and stairs as part of the process of perception, rather than just functional elements in their own right. This expansion is most obvious in his rotation of the main stair as the central component of the entrance sequence. He also uses this as a sculptural element, flipping it over at a 90 degree angle, using the triangular form as the face of a second internal stair on the front elevation as well. This play of forms may initially seem to be similar to the kind of semiotic experimentation that Robert Venturi introduced in his design of his mother's house in Chestnut Hill at the same time as the Hanselman House was being built. However, Venturi's interests were more related to mass media and the way it had subliminally invaded the public consciousness at this time as a largely unrecognized ideological force, and the place that architecture had in this process.[20]

The Benacerraf House Addition Two years after the Hanselman House was completed, Graves designed an addition to a conventional, single-family house in Princeton, New Jersey. It was originally intended to be a freestanding pavilion in the back yard to be used as a playhouse for the children, but ended up being attached to the eastern side of the existing house, which Graves also renovated as part of the process. In its final, dependant position, it allows for close supervision of the children's area from the kitchen, adjacent to it on the ground floor, and as an open terrace next to the master bedroom and bath on the first floor. The two levels of this playhouse-deck addition are connected by an external stair, which serves as its public, street front elevation.

As in the Hanselman House, Graves started his design process with a grid, which he extended into the original house, in this instance, as an obvious gesture of continuity with the Corbusian five points. The free plan and free elevation, as the second and third components of that formula, are also obviously present, as are the strip window and roof garden, which Graves uses as a terrace. But once again, as he had in Fort Wayne, the architect ventures into perceptual explorations involving building elements such as the stair, the columns, and the wall, used as a screen primarily on the front elevation. That entire surface is treated as a three-dimensional collage of parts with the stair connecting the playroom on the ground floor with the terrace above flattened against the wall surface to exaggerate its triangular form, and the dual purpose of the screen it is attached to, as a demising wall on the ground floor and perforated partition above. A wide railing in front of the stair, which is made to look like a column that has been placed on its side, completes this tectonic collage. The result is a visually arresting three-dimensional exercise, deliberately intended to confuse perceptions of interior and exterior space. There is once again a temptation to group it with the syntactical explorations being made by Venturi at this time, but is a test of the mental process by which meaning is created.[21]

The Snyderman House Back in Fort Wayne, three years after the Benacerraf *folie*, Graves designed the third house in this historical series. This one, for the Snyderman family, is the largest of all. It is located in the middle of a 40-acre site and is surrounded by trees. Graves identified a cross-axis, created by a natural line of entrance to the site, on the one hand, and a pond and a flat plateau that form a secondary axis, on the other. In his earliest "napkin" sketches of the house, Graves graphically reacts to those two axes by drawing a square plan footprint deformed in the middle of each side by the impact of the axis that penetrates the house there. Once again, as in the Hanselman house, the form of choice is the square, which is a reminder of the fact that rationalism was a large part of the Corbusian heritage, at least in his early work. This included a love of Platonic solids, such as the square, which Graves replicated in his first sketch of his idea. But, a square was also the perfect form to reconcile the potentially conflicting requirement of the cross-axis he had identified, and so it was easily assimilated.

Because of its larger scale, bigger site, and more involved contextural conditions, the Snyderman House is complex, but much of that complexity is self-imposed by the architect. In this respect, he also reminds us of Robert Venturi, for whom complexity was the entire rationale for his departure from the Modernist fold. A description of the ground floor plan of the Snyderman House must begin at the front door, which opens in from an "entry terrace" raised up six steps on a slight podium base. The terrace is larger than most suburban houses are today. A living room, dining room, and kitchen rotate out from the front entry, in an open plan arrangement, orbiting around a large stair, placed off the center of the square to avoid the cross-axis. The master bedroom and bath are located in the northwest corner of the plan, protected by a thick, L-shaped wall that also contains the toilet, tub, and sink, if not the shower, which is freestanding.

Michael Graves himself has described his intention in determining this arrangement by saying that:

the rooms are organized both to take advantage of the appropriate exposure to the sun and to establish a progression from the entrance to the most private spaces. By its east-west alignment, (the house) is in an ideal position in relation to the sun whose path from front façade to the back traces both the course of a day's activities in the rooms and the movement from collective to more individual private spaces.

This idea of arranging the internal spaces of a house to take advantage of external environmental influences, now referred to as diurnal zoning, is nothing new, having been used for thousands of years in the traditional architecture of preindustrial societies. What is new here is its implementation by an architect who was, at this point in his career, a self-declared Corbusian Modernist, since concern for nature was not the primary consideration of his mentor. But, Graves demurred soon after that in the same statement by shifting the discussion to the idea of a machine in the garden metaphor, which is a refrain that is more familiar to the rationalist tradition. In this iteration, the house is an artificial implant into the natural environment, and so should be expressed differently, as a foil. Graves goes further by matching spaces, which refer to or touch the earth, that he describes as being characterized by "irregularity, lyricism and movement" with colors that relate to it, such as brown, and using white on the grid, which is extruded three dimensionally as a white screen around the house, representing "idealized form, geometry and stasis."

The Walter Gropius House, Lincoln, Massachusetts

On the eve of the Second World War, late in 1936, Walter and Ise Gropius started the process of relocating from Berlin, Germany, to Cambridge, Massachusetts. Gropius had been named Director of the School of Design at Harvard, with Joseph Hudnut as its Dean. Gropius and his wife were about to undergo a degree of culture shock that neither of them could have fully anticipated.

A Founder of the Modern Movement It would be simplistic to say that Walter Gropius was single-handedly responsible for establishing the Modern Movement in architecture. There were many different stands of influence in its formulation, beginning with the Industrial Revolution in the early part of the eighteenth century. But it would be fair to say that it would not have happened at quite the same time, in quite the same way, without him. Before Gropius, there was still a lingering sense of nostalgia for the past and the wish to reconcile history with the technological breakthrough of the present and the future. Otto Wagner was one example of an architect who was trying to hold on to tradition while embracing the new, and Charles Rennie Mackintosh was another. The clearest evidence of the change in attitude that Gropius helped bring about is the stark contrast between two buildings, designed by both him and his mentor Peter Behrens at about the same time in Berlin. Behrens was the corporate architect for the *Allemagne Electrichich Geselshaft*, or AEG, the Germany Electric Company, prior to World War II. He designed a turbine factory for it that adheres closely to the mechanistic language of the Modern Movement, or the New Architecture as it was being referred to in Europe at that time. But, as Wagner and Mackintosh had before him, Behrens attempted to make historical references in this building, as well. These are layered into both classical and rural associations that were intended to elevate the workplace to an almost sacred space in the first instance, and to make the workers, who had mostly come to the city as a result of rural urban migration, feel more at home on the other. The temple-like, classical metaphor is conveyed in the AEG Turbine Factory, through a tripartite division of the building into a podium base, colonnaded middle, and segmental pedimented top. The rural symbolism is also conveyed by that roof, which has been compared to a barn gable elsewhere.[22]

Gropius Was Not Sentimental In his own design for a shoe factory that he completed about the same time as the AEG Turbine Hall was built, Gropius clearly demonstrated just how free of similar sentiments he could be. Instead of the ennobling intention of classical associations or the rural reference of a segmented gable roof, Gropius eliminated all connections to history in the Fagus Shoe Factory by making the roof entirely flat. Instead of the columnar bay and temple-like division into base, middle, and top that Behrens has also used to elevate the workplace to a nearly sacred status, Gropius wrapped his factory entirely in glass, as if to tell the workers and the public that management was in charge and that employees would have nowhere to hide. A clock above the front door completed the image.

Gropius was a leader of a rationalistic school of thought that eventually prevailed within the New Architecture Movement, toward a more objective position. He was among the most influential members of that nonaffiliated group, and while Le Corbusier was inarguably its most dynamic and charismatic figure, Gropius had equal influence because of his role as an educator. He had been instrumental in the establishment of the *Deutsche Werkbund*, which was an institutional approach taken by the German government to ensure an improvement in the national competence in industrial design as well as in consumer culture in general. Gropius went on to refine this mission by reconfiguring the Bauhaus in Weimar, and then reestablishing that school in Dessau, prior to his departure for America. During this period he had a central role in formulating the intellectual platform of the Modern Movement.

The Gropius House in Lincoln, Massachusetts Walter and Ise Gropius arrived in Boston in the spring of 1937 with little money, having only been able to ship to their new home some household belongings, including some furniture prototypes that had been produced in the Marcel Breuer studio at the Dessau Bauhaus. Breuer followed Gropius to the United States, and the two joined together in partnership for a brief period afterward, although it ended in 1941. Through a mutual friend, the couple met Mrs. James Storrow, who offered to help them find a suitable property to build on and to financially assist them in doing so. She was unaware of the ideological position that Gropius represented, believing only that newcomers coming to America from abroad deserved a chance, and she wanted to help them get one.[23]

After rejecting a suggestion by Joseph Hudnut, dean of the Graduate School of Design of Harvard University, that they look for an existing house on Beacon Hill in Boston, Walter and Ise Gropius decided to buy land and build a house of their own. They had been looking at small towns in the area around Cambridge and started to focus on the three small villages of Lexington, Concord, and Lincoln of Revolutionary war fame. They were attracted to Lincoln, in particular, because of its rural New England character and small size, as a welcome contrast to their hectic life in Berlin. They rented a house there as a temporary measure, while their search for property continued.

Studying Vernacular Precedents Before embarking on a site search and house design, Gropius and his wife traveled throughout Massachusetts and to neighboring New Hampshire and Vermont as well, to study local, indigenous New England architecture. Mrs. Gropius remembered that her husband was impressed with the regional adaptations to an original Georgian model that he saw on these trips, and the way that the early builders had used different materials due to climactic conditions and budget restrictions. This resulted in the replacement of brick, which was the material that was favored in England and in British Colonial cities such as Boston and Philadelphia during the Georgian period, with painted wood clapboard. He also noted other environmental adaptations such as the consistent opposing placement of the front, entrance door to the Colonial house and the rear door leading to a back garden to encourage cross ventilation, which was necessary in an area where summers can get very hot and humid.

This recollection by Ise Gropius seems innocent enough until one remembers that Gropius, like the rest of the proponents of the New Architecture, has the historical reputation of being unconcerned about contextural issues, and was supposed to believe that scientific solutions could be found to any climactic

The Walter Gropius House   Courtesy of Daniel Malantic; Flickr

condition. Vernacular adaptations of the kind that impressed him in New England were not supposed to be of any interest.

This is not the only surprise provided by the design process behind the Gropius House, which shatters several other stereotypes that have been attached to the Modern Movement as well. The couple ended up choosing a 5-1/2-acre site very close to the house they were renting at Sandy Pond that attracted them for several unexpected reasons. The first of these was that it was located on a low hill, surrounded by an apple orchard with nearly 100 trees. The second point of interest for them was the view that the house at the top of this hill would have of Mount Wachusett, nearby. The third reason, which reveals an even more romantic streak in someone who was reportedly an unrecalcitrant pragmatist, was the fact that the site was within walking distance of Walden Pond. In his writing about that pond, Henry David Thoreau praised its simple, primeval beauty, revealing that Gropius had a soft spot for nature after all.

The house that he designed on Baker Bridge Road at the top of a low hill demonstrates how well he absorbed the lessons he had learned from the local vernacular architecture, as well as how thoroughly he understood natural forces. But, in keeping with the Rationalistic, functionalist tendencies ascribed to him, he also decided to use the construction of the house as a test case in mass production techniques, to demonstrate how products that were readily available on the market in America could be used to produce a modern house. He succeeded in doing this, with only the curved railing of the one main staircase being custom-made.

Efficiency Combined with Tradition In spite of the deference that Gropius paid to local tradition in siting and in using local materials for the fieldstone foundation, brick chimney, and white painted vertical wood strips for siding, the house as finally built is very reminiscent of others that Gropius and Breuer had designed for faculty members on the grounds of the Dessau Bauhaus. It is sleek and box-like with long strip windows and a flat roof. Its rectilinear forms are relieved only by an angled covered entry leading in from a circular driveway on the north side and a spiral stairway that goes up to a roof deck farther back on the same elevation.

Gropius was working within a tight budget, which, in addition to prompting his interest in readily available, off the shelf parts, also resulted in minimal room sizes. The bathrooms are stacked above each other in the two-story plan to save on plumbing, and with the exception of the roof deck, which takes up about 30 percent of the upper floor, other spaces are fairly tight. There is also a sizable screened-in porch on the ground floor, which projects out at a 45 degree angle from the long southern side of the rectangular house, and these exterior living spaces must have seemed luxurious indeed to the former urbanites from Berlin.

Landscape a Major Factor The extremes of climate in this part of New England, of extremely cold winters and hot, humid summers were another factor behind the decision to make the house as compact as possible. Climate also contributed to the need for a tree planting program around the house to protect it from cold winter wind and hot summer sun. Even though there was an abundant apple orchard at the bottom of the hilly site, the top was devoid of trees, and so a selection process of the right species to use as well as a planting program took equal priority with the construction of the house itself. The entire field of landscape architecture that would complement its Modernist equivalent was then in its infancy, and Harvard led the way in this area, producing designers such as Garrett Eckbo, Dan Kiley, and James Rose during the Gropius years.[24] In addition to a purely functional purpose of environmental mitigation, the trees around the Gropius house were strategically placed to help blur the boundaries between inside and out, and to break down the severe angularity of the rectilinear surfaces of the house.

The House The jauntily angled marquee that connects the circular entrance driveway to the front door to protect people from rain or snow leads into a modest entrance hall at the core of the rectangular plan, containing an open alcove for coats and the main stair. A long narrow galley kitchen perpendicular to this hall separates it from the screened-in porch, of the same width as the entry space, which projects out, in line with it, toward the back garden. This was a deliberate decision proudly described by Ise Gropius as the desire to make "the design of the house totally asymmetrical, showing no conventional façade and departing from all accepted rules of that time by extending the screened porch at right angles to the rear of the house."[25] The ceiling height of the lower floor, however, is fairly conventional being just over eight feet high, while that of the upper level is seven inches less. Gropius covered some of the walls in vertical clapboard, also painted white, as a deliberate twist on the regional tradition of using it on the exterior of a house in a horizontal configuration.

The master bedroom and bathroom suite is located at the far end of the upper level, opposite the roof deck, on one side. The bedroom and bath suite for the couple's daughter is located at the other, and a guest room is placed in between, closest to the stairway.

Using the Bauhaus furniture that they had brought with them from Germany was another important consideration for Walter and Ise Gropius as they planned their house, with spaces kept as open as possible to accommodate all of it.

All of the other rooms on the ground floor spin outward from the entrance hall, which is slightly left of center, such as a study, living room, and dining room to the right of it, and a maid's bedroom and bath, accessible through the long galley kitchen, at the left. The upstairs was retained as a private zone, with all rooms except the roof deck at the western end also being directly accessible from the central hall.

The Philip Johnson Glass House

Philip Johnson, who died in 2005 at the age of 98, was almost single-handedly responsible for introducing the architectural aesthetic of High Modernism into the American context. Johnson wielded enormous influence as a tastemaker in the early part of his career in his role as a curator in the architectural section of the Museum of Modern Art in New York City in the early 1930s. Even after he left that post, he continued to exercise that self-designated authority throughout the rest of his long career.

Johnson traveled throughout Europe just prior to World War II, with a specific focus on Germany. While he was there, he met with many of the leaders of the Modern Movement just before they emigrated to the United States. Several of these were closely associated with the Bauhaus, which was closed because of political pressure. While he was visiting Germany, he was able to identify a consistent set of architectural principles, resulting in a formal tectonic position that he and historian Henry-Russell Hitchcock would later refer to as "The International Style." They grouped these together and presented them in an exhibition they had organized at the Museum of Modern Art after Johnson's return to New York. This exhibition had a profound impact that, in retrospect, may now be seen to be directly proportional to the growing influence of the media at that time and its ability to shape public opinion.

Universal Applications Johnson and Hitchcock chose the name "International Style" for the collection of projects that they included in their groundbreaking exhibition because each of them conformed to the basic Modernist belief in the need for a contexturalism and a historicism, as well as because of the fact that the selection included countries other than Germany. The basic idea that all of the work conveyed, however, was that of uniformity, pragmatism, standardization, and interchangeability, centered in the idea that technology can level out all environmental extremes. Different architectural strategies were not felt to be necessary to do this.

Ludwig Mies van der Rohe was one of the most prominent and doctrinaire members of this movement in Germany, and he became Johnson's mentor. The young curator, who was the scion of one of the wealthiest families in America, facilitated the German master's decision to emigrate to America, where he became the head of the architectural program at the Illinois Institute of Technology. In turn, Mies van der Rohe was instrumental in convincing Johnson to get an architectural degree, and he enrolled at Harvard, where Walter Gropius was the director, just prior to the war.

After he graduated, Johnson collaborated with Mies van der Rohe on the design of the Seagram Building in New York City, which in retrospect represents the apogee of the public representation of the style in America. The Lever House tower by Gordon Bunshaft, at Skidmore, Owings, and Merrill, completed in 1951, illustrates the virtues of the Seagram Building by comparison, since it replaces the custom-made technology utilized by Mies van der Rohe and Johnson, with the more standardized approach that would then become the norm in corporate buildings in America for the next decade.

Johnson helped Mies van der Rohe assemble a collection of Mies van der Rohe's work for exhibition at the Museum of Modern Art between 1946 and 1947, and this was to have seismic reverberations throughout the architectural community in America as well. Coinciding as it did with the end of the war and the crest of optimism and joy that this caused, the Mies van der Rohe exhibition held out the promise of a minimal, efficient, and technological future, free of the stuffiness and burdens of the past. Charles and Ray Eames, for example, who were soon to produce their own estimable contribution to the movement toward Modernism in America in their design of a house and office for themselves in Pacific Palisades that is now considered a classic in its own right and is discussed elsewhere here, changed their original concept after attending the exhibition. They were concerned that it coincidentally seemed similar to one that Mies van der Rohe had included in the show, and they did not want to be seen to be derivative.[26]

Farnsworth House During the preparation for that exhibition, Johnson saw the drawings for a house that Mies van der Rohe was designing for Edith Farnsworth in Plano, Illinois, not far from the IIT campus where Mies van der Rohe had begun to hold court. The Farnsworth house consists of two side-by-side, shifted rectangles, which are each raised up above the ground by steel columns. The first of these, which is just a flat, open platform, is used as an entrance deck and is offset from the main house, which it is joined to. The house, as the second rectangle, is raised even farther off the ground, and it is sheathed entirely in glass between the columns from the flat floor to the flat roof of the long, thin, one-story structure. This design is a severe rationalization of the Tugendhat House in Brno, Czechoslovakia, which is more compartmentalized as befits the needs of a larger family with servants. The Farnsworth house was designed for a single woman, and a modest one at that, and so it created a great deal of controversy when it was built because of its lack of privacy.

The Glass House In 1949, Philip Johnson built a 1,728 square foot glass pavilion of his own at the edge of a ridge near the middle of a 47-acre estate he owned in New Canaan, Connecticut. Although it is similar to Mies van der Rohe's Farnsworth House in its almost complete glass wrapper and flat roof, it differs from it in several important respects.

The first difference is that unlike the Farnsworth House, which is elevated above the ground on steel columns that then continue upward to support both the floor and the roof, and which also has a separate adjacent platform that Mies van der Rohe used as an entry deck, the Johnson House is a single rectangular volume that sits on a brick pad, directly on the ground. The reason for the difference relates to the site conditions in each case. The Farnsworth House is located in a low-lying field near a stream, and so it had to be raised to be above the flood plain. The Johnson House is located at the edge of a ridge overlooking a park-like setting below, with a stand of oak and maple trees around it. While both houses are built of structural steel, the Farnsworth House is painted white, and the New Canaan pavilion is painted black. The choice of color in each instance reveals a deeper attitude toward nature. The Farnsworth House has the appearance of an elegant yacht sailing across a sea of grass, surrounded by a forest. Following that metaphor, nature becomes the background to a fantasy of escape from the real world into a private realm, and is not meant to be engaged. The platform in front of the house is an intermediated zone between nature and the rarefied world inside the glass walls of the house, but unlike the Japanese *engawa*, which is used as a seating area from which to contemplate the beauty of the garden just beyond the final step down to ground level, the platform of the Farnsworth house is little more than a glorified, open foyer.

Johnson's Glass House, on the other hand, is literally grounded in nature and is a viewing platform from which to appreciate the verdant beauty of the wooded estate around and below it. Its brick floor is a processed version of the earth on which it rests, eloquently mitigating between technology and the environment. The glass panels that enclose the house are fixed, and so there is no doubt that the house is also a hermetically sealed capsule, in the same way that its Miesian precedent is, but Johnson obviously did share the particularly American sensibility of having a love of the outdoors.

Robert Venturi: The Vanna Venturi House

The Vanna Venturi House is one of the most important works of architecture from the twentieth century. In order to fully appreciate its significance, it is necessary to describe the role that its architect, Robert Venturi, and his partner, Denise Scott Brown, played in challenging the prevailing attitudes of the time, and the way in which the house reflects that apostasy.

Robert Venturi is as well known as a theoretician as he has been for the buildings he has designed. He has been somewhat of an anomaly throughout his distinguished career, consistently outdistancing even the most original thinkers in the architectural avant-garde with the freshness of his ideas. Venturi and Scott Brown continue to personify and perpetuate the original spirit that began in Philadelphia in the late 1950s and early 1960s. If the attentions of an increasingly fashion-conscious profession and the public that followed it may now have focused elsewhere, something very substantial took place in Philadelphia during a period that lasted roughly from 1955 to 1974, with architectural repercussions that continue to surface in surprising and unexpected ways today. The University of Pennsylvania, under the leadership of Dean G. Holmes Perkins, then began to be the focal point of a daunting array of talent at that time. Louis I. Kahn was unquestionably the spiritual leader of the school, and others, such as Aldo Giurgola and Ian McHarg, had, and still continue to have, considerable influence. But the work that Robert Venturi was doing there in the early 1960s unquestionably generated great excitement, and he developed a sizable following.

Complexity and Contradiction Venturi's book *Complexity and Contradiction in Architecture*, which was first released in 1966, had received an extensive preview in the Yale journal *Perspecta* one year earlier. The issue soon spread quickly through the studios of schools throughout the country.

The book itself began as personal footnotes to a course in architectural theory that Venturi taught at Penn, with more than 350 small examples used as a series of lecture slides to incrementally establish an irrefutable thesis that has now been widely recognized as having totally changed the direction of architecture. Rather than simply being an attack on the Modern Movement, *Complexity and Contradiction* was a plea for a more interesting and humane alternative.

The thesis of the book is simply that buildings that have several complex design criteria are far more interesting than those that do not, and that less, rather than being more, as leading Modernist Mies van der Rohe famously said, is simply a bore. As the architectural equivalent of a child's recognition of a king's nakedness in the fable about the emperor's new clothes, Venturi's book eventually served to expose the weaknesses of the Modern Movement and was a critical factor in its decline. As a member of what author Tom Wolfe has called the "academic compound" himself, Venturi was able to put forward arguments that others outside of it had not dared to formulate. He knew how to structure those arguments most effectively. Since *Complexity and Contradiction* is organized in a lecture format, with points emphasized with images, there is a real, cumulative sense of an irrefutable position being established, and of a limiting intellectual barrier being dismantled piece by piece. As such, the book is a legitimate antidote to *Vers Une Architecture*, which was written to proclaim the beginning of the Modern Movement more than four decades earlier, serving as a self-proclaimed "Gentle Manifesto" set in opposition to that more strident call by Le Corbusier. The proposals put forward by Venturi for an architecture that was complex rather than simple, related to history and context rather than being dismissive of it, symbolic and ornamental rather than intentionally codeless, and humorous rather than deadly serious, were all part of what he called the circumstantial and ordinary aspects of everyday life. His recognition of the important place of all of these elements in the significant architecture of the past, as well as in meaningful direction in the future, elicited an eager response, and eventually served as one of the main building blocks of the Postmodern Movement that followed.

Venturi's "Gentle Manifesto" also shared space with Louis Kahn's latest projects in that prescient 1965 issue of *Perspecta*, the journal of the Yale School of Architecture, reflecting the symbiotic as well as competitive relationship that existed between them. In briefly comparing the two, it should first be noted that each had a firm basis in Modernist theory. As Robert Venturi himself has said: "I have never intended to totally reject Modern architecture in words or work because I do, and I think our architecture should, in important ways, evolve out of it, not revolt against it. Its masterpieces hold their own with those of any age."[27] But, what are those "important ways"? For Kahn the answer has much to do with buildings such as the Richards Medical Laboratory and the Dacca Assembly Hall, which are examples of a kind of historical abstraction that was considered to be acceptable by the Modernists. In this abstraction, specific monuments from the past were deemed suitable for inspiration, but not direct quotation, leading Kahn to include Scottish castles, the towers of San Gimignano, and the temples at Paestum among his sources. For Venturi and Scott Brown this kind of abstraction has also been consistently present, but because a more comprehensive, and virtually encyclopedic, recollection of architectural history lies behind the selection of the references, they tend to be overlaid upon each other in ways that are frequently unintelligible to those who are less knowledgeable.

The Vanna Venturi House, which will be examined here, was designed for the architect's mother and is one of the first instances of this kind of overlay; Michelangelo's Porta Pia, Le Corbusier's Villa Stein de Monzie at Garches, and Palladio's Villa Barbaro at Maser, as well as the fundamental generic symbol for a Classical pediment are all present, just for a start. Such multiple references can be identified in virtually every design that the firm has produced, paradoxically becoming one of the ways that it makes a commentary on Modernism.

Venturi and Kahn may have shared a penchant for historical abstraction to varying degrees, based on the differences in their awareness of sources, but they most certainly parted company over a strong emphasis on structuralism that was promoted by Kahn's engineer, August Kommendant, as well as on the concepts of "existence will" and "served" and "servant" spaces, which Kahn used as further refinements of Functionalism. While *Complexity and Contradiction* may have shocked purists who still believed that less was more, its historicism was still understandable and acceptable. With the publication of *Learning from Las Vegas* in 1972, however, a definite schism was opened between the two. Aside from the obvious heresy of proposing that such a crassly commercial example as Las Vegas could help teach architects how to synthesize irrefutable aspects of popular culture and the built environment and to communicate them more effectively to others, the final formalization of Venturi's ideas of the "duck" and "the decorated shed" make this book just as significant. As *Complexity and Contradiction* Kahn's "wrapping ruins" around the unbuilt meeting place of the Salk Institute and the exterior zone of the Dacca Assembly, which many feel had been inspired by Venturi's first use of layering at the North Penn Visiting Nurse Association Building in Ambler in 1961, show a flirtation with the separation of form and function, but falls far short of the divorce from Modernist doctrine represented by *Learning from Las Vegas.*

Denise Scott Brown Robert Venturi's collaboration with Denise Scott Brown started in 1964, just before the Vanna Venturi house appeared. It added an entirely new and much more humanistic dimension to the firm, leavening it with social consciousness as a more inclusive and wide-ranging agenda of concerns began to emerge.

Denise Scott Brown entered the Architectural Association in London as a fourth-year student in 1952, and soon became interested in the work of Alison and Peter Smithson, who were part of the Independent Group at the Institute of Contemporary Art. She, with a small number of students from the AA, sought them out before they became well known in the profession, and their ideas had a lasting influence on her.

> "As I understood the Smithson phrase 'active socio-plastics,'" she has said, "it meant that architects should design for the real life of the street and for the way communities actually work, even if the results are not conventionally pleasing. There was, I think, an unspoken desire to derive, from a community life that was not immediately beautiful, a deeper beauty, and an intention not to abandon architecture but to make it socially relevant."[28]

Following this, she went to the University of Pennsylvania in 1958, where she was taught by the urban sociologist Herbert Gans, who reinforced the Smithsons' idea that processes and patterns could be discovered and built upon if approached with an open mind.

Learning from Las Vegas; *a Second Manifesto* Finding and expressing those patterns, as well as the significance behind social norms, has been one of the main goals of the firm since Scott Brown has become involved with it. That determination is certainly evident in *Learning from Las Vegas*, which is unequivocal in its expression of support for variety over uniformity. For evidence of this view, it is only necessary to read the chapter in it entitled, "Theory of Ugly and Ordinary and Related and Contrary Theories," which presents one of the clearest and most perceptive criticisms of the Modern Movement that has ever been written. This analysis has lost none of its polemic pertinence. As a plea to architects to look at the world as "what it is" rather than "what it ought to be," the "Theory of Ugly and Ordinary" is a statement of disbelief in the prevailing attitude of exclusivity that was an essential part of the Modern Movement at the time. While representing a natural extension of the ideas first put forward in *Complexity and Contradiction*, *Learning from Las Vegas* presents them in a more empirical and less historically referential way. In expanding upon the innovative work by Donald Appleyard, Kevin Lynch, and John Myer in *The View from the Road*, for example, Venturi, Scott

Brown, and Steven Izenour have added a qualitative dimension to this underestimated but important field of study, and they confirm a reality that has yet to be acknowledged by architects today.

An Enduring Contribution The contribution that Venturi and Scott Brown have made to the diverse architectural scene today as well as the revolution they started, and the rancor that surrounded it, has largely been forgotten today, which provides a poignant reminder of the selective public memory that has become symptomatic of the Information Age. In the relatively short period of time since the Vanna Venturi house appeared and *Complexity and Contradiction* and *Learning from Las Vegas* were written, a social cycle, at least in the Western world, has been completed. The consequence of too much information and too little time to absorb it, this condition has not only been accompanied by collective amnesia but also by a baffling proliferation of literary allusions that go far beyond the original intention of Venturi and Scott Brown to use words in order to prompt linguistic associations with architecture. As a consequence, words have become an indispensable aegis of authority for all aspiring architects and books have become shields to hide behind rather than sources of fresh ideas. Where it may once have been necessary to do professional battle in order to establish the fact that architecture, like language, has semiological components that can be effectively utilized to send signals to those experiencing it, words are now seen as being substitutes for, rather than analogous to, built reality. Architecture is no longer considered to be like a text, but has become the text itself, and, as a result, each new movement is considered to be illegitimate without a titular sage to give it literary credibility.

A Continuing Tendency toward Exclusivity The tendency toward exclusivity, which has plagued the profession since architects began to think of themselves as individual creative agents, now seems to have been magnified. Architects in the developed world, at least, still appear to be closed off, and architecture remains a highly ritualized profession with an elaborate initiation procedure. The double-edged literary sword that Venturi and Scott Brown introduced so effectively in their books is now being used to attack their basic premise.

Venturi, in both a lecture entitled, "Diversity, Relevance and Representation in Historicism, or *Plus ça Change*," delivered in 1982, and a joint presentation with Denise Scott Brown called "Architecture as Shelter, City as Decon" given ten years later in London, has stated that postmodernism, in spite of all the convoluted theorizing of its advocates, turned out to be just as restrictive as its exclusive Modernist predecessor. In "Diversity, Relevance and Representation in Historicism or *Plus ça change*," which was also published in *Architectural Record* nearly 20 years after *Complexity and Contradiction* appeared, Venturi described how postmodernism had used different images than Modernism, but had retained the same exclusivity and rigidity of principles. As such, it had become nothing more than a lockstep sequel to the ideology it had sought to democratize, and had even failed in the relatively simple task of contextual fit that it had set for itself. It once again developed into a conversation between architects, replete with in jokes, rather than the dialogue between architects and the public that it was originally intended to be.

From Exclusivity to Plurality In his own work, Venturi has consistently sought to do otherwise, and in the process has managed to convince several generations of architects that the commonplace and everyday built environment cannot be willed out of existence, and is "almost alright." The mere thought of using conventional elements in a building at first shocked many practitioners, but Venturi's own deft handling eventually convinced even the most reluctant of them that the ordinary could become extraordinary in the right circumstances. Where the Modernists had felt it was necessary to educate and elevate public taste, Venturi and Scott Brown have instead been able to convince architects to accept and improve upon it.

The Vanna Venturi House As expressed in his architecture, his original thesis in *Complexity and Contradiction* constantly surfaces as a struggle between the interior requirements of a building and those of its exterior envelope. This, in turn, typically leads to conflict, ending in the separation and eventual divorce of the two. In one of his most well-known designs, for Venturi's mother's house in Chestnut Hill near Philadelphia, this struggle is acted out between the topographical requirements of a formal, front entry and the main interior stair. The most obvious example of this deliberate conflict is the clash between the main entrance and the central hearth, which is deliberately placed in the path of entry to provide privacy for the interior. This battle is further complicated by the insertion of a stair between the entry and the hearth, which is distorted by the demands of each. As in a project simply called the Beach House in New Jersey that preceded it, this intentional dichotomy, once accepted, eventually seems to give the entire plan a focus. As Venturi has described it:

> This house has a central core containing fireplace, chimney, and stair, as well as entrance. This is not a Classical configuration, because Classical plans usually contain

The house that Robert Venturi designed for his mother Vanna, which is located in Chestnut Hill, north of Philadelphia, Pennsylvania, has historical significance far beyond its modest scale. *Source:* Venturi: Scott Brown Associates

space at the center; but the core generates axial symmetry. The symmetry disintegrates however at the edge, to accommodate particular requirements of the plan. We think setting up an order and then breaking it is in the Mannerist tradition of Classical architecture.[29]

The axiality and the violation of it that he speaks of begins in the siting of the house, slightly off-center of a long, gently angled driveway, only lined with trees along its southern edge. The façade facing this quasi-formal approach, which has now become as iconic in the history of contemporary architecture as that of the Villa Savoye or Fallingwater, which keep it company at that exalted level, is testimony to Venturi's idea of the decorated shed, put forward in *Complexity and Contradiction*. It is intended to send both conscious and subliminal messages rather than being an expression of form follows function in the conventional Modernist sense. The use of various parts of this house as a built syntax with which to speak to observers and those who live in it paralleled a growing interest in semiotics and linguistic theory at the time the Vanna Venturi house appeared, as a way of literally communicating more effectively with the public. In the instance of the Venturi house façade, the level of that communication is nuanced. It begins with the scale, which is much larger than it has to be to convey the intention that the front elevation is a sign, or billboard announcing its purpose, rather than a literal description of its function. The top of the sign is angled to recall a gabled roof and, more essentially, the idea of shelter. The gable, however, is split at the top, which implies a fissure, in reference to the growing stress on the conventional family of America in the early 1960s when this house was built and to the rising divorce rate that tracked that shift. A wide vertical shaft behind the rift, which looks like a chimney and initially conveys the image of hearth and home associated with a fireplace, is actually much wider than it needs to be. This only becomes apparent when viewing the house from the park behind, when the small flues of the real fireplace become visible. Once again, the metaphorical message is that the image of domesticity conveyed by the chimney-like element on the front is not what it seems. This kind of distortion continues with the door, the windows, and an oversized dado on the front elevation. The front door, or what appears to be the main entrance, is really just an oversized covered opening, which is still outside, leading to a pair of doors that are hidden from direct view, inside on the right. Windows are used in symbolic ways, as well, most notably a large square one on the far left side of the façade. Here Venturi wanted to return the window to its traditional role of being what he described as "a hole in the wall," in contrast to the Modernist idea of the wall being an integral surface that should not be violated. "In Modern architecture," he said, "the ideal was not a hole in the wall, which negated the integrity of the wall, but an interruption of wall, an absence of wall, which promoted flowing space and abrogated enclosed space." [30] His large square window, divided by mullions into four equal parts is intended to be reminiscent of traditional windows, even though those in vernacular residential American history were never of this scale or configuration.

Lastly, the stylized overscaled dado that Venturi uses on the exterior of the front wall reiterates his theme of domestic tranquility being threatened by social forces as yet unseen in America, first hinted at in the splitting of the gable and the false solidity of the chimney. The dado was typically used in houses in the past on the inside, in heavily used rooms where chair backs, pushed against a plaster wall could cause damage. It disappeared, except when used as a conceit, in contemporary houses, because drywall or plasterboard is used extensively now, and if it is dented it can be easily repaired using spackle and paint. By placing an overscaled replica of a dado on the entrance façade, Venturi seems to be implying that domestic values have now been turned inside out.

Distorted Symmetry as a Concept Such symmetrical considerations are also prevalent in another house in Greenwich, Connecticut, of 1970, which in spite of its apparent disregard for balance, conforms to a grid similar to that used by Palladio at the Villa Thiene at Cicogna. This provides a tantalizing hint that Rowe's *The Mathematics of the Ideal Villa* might profitably be extended in this direction as well. While its siting at the crest of a trimmed greensward, as well as the unbuilt English manor house that was later proposed as an addition, would seem to argue for the predominance of a romantic aesthetic here, repetition of the "broken order" seen in the Vanna Venturi house as well as an inverted bow fronted "Palladian" façade tend to prevail.

A similar kind of duality is evident in the Trubeck and Wislocki Houses built in the same year on Nantucket. In this case, however, a local Wauwinet cottage type contends with the Classical influence, which is only subliminally present in the pedimented temple forms of both houses, as well as their inflected conversational orientation toward the sea, which intentionally recalls the positions of Temples E and F at Selinunte. Rather than being organized along a longitudinal grid, each of these cottages related to a cross-axis, with the Trubeck House stair breaking the symmetry more obviously than any such disruption in the plan of its diminutive partner.

A Local Prototype A similar local prototype also governed in the planning of the house in Delaware built in 1978, which is reminiscent of the barns that are common to the area. Like the house in Connecticut, it also commands a large green, tree-lined site, and the bucolic, farm-like image that it conveys is further amplified with small details, such as a stylized garden trellis/pergola that acts as a gateway between the driveway and the woods beyond. Two overscaled lunettes, however, layered over the east and west elevations of the house, compete with this image, to superimpose a separate meaning of their own. While only the lunette on the western elevation uses an exaggerated, flat Doric colonnade for support, both arches are combined with a pedimented gable to evoke primal, basilican forms that might seem totally extraneous to the rural idyll as first perceived.

While contradictory at first sight, the flattened Doric colonnade of this house, which initially looks like a caricature of the Order it mimics, actually answers to a nearby wood that comes close to the house at this point. In this way it is similar to the monumental order of the Temple of Poseidon at Paestum or the Heraion at Olympia, which both clearly show the evolution of Greek construction from timber to stone and relate to their own natural surroundings. In a discussion of the relations between the column and the tree trunk, which was its original form, Demetri Porphyrios has used a comparison between David Humes's analyses of entasis in *A Treatise on Human Nature* with Le Corbusier's geometric view of the same relationship. As a conclusion to this, Porphyrios has said:

Both Hume and Le Corbusier speak of the way in which the column imitates the tree. Neither of the two speaks of actually reproducing a tree. Hume discovers in nature's workings an anthropomorphic image. Le Corbusier, on the other hand, discovers in nature a geometricity, which is made pertinent by his admiration for the precision and exactitude of the machine. The Classical imagination looks at the tree trunk and sees in it an image of stability which it commemorates in the form of the entasis of the column.[31]

In the exaggeration of the entasis then, the essence of the natural beginning of the column is isolated here. The columns were originally designed to be round, but were later made flat, so that they become a caricature of a Classical column, serving as a signifier rather than a literal copy of the original.

In this sense, this arcade also recalls a particularly Albertian attitude toward the colonnade as ornament, rather than structure, as it was in antiquity. Whether it was determined to be this way through an intentional revision of Classical archetypes, as some would have it, or was the result of ease of access to late Hellenistic and Roman examples, the fact remains that Alberti did not view the column as an independent element, but as the load-bearing part of a solid wall, and the linear equivalent of a vertical line of force. The multivalency presented by this one part of the house in Delaware, where a single colonnade represents the exaggerated, vernacularized shadow of nearby trees, an Albertian translation of an ornamental absence of wall, and the formal echo of the nostalgically rural typology embodied in the house itself, is indicative of the level of sophistication present in the exploration of these two themes.

As incongruous as the connection may seem, Venturi himself has stated that he sees his work as an extension of Modernism rather than the antithesis of it, and as such, his fascination with these themes places him within the tradition of German Romantic Classicism on the Miesian side of the movement rather than in sympathy with the machine aesthetic of Le Corbusier. In his sympathetic alignment with Schiller and Schinkel, rather than Chandigarh, Venturi extends the sympathetic humanistic strain of Modernism that is frequently forgotten today, and while Mies van der Rohe has now been faulted for his cold, antisocial minimalism in glass and steel, it should be remembered that the Carolingian Cathedral in his hometown of Aachen remained a frequently quoted source in his early work, and he saw the New National Gallery in Berlin, which was one of his last buildings, as the contemporary parallel to the Neoclassicism of the Altes Museum.

Complexity and Confrontation An unequivocal attitude toward the importance of the wall, as well as to the house as a shelter, rather than the Modernist glazed pavilion exposed to public view, is especially evident in the early plans of the Wike and D'Agostino projects, as well as in the roof forms of Vanna Venturi, the Tucker House, and the ski lodge at Vail. This feeling for the protectiveness of the wall, in particular, has had a singular influence upon many architects today, who have generally tended to mistake introspection for living under siege. The consistent theme of conflict in each of these houses comes from the discrepancies that are frequently discovered between form and function in both plan and elevation, and are always consistent with Venturi's thesis of *Complexity and Contradiction*.

If these conflicts seem disconcerting and possibly avoidable, they begin to take on certain logic with familiarity, as is the case in the house in Tuckers Town, Bermuda, completed in 1975. The "broken order" first mentioned by Venturi in reference to the Vanna Venturi house is repeated here, most noticeably in the shifted axis of the main entrance. In this case, the front door slides across the façade to accommodate the hierarchical claims of the library on one hand and the guesthouse on the other, which both share a vestibule with the main reception rooms in the center. The angular contortions and intersections that result from this tripartite need also produce a house that is delightfully comfortable on its hillside overlooking the sea.

Two subsequent houses, on Long Island and in Maine, are even more gracious, in the best Shingle Style tradition, and are reminiscent of the mansions designed by Peabody and Stern, William H. Dabney Jr., or Mckim, Mead, and White just before the turn of the century. Rather than being stiff, formal exercises in this genre, these houses evoke a genuine sense of nostalgia for an idyllic time in America's past, recalling straw hats and white linen, as well as long hot summer nights spent sipping lemonade on a veranda overlooking a vast expanse of green lawn. This is a dignified, rather than introspective or antisocial, architecture, which is particularly noteworthy in that it comes from the same office that first charted the course through the collapse of idealism for many in the past. While they have now taught generations of architects how to cope with this age of diminished expectations, Venturi and Scott Brown have shown in these last houses that it is also possible, against all odds, to discover ideals once again, and the reasons for doing so defy the referential analysis that has typically been used to attempt to explain their intentions. The latest houses go far beyond the artificial creation of a heritage that has been so common in a comparatively young country that has always had such a craving for history of its own. They mark a turning point at which America needs to be reminded that it is now in danger of losing the traditions that it has, and they point toward the future by effectively reinterpreting the past.

The White House

The White House in Washington, D.C., has become such a ubiquitous national symbol that few Americans ever give a second thought about its origins, let along the fact that it is actually a house. As for its sources, it can have no more valid historical authority than it has, having been initiated, planned, approved, and staked out by none other than George Washington himself, just before and during the start of his tenure as the first President of the United States of America.

A Basic Contradiction The need for a house for the presidential family was not a foregone conclusion in America after the Revolutionary War had been won. It was as much in question as the idea of a capital city itself to a group of leaders and a nation that had just freed itself from the domination of a world power. It was Washington who promoted the idea of a federal capital, and he wanted it, and the presidential residence within it, to be the equal of anything in Europe. An area called Columbia, with obvious reference to the discovery of America by Christopher Columbus, was set aside as a separate district on land ceded to the new federal government by the States of Maryland and Virginia. The plan for the new city was designed by French urbanist Pierre Charles L'Enfant and is a brilliant solution to problems posed by difficult topographical conditions, accommodating a low-lying wedge-shaped piece of land at the intersection of the Potomac River basin. L'Enfant's plan is essentially a gridiron layout, but it is crisscrossed with a series of diagonal avenues that roughly conform to the divergent angles of the two branches of the Potomac that make up the southern border of the city. These diagonals provide sweeping vistas in a way that a gridiron plan cannot, regardless of the width of the streets used in it, and they encourage monumental landmarks at their intersections.

The President's House was intended to be one of these landmarks and was originally planned at a scale felt to be large enough to hold its own in that category. A Residence Act, passed by Congress, finally gave official governmental approval for the house in 1790, setting a mandatory date of 1800 for its completion. As the construction of the infrastructure for the new capital city on the Potomac advanced, a basement was dug for it, based on preliminary estimates of its size, and the search for an appropriate design was then underway.

Thomas Jefferson as a Contender It is ironic that Thomas Jefferson, who was Washington's Secretary of State at the time, was available for consultation on the design of the President's House but was not selected to do so. He was certainly capable of giving it, since he was an exceptionally talented, self-taught architect, who had designed his own residence, called Monticello, in nearby Virginia and had consulted on the layout of the University of Virginia as well. And yet, there was a sense of competition in this area between the two since Washington was confident of his own abilities in this area because he had planned his own private residence of Mount Vernon as well and was probably too proud to ask Jefferson for advice. Instead, Washington agreed to open up the search to a national competition, while searching privately for a likely candidate to design and build the house. Jefferson was forced to resort to the humiliating subterfuge of having a surrogate submit his design, which looks remarkably like *La Rotunda*, or the Villa Capra, by Andrea Palladio, complete with its four distinctive temple fronts and dome.[32]

James Hoban to the Rescue Henry Laurens, who was a friend of Washington's and who lived in Charleston, South Carolina, recommended an Irish-American architect and builder named James Hoban to the President. Hoban was young, energetic, and accommodating, and Washington liked him.[33] He started by surveying the foundation that had already been built and based his design on a residence, called Leinster House, that he had come to know while he was a student at the Drawing School of the Royal Dublin Society. Washington knew the family that lived there, especially Edward Fitzgerald, who had fought on the American side during the war, and had been held in Charleston as a prisoner of war by the British.[34] Hoban had been apprenticed to an architect who was an advocate of Neoclassicism, and so would have been well versed in the Palladian Revival then taking place during the Georgian Period in London. Washington officially selected James Hoban as architect on July 16, 1792.

Hoban had difficulty accommodating the dimensions of the existing basement to the scale of Leinster House, but quickly made the adjustments necessary to each to make his design work. It was a three-story high Palladian mansion, about one-fourth the size of the house Washington and L'Enfant had anticipated, but still much larger than any public residence that Americans had seen before. Several pretenders had been built by city authorities in New York and Philadelphia during the 1790s, in the hope that both the federal capitol and the President's House that had been planned for the District of Columbia would not materialize, and that Congress and the president, would turn to them as an alternative. Each of the houses that were built to lure Washington to them were similar in some ways to Hoban's design, with the one built in New York being closest in intent. It also has a raised podium base and projecting temple front, but is not even close to the scale of the residence that was finally completed in Washington, D.C., in 1798.

Washington had been a surveyor before his service in the French and Indian War. He was the one who finally settled the debate about where his house should be sited. He selected the northern edge of the larger rectangular basement that had been prepared for it and in doing so, pulled it back from Pennsylvania Avenue toward a park to the north. This denied L'Enfant's original intention of having the house terminate a vista along the avenue and of having it and the United States Capitol Building at the other end act as visual anchors for the wide thoroughfare.

But, this adjustment did allow for the house to more easily accommodate its difficult, double function as both a national institution and a private home, with the north side, facing Pennsylvania Avenue becoming the public side, and the south side, facing a park that has now been reduced to the South Lawn, serving as the presidential residence. A cornice, which wraps around the entire rectangular perimeter, unites the front and back, but their elevations are different. The rusticated podium base, which is evident on the south side, is missing on the north, where a prominent temple front, that once intended to act as a *porte cochere*, projects out, pulling visual emphasis on the main entrance.

The front, as it exists, has a pediment supported by Ionic columns, over a pair of doors that serve as the main entrance, covered by a fan lunette. It is flanked by five windows on each side, crowned by alternating arched and angled pediments in the manner favored by Michelangelo, in such projects as his vestibule for the Laurentian Library in Florence. These windows have very low sill heights, giving them a long elegant profile, while those on the third story directly above them, which have no pediments, are shorter. Both the longer, lower rank and the shorter, upper one have supporting brackets under each ledge, which, while modest, reinforces the connection between this presidential residence and its Palladian heritage, as well as between that reinterpretation of Renaissance principles, and its origins, in the work of Michelangelo, who was the greatest Renaissance architect of all.

Remarkable Stonework Perhaps the fourth major surprise to a layperson with little knowledge of the history of the White House, following the revelations that Jefferson surreptitiously entered the competition to design it, and that Washington not only skirted the competition process to find a designer that he liked, but also drove the stakes for his house himself, is that it is made of stone. Its anonymous white shell hides its substructure so well that it is difficult to tell what it is made of. But, the White House, as it came to be called because of its thick coating of paint over the whitewash necessary to seal its Agua Creek sandstone walls because of their porosity, is decidedly a masonry building. Scottish masons from Edinburgh were brought over to cut the stone, build the wall, and carve the rustication, the quoins, and other decorative elements to a level of excellence rarely seen before or since.[35] Their skill is most evident on the south side, looking up from the South Lawn. When the building received a major cleaning and repainting in 1990, and layers of covering were removed, the individual marks of the original stone masons were exposed, showing that the crew followed a custom dating back to the building of the pyramids in which each mason was paid at the end of the day according to the number of his "banker" marks cut into the stones that he had completed, rather than being paid an hourly wage.[36] More than 30 professional masons built the White House, according to the different marks that have been found. As soon as it was completed, however, the house was covered with whitewash to seal the stone, which was pale grey, and the whitewash was mixed following a unique recipe that included salt, glue, and ground rice, as well as the usual mixture of lime and water, that allowed it to be applied like paint.[37]

A Tragic Loss Washington managed to serve out his entire presidency, from 1789 until 1797, while living in the house that he had played such a formative role in having designed and built, but the British were not through with America just yet. The War of 1812, based mostly on the economic competition that the young nation was beginning to present to Britain, acted out mainly through naval clashes on the trade routes across the Atlantic and in the Caribbean, led to British invasion. They marched on Washington in the late summer of 1814, and, after setting fire to the Capitol and helping themselves to food that Dolley Madison had set out for guests before fleeing for her life, they torched the White House.[38]

After the British were defeated by Andrew Jackson at the Battle of New Orleans in January 1815, the rebuilding of the house that had soon become one of the most potent symbols of American identity became a national priority, quite unlike the hesitation that had plagued its construction in the first place. President James Madison helped to ensure that, as it was rebuilt, the White House was as close to the original as possible.

THE SOUTH

The Shotgun House

The shotgun house type has been traced back to New Orleans in the early 1800s, when a group of Haitians, who had left the island after a slave rebellion against the French had settled there, built a community of the houses that started the form. From that point, it has been tracked further to the Yoruba compounds of West Africa, which is where a majority of slaves came from.[39] At the Yoruba source, houses are placed in a cluster around a central space. The emphasis is on the group, or the tribe, rather than the individual, and the family and its extended members were more important than any single member of it. This focus included the recognition of deceased ancestors as well.

Like the Yoruba houses, the dwellings in New Orleans also had one room, and they were built in rows on both sides of a block so that the backs of the long narrow units faced onto a common open space between them, like an elongated open courtyard. This court served as a combination social space, cooking area, playground for children, place to wash laundry and hang it out to dry, and area for entertainment.

After slavery was abolished in the United States, African Americans adopted the shotgun house as their own, and it has since come to be identified with their history and cultural traditions.[40] The name of the house comes from the fact that the circulation of the long narrow plan runs continuously along one side from front to back, so that a gunshot fired through the front door could go straight out the back door without hitting anything.

As the house evolved and became even more closely associated with a collective identity, slight refinements were made to improve on its already abundant climactic and social advantages. The single-story units, which rarely exceed 600 to 700 square feet in area, started to become the beneficiary of the same mass production techniques that were used on the bungalow, which became extremely popular in America in the decades just before World War I. Like the shotgun, the bungalow is also raised up off the ground to allow cross ventilation to flow underneath, but the so-called "crawl space" beneath it is actually high enough to allow someone to get under it, for whatever reason. The main living floor of the shotgun is typically only three steps, or little more than two feet above grade, which is enough for air movement, but not for access. The two types both started to use clapboard siding, which was run up in great quantities after the turn of the twentieth century, as well as air vents right below the roof ridge to allow for the heat that would build up at the top of the attic space to escape. The bungalow typically also has a front porch, but it is much larger than that provided on the shotgun, which is recessed and concentrated only where the front door is located, on one side. Precast concrete steps started to be used on each type of house as well, to save construction time and cost. The shotgun is also identifiable by one square wooden column holding up the roof above the porch.

The differences between the two residential forms have much to do with variations in social patterns. The front porch of the bungalow, facing the sidewalk and the street, was initially used as a social space, from which residents could greet and converse with neighbors, so it typically extends the full width of the house. There is usually no back porch, however, although some types did have that option. The shotgun, on the other hand, presents a relatively blank façade to the street for security or protective reasons perhaps, and the porch, which occupies a little under one-third of the entire front elevation and is called out by a small pent roof above it, is not wide enough to be a social space, being primarily intended as an entrance portico. Six to eight feet separate the front step from the front door, recessed far behind the pent roof. The real social space for the residents of a shotgun house was a porch that projected out into the common courtyard in the back. Old photographs show people sitting on these porches or washing clothes there on metal washboards placed in metal or clay pots of water.

Unlike the shingle-roofed bungalows, tin sheeting was the material of choice for the shotgun houses, and they also had lower window sills that allowed more light and air into the small, sequential rooms lined up along the circulation spine along the side.

The Stretto House

The Stretto House, which was designed by Steven Holl in 1989 and completed in 1992, is located near Dallas, Texas. The clients had originally intended to build on a site they had purchased near the Turtle Creek section of that city, but were dissuaded from doing so by the architect because he felt that it was too small. Holl helped them find a new property, which also has a stream running through it. As it crosses the property, this stream is divided into three sections by dams that form ponds behind them.[41] During his first visit to the site, Holl noticed that the water falling over each of the dams created a murmuring overlapping sound. This inspired him to consider that the beginning concept of the house might be based on the idea of musical layering. Discussions with a friend, who is a pianist, led him to focus on the fugue stretto form, in which each note is echoed before it is completed.[42] He then found a classical example of this form in the "Music for Strings, Percussion and Celeste" by Béla Bartók. He recalls that he concentrated on the fact that the piece is divided into four movements and "has distinct divisions between heavy (percussion) and light (strings)." [43]

Four Sections To establish a metaphysical connection between the house and this musical form that replicates the sound of the stream, Holl divided it into four distinct zones, each having heavy and light materials that correspond to the percussion and strings of the stretto. For the heavy section he has used masonry with

Stretto House. © Paul Warchol Photography

49

metal roofing acting as the lighter foil for its mass. These four sections extend in a syncopated line along the back edge of the site, beginning with the entry on the south and ending at the bank of the stream that crosses the property along its northern boundary. The house is anchored by a separate pavilion in which the guest quarters and a small library are located, placed on the far side of a square parking lot at the end of the driveway. This pavilion, which is a major effort in its own right, is more introspective and solid in appearance than the residence across the drive, with a minimum of openings to protect the books and artwork inside it from the hot Texas sun, as well as the privacy of the guests living there. The walls are made of tilt-up concrete slabs with a moss green admixture used to soften the harsh whiteness of the cement. The main entrance to the main residence, located across the bluestone gravel motor court from this pavilion, is indirect, preceded by a raised porch covered by the first and the lowest of a playful series of canopy-like curved metal roofs that echo the vernacular form buildings of this region. After moving under this open canopy and through the protected and deeply inset front door, passage through the house is then modulated by a series of four 10 feet wide and 45 feet deep service blocks, spaced 35 feet apart, with the last of these partially planted in the stream.

Served and Servant Zones These zones, which appear as vertical towers on the main street facing eastern evaluation, establish a regular visual order that evokes musical transcription on a scale, especially since the curving metal roofs move so lyrically up and down between them. The first of these service bars, which are also reminiscent of a similar method of modulation used by Morphosis in the Crawford House in Montecito, California, discussed elsewhere here, contains a stairway as well as the majority of the chimney behind a fireplace facing into a large living area adjacent to it. This servant–served relationship continues through a second, more open band, to a third that contains the kitchen. To alleviate the narrowness that the 10 feet width of the masonry service bar imposes, Holl projects a U-shaped section of a kitchen counter out from it into the dining space that it faces. The fourth and final bar, which spans, or delicately mitigates between land and water, also appropriately serves as the termination of a long, narrow swimming pool, placed in an open court, also covered by a curved metal canopy. The entire house is a fascinating study in scale, rhythmical movement, and balance, between solid and void, open and closed, curved and straight, so that the carefully choreographed passage through it becomes a journey of discovery.

THE CENTRAL REGION

The American Townhouse

In America, the townhouse is now taken for granted as a residential type, but it is really a relatively recent innovation with a rather turbulent European lineage. A townhouse may be defined as a subgroup of the row house, being attached to similar houses on each side, with several stories, a long narrow, rectangular plan, and windows only on the narrow front and back ends.[44] It differs from the row house in that it is usually associated with a higher economic level of ownership.

Its European heritage may be traced first to both Britain and France, beginning in 1612 in the *Place Royale*, which was instituted by King Henry IV. This *place*, or urban square in Paris, which later became the *Place des Vosges* after the Revolution, was formulated by the king as a commune that was intended to develop and promote the French silk-making industry. He visualized the square as being surrounded by identical, attached houses that would have shops for the artisans at street level and living quarters for them above. At that time, during the Renaissance, Italian artisans dominated the market and Henry IV successfully persuaded several of them to set up shop in the *Place Royale* so that local craftspeople could learn from them. The houses that were built there, which are described in detail in Volume II of this series, were rather rustic and wide by contemporary townhouse standards, with a steeply angled, overhanging gable roof that was intended to keep the rain from penetrating the half-timbered wattle and daub façade. The king wanted to emphasize royal support for the enterprise by having a townhouse built for himself on the square, but, instead, unwittingly doomed it to failure by doing so. His association with the project and sporadic presence there encouraged courtiers to follow him, and they eventually displaced the original occupants. They also changed the construction type from wood to brick and stone giving the *Place des Royale*, renamed the *Place des Vosges* after the Revolution, the elite appearance and constituency it has today. This contributed to the aura of social exclusivity that the townhouse has as well.

Covent Garden Under the patronage of Charles I, the Earl of Bedford developed a similar kind of combined commercial and residential endeavor in London at Covent Garden in 1630. This area was already being used as a farmer's market, and the Earl's architect, Inigo Jones, simply placed a row of shophouses on each long side of the rectangular plaza and designed a small church, named St. Paul's, for one of its short sides. Unlike the elegant townhouses that now line all sides of the *Places des Vosges*, those on the Covent Garden plaza have not survived, but we know that Jones was converted to Neoclassicism during his prolonged stay in Rome, resulting in the transplantation of Palladian principles from Italy to England when he returned in the early 1600s. King Charles I was also responsible for encouraging a similar kind of urban form at both Great Queen Street and Lincoln's Inn Fields, which have evolved from their original form, setting a standard for townhouse clusters that followed. As a result of the fire of 1666, wood was replaced by masonry. George Dance, who was the mentor of Sir John Soane, who created one of the most famous townhouse groups of all in the Lincoln's Inn Fields cluster, was then instrumental, along with Sir Robert Taylor, of further codifying the townhouse into four categories, in the Building Act of 1774.[45] London was in the midst of a building boom at that time as a result of the Industrial Revolution, and those who benefited from that economic surge created a demand for a house type that suited their newly acquired social position.

The Royal Circus and Crescent in Bath Somewhat unexpectedly, because it occurred in a smaller setting, the next biggest advance in the evolution of the townhouse type occurred in Bath, west of London. This was due to the growing popularity of the resort among the upper middle class and the aristocracy, who prospered from the wealth that was generated by the Industrial Revolution. A father and son team, referred to at the time as John Wood the Elder and Younger felt that the Classical style was most appropriate for a series of projects they completed in Bath between 1754 and 1775. The small city has natural hot springs that once attracted Roman visitors when they occupied Britain in the past, and these builders decided to capitalize on this Classical connection. John Wood the Elder designed a three-story high, circular group of houses called the Royal Circus based on the Coliseum in Rome. Like its progenitor, the Circus also has column styles that progress from Doric at the ground floor to Ionic in the middle and Corinthian at the top of the inner façade. The ground and second stories also have floor to ceiling windows that fill the entire wall between these colonnades, in which the columns are arranged in pairs and span from cornice to cornice. The top floor, which was typically reserved for servants, had a smaller window, and this occupied about half the wall surface between these column pairs, and was placed in the middle of it. This composition resulted in an elegant, restrained image of dignified privilege that had an enormous influence on later designers.

The Royal Crescent, begun in 1767 by John Wood the Younger, follows the same prototype, but is laid out in a wide arc at the crest of a slope, open to the view of the rolling landscape, just beyond the bottom of the hill on which it is sited.

Robert and James Adam Scottish brothers Robert and James Adam were responsible for the next iteration of the townhouse type in their speculative design of Adelphi Terrace in London. This helped to solidify the reputation of the townhouse as a precinct of the upper classes because the brothers raised the attached units up onto a plinth base. They differentiated between the ends and the middle of the complex so that it resembled a large royal palace, rather than a series of individual houses. John Nash followed their lead in his design for townhouses, also known as terrace houses, in Regent's Park, elevating the contributions of the Wood and Adam families to a new level of urbanism by using the townhouse to define a new street pattern carved through the northern part of London.

Transplanted in America The townhouse was introduced to America by the British during the Colonial Period, appearing first in the most strategically important East Coast settlements at that time, such as New York, Boston, Philadelphia, and Savannah. Several architects adopted the typology and adapted it to regional conditions, since the early settlements were far less organized than London or Bath, and far more crowded. In 1794, Charles Bulfinch, who had studied architecture in London, designed the Tontine Crescent in Boston, which borrows heavily from both its semicircular antecedent in Bath and the Adelphi Terrace in London. Like them, it is also Neo-Classical, opens up to a park and is raised up on a stately base, with larger units, like bookends, on both sides to complete the series. These larger units are more ornately detailed than the three-story attached houses in the middle of the graceful curve, but the tripartite division of the floors as well as the window pattern used by John Wood the Elder and Younger have been maintained.

A Symbol of Democracy It is ironic that the townhouse, which is now viewed as a symbol of social prestige and refinement, was originally considered to be just the opposite when its popularity began to spread in the United States. Soon after the American Revolution, the image of similar, tall, narrow houses joined together in a row may have conjured up images of Continental soldiers marching into battle. They also mirrored the democratic aspirations of the new nation perfectly at that time of their own uniformity and clusters of this new type of housing started to appear in many of the major cities along the East Coast. Those urban areas with the strongest strain of British influence, which played the most central role in the struggle for independence, have the oldest and most influential examples. New York, Boston, Philadelphia, Baltimore, and Annapolis each have an equal share of this heritage.

Benjamin Henry Latrobe, who was born in Britain in 1764 and is perhaps best known for his design of the U.S. Capitol in Washington, D.C., applied his thorough knowledge of Classicism to several townhouse projects in Philadelphia and elsewhere. He built a number of these with fellow Neoclassicist advocate Thomas Carstairs in central Philadelphia in the early 1800s, with red brick façades that helped them to match their Georgian prototypes, which were built in that city several decades before.[46] Several of his disciples, such as Robert Mills, followed Latrobe's lead. Mills designed Franklin Row in Philadelphia in 1809, which is generally considered to be one of the finest examples of townhouse planning during the early years of the Republic.

Charles Bulfinch, who was based in Boston, rivaled Latrobe in his knowledge of British Neoclassicism. He complemented this with travels throughout the United Kingdom, during which he surveyed the best examples of the style. Bulfinch tended to focus more loosely on Palladian principles and excelled at adapting them to the unusual urban patterns that started to emerge in America as the country continued to mature. Tontine Crescent, which Bulfinch built in Boston in 1794 as a speculative venture, demonstrates his high level of skill at translating a style that had become so closely identified with England into a different national dialect. The growth of print media in America at the same time provided a conduit for Neoclassical style in general, and the idea of townhouses lining a residential urban square specifically, to reach the mass market, and builders, developers, and contractors with far less aesthetic judgment and skill than Latrobe or Bulfinch started to adapt designs published in pattern books into speculative developments.[47] In less talented hands, at a lower budget, and as intended for a less discerning clientele, these became the row house.

The Greek Revival After the War of 1812 with Britain, the Palladian style lost its appeal because of its association with the enemy that had invaded Washington, D.C., burned the White House, and was finally routed by American forces led by General Andrew Jackson at the Battle of New Orleans. Architects turned to Greek Classicism instead, with its allusion to democracy and philosophy. By the 1840s, the Greek Revival style had all but replaced British Palladianism and was prevalent in both the townhouse and row house permutations. It held sway for about a decade. All that had really changed were the details, which were finer in proportion, with Ionic and Doric columns, dentils, broken architraves, and thinner pediments being the defining features. New York City, which was then in the process of becoming one of the most important cities in the country and experienced a sevenfold expansion of its population between 1825 and 1867, was replete with Greek Revival townhouse clusters. These include LaGrange Terrace, also known as Colonnade Row, which was located at Lafayette Place, designed by Seth Greer, built in 1833. It is unusual because of a row of 12 two-story high columns rising up from a projecting, rusticated ground floor to a continuous cornice above. The second and third floor façade is recessed behind this row, which gives the unit its name and provides a distinct image of unity and elegance to it.

The Brownstone The Greek Revival was then displaced in mid-century by the brownstone, which has come to be synonymous with the townhouse. This is especially the case in New York City, where many of the best examples still remain. There is some debate about exactly what a brownstone is, but there is little dissent about the key role that this type of townhouse has played in helping to establish the image of upscale urbanity in the consciousness of the general public. This is partly because of the large number of them that were built due to their popularity, leading to their ubiquitous presence as the background for stories, films, and plays about city life. This acceptance by both builders and buyers has been explained as being the result of three key factors. From the perspective of the builder, sandstone was easy to carve and detail, saving on construction costs. Second, the deep reveals that this carving produced set the façade of the brownstone distinctly apart from the wooden profiles of the Greek Revival townhouses that had preceded them, making them memorable, seemingly more durable, and ultimately more desirable to an increasingly wealthy middle and upper middle class clientele. The third factor was that of the color of the sandstone, especially the light mocha shade quarried in Little Falls and Passaic Heights in New Jersey, used in New York City. It matched the color range of furniture materials and wall coverings that were popular in the post–Civil War period.[48]

The brownstone townhouse not only changed the visual character of New York City and the other major American cities where it was built, but altered the essential structure of these urban areas as well. As one historian of this housing type has described this shift:

> Brownstones redefined older American cities in two ways. First, rows of them dominated the streets of all of the larger cities that grew dramatically in the decades around the Civil War. Second, they were used by developers in the way that earlier row houses had been used, that is, to define the boundaries of parks and squares that served as oasis in the densely built cities.[49]

Queen Anne Brown sandstone was not as feasible in earthquake country, however, and a highly ornate version of the Queen Anne style that had swept Britain by storm decades earlier became extremely popular on the West Coast of America, especially in San Francisco. The wooden houses built along the hilly streets of the city by the bay, which are generally referred to as "Victorian Gingerbread," are more accurately Queen Anne style, but not a particularly authentic version of it.

By the time of the devastating fire that destroyed huge areas of San Francisco and led to fire codes that discouraged wooden construction, the townhouse typology was well established in the United States. It continued to evolve through several more iterations from that point forward, but its essential function as urban anchor and catalyst was well established.

Bruce Goff: The Bavinger House

Bruce Goff was born in Alton, Kansas, in 1904. He started his architectural career as an apprentice with Endacott and Rush in Tulsa, Oklahoma, just before

World War I. Because of a shortage of books on architecture at that time, Goff voraciously read every periodical he could find, including an issue of *Architectural Record* that was dedicated to the work of Frank Lloyd Wright. The issue had a profound influence on Goff, who wrote to Wright for more information about his work. Wright sent him a copy of the Wasmuth portfolio by return mail. This portfolio, which had already caused a sensation in Europe among the leaders of the Modern Movement there, became the inspiration for the direction that Goff was soon to take. In addition, Goff was also influenced by the graphic designs of Beardsley, Erté, and Klimt, as well as the architecture of Mendelsohn and Taut, indicating his decidedly expressionistic tastes.

While with Endacott and Rush, Goff designed the Boston Avenue Methodist Church in Tulsa in 1926, but it is one of the rare examples of his nonresidential work. In 1936, Goff began to work for Libby Owens Ford Glass Company because that was the only work available to him during the Depression. This turned out to be a beneficial experience and was of great value to him in his design work.

After serving in the Seabees during World War II, Goff joined the University of Oklahoma at Norman in 1947, which opened up a new, academic phase of his career. But, his residential work also increased during this time.

The Bavinger House The Bavinger House, built near Norman, Oklahoma, in 1950, repeats these themes in an even more primitivistic way. The plan of the house is a spiral, like that of a chambered nautilus, which continues upward at its core to become a tower. The roof is attached to this increasingly smaller coil in the center like a sail that is then also connected to the base, giving the entire house the image of being a temporary encampment by shipwreck survivors on a desert island.

The Farnsworth House by Ludwig Mies van der Rohe is located very close to it, and Mies van der Rohe visited it while supervising work on his own house. It is difficult to imagine two more diametrically different approaches to architecture than those represented by these two architects, since Goff seemed to exemplify the naturalistic and antinatural side of Frank Lloyd Wright's approach.

Goff left the University of Oklahoma in 1956 and serendipitously set up his office in the Price Tower in Bartlesville, nearby, designed by Frank Lloyd Wright. After the Bavinger House, his

Bavinger House. *Source:* A. Y. Owen/Time & Life Pictures / Getty Images

work became even more *ad hoc*, as can be seen in the Gutman, Gryder, Dace, and Nicol Houses that were built between 1958 and 1964. Each of these focuses on centrally located, stepped, and carpeted "conversation pits," extreme geometric forms, and a novel use of color. The Price House of 1956, which was commissioned by the same client that built the tower in Bartlesville, typifies the extent of Goff's stylistic approach.

Between 1970 and 1978, Goff returned to the circular and spiraling themes that he had used earlier in residential projects such as the Bavinger House. He has come to represent an identifiable school of Frank Lloyd Wright followers that share his middle American background, expressionistic tendencies, and theory of an organic architecture that complements natural systems.

Frank Lloyd Wright: The Oak Park, Robie, Hollyhock, Jacobs, and Fallingwater Houses

Of all of the architects in the relatively brief history of the United States, Frank Lloyd Wright is certainly the most well known and the most prolific. He boasted of having completed at least one building in every state in the Union, and the majority of these are houses. It is difficult to select those that would present a truly representative sample of his work because he was constantly reinventing himself, and during his long career he went through five distinct phases. But, any survey would of necessity begin with the residence he built for himself and his family in Oak Park near Chicago when he started his own practice there. It was a labor of love and was added to several times as his family grew, also serving as a personal laboratory for ideas he was developing at the time. These were related to Arts and Crafts theory and the beginning of the Prairie House style, inspired by Japanese traditional architecture that evolved over the years he remained in Oak Park.

The next residence that must obviously be included then is the Robie house, which represents the culmination of the Prairie House style and was among the last projects that Wright completed before beginning a new chapter in his life in Los Angeles. Aline Barnsdall was the catalyst for this change, since she brought Wright to California to oversee the construction of his design for her residence, called Hollyhock House, at the intersection of Vermont Avenue and Sunset Boulevard in Hollywood. This was the beginning of another line of thinking for Wright, related to the idea that Mayan tradition rather than its Japanese equivalent was the real precursor of a true indigenous American heritage. The "textile block" houses, such as the Millard, Storer, Ennis-Brown, and Freeman residences that he realized in Los Angeles, represent an effort by this talented architect to finally integrate industrial materials and techniques with natural processes, in true Arts and Crafts tradition.

Wright was also far ahead of the ecological, or sustainable, movement that now holds sway in contemporary architecture, as his first house for the Jacobs family clearly demonstrates. It is built almost entirely of material gleaned on or near the site. It is also half buried in a hill that blocks the cold wind from the north and opens up to receive passive solar gain from the south. This keeps it cool in the summer and warm in the winter, without predominantly relying upon mechanical systems to do so.

Wright was prone to contracting pneumonia in his later years, and his physician advised him to move to a warm, dry climate to avoid the problem. He, along with his wife, Olgivanna, decided to found a school for architects near Phoenix, Arizona, which Wright named Taliesin West, in honor of his homestead, Taliesin, in Spring Green, Wisconsin. Without a great deal of financial backing, Wright devised an inexpensive means of construction that prospective students could manage to use to build the school, involving local stone placed in rudimentary formwork and then surrounded by a concrete admixture that was poured in to hold the boulders together. Wood taken from the site was used for roof beams, and canvas was used for roofing, since rain in the region is sparse.

Wright's most memorable house, however, is undoubtedly Fallingwater, which was his *riposte* to the Modern Movement, then gaining strength in pre–World War II Europe, and to the Ville Savoye by Le Corbusier, in particular. In the Fallingwater design, Wright has demonstrated his belief that nature and industry, in the form of stone quarried from the site, used in combination with concrete, steel, and glass, must work together, and not to the exclusion of each other.

The Oak Park Studio and Home Frank Lloyd Wright had strong Welsh roots on his mother's side. The Lloyd-Jones family had emigrated from Wales in 1844, just 20 years before he was born. The patriarch of the clan was Richard Jones,

Oak Park House and Studio.   *Source*: Dongjin Sah; Flickr

whom Wright described in his autobiography as "an impassioned, unpopular Unitarian."[50] He married Mary Lloyd in Wales and changed the family name to Lloyd-Jones. They settled in Ixonia, Wisconsin, on a farm in what they referred to as "the valley." Richard Lloyd-Jones appropriated a Druidic symbol, resembling a three-pronged fork turned upside down, as the family symbol. It means "Truth Against the World."[51]

Maternal Encouragement Richard Lloyd-Jones was Frank Lloyd Wright's grandfather. His mother, Anna, was the fourth child of Richard and Mary Lloyd-Jones. She became a teacher and married a Methodist minister named William Russell Carey Wright, from Hartford, Connecticut, whom she met while he was preaching in Lone Rock, Wisconsin. He was also an accomplished musician, especially on the piano and organ, and when Frank was born, the family lived in Richard Center, Wisconsin, since his father was a minister in a church there. Frank Lloyd Wright's mother doted on him to the extent that it caused the couple to argue and drove them apart. For some reason, she was determined that he would be an architect, framing pictures of English Gothic cathedrals that she had taken from periodicals and hanging them on the walls of her son's bedroom. She also gave him a set of wooden Froebel building blocks that she had found out about at the Philadelphia Centennial, which had a profound effect on Wright's understanding of three-dimensional, geometrical relationships.

The family moved to Waymouth, a suburb of Boston, when Frank was three years old, so that his father could take up a position at a church there. He was later sent back to the Lloyd-Jones farm in Wisconsin to work there during the summer. This connection to nature, combined with his exposure to Transcendentalism in New England and the Unitarianism on the Lloyd-Jones side of the family tree, were also important formative influences on Wright's character. The anti-rationalistic thrust of Transcendental theory, which gives priority to intuition rather than empiricism, continued to set Wright apart from his European counterparts throughout his career as an architect. He was especially influenced by Emerson and Thoreau.

After moving back to Wisconsin once again, to Lake Mendota, near Madison, family life became strained by poverty and his father left home. His mother took him to be interviewed by Allen D. Conover, the dean of engineering at the University of Wisconsin, and he was admitted into the program. He continued to live at home and walked several miles to class each day. He liked mathematics, which he compared to his love of music, seeing the similarity between the two. He also took English composition and French, stereotomy, graphic statics, analytical and descriptive geometry, and drafting. He particularly liked drafting, taught by Professor Conover, and his frustration with his progress in English composition prompted him to organize his own course of self-study by reading as much as he could. The authors that interested him most, which should not be surprising given his Celtic background and Transcendental foundation, were the Arts and Crafts theoreticians: Thomas Carlyle, John Ruskin, and William Morris. He also read Goethe, William Blake, and Viollet-le-Duc. Wright did not thrive at the University of Wisconsin, chafing from the need to compete and the rules and regulations, which he characterized as "doctrine."[52]

He left the University of Wisconsin halfway through his senior year for Chicago, to find work in an architecture office there, in 1887. He had $7 in his pocket after paying for his train fare, which he had gotten by pawning his father's books and a mink collar taken off his overcoat. He had no prospects and no place to stay when he arrived at Wells Street Station, and he got a cheap room in a boarding house on Randolph Street. With his $7 down to $3, he chose architects' names out of a city directory, including the firm of J. L. Silsbee, since he had designed a church that Wright knew of. But he wanted to try better firms first, such as the office of William Le Baron Jenney, where he was turned down because he had no examples of his work. After more refusals, moving to an even cheaper room, and foregoing food for four days, he finally went to Silsbee's office and not only discovered a sympathetic interviewer named Cecil Corwin but also found they had something in common in both being minister's sons. He liked the warm and friendly atmosphere in the office. He changed boarding houses, moving to one that was more upscale. He began to socialize at Cecil Corwin's church called All Soul's and met a young woman named Catherine Tobin. She was 16 at the time and he was 19. They were married two years later in 1889. In the meantime, he asked J. L. Silsbee for a raise, and when he was turned down, moved to a firm called Beers, Clay, and Dutton. After deciding he had nothing to learn there, he quit after a few weeks and asked Silsbee to take him back. Silsbee was astonished that he had quit without any assurance of being able to return, and admired his honesty and confidence. He hired him back, with the raise he wanted in the first place.

After a year at J. L. Silsbee's office, he encouraged his mother to sell the house in Lake Mendota and come to Chicago, and they both moved in with a family friend who lived on Forest Avenue in Oak Park. Wright was repelled by what he later described as the "Eastlake mimicry" evident in a "suburban house parade" there.[53] In the same year, he heard about an opening at the office of Adler and Sullivan, doing work drawing details of ornament for the Auditorium Building. He had been fascinated with Owen Jones's *Grammar of Ornament* and had traced all of the details from it. He showed these, as well as some drawings he had done in Silsbee's office, to Louis Sullivan and was hired at $100.00 a month, which was quite a high salary at that time.

A Master-Student Relationship Wright and Louis Sullivan got along well, and because Sullivan favored him, Wright had a difficult time at the start. He literally had to fight to retain his place there, and he ended up getting stabbed in the back with a drafting knife. He later wrote that "then and there, I made up my mind to stay in that office till I could fire every one of the gang" that had tormented him.[54] Sullivan had attended the *Ecole des Beaux Arts* in Paris, as had Henry Hobson Richardson, whom Sullivan admired and who had an equally important role in what came to be called the "Chicago School" of architecture. This involved a radically new approach to technology in relationship to traditional principles. Wright, with his midwestern background and incomplete education, came from a different world and was in awe of Sullivan, who he always referred to as "the Master." They shared an appreciation of the poetry of Walt Whitman, and Sullivan introduced Wright to the work of Herbert Spencer. Wright said he became "like a pencil in the Master's hand."[55]

After his marriage, Wright approached Sullivan with the proposal of a five-year contract in exchange for an advance on his salary large enough to buy a lot in Oak Park and build a home for himself, his wife, and the family they anticipated. Sullivan agreed and even went to see the property that his apprentice had in mind at the corner of Forest and Chicago Avenues. At this point, Wright recalls, he was the highest paid draftsman in Chicago. Frank Lloyd Wright and Catherine Tobin eventually had six children.

Even though his salary was high, his rapidly expanding family stretched Wright's finances. He had been earning overtime pay by working on houses for important clients of Adler and Sullivan at home, and then he began accepting clients of his own, which was not allowed in the contract he had negotiated with Sullivan. It also stipulated that his employer would retain the deed to Wright's house and property until the money they had loaned him had been paid in full. The debt had been paid, but Louis Sullivan was so offended by what he saw as his apprentice's disloyalty that he refused to release the deed. Wright asked Dankman Adler to intervene, but Sullivan was adamant, so Wright quit, having then spent six formative years in that office. He did not speak to Louis Sullivan for 12 years after that, until he visited Sullivan on his deathbed, and the deed, signed by Dankman Adler, then followed.

The Oak Park House Grows When Wright left Adler and Sullivan, he rented an office in the Schiller Building and asked Cecil Corwin to join him in the new firm, Frank Lloyd Wright, Architect. His house in Oak Park, as first designed in 1889, was straightforward, due to the limited amount of money available. It was a modest two-story house with a direct entry into a stairwell, living room, kitchen, pantry, and dining room downstairs and a master bedroom and bath, nursery, and studio above. It had a large fireplace and gabled roof because Wright saw these as being symbolic of domesticity, and there were wooden benches built into the wall on either side of the hearth to underscore this point, even though the family's initial budget was tight. But the pressures of a growing family forced the young architect to add on to the original plan. In 1895, a study replaced the dining room, which was flipped over to where the kitchen had been and lengthened to accommodate a growing number of children, and a new kitchen wing was added, along with a maid's room and a second stairway on the ground floor, leading up to a large playroom above. The master bedroom remained where it was, but Wright's studio space was converted and divided to make two more rooms for the children, and the nursery was extended to make an additional, larger bedroom on the south side of the house. Three years later, in a third phase of addition and renovation that continued until his departure from Oak Park in 1909, a separate entrance for the maid was carved out of the space between the servant's room and the kitchen, and a loft was added as a mezzanine space above the playroom where a piano was installed.

A New Studio More substantially, however, Wright decided to reclaim the private territory he had lost when his studio was converted to bedrooms for his growing family by building an entire office along the north edge of the property, with its own separate entrance. This office component, which is as large as the house it is conveniently attached to by a small connecting passageway and stair, is articulated into clearly differentiated parts that counterbalance the house itself in their form. In addition to the reception area at the center and Wright's office, which is separated from the entrance by a wall, these are an octagonal library, which projects out to the right of the reception area, and a square drafting area to the left. There was also a vault attached to this square room as a separate form between the office and the house, in a secure location at the end of the connecting passage between the two to hold the steadily accumulating amount of money that Wright was making. The library could be used as a private conference room, as a place to meet with clients or employees.

An Arts and Crafts Aesthetic The feeling throughout the Oak Park house and studio is one of warmth and security, due to the large amount of wood that Wright used for the floors, stairs, railings, trim, and furniture, which were all designed by him. This, along with the earth tones used for carpets, stained glass, and paint all coordinate to create a very comfortable domestic environment.

The Winslow House Wright had remained in the Schiller Building office for more than three years until the new home-office was complete, which was intended to save him time and money. His wife, Catherine, used the playroom as a space for her private kindergarten, and so husband and wife each had his/her own realm, coming together at the end of the day for meals with all of the children.

Soon after Wright left Adler and Sullivan and opened his first office in the Schiller Building, he was visited by his first client, William H. Winslow, who asked for a house to be designed for a lot in River Forest. Wright responded with a scheme that was highly unusual for its time due to its minimal profile, low gable roof with wide overhanging eaves, and lack of ornament, except, perhaps, for a horizontal vegetal frieze that is reminiscent of Louis Sullivan's organic detailing, which takes up the top third of the elevation under the eaves. By using a plain surface for the relatively solid massive walls of the bottom two-thirds of the house and this highly rendered band for the top third, which is slightly inset from the base, Wright creates a telescoping effect that makes the house seem to rise. Square window openings, cut into the base, contribute to this effect since they make the wider, lower band seem more solid, with the longer, rectangular windows above them, which cover the entire distance between the sill and the soffit of the wide eave, to extend the visual effect.

The Winslow House was to be the first of an astonishing list of 125 projects, most of which were houses, completed in 11 years at both the Schiller Building and in his Oak Park Studio in Chicago after leaving Adler and Sullivan. This represents a quarter of the projects he completed over his entire long and productive career.

The Robie House Frederick C. Robie came to Frank Lloyd Wright in 1906 with an unusual site for the house that he wanted to build for him and his family. It was a narrow lot sold off the front of a neighboring property, with the obligation that the new house cost at least $20,000 to build so that it would fit into the wealthy neighborhood at 58th and Woodlawn Avenue in Chicago's Hyde Park. Frederick Robie and his wife, Lora, were the beneficiaries of a successful family business of manufacturing bicycles and motorcycles, and Frederick anticipated expanding into the production of automobiles, which were just starting to be used at that time. He presented Wright with a rough sketch of what he wanted, as well as a list of requirements. Prior to World War I, servants were commonplace in the homes of wealthier families, and so this list included two rooms for maids as well as a separate dining room for them. In addition, the requirements included a living and dining room, a kitchen, a master bedroom and bath, two bedrooms for the children, and a guest room. It also included a playroom for the children, a billiard room, and a three-car garage that was a novelty at the time.

Wright met the challenge of accommodating such an ambitious program on an unusual site by splitting the plan into two long narrow bars that slip past each other on the east-west axis, creating an entry level hall in the open area that this creates on the east end, and a walled-in courtyard and a garage for the cars on the west. He also pushed the house as far forward on the site as possible, going against a neighborhood convention of maintaining a 38 feet setback from Woodlawn Avenue in doing so. As in his other Prairie style houses that precede this later, and many would say finest, example of the style, Wright used no basement level here, even though this would have gained him preciously needed space. Instead, he divided the house into three vertical layers of increasing privacy, bringing functions that might otherwise be associated with a basement, such as a billiard room, children's playroom, laundry room, and mechanical room, up to the ground floor. The pinwheel *parti* begins with the offsetting of the two long bars, which are each about 20 feet wide, and is completed by a bedroom block on the third floor that acts as a fulcrum in the middle of the plan.

Wright treats the ground floor like the lower level on an Italian villa, as a service level supporting the *piano nobile* and private domain that superimposes it, above. And, this makes sense as the place for a playroom for the children since it would have been acoustically segregated from the social spaces on the first floor and the bedrooms on the second. That playroom has access to the motor court around the garage, which was probably not the most salubrious place for them to play outside, but the restriction on open space presented by the small site left Wright with few options.

Through the use of a wall running the length of the house along the south elevation, at grade, combined with a long balcony above it that spans between the living rooms above, Wright does manage to make this entrance level suite of rooms seem to visually regress as part of a powerful podium base. The wall and balcony almost conceal the long line of windows that light the suite of rooms at entry level.

A Complex Processional Sequence There are two entrances into the Robie house. The first is from the west side, along a low wall that leads into an entry hall, and the second is from the garage at the east end of the house, which reaches the same point after crossing a hallway that is open to the children's playroom. In each case, the only option then available, other than service stairs that are hidden from view and intended for the hired help, is a scissor stair with runs that are 4 feet wide each that starts in the midst of a large masonry pier that also includes the hearth. It returns on its upward trajectory into a corridor directly above the entry hall at the midpoint between the living and dining rooms, which are each still mostly hidden from view. There is no real reception area on this main floor of the house, so this 8 feet wide by 24 feet long intermediate space performs a double function as both a secondary entry and a wide corridor. It is open at both ends to allow access to two of the most important rooms in the house as well as a second family stair, which also has a double run leading up to the bedrooms on the second floor.

The Symbolism of the Hearth As he completed the Robie House, Wright's own version of domestic bliss fell apart due to his affair with a client, Mamah Borthwick Cheney. He had completed a house for her and her husband, Edwin H. Cheney, in Oak Park in 1903, three years before the Robie House was realized, and he gave up his practice and left his family to travel throughout Europe with Mamah in 1909. So the Robie House, as well as the Avery Coonley residence of 1907–1908 in Riverside, Illinois, was completed at a time when his own carefully constructed world was disintegrating. There are many other projects on the office ledger during the six-year period between the time that he met Mamah and decided to start an entirely new life with her. There are many public works, such as Unity Temple and the Larkin Company Building among the more than 50 buildings he designed during that time. But the Robie and Coonley Houses present two of the clearest examples of a shift that would soon take place in his sensibilities. In each case the hearth, which is an elemental symbol of family and home, is central to the plan, serving as a centerpiece of the large living room that dominated the Avery Coonley home, and as an even more obvious metaphor in the Robie House, since you literally have to walk through it to get from the ground floor to the first. However, that would soon change and the hearth would begin to move farther away from the center toward the periphery.

Robie House.   © Steve Skjold / Alamy

Free Flow of Space Much has been made about the freedom of the Robie House plan with claims often made for a new approach to domestic space being made there due to its openness. It is different to be sure, but the interior of the house has been changed a great deal since Robie sold it in 1910, due to a crisis in the family business and the subsequent breakup of his own marriage as well. Photographs taken soon after completion convey an entirely different impression, which is unconventional to be sure, but open in a much different way than the house is today.

Wright believed in the Arts and Crafts idea of the total work of art, in which the architect designed not only the house but everything within it, such as furniture, lighting fixtures, windows, carpets, and even silverware, to provide a complete aesthetic experience for the occupants. All of these are integrated to an extensive degree in all of his houses, but because of the lightness caused by the unusual site restrictions related to the Robie House, furniture design and groupings were even more important to him. Rather than just having a conventional railing, the hearth stair connecting the ground level with the living-dining floor above was wrapped in a screen of closely spaced wooden slats that extends up to 60 percent of the height of the room. This was stabilized by a large square pillar at the corner and had narrow sideboards built into it, facing the dining room on one side, with a long corridor running the entire length of the southern street edge of the house on the other. The dining table and chairs were custom designed for their 20 feet by 20 feet space, on axis with a second, longer console built into the wall separating the dining room from the kitchen to the north. Rather than having legs, in the usual sense, the table was supported by square piers that were similar in proportion to those that supported the screen around the entry stair, and had metal vases intended for flowers on top to solve the problem of arrangements in the middle of the table that block conversation and view. The six chairs that Wright designed for this rectangular table, with one at each end and two on each side, had no arms. They also had high, just slightly curving uprights that went from the floor to about three feet above the leather seats, with open slatted backs supported by solid horizontal top and bottom rails. These backs echoed the slatted screen around the entry stair, just as the posts that supported it did the solid corners of that layered wooden veil, creating a room within a room in which the family members, once seated for dinner, were united and secure. Wright continued to use this tactic even after his departure from Oak Park, but often for different reasons. In the Hollyhock House in Los Angeles, for example, which he designed nearly 17 years after the Robie House, he did the same thing in a living room grouping for Aline Barnsdall and her young daughter. But in that case the intention seems to have been the provision of a smaller scaled enclosure, closer to the size of the diminutive occupants of the house that would make them feel more comfortable within the large expanse of its most important social space.

Wright created intimacy in the living and dining rooms of the Robie House in other ways as well, most notably in the repetitive placement of custom-designed built-in light fixtures, which project from the soffits that run down each side of the living-dining level. These are connected pair by pair across the room, with stripes of color between pairs of wooden strips that visually slice the long continuous space up into narrow bits. These are related to the 15 columns that support the window wall along the south-facing street elevation of the house, and the pairs of doors between them that lead out to the extended balcony along that side. The lights and the strips on the ceiling that connect them have remained, although they are now completely out of context. The carpet that Wright designed for this floor was intended to convey a sense of cozy domesticity, but here especially so, to offset the hardness of the wood screens and brick hearth. It was wall-to-wall carpet in a consistent pattern that unified the large area.

One of the Last Examples of a Type Wright never referred to any of the houses that he designed during his Oak Park years as being "Prairie style." His followers, who became known as the Prairie School, did so later, based on his conversations, lectures, and writings about his love of the American Midwest, and the need to evolve a new house type that would respond to the prairie.

The Robie House is not the last of Wright's Prairie houses, but it is the most memorable because of its distinctive form, and Wright did all he could to ensure that it would be so. The seed of the idea for the Prairie house type was planted when Wright went to the World's Columbian Exposition held in Chicago in 1893. He was impressed by the *Ho-o-den* Temple there, which was part of a Japanese pavilion that was based on vernacular principles rather than the Classical style required of most of the other participants by the Exposition planner Daniel Burnham. The horizontal, tripartite organization of that grouping into the characteristic columnar base, raised platform middle, and large overhanging roof on top defines traditional Japanese religious and residential structures. Wright also responded to the sensitive use of natural materials that had a far greater impact on him than the classical orders, columns, entablatures, pediments, and domes used elsewhere in an exhibition that Burnham hoped would result in a mandate for a national style for America.

The alternative Prairie style evolved relatively quickly in Wright's imagination and was fully formed by the time the commission for the Robie House came along. Like its Japanese predecessor, the key element for the Prairie House was horizontality, to help it blend in with flatness of the grasslands around it and the horizon in the distance. Wright exaggerated that characteristic by having the balcony along the street appear to span 40 plus feet above the windows on the ground floor level, by the extraordinarily wide overhanging eaves that stretch out along the long, east-west axis of the site, and by having the masons only strike the horizontal joints of the brick walls, leaving the vertical joints flush.

The Barnsdall or Hollyhock House Frank Lloyd Wright's Barnsdall commissions in Los Angeles, including the Hollyhock House, are the most conspicuous, followed by the Robie House. Wright was introduced to Aline Barnsdall in 1914 while she was a co-director of the Players Production Company at the Fine Arts Building in Chicago. She originally came from Pennsylvania, and when Wright met her, she was due to inherit the fortune accumulated by her father, Theodore, following his discovery of oil near Bradford after the Civil War. Wright was then involved in the design of the interior of the Fine Arts Building, where he had sporadically occupied an office between 1908 and 1911 due to his problems at home. He had recently gone through the burning of Taliesin, which had resulted in the death of Mamah Borthwick Cheney and her children in the summer of 1914. This was a tragic end to a relationship that had caused him to be ostracized from the Oak Park community where he had lived with his family from 1889 to 1909.

Aline Barnsdall was extremely interested in the idea of small theatres that would be more accessible to the public and especially to children. She was introduced to Wright by Henry Blackman Sell with the specific idea that he would design a small theatre for her, and the heiress first considered building a theatre of this kind in Chicago. This was intended to take advantage of the organization that already existed there. She changed her mind after returning from a trip to Los Angeles.[56] She then asked Wright to design an entire complex for a site that she wanted to put there.

Aline Barnsdall moved her Players Production Company to California in 1916, but was unable to go ahead with plans for a theatre there due to the death of her father the following year. Wright subsequently became deeply involved in the Imperial Hotel project in Tokyo in 1916, and for the next three years, until Olive Hill in 1919, Barnsdall and the architect communicated by letter or telegram.

Olive Hill The 36-acre tract of land that Aline Barnsdall purchased between Sunset and Hollywood Boulevards, and Edgemont Street and Vermont Avenue in North Hollywood is special in many ways. Olive Hill was named after an olive orchard that existed there for nearly 30 years before the purchase. This was very unusual in California in the early 1900s.

The relatively flat area below the site has now been completely urbanized, but Olive Hill still retains the same insular, almost sacred quality that it had when Barnsdall and Wright first saw it. It gradually rises up to nearly 500 feet above sea level, providing dramatic views in all directions and giving it the quality of a unique place. Both architect and client thought of it as a lush acropolis, covered with pines and eucalyptus along with the olive trees and hollyhocks that were already growing there. It is the ideal location for a private house, but they also saw it as the start of a self-sufficient, creative community that would be supported by commercial activity on the northern edge of the property.

Their ambitious plan, which appeared in the press in July 1919, included a theatre and roof garden for 1,250 people on Vermont Avenue and eight pairs of stores combined with terrace apartments to house actors, artists, and musicians. These shops were lined up along Hollywood Boulevard and ended at a movie theatre at its intersection with Edgemont Street. The site plan also included an apartment house, called the "Actors Abode," as well as housing for the artistic director of the theatre and two other houses, now known as Residences A and B, with Aline Barnsdall's house, named "Hollyhock" after her favorite flower, in the middle.

Siting the house at the top of the hill was an exception for Wright. He had previously always selected a site below the brow of the hill as he did in his own residence at Taliesin, Wisconsin. The reason for his decision not to do so here becomes apparent when one stands near the house. It addresses cardinal reference points. Wright established the sun path as the primary axis, instead of choosing either the quality of the natural light or the best views toward the San Bernardino Mountains to the east and the Pacific Ocean to the west. The cross axis, which is longer on the north to relate the line of entrance, serves as a compass that leads into the heart of the house. It ends in a glass-enclosed loggia overlooking a central garden court. Wright had used such a device before but the absence of the fireplace that normally occupies this intersection in earlier Prairie House plans is new here. Perhaps this had something to do with his own change in marital status and his evolving attitude about hearth and home.

The beginning of the entry axis is marked by a thin, rhythmical line of paired columns supporting a thin cantilevered roof. It also has a thin niche recalling the *Tokomoma* of a Japanese house. Wright's role as a dealer in Japanese artifacts has only recently become more well known, and he sold objects he had purchased in Japan to clients such as Aline Barnsdall.

The entrance into Hollyhock House is quite narrow as it is in many of Wright's houses. This intentionally evokes primal memories of shelter. It also makes the controlled views into the large interior and garden court in the middle of the house even more dramatic. This contrast is heightened by the raised level of the entrance, which constricts the height of the ceiling even more, and by the imposing double doors that end the entrance processional.

These doors are made of precast concrete, and each leaf weighs more than 300 pounds. An ingenious hinge detail allows them to give the impression of weight that Wright wanted to convey, while still allowing them to open quite effortlessly. This is all part of the carefully planned experience of entrance.

While higher than the roof of the entry canopy, the foyer directly inside these doors is still lower than the conventional ceiling height used in most homes today. Only in the loggia, where procession from exterior to interior ends, does the vertical scale begin to increase. This technique of collapsing spatial volume at an entrance is made more memorable here by the extremes of darkness and light provided by a deeply recessed doorway and the brightness of the interior garden revealed by the wide glass doors of the loggia.

From this final, central vantage point inside the house, the relationship of each of the individual segments that flank the four sides of its central courtyard become clear. The living area, which is the first social space of the house, serves as an anchor for two longer wings that project out from it to the east. The central part of this base is the living room itself, which is rectangular, with a longitudinal axis running from east to west.

A Dislocated Hearth A fireplace dominates the south wall of the room, and it is the first thing that comes into view when one turns into it from the loggia. It offers several important clues to Wright's basic intentions for the house. First, it is not placed symmetrically in the middle of the space, as was his habit in his earlier houses, where the centrality of the hearth was purposely intended to symbolize domestic stability.

The symbolism used on the hearth can be accurately interpreted. It is pictographic to an extent that is unusual for Wright. The fireplace, which is built of randomly sized, smoothly dressed stone blocks, is divided between base, middle, and top. It is dominated by a rectilinear panel that projects from the mantelpiece. The left side of the composition is filled with a tightly organized group of interlocking circles, with the smallest, near the center, suggesting a head. A vertical line running through all of the circles is similar to the hollyhock motif used extensively on the outside of the house.

Each of these symbols makes specific associations with Aline Barnsdall and the location of the house perfectly clear. Vertical striations running across the entire top of the frame represent the sky, and horizontal lines represent water, which terminate in a group of diamond-shaped forms at the bottom to complete the picture. In addition to being a cosmological symbol, this ideogram is also an abstract reference to the use of water in the house, and it shows Wright's facility in three-dimensional visualization, which other drawings on the fireplace confirm. One of these carries an elevational detail of a brass fire screen on into a plan in which a cast iron grate continues the theme begun in the panel. The pictogram, according to the architect's son Lloyd Wright, is meant to show Aline Barnsdall as an Indian princess, sitting on a throne, looking out over a desert to mesas in the distance.[57]

The Four Elements The theme of the four elements of earth, air, fire, and water, shown in the panel, is physically continued on the mantlepiece, as well as with the intricate skylight above it and the moat partially surrounding the apron on which the logs are placed. The water that surfaces to fill this moat completes its axial line across the site in a square pool that comes right up to the front of the living room on the west. From here, it runs under the foundations to the pool at the hearth, going underground again until it reaches a circular pond in front of the rows of auditorium seating that close off the atrium court, which is its source.

This channel originally continued onto the crest of this side of Olive Hill, coming out of the ground again as a small waterfall that filled a long, rectilinear pool behind the main theatre below and an organically shaped lake that was intended to serve as a visual buffer between the arts complex and Vermont Avenue, along one entire edge of the site. The pool in front of the hearth, which was dry for many years, has now been restored to its original condition. Small gold mosaic squares cover the bottom and form a single course at the water line, while concrete is used on all other surfaces. The bottom of this container had to be raised by six inches, due to safety regulations related to swimming pools that were enacted in Los Angeles in the 1970s, in order to avoid having to surround it with an unsightly protective railing, so the desired impression of depth has now been slightly changed. The level of consideration that Wright gave to the way in which water is symbolically used in the Hollyhock House demonstrates his capacity for thoroughness.

Photographs taken shortly after construction, as well as visitors' verbal descriptions, indicate that the water here did serve as a mirror for sunlight as well as the moon and stars just as Wright had intended. But he misunderstood the level of glare during the day in Los Angeles, which made the installation of a thick velvet curtain a necessity. Eventually, this also required that a shed roof be built over the skylight, cutting off the direct connection with the sky, which had been such an important part of Wright's whole composition.

The purpose of this grouping is also implicit in the built-in furniture designed for the living room. There are two long banquettes flanking the hearth. These are located on either side of its central axis. They were built at the same angle as the fireplace upon projecting into the pool, demonstrating the permanent connection that Wright wanted to establish between the furnishings and the offset fireplace. Tall, built-in *torcheres* connected to the end of each banquette underscore this relationship. This furniture had been removed during several renovations over the years, but was replaced, in the spring of 1990, with reproductions built according to survey drawings by Roderick Grant. Olive Hill was originally intended to serve a social as well as residential function, but that left little private space for Miss Barnsdall and her young daughter. To bring down the scale of the living room, Wright designed two couches with high backs and sides to provide a sense of protection for them.

The Dining Room The dining room in Hollyhock House, like the hearth, is off-axis from the entrance. This effectively makes the music room more prominent, as part of the plan to have the house be an entertainment center as well. This location had the added advantage of allowing Wright to extend the necessary service functions of the kitchen and the servants' quarters along the northern edge of the garden court, placing that area so that it did not interfere with the main entry into the house. A short flight of stairs from the entry level up into the dining room makes this separation clearer. While the dining room is square, the entrance into it from the foyer and from the kitchen is located on one side of the space. This makes half of the space for circulation, so that the rectangular area that is left along the northern wall is the only logical place for a table to be located. Windows along this wall relate to the landscaping in the garden outside, and the dropped ceiling in this half of the space reinforces the impression of a space reserved for the family.

A Tree House for Sugar Top A hexagonal table and tall, hollyhock-shaped chairs that were custom designed for the dining area have now been restored to their original positions, but the division between circulation and dining areas that was once underlined by a Persian rug covering this part of the wooden floor has now been eliminated by the addition of a wall-to-wall carpet. In general, however, the entire dining room seems very small in scale for a house designed around the concept of entertainment. This also underscores the idea that Wright made a concerted effort to humanize the spaces that Aline Barnsdall and her daughter used on a daily basis.

A guest wing, across the courtyard from the dining and kitchen wing, had a long, glazed gallery. This served as an intermediary sun space between these rooms and the central court. Both guest rooms, which were of equal size, looked out to the south onto a patio surrounded by a high wall to protect it from prevailing winds. Beyond this wall there is a lower garden formed by a semicircular retaining wall, which holds back this slope of the hill. The glass-enclosed pergola to the guest rooms also served as a wide corridor leading to the bedroom of Miss Barnsdall's daughter, Aline Elizabeth, whom she nicknamed "Sugar Top." This room turns on axis to effectively terminate the line of the spaces beside it. With an extended alcove on one end, a nurse's room at the other, and a deep bay window, projecting out into the garden from a dressing and sleeping area in the center, this suite gives the impression of a self-sufficient house of its own. A winding path, leading from the bedroom down to the garden portion of the semicircular amphitheatre at the end of the central garden court adds to the sense of privacy of this wing. This was intended to provide Sugar Top with an enclosed, protected place to play.

This miniature house has hard materials and open, interlocking spaces, and it is difficult to imagine it being used as a nursery. The only move toward intimacy is a finely detailed wooden partition wall, with a hinged doorway that separates the dressing area from the rest of the space. A stairway located between the nurse's room and Sugar Top's bedroom connects it with Aline Barnsdall's suite, on the floor above. This congruity extends to the location of a fireplace, which is located above that in the nursery, in order to group the flues together, as well as to the bay window, which is carried up to the second story to become a glassed-in sleeping alcove in the trees.

Wright's working drawings show that he originally intended this long alcove, which has a sunken floor that causes a dropping ceiling in the corresponding space in the bedroom below it, to be separated from the rest of the space by a thin wooden screen connected to both the floor and the ceiling to ensure privacy. The construction documents also show a bed built into steps leading down to the alcove. It is clear that the intention was that this bed and the skylight above it should be aligned. These details confirm his view of this part of the residence as a tree house in the forest, open to the sky. A bridge across the garden court, held up by two "I" beams that represent the only significant use of steel in the house, connects the Barnsdall suite with another guest room on the north side of the second floor.

Flight of Fancy Wright mentions the Hollyhock House in his autobiography. He begins his description with a musical metaphor by saying: "As I have since learned, music is the language—beyond all words—of the human heart . . . I now felt Architecture not only might be but ought to be as symphonic in character: the same in mind." He compares the house to a romanza, which he describes by saying that

> A musician's sense of proportion is all that governs him in the Romanza: the mysterious remaining just haunting enough in a whole so organic as to lose all evidence of how it was made. Now translate "sounds and the ear" to "form and the eye," romanza seems reasonable enough to Architecture? In California or anywhere else.[58]

Wright's decision to embark on an uncharacteristically romantic adventure here is clearly expressed in the materials and construction techniques used in the residence. The surface of the Hollyhock is often mistaken for poured concrete. However, the wall system that Wright actually used starts with a poured concrete footing and concrete block stem wall foundation below grade. This supports a hollow tile wall covered with stucco above, and a timber trussed roof. The only place that poured concrete is used in the house itself is in the massive front doors, in the mantle over the fireplace, and in columns and sills.

Wright's brief description of the house in his autobiography ends in a far more negative way, however, as he describes the ways in which his working relationship with Aline Barnsdall began to deteriorate. He agrees that this was probably caused by his long absences from the site, since he was in Japan for the construction of the Imperial Hotel during a majority of the time Hollyhock House was being built. Cost overruns and misunderstandings with the contractor who had difficulty in interpreting an unusual set of plans contributed to Wright's difficulties.

Aline Barnsdall had a circle of close friends who convinced her to stop construction at one point. Wright's response to this setback is instructive, because he basically dismissed it as Aline Barnsdall's ignorance of what he saw as her responsibility as a guardian of a work of art that she was paying for, but did not truly own, since Wright saw it as belonging to posterity

After identifying the "agonizing triangle" of owner, architect, and contractor as what he considered to be the basic cause behind this and all other difficulties related to building, Wright resolved to have his own way regardless of the effect this had on the architect-client relationship so that the house could be built according to his original concept.

As an immediate result of these difficulties, Rudolph Schindler was appointed as project architect. He had been working for Wright at Taliesin. He initiated a series of small changes that were his influence but became more substantial as time went on. Schindler arrived in Los Angeles in December 1920, and building permits totaling nearly $40,000 were taken out for Residences A and B in that same month. He appears to have restored the client's confidence and so Wright's strategy worked. Construction on Hollyhock House had reached the upper level at this stage, and so Schindler's main contribution to the interior was in the completion of Miss Barnsdall's bedroom and the detailing of the ceiling and the sleeping alcove. He was also involved in the detailing of the escutcheon plates on the front doors, the location and installation of lighting throughout the house, and the design of a pergola and wading pool near the perimeter.

In 1921, however, Aline Barnsdall's disenchantment with the entire process increased, since newspaper accounts described her intention to scale down the size of the theatre on Olive Hill and to offer it to a local repertory company. The commercial spaces that Wright had designed along Hollywood Boulevard, originally meant for actors, artists, and musicians-in-residence, were also redesigned as more upscale shops, signifying a shift in her ideas for the project. She commissioned another house in Beverly Hills in 1923, which is a sign of her restored faith in Wright, but it was never realized, and her intentions to live elsewhere show her increasing disinterest in Hollyhock House and her unwillingness to stay there. In 1926, after the Beverly Hills commission, Aline Barnsdall decided to dedicate 11.4 of the 36 acres of the Olive Hill tract and all buildings except Residence B to the Department of Recreation and Parks of the City of Los Angeles. This ended her plans for an experimental creative community in California. Following the completion of Hollyhock House, Frank Lloyd Wright continued to show a personal liking for the project. He lived in Oleanders, or Residence B, at 1600 Edgemont Street on the northwest side of the site for a period of about a year while he retained a studio on Harper Avenue.

Residence B is located on a steep slope and was designed to align with the contours of the hill. Its walls are battered to an even more dramatic angle than those of Hollyhock House and have horizontal banding to accentuate unity with the landscape. This angled outline is topped by an extended cornice line that is a reminder of earlier Prairie School designs, but several details give it an identity of its own.

It would seem that such a generous bequest would be quickly accepted by the City of Los Angeles, but the conditions that Aline Barnsdall attached to the gift ended in protracted negotiations that delayed transfer until January 1927. Aline Barnsdall and her daughter continued living in the house during this time. From its completion late in 1921 until it was taken over by Los Angeles, she had been in temporary residence there for less than six years.

One of the stipulations she placed on the transfer was that the California Art Club would have use of the house for 15 years. It was officially designated as their headquarters on August 13, 1927. A monthly bulletin produced by the club has proved to be an invaluable source of information about the original condition of the house.

At the time of the turnover the wall color of the living room was described as "unevenly tarnished gold" with beige drapes combined with "gold and wisteria silks." Earlier sources, however, had called the ceiling gray-green, which corresponds with Wright's term for the color of the olive trees that gave the site its name, and nile green mixed with bronze. These colors also match the palette used in a large Japanese screen that Aline Barnsdall bought from Wright. The main colors in this screen are dark green on a gold background.[59]

Sources and Significance There was a complex set of influences behind Hollyhock House as it was built. However, various layered sources can be traced. The first of these is Wright's interest in Japanese architecture, especially since Wright described his love for Japan in his autobiography and was also involved in the design of the Imperial Hotel there while working at Olive Hill.

Wright's first awareness of this culture prior to his initial visit to Japan in 1905 came during a visit to the Chicago World's Fair of 1893. This occurred at the same time that he rented an office in the Schiller Building. He criticized the Fair as an example of *Beaux-Arts* Classicism, and the *Ho-o-den* Temple, Nippon Tea House, and Exhibition of Japanese Art that he saw there must have been an exciting contrast to it. Soon afterwards, he started using a similar division of platform, skeleton-framed walls, and wide-eaved, steeply gabled roofs that he saw on these Japanese buildings as the basis of his new "Prairie" architecture. Individually confined rooms were replaced by the free flow of space usually associated with the traditional Japanese house.

Wright's self-described "breaking of the box," as seen in the Darwin Martin, Robie, and Avery Coonley Houses of the following years can be traced as the beginning of the spatial relationships used in the living area of the Hollyhock House. This relocation of the fireplace is the only notable exception to this evolution.

The central courtyard is Wright's essential concession to the idea of a California typology, clearly expressed in his belief that the design should be as much open as closed. There were other precedents for this type of openness before the Hollyhock House, such as the Midway Gardens project, completed in 1913.

The square, open, central space of the Gardens was surrounded by two wings that projected out from a covered, stepped pavilion. This is reminiscent of the arrangement used in reverse order at Hollyhock House, where the roof over the loggia was used as a stage for those seated in the amphitheatre across the courtyard.

Concentric arrangements of the type used in the Hollyhock House appear several times in Wright's early work, for example, in his scheme for a resort on Wolf Lake in Indiana, designed ten years before Olive Hill. In that scheme, which Wright chose to include in the Wasmuth portfolio, projecting arms also appear on either side of an axis, and a bridge between them forms a key part of the composition.

Modular layering of the type seen in the Midway Gardens pavilion and Holly-hock House elevation also appears in the Kehl Dance Academy, designed for an urban site in Madison, Wisconsin. In addition to its symmetrical plan, this theatre-like building has a richly ornamented façade and flat roof. The Kehl project mirrors the exterior appearance of the Barnsdall residence in other details such as Wright's use of a hollyhock motif on lamps on exterior terraces.

The Imperial Hotel in Tokyo was the second major precedent in which Wright used a central court. As in the Midway Gardens, it was also organized along a central axis with guest room wings extending out from a central lobby to protect landscaping and pools inside. The Imperial House looked like a fortress built against the natural threats that it was meant to withstand, such as the earthquake it eventually survived.

Wright's pride at having created an earthquake-proof building is well known, and while he was living in Residence B on Olive Hill, he received the telegram from Baron Okura telling him that it had prevailed. He produced several other projects in Japan while he lived there, but several of these, such as his scheme for a large hotel in Odawara in 1917 or his projects for the Immu, Inouye, Goto, and Mihara Houses of 1918, were never realized.

The Tazemon Yamamura House in Ashiya was built and provides many insights into houses he was designing in Los Angeles at the same time. While the absence of any drawings of the Yakamura House in the Taliesin archives indicates that Wright may have delegated it to his assistant Arata Endo, it is still recognizable as Wright's design.

The Yamamura House does not have a large courtyard, but steps down a steeply sloping site in three distinct stages. Oya stone, alternating with plaster walls, is used to designate changes in level. In spite of this difference, its angled walls and distinctive use of ornaments make comparison clear to the Hollyhock House, as does its roof, which is also used as an outdoor terrace. Tall chimneys projecting up through a thick pine forest give the profile of this house a different, more vertical emphasis than Olive Hill, however.

Mesoamerica Sources Replace Japan There has been a great deal of speculation about the influence of Mayan architecture on Hollyhock House. Lloyd Wright confirmed that his father wanted to convey the image of a pueblo.

But a Mayan influence is very clear. At the same Chicago Exposition of 1893 where Wright saw the *Ho-o-den* Temple, several Mayan ruins were reproduced by Edward H. Thompson, who had served as the American Consul at Merida in the Yucatan from 1885 to 1910. These included parts of the Nunnery at Uxmal and the corbelled arch at Labna, which were surrounded by a simulated jungle overgrowth to add to their exotic appeal. Wright also produced two designs, for the A. D. German Warehouse at Richland Centre, Wisconsin, in 1915 and the F. C. Bork House in Milwaukee in 1915, which owe obvious allegiance to Mayan prototypes, and each of these also had roof terraces.

Before the World's Fair Wright may have had other exposure to Mayan architecture, since important studies on Mesoamerica had begun to appear while he was a student. Sir Alfred Maudslay had been one of the first to undertake a complete archeological survey of British Honduras, Guatemala, parts of Campeche, and Chiapas between 1880 and 1894. He published his findings in a five-volume set.

Desiré Charney, who traveled extensively throughout Central America between 1858 and 1860, also published photographs of the expeditions in *Cities et Ruines Americains* in 1863. A second expedition in 1880, which was partially financed by Pierre Lorillard of Tuxedo Park, New York, resulted in a second book entitled *Les Anciennes Villes du Nouveau Monde*, which appeared in English in 1887. Wright was 19 years old at that time and had just arrived in Chicago after leaving the University of Wisconsin.

Wright read widely from a broad variety of sources. Historian Vincent Scully has pointed out similarities between Wright's Oak Park studio-house and two residences for Bruce Price in Tuxedo Park, making it possible that he also knew Lorillard.[60]

Specific similarities occur in the platform base, tripartite ordering of elongated windows, unbroken band of ornament, and high truncated roof used on the predominant, western elevation of Hollyhock House and Temple 33 in Yaxchilan, on the Mexican side of Usumacinta River, near Guatemala. These features are used in almost identical proportion in the Mayan example, also recorded in reconstructed drawings in Maudslay's studies, since Temple 33, and it is doubtful that was the model since it had yet to be restored and is still covered in undergrowth.

Temple 33 was built on a terrace 200 feet above the main plaza of the city, as many Mayan temples were. Wright has said,

> I remember how, as a boy, primitive American architecture, Toltec, Aztec, Mayan and Inca—stirred my wonder, excited my wishful admiration. I wished I might someday . . . join in excavating those long slumbering remains of lost cultures; mighty, primitive abstractions of man's nature. Those great American abstractions were all earth architecture: gigantic masses of masonry raised up on great stone paved terrain, all planned as on a mountain, one vast plateau lying there and made into the great mountain ranges themselves; those vast areas of paved earth walled in by stone construction. They were human creations, cosmic as sun, moon and stars.[61]

In many of the preliminary sketches that Wright made of Hollyhock House, the western elevation as seen from Edgemont Street is treated as the most important. This is also the position that acts as a gateway between the slope that leads up to the house and the snow-capped mountains in the distance. The earliest of these sketches show his gradual assimilation of the rare, primal quality of the hillside. In it two large vertical piers are clearly visible. They are part of a familiar, Prairie School language, and emerge in the final design of the house.

In another sketch, this profile is replaced with a triangular form, like a tepee, over the living room, and a deeper pitch over each of the projecting wings. A tall chimney also adds to the vertical thrust of the massing. A final elevation shows that this vertically has been replaced by a *talud* and *tablero* profile. Considering the pictogram that he has used to present Aline Barnsdall on the mantle of the living room fireplace, in which she is depicted as an "Indian princess," his rejection of a steep-sided, triangular roof symbolic of Plains Indians in favor of a Mesoamerican form may seem curious. The teepee form does emerge again in projects like a resort on Lake Tahoe in 1922, the Nakoma Country Club in Madison, Wisconsin, in 1924, the Steel Cathedral in 1926, and Beth Sholom Synagogue in Elkins Park in 1959, however.

Wright's decision not to use it at Olive Hill may be explained by his relative unfamiliarity with West Coast culture at that time and doubts about the ability of this sharp profile to stand up against the visual power of the mountains that he consistently drew as a background in each sketch. Wright relied on the modular grid in the plan of this and many others of his houses, and the extension of Cartesian coordinates up onto this final one also implies that regulatory considerations were as responsible as any historical prototype for the visual layering that finally resulted. Wright's intention to use one native American style or another, however, never changed due to his self-image as the champion of a democratic ideal. Debate continues on his sources but there is no argument that the Barnsdall house sparked a Mayan revival in the United States. It reached its apogee in the interpretive work of Robert Stacy-Judd in Los Angeles just before World War II. The Hollyhock House played an important role in Wright's career. Personal calamity occurred in his life with almost Biblical predictability, marking phases that have a definite beginning and end. His Prairie School years, beginning with the Willets House of 1902 and ending with the Robie House seven years later, changed architecture in America and abroad, encouraging designers to follow Wright's lead in "breaking the box," and opening up room plans.

Wright's decision to leave Chicago because of the breakup of his first marriage was irrevocable, and the destruction of Taliesin by fire soon afterwards provided tragic confirmation that the first chapter of his life had ended. The Barnsdall commissions, and Hollyhock House in particular, gave him the chance to make a fresh start in totally different circumstances and to express what he found in them in a new way.

No place in the United States could be more different from the flat grasslands of the midwestern prairie than Los Angeles, where heavily forested snow-capped mountain ranges come up to the edge of the Pacific, and earthquakes, torrential rains, mudslides, and violent windstorms intermittently interrupt the illusion of paradise. These natural extremes must have been even more obvious to an architect of Wright's sensibilities, since he had such empathy with the land. He once described the appearance and smell of each of the trees surrounding his beloved Taliesin as they began to bloom in the spring. As Vincent Scully commented on this aspect of his talent, saying that Wright:

> built almost everywhere on the North American continent without relinquishing his attempt to celebrate in architectural form the specific landscapes with which he happened to be involved ... that is he tried, though in abstract form, to echo the shapes and dominant rhythms of the landscapes in which his buildings were set.[62]

Hollyhock House, as well as the Tazemon Yamamura residence that is its spiritual counterpart across the Pacific, is the result of an emotional response to context. It represents a victory of nature and art over technology and the Modernist prerogatives of honesty of structural expression.

Taliesin East.   Courtesy of Scott Beveridge; Flickr

Wright succeeded in establishing a California typology here, which he contin-ued to elaborate upon in the Ennis, Freeman, and Millard Houses that followed. This served a point of departure for many influential architects soon afterward. Because of worsening economic conditions leading up to the Depression in the de-cade following Wright's Los Angeles hiatus, he was not given the same opportu-nity to express the natural beauty of a site until 1936, when he designed Fallingwater for the Kaufmann family in Ohiopyle, Pennsylvania. This is the project most frequently associated in the public consciousness with his ability to link architecture with nature.[63]

Except for the house within a house containing the Aline and Aline Elizabeth Barnsdall suites on the southwestern corner of the central court, which has a dis-tinctive image of its own, the sense of a public forum remains alive on Olive Hill. This fits easily with the personality of a client who initially wanted everything there to be imbued with the possibility of performance. She commissioned Hollyhock House, but Wright never intended it to belong to her alone, and so the public role that it plays as a gallery for artists and a background for musical and dramatic per-formances, as well as being the centerpiece of public attention, was intended by its architect from the start.

The Jacobs Houses In 1937, Wright made a second attempt to create a truly American style, following the completion of his Prairie House series, his departure from Oak Park in 1909, and the Olive Hill experience. In the midst of the lead up to World War II, he launched what he called the Usonian house with his design of a residence for the Jacobs family in Madison, Wisconsin. He wanted this house to be the prototype for an efficient low-cost residence for the average, middle class American family that would be easy to build and could be customized, within limits, to fit any site in the country. He had just experienced the success of Fallingwater in Bear Run, Pennsylvania, which was certainly far from average and middle class. It had brought him international recognition, followed by the commission to design the headquarters building for the Johnson Wax Company in Racine, Wisconsin. His long career had been reborn, yet again, and he was in a much stronger position to put forward an ambitious idea of this kind than he would have been a decade earlier. But, there are many elements in the first Jacobs house that he had used earlier in what he referred to as his "board and batten cottages."[64] Like the Usonian prototype, it also had a modular plan, flat roof with cantilevered eaves, continuous south-facing windows, and horizontal wood cladding, and it had only one level. Like the Prairie house, the Usonian house was also intended to express the American spirit of independence and freedom of expression, as well as a "can do" spirit of innovation and entrepreneurial invention.

The first Jacobs house is relatively modest in size at 1,500 square feet, but seems much larger because of the lack of conventional room divisions and its relationship to a garden on the inner, protected side of an L-shaped plan. Wright used this plan shape to best advantage to segregate public and private zones inside, in conjunction with the garden. He provided two entrances for the same reason, with the first leading into the more public end, where the living room is located, and the second providing access from the bedrooms to the garden. The service spaces, such as the kitchen and the bathrooms, act as transition spaces between the two zones at the middle of the "L." Wright also used different materials to draw attention to the different areas, blending brick with wood siding in the more public end of the house.

The Garden Consistent with his notion of independence, the garden was not simply intended to replicate nature, but to be planted with vegetables and herbs so that the family could be partially self-sufficient in their food needs. The Usonian house was meant to integrate architecture and agriculture as a true symbol of American life.

A First Attempt The first Usonian house was built for Herbert and Catherine Jacobs in Madison, Wisconsin, in 1936. At 1,500 square feet (150 square meters), it was relatively small and cost approximately $5,500. Shortly afterward, the Jacobs family moved to a 52-acre farm in Middleton, Wisconsin, and asked Wright to design another home for them there. While his first house was rectilinear, the topography of this more wide-open site suggested a curvilinear or semicircular plan, the first of a series of houses that Wright built with curved plans. By early 1944 he had produced a house that was unlike anything he, or anyone else up until that time, had done and that is now seen as a pioneering attempt at passive solar design. The house is a half circle with its rear, north wall protected from the cold winter wind by a berm that rises to the top of it. The entire south façade has large windows and glass doors covered by the deep eave of a flat overhanging roof to let the low winter sun in and to block the higher summer solar angle. This is in response to a midwest, northeast temperate zone where temperature can range from subzero to more than 86 °F (30 °C) and where summers can be very humid.

In this humid zone, which has higher temperatures than are typical in the Midwest, Wright realized it was especially important to open up to cooling breezes, and so these large doors on the south side open wide to connect the long, narrow interior space to a sunken, outdoor garden protected by the hill and the curved form of the house. The interior is basically one large room, 17 feet (5 meters) wide and 80 feet (17 meters) long, with a kitchen and bathroom kept apart in a masonry core. There are bedrooms on an upper level, reached by a narrow stair in a circular stone core; but to keep the lower level open, this floor is suspended from the roof beams by steel rods. These beams, which are relatively small, radiate out from the buried berm wall on the north and are doubled up to embrace the mullion posts of the glazed south wall, to which they are bolted on either side.

A Lesson, Ahead of Its Time The second Jacobs house is in perfect harmony with its surroundings and is a model of passive solar design, which was not to become popular for another 30 years. It integrates a relationship to its particular context with strategies for natural energy and spatial organization in many important ways. Burying the back of the house in the earth protects it from the prevailing wind and keeps it warmer because of thermal mass, and the limestone walls and floor serve the same purpose. Rather than being coincidental, the curved shape derives from the structural requirements of this earth berm, which is very heavy. The orientation toward the south/southeast is ideal for passive solar gain, captured by clever use of glazing.

The curved shape of this façade is also the most efficient in increasing solar gain. The large roof eave protects the interior from direct solar radiation in the summer and allows it to come in during the winter when the sun is lower on the horizon. The irregularly laid limestone bricks, rather than being a stylistic gesture, also increase the surface area of material used for thermal storage, soaking up heat during the day and reradiating it into the interior at night. The suspended second floor, recessed 4 feet (1.2 meters) back from the south window wall, allows heat to rise from the lower level to heat the upper floor during the winter. During the summer, the wall on the north as well as the windows on the south have openings that allow the house to be cross ventilated, and this natural ventilation, combined with the thermal inertia created by the stone walls and floor, contribute to a cool interior environment. The Jacobs Hemicycle was followed, in rapid succession, by the Martin House in Akron, Ohio (1947), Meyer House in Galesburg, Michigan (1948), Laurent House in Rockford, Illinois (1949), and Pearce House in Bradbury, California (1950), as well as similarly shaped houses for his sons David, in Phoenix, Arizona (1950), and Robert Llewellyn, in Bethesda, Maryland (1953). None of these, however, has the direct simplicity of their pioneering predecessor.

Taliesin West Just before the second Jacobs house was built, Wright was also consulting on the Arizona Biltmore Hotel, designed by a former employee at the Oak Park Studio, Alfred Chase McArthur. Wright stayed in Phoenix for four months and, while he was there, also received a commission for another hotel, San Marcos, in the desert. Escaping the cold Wisconsin winters, in 1929 he established a site, which he called Ocatilla, at Salt River Mountain as a studio and living quarters for 15 people who came from Taliesin. It was built of readily available, inexpensive materials appropriate to its temporary status: wood and canvas units laid out in an angular geometrical plan that echoed the mountain peaks nearby. The rooms were grouped around an internal courtyard, which offered some protection from the harsh desert landscape.

The San Marcos project was sidetracked by the stock market crash, but the brief experience at Ocatilla, and a bout of pneumonia, planted the idea of establishing a permanent studio there. In January 1938 Wright bought 800 acres, 26 miles northwest of Phoenix in Paradise Valley, and the entire Wisconsin studio traveled there to help construct Taliesin West. It is angular, like Ocatilla, in reference to the McDowell Mountains, which form a 4,000 feet (1,300 meters) high backdrop on the north side of the site.

The materials used in the construction of Taliesin West were also mostly taken from the site, as they were for the Ocatilla Camp, but the more permanent volcanic stones at hand were placed in rough wooden forms and concrete was poured in around them to hold them together without using steel reinforcing bars. Heavy redwood truss frames were placed at intervals along these walls. These hold up a sliding canvas panel roof between them, creating the feeling of a sophisticated tented camp that is in perfect harmony with the desert landscape.

Brendan Gill broke the unofficial and unspoken code of silence that surrounded Wright for years after his death in 1959. This was imposed by his inner circle, especially his wife, Olgivanna Labovich, who was very protective of his image and reputation. Gill has written about Wright's paradoxical character, especially his ability to endure great hardships for the sake of his work and his equivalent love of luxury. Taliesin West is an enduring symbol of that ambivalence.

After the first phase was completed in 1941, the permanent composite included a residence for the Wrights, a drafting room and workshop, but also a "teaching theatre" for performances and films, where Wright and his wife were the center of attention. There was also a communal kitchen, consistent with Wright's idea of a fellowship in which people lived and worked together. Wright's wife had been a Gurdjieff disciple at his Institute for the Harmonious Development of Man, so her involvement in the formation of Taliesin West introduced a spiritual component into Wright's idea of an organic architecture, taking his notion of unity with nature to an almost mystical level, as a way of enhancing human perception.

After Phase I was completed, there was an annual western migration from Wisconsin to Arizona until Wright died. Photographs and films taken during the early days at Taliesin West show the contrasts best: one indelible image is of Wright and his wife in a Cherokee Red Lincoln Continental Cabriolet, in front of their elemental rock, wood, and canvas commune.

Fallingwater Fallingwater, which has consistently been chosen by design professionals in annual polls taken by several leading journals as one of the most influential works of architecture ever produced in America, is all the more significant because of the special circumstances behind its creation.

An overview of Frank Lloyd Wright's entire career shows that the period immediately preceding the design of this house was one of his least productive in terms of actual work built. This inactivity as mentioned eventually led both him and his wife Olgivanna to conceive the school at Taliesin as a means of sheer professional and financial survival. Edgar Kaufmann Jr. was one of the first students

An exterior view of Fallingwater. © Mark Hiser, http://MarkHiserPhotography.com. Used with permission.

at Taliesin, and he was so impressed with what he saw that he suggested to his father that Wright be the architect of a new vacation house that the family was then considering on a large plot of land at Bear Run, near Ohiopyle, Pennsylvania. The site, which had been used as a family campground for many years, is dominated by Bear Run Creek and is surrounded by gently rolling hills, dense woods, and the ever-present pink mountain laurel that is also the state flower. This area is typical glacial moraine with rocks and boulders from its geological past strewn everywhere.

On his first site visit with Edgar Kaufmann Sr., Wright characteristically took in far more than the area immediately surrounding the primitive log cabin that the family had built on a high bluff overlooking the rushing stream below. Kaufmann had automatically assumed that this would be the logical position for his new home. Several stories that have come down from his apprentices, and may be partially apocryphal, tell of an impatient call from Kaufman after months of waiting for word from Wright and a preliminary design accomplished in a single night, all following a long period of reflection after this single site visit. This frenetic burst of creative activity produced a set of sketches on yellow tracing paper that Wright asked his students to draft up for the client visit that day, a design that stayed appreciably the same throughout the construction process. The design revealed in those sketches presented Kaufmann with a totally unexpected vision. It showed a living environment distributed among several horizontal levels and dramatically projected out over the large waterfall in the middle of Bear Run that the family had admired from a distance for so many years. What Wright had gleaned from his short visit to the ravine with a rushing stream running through it was that a waterfall and the rock ledge it fell over was the epicenter of the site. He had determined very quickly and quietly during his short visit that he wanted to project the house over that point so that it would participate in the natural cycle that was constantly unfolding there.[65] He echoed the rock ledges that caused the cascade by building vertical towers, enclosing stairs made of stone taken from the site, and in cantilevered concrete slabs; nature and "the machine," as he referred to non-natural materials, are placed in perfect balance. He later wrote that he really disliked concrete because it is inert and nonorganic, but nothing else could have achieved his goal of cantilevering slabs out 30 feet over the waterfall to make nature and architecture seem to blend together.

As he had in his Prairie houses in Chicago, Wright used an emphasis on the horizontal to help to visually tie the house to the ground.[66] In Fallingwater, however, that tactic takes on additional symbolism due to his use of concrete and stone. Industrially produced material extends out to connect to its surroundings, while the stone from the earth on which the house sits seems to shoot upward, providing an anchor for the composition. This balance continues between the amount of indoor and outdoor space in the house. Wright often used the strategy of a small entrance leading to a progressively larger series of spaces, as previously seen in the Hollyhock House. He does that in the Kaufmann house as well, making the doorway, which is hidden between vertical stone piers, seem like the entrance into a cave. The surprise that awaits is the view out over the stream to the opposite side of the ravine beyond. It is covered in dark green mountain laurel, which has pink blossoms in the spring, creating a seemingly unobstructed vision of a natural paradise just beyond the glass wall of the living room. The living room has no walls to allow as much of an open vista as possible. The secondary focal point, after this external view, is a massive fireplace, located to the right, and a boulder projecting up through the floor in front of it. Wright identified this on his site visit as the structural fulcrum on which he would balance the intricate cantilever system he has used. A vertical stone tower projects upward from this point, containing stairs, mechanical flues, and electrical chases to the floors above. It counteracts the interlocking concrete cantilevers that project outward in alternating directions above the stream. Each of these projecting floors has a grillage of concrete beams as its support structure, covered by a slate floor that unites the outside decks with the interior space. Wright later admitted to having many sleepless nights worrying about the weight that these slate slabs added to the cantilevers. Later events would seem to bear out his concern, since the floors eventually deflected enough to cause the house to be supported by scaffolding in the late 1990s. Further investigation later revealed that the deflection was not caused by the slate, but by inadequate reinforcing in the grillages themselves. Wright had calculated the reinforcing correctly, but the contractor had put in only half of the bars to increase his profit.

Aside from the living room, which is the main space of the house with its dual focus on both the outside terrace and the hearth, there is a small kitchen and dining area that is a reminder that this was just a vacation house and not a permanent residence. This balance between indoor and outdoor space, of each room having its own terrace, continues with the bedrooms on the floor above, which are treated the same way.

Independent engineering studies, commissioned by Kaufmann without Wright's knowledge when construction started, cast immediate doubt on the structural stability of the house. The cantilever system that the architect was proposing was unfamiliar, and engineers doubted the wisdom of choosing a single boulder in the middle of the stream as the fulcrum of that cantilever.[67]

This study, when presented to Wright, prompted the first of several confrontations between architect and client that came to characterize the progress of the house. Upon receiving word of the study and its conclusions, Wright fired back a cable to Kaufmann, telling him, in essence, that he "did not deserve the house" and requesting the return of all working drawings. Temporarily reassured, Kaufmann apologized but continued to commission further studies. Perpetual doubts eventually prompted the client to surreptitiously arrange for a brick wall to be built in the dark shadow beneath the longest cantilever of the first floor to prevent what he and his engineers felt was sure to be imminent collapse. Wright, who had purposely chosen both an inexperienced project manager and contractor so that he might better control each of them, happened to be in the area giving a lecture at the University of Pennsylvania in Philadelphia at the time, just as the wall was being built and decided to make an unannounced visit to the site to check the progress of the work. He was infuriated when he saw the wall but asked the contractor to continue building it, except for the final closing course. He wanted it to appear to be complete, but have it give no structural support to the cantilever.

On the day of the opening dedication, when the house, which had already been proclaimed as "the beginning of a new era" on the cover of *Time* magazine, was complete, Kaufmann sheepishly told Wright about the wall, which he thought he had not seen hidden in the darkness amongst the rocks. After Wright told him that he had known about the tactic as well as about the missing last course, both agreed that the entire stack of engineering reports should be buried under the hearthstone, which was the last piece to be put in place, as a testimony to Wright's innate structural instincts. More than any other of Frank Lloyd Wright's projects, Fallingwater has come to symbolize his strong principles and his key philosophy of uniting architecture with its natural surroundings. The vertical towers of stone quarried on the site visually and structurally counteract the horizontal planes of the cantilevers, and are in turn softened by having each course laid up rough, so that the ledges once again unite the building with the ground. This kind of sensitivity abounds throughout the house, revealing an organic relationship between the natural and the man-made as the core of the architect's concern. The entry sequence into Fallingwater today also shows the architect's skill in the manipulation of scale, the contrast between open and closed, and the element of surprise, which is found so rarely on the contemporary scene.

Fallingwater is Wright's *riposte* to Modernists such as Le Corbusier, who were getting so much attention at the time he designed this house. He demonstrated that industrial materials and nature need not be mutually exclusive, but can coexist.[68]

THE WEST

Buff and Hensman: The Bass House

Like many avant-garde members of their generation in and around Los Angeles, Conrad Buff and Donald Hensman tried to oppose the stultifying introspection typical in prewar housing and accommodate the radical shift in lifestyle brought about by the end of World War II, a less formal, more casual approach demanding freedom and openness in living arrangements.

The modern architectural language, notably flat roofs to avoid historical reference; white surfaces to obliterate class distinctions; material limitations to exclude nonindustrial products; a predominance of glass associated with political transparency, generic spirituality, and reliance on functionality; all evolved in Europe, primarily Germany, from the turn of the twentieth century to the outbreak of World War II. This language was introduced to the United States by the media, by Philip Johnson, curator of the International Style Exhibition at the Museum of Modern Art, and a group of émigrés: Walter Gropius, Ludwig Mies van der Rohe, and Marcel Breuer, who fled to America to avoid the National American converts such as John Entenza, who promoted it in his restructured *Arts and Architecture* magazine.

Eager to use newly developed technology, the United States heralded the arrival of European Modernism as an opportunity to experiment. Many architects adopted forms without understanding their meaning and cultural attitudes without grasping their significance. Such doctrinaire positions extended to clients; architects often felt clients needed educating rather than serving. Buff and Hensman sought to accommodate rather than dictate, but retained the aesthetic principles of the Modern Movement. Their attitude and the lack of hubris that it requires are a constant theme, as is the aesthetic sensibility that guided the following projects. Such a delicate balance takes confidence and certainty, remarkable in architects of their age, especially considering peer pressure to treat clients otherwise.

Case Study Innovation There is a mystique surrounding the Case Study House Program that is difficult to unravel, but any attempt to do so must begin with the founder, John Entenza. Charismatic by all accounts, he was also determined to convert the entire nation to Modernism through the vehicle of *Arts and Architecture* magazine and the Case Study houses he featured in it. His concept was brilliant in its simplicity, allowing all concerned to benefit. Clients with land to build on got a new house free of charge, as long as they gave Entenza and the architect he selected free aesthetic rein. The architects involved were asked to waive the fee, but since many of these were in the early stages of their careers, they welcomed the publicity and exposure that *Arts and Architecture* gave them. Contractors and suppliers were asked to contribute building services and material in return for free advertising in Entenza's magazine, thus making the circle complete.[69]

This revolutionary experiment in media promotion brought a new generation of California designers, as well as some who were not so new, into the national spotlight, putting many promising careers on a fast track to fame. Entenza had an unerring eye for talent; he was especially adept at identifying young people who were just about to break through the barrier of anonymity, with or without his help. Conrad Buff and Donald Hensman were selected to this illustrious company because of a sensibility they shared with Entenza—an acute appreciation of space, elegant and honest expression in the best contemporary California tradition—and because John Entenza had the prescience to realize the potential that these two young architects possessed.

Bass Residence, Case Study House No. 20
Altadena, California, 1958–1960 This residence for Ruth and Saul Bass had several factors determining the primary concepts of the project. As architect Donald Hensman recalls it:

> Initially, we recognized the unique qualities and limitations of the site and considered a structural frame that would enclose it entirely. Second, consideration of the client's specific needs and budget led to our placing particular emphasis on the structural and spatial aspects of our architecture rather than the use of excessively refined and costly techniques, equipment, and materials. Finally, we saw the necessity for organized space in major areas devoted to specific needs, functions, and age groups, to be separated by courts and open spaces. This would then segregate the parents' private living areas, children's rooms, social and dining facilities, and studio work areas. We thought this kind of zoning, with its direct and orderly circulation, would help to create a harmonious and satisfying environment, conducive to the happiness of all members of the family in response to nature.

Case Study House No. 20 was unique in that it was based upon the experimental use of several prefabricated Douglas fir plywood products as part of the structure concept. This system consists of a series of continuous plywood box beams, stress-skin plywood panels, and hollow-core plywood vaults, all fabricated by the Berkeley Plywood Company. The component parts, fabricated in northern California, were trucked to the site and handled by forklift hoist, making for rapid construction. The plywood walls in the central area of the house were positioned and initially secured in less than two hours. These walls, the stress-skin panels spanning the 8-feet base, and the flat roof area of the house are composed of two layers of Douglas fir plywood, the top one being 1/2-inch thick and the bottom 3/4-inch thick. These were spaced by 1-1/8-inch by 1-3/8-inch ribs, and the central void area was filled with fiberglass insulation. The panels were bent and pressure glued into the required forms, thus achieving lightweight modular layers.

The primary exterior surface is the same material that is used as the structural skin over the light wood framing members: 3/8-inch Douglas fir plywood with a medium density overlay face. This material requires extreme rigidity to resist horizontal loads and makes an excellent surface for subsequent painting. The 4 feet by 8 feet panel size directly integrated with the 8 feet structural module vertically and horizontally, eliminating the necessity for job cutting each panel. The joints between panels were treated directly with a slender applied lathe, which covers structural nailing, provides weather strip closures, and echoes the modular rhythm of the building. In contrast to the smooth paneling, the remainder of the exterior walls were clad with 5/8-inch surface groove structure 111 Douglas fir and plywood. The house and garden plans are unified through the use of a spline quarry tile that links the entry court, the main dining areas, and all the major garden terraces adjacent to the swimming pool. All major rooms open directly into a garden court and deck by means of full height (8 feet by 8 feet) sliding steel doors with adjustable glass and stainless steel louvers that provide natural ventilation. Glazing of the public approach was done with a new type of glass manufactured by the Mississippi Glass Company. Aluminum framed, plastic, heat-reflecting skylights were used in the interior as well as service areas. Lighting is provided mainly by fiberglass soffits that create diffused, continuous planes of soft light throughout the house. Cove lighting at the base of the vaults emphasizes their form as well as providing general illumination in the living and dining areas.

Landscape development by Eckbo, Modine, and Williams complemented the architectural space organization as well as the existing trees and undergrowth. We designed an unusual swimming pool to make a central focus for the rear garden, its form subtly echoing the curvilinear nature of other elements of the design.

This project has substantiated our conviction concerning the use of factory, processed, prefabricated wood products. In particular, the success of the roof installation offers encouragement for further exploration in the development of structural panel systems. Lamination, pressure gluing, and plastic impregnation give new significance to this traditional material, indicating another direction for its rational use as part of a contemporary vocabulary of structural techniques.

Morphosis: The Crawford House

The Crawford House is located on a 2-acre parcel of land that slopes away from a street on one side of the site, favoring the view toward the Pacific Ocean, which is about one-half mile away. It was designed and built between 1987 and 1991 while Thom Mayne and Michael Rotondi were still partners in the firm Morphosis. They have since split up, with Mayne keeping the name of the firm and Michael Rotondi creating a new one, called RoTo, with Clark Stevens. The house is large, with its 8,000 square feet arranged in linear formation along a north-south axis. It carves into the site so that it only appears to have a long low profile from the street, looking like a one-story structure, with a multicar garage on the right-hand, north end of the elevation, and a guesthouse, which is broken off the left-hand, southern end, located farther down the hill.

This strategy, of siting the house as far back on the property as possible, allows the majority of it to be on the oceanside. Mayne, who was the designer, began with the concept of a circular boundary wall, which becomes a retaining wall on the entrance side near the street, with a gap to indicate the pathway to the front door. This circular enclosure begins to fragment on the western oceanside, protecting and enfolding the southern edge of the guesthouse at that edge, and only emerging as a small segment on the north to serve as a reminder of its presence, before disappearing completely on the horizon at the bottom of the hill, to the west. One of Mayne's first, if not *the* first, concept sketches shows the idea clearly. It indicates a crescent-shaped enclosure that embraces the main central portion of the long, linear house that runs across and eventually bisects it, with a gap, drawn as an arrow and eventually, built that way, in the middle to provide access to the front door, and the guesthouse attached to the left-hand arm of the crescent, on the west. In that same concept sketch the house itself is shown as a series of repetitive structural bays, simply drawn as grid lines, to provide a sense of hierarchy and order to it. In addition to becoming the main column bays, these would later emerge as a rank of seven rectangular light monitors on the roof syncopating the extended elevation along the street and giving it momentum and life. The final embryonic part of that initial concept diagram is a cross-shaped piece extending from the front entrance on the street side to the east down and out of the house toward the west. The long upright shaft of the cross is perpendicular to the predominant, north-south axis of the house, while the crossbar, which is parallel to the residence, is much thinner and shorter. This initial cursive drawing has very few lines but contains all of the information necessary to understand the architect's design intent. It falls into that wonderful tradition of the napkin sketch that turns out to be the final scheme when drawn by a talented designer, which is becoming very rare as the computer revolution continues to reshape the architectural profession, and the skill of sketching, which has been a part of architecture since the Renaissance, is being forgotten.

The three elements in the sketch, the semicircular wall, the elongated bisecting row of grid lines running parallel to the street, and the cross-shaped blob on the central east-west axis of the crescent that is perpendicular to that, are the essence of the house. At the time he designed it, Mayne described these three elements as first, "the mercator," which is the semicircular wall; second, "a series of linear progressions perpendicular to the axis of the major view orientation," which are the grid lines, providing order; and third, "a deserted center," which is the open entry axis, allowing views through the house, across the cross-shaped swimming pool in an open garden in the back, to the Pacific Ocean in the distance.[70]

This central view axis that cuts through the middle of the house, from the front door to the pool and then the ocean, literally begins with an arrow-shaped space that points toward the view. This is a reminder that Mayne belongs to a growing cadre of younger architects who have been actively engaged in redefining Modernism. They have taken it out of the dustbin of history to which it had been relegated in the mid-1960s and early 1970s, have begun to reexamine its basic principles, and have found them to be sound. They have been dedicated to improving only those parts of that language that caused it to be questioned by an increasingly disillusioned public in the first place, such as lack of environmental and contextural sensitivity, a shortage of interior softness and comfort, a dearth of legibility, in terms of being able to find front doors, stairs, elevators, and bathrooms, and a disconnection with the past.

A New Modern House The designer of the Crawford House obviously took these criticisms to heart. It falls within the modernist canon because of the emphasis that Mayne has placed on making forms adhere to function, the use of a strictly hierarchical order, the sense of progression through a carefully calculated series of interior and exterior spatial experiences, and his use of an industrial palette of materials, most notably in the exposed steel used for the steel columns and vaulted steel beams that predominate in the main living spaces. There is also a concerted attempt to zone the house into what Louis Kahn defined as both "served" and "servant" spaces, that is, the main living areas and those that service them, including mechanical rooms, bathrooms, storage areas, and circulation. This zoning in the Crawford House involves a complex layering of zoning, beginning with a linear spine that is visible on the roof as a counterpoint to the light monitors behind it. This is a three-dimensional expression of a long thin zone that runs the length of the house, almost as a corridor that provides access to both the enclosed and the open spaces on either side of it. Conceptually, this is a very effective way to organize circulation and is reminiscent of a similar method used in the Brighton Pavilion design by John Nash, built for the Prince Regent. This is a reminder also that good ideas do indeed resurface, in spite of the differences in historical period, culture, and lifestyle, to deal with a complicated circulation pattern. In the Royal Pavilion at Brighton a long gallery leads straight from the entrance to this circulation spine, placed at right angles to it. The spaces are then distributed from right to left in increasingly private order, ending with the Prince's apartment on the far left. In the Crawford House this distribution moves counterclockwise along the arc or crescent, which Mayne has used as an additional counterpoint to the spine, from the guesthouse halfway down the arc on the left, through to the bedroom zone, then the living room and dining room area, ending with an artist's studio on the far right of the main spine, which is also perpendicular to the entrance axis. A further complication, or layer of meaning, that Mayne has introduced to this mix is his ingenious use of the sloping site to shield spaces on the street side, but also to expose them, as the ground falls away, to the oceanside. There are bedrooms in their own private zone stacked on both the upper and lower levels. The living room, dining room, and kitchen are on the entrance level with a maid's room, directly accessible by a stair in the service spine below. The family garage, which is by necessity on the street level, is above the artist's studio, which opens onto the courtyard below.

The Mercator The arc, or fragmented circle, which is also the retaining wall that makes this flip from upper to lower and front to back possible, has been referred to as a "mercator" by Mayne, raising the question of any additional symbolic intention he had in mind for this part of the plan. This is not the first time that Morphosis has used a circular or partially circular element such as this in their design vocabulary, and have referred to it in the same way, most notably in the Kate Mantellini Restaurant on Wilshire Boulevard in Los Angeles where an ocular-style light well elevates a self-described high-level diner to cosmological status. This is a distinct advantage in a city that bills itself as the global epicenter of entertainment and the home of the stars.

The Japanese Connection The explanation of possible reasons behind the use of this conceit in Montecito, however, is a bit more involved, combining an American fantasy of the frontier, a duality of identity, and a rapidly contracting world. The buzzword "globalization" is used frequently these days, but few understand its myriad implications. These were first felt in America as early as the establishment of the British colonial outpost at Jamestown, Virginia, when foreign capital was responsible for the introduction of alien cultural systems, including both agricultural and financial structures that revolutionized this new unexpectedly positive vulnerable context in both positive and devastatingly negative ways.

One of the most important foreign exchanges after that, as far as the history of architecture in California is concerned, took place in the opposite direction, when flotilla that was part of the United States Navy under the command of Commodore Matthew Perry sailed into Yokohama Harbor in 1852, demanding that the

Tokugawa Shogunate open Japan up to international trade. The loss of face that this brought about for the ruling regime, which had been in place for more than 200 years, had far-reaching repercussions for the future of Japan, but the aesthetic earthquake that this unleashed is of more relevance here. This had a substantial impact on the Arts and Crafts Movement on Britain, and subsequently on its most dedicated followers in America, such as Frank Lloyd Wright and the Greene brothers, based in California. The results of this exposure on Wright are now well known. The effects on Charles and Henry Greene, as well as a spate of Los Angeles architects that followed after them, ranging from the Bay Area School to Rudolph Schindler and Charles Eames, still requires definitive research.

That influence would surely include Frank Gehry, who greatly admires Wright, and whose early work honors him. Gehry was once referred to as the headmaster of the Los Angeles School of Architects, which in the late 1900s when the Crawford House was built was contrived to be a loosely affiliated group of architects that included Eric Owen Moss in addition to Morphosis. In his eclectic Norton House in Venice Beach, also realized during this ecumenical period in the history of Los Angeles before he achieved global superstar status with his Bilbao Museum, Gehry made homage to the special relationship that his city on the western edge of the Pacific has with Japan to the east. A primitive *torii* gate, made of amputated parts of telephone poles, are used as a shade structure there serving as a rough-hewn canopy over the sliding doors of a quest flat facing onto the Venice boardwalk and the beach.

Although the existence of the Los Angeles School was largely a myth invented to sell magazines, there was a noticeable similarity of awareness that was shattered among the people who were alleged to share that curriculum, and one of these was a growing awareness of the rising importance of Asia. Los Angeles is like Athens during the Classical Age, which Socrates famously described as being in the center of a frog pond, in which one member of the Hellenic league could easily call out to others, across the water. Los Angeles is now purported to be one of the capitals of the Pacific Rim, and as such is increasingly cited as a paradigmatic city of the future. Mayne, in the Crawford House in the late 1980s, was attempting to connect his project to that network.

Charles and Ray Eames: The Eames House

The Eames House has had a profound impact on the history of contemporary architecture in the developed world, having inspired several generations of architects who have been thrilled by its mixture of high technology and humanism. It is part of the Case Study House Program, which was instituted by the publisher and architect John Entenza just before the end of World War II in Los Angeles. Entenza's idea was to promote modern architecture through the vehicle of a magazine he had purchased called *California Arts and Architecture*. He simplified the name, making it just *Arts and Architecture* in order to appeal to a wider national and international audience. His strategy, which in retrospect was a brilliant one, was to approach young architects who would be willing to design a protypical modern house for no fee, for clients who would also be willing to build such a house. His inducement to each of them was that the houses would be published in his magazine as part of a Case Study series. He then approached contractors and material suppliers as well as kitchen suppliers, and offered them free advertising in his magazine if they would contribute their labor and products to this process. By doing this, he was able to promote modern architecture by having these houses built at no cost to himself. This program lasted for almost 20 years and was remarkably successful. Entenza's hidden intention was to produce a prototype that could be repeated in other contexts throughout the country, and in later years, this led to the use of steel as a building material by Case Study architects such as Pierre Koenig. Koenig's work, which is described elsewhere here, was predicated upon the idea of mass production, in which a steel house could be manufactured in much the same way as an automobile on an assembly line from prefabricated parts. Noted architectural critic Reyner Banham in his classic book entitled, *Los Angeles: The Four Ecologies,* referred to the Case Study House Program as "the style that nearly."[71] The unspoken part of this sentence might be "revolutionize house building in the United States," but, for various reasons, this style did not catch on at the time. One of these reasons is the fact that the unions in the United States involved in home construction resisted the idea. A second hurdle was the resistance of manufacturers to the process that the Case Study architects proposed to them. Another difficulty was that the American public at that time was not ready to unanimously adopt the idea of living in a steel house. The Case Study House Program is now seen as being prophetic, and many of the principles that it promoted are now being adopted by the architectural avant-garde. The general public is still far away from accepting the idea of a mass-produced, prefabricated standardized house built mostly of steel and glass.

Charles and Ray Eames The Eames House was the eighth entry in the Case Study House Program. It was built by architects and industrial designers Charles and Ray Eames. Charles Eames came from St. Louis, Missouri, where he was born in 1907. His early interests included amateur photography, and he was passionate about it to the extent of building his own cameras. In his early teens, he worked at the Laclede Steele Mill in Venice, Illinois, and then also worked on a construction crew involved in making concrete formwork. After graduating from high school, he was offered a scholarship in architecture at Washington University in St. Louis, and he entered that program in 1925. Soon after he entered, he also started working in the office of Trueblood and Graf. He left Washington University at the end of his second year to open his own office with partners, Walter E. Pauley and Charles M. Gray. His timing could not have been worse because the Depression started soon afterwards. The partners closed their office in 1934. Charles Eames then worked for the Public Works Administration as part of the Historic American Buildings Survey, after which he returned to St. Louis and opened a new firm called Eames and Walsh. Among other notable buildings, this firm designed St. Mary's Catholic Church in Helena, Arkansas, which was completed in 1936. The church was published in *Architectural Forum*, which brought him to the attention of Eliel Saarinen. He offered him a fellowship to study architecture at the Cranbrook Academy of Art, in Cranbrook, Michigan. He entered the academy in 1938 along with other members of that illustrious class that included Edmund Bacon, Harry Weese, Harry Bertoia, and Ralph Rapson. He became the head of the Department of Industrial Design at Cranbrook in 1940 while also working part time in the office of Eliel Saarinen. In that year, he also visited California for the first time and through a mutual friend was asked to design a film studio in Hollywood for Irene Rich. This project was never realized, but through it Charles Eames became interested in relocating to Los Angeles.

The year 1940 was important in other respects as well, since he also entered the "Organic Design in Home Furnishings" competition organized by the Museum of Modern Art in New York City, along with Eero Saarinen.[72] One of the conditions of the competition was that the winners would allow their entry to be manufactured. The Eames-Saarinen entry was based on new manufacturing techniques involving the pressure molding of wood into compound curves and the combination of rubber and wood. The production of the furniture that they designed was restricted by the shortage of materials caused by the Second World War. But techniques that were introduced in the Organic Design Competition formed the principles for the furniture that Charles Eames was to design in the future. This competition was also important to him on a much more personal level because it resulted in his meeting Ray Kaiser who helped him prepare the models and drawings for this competition. They were married in the spring of 1941. Ray was also a student at Cranbrook, beginning her studies there in 1940. She was born in Sacramento, California, and was instrumental in convincing Charles that they should move to Los Angeles, which they did soon after they were married. Charles Eames struck up a friendship with John Entenza, who helped the young couple find an apartment in the Strathmore Avenue Building in Westwood, designed by Richard Neutra. Charles Eames was hired by Metro-Goldwyn-Mayer and worked in their studio in Culver City designing and building movie sets. In the meantime, he and Ray continued experimenting with molded plywood, continuing ideas introduced in the Organic Design submission. Their intention was to develop a series of furniture prototypes that could be made on the assembly line and would need no additional upholstery. They soon expanded to the point that they were forced to move into a separate studio, off Santa Monica Boulevard, in 1942, as well as to open a production factory at 555 Rose Avenue. They used the production factory as an architectural office as well.

In 1943, Charles Eames became involved with the Case Study House Program portion of *Arts and Architecture* magazine especially in advising on graphic design. In that year John Entenza announced a competition in the magazine called "Designs for Post-War Living," and he included the winning entries in an issue published in 1944. This was an introduction to the Case Study House Program, since this issue was used to promote ideas of mass production and prefabrication applied to residential design. This issue also included an article by Charles Eames and John Entenza entitled, "What Is a House?" In this article, they argued for the conversion of the industrial technologies developed for wartime production to solve the problem of the housing shortage in the postwar period.

The Case Study House Program was officially introduced in an issue of *Arts and Architecture* magazine published in January 1945. John Entenza selected eight architects who were instructed to redefine the American lifestyle to conform to the desire of people returning from the war for more carefree and casual ways of living. The architects that were chosen for that issue were Thornton Abell, J. R.

Davidson, Charles Eames and Eero Saarinen, Richard Neutra, Ralph Rapson, Whitney Smith, Spaulding and Rex, and Wurster and Bernardi.

The Eames House The house that the Eameses built for themselves was Case Study House No. 8. It is located on a three-acre site on a 150 feet high cliff in Pacific Palisades. It overlooks the ocean, which is visible through a line of Eucalyptus trees that run in front of it. John Entenza had originally purchased five acres here from the Will Rogers estate, selling off three acres to the Eames and keeping two acres for himself. The first design that the Eameses produced for their house was in the shape of an "L" with the living area jutting out from a steep embankment at the northeast side of the site so that the occupants could have an unobstructed view of the ocean and the privacy of the Entenza House to the south would not be compromised. The Eameses, along with their structural engineer, Edgardo Contini, arrived at the idea of using a bridge-like form to deal with a slope beginning at the embankment, and continuing down to the center of the site. The Eameses referred to this as their bridge house, and they intentionally designed it to work in conjunction with the Entenza house, which was Case Study House No. 9 and is square in plan. The Eameses conceived their house as being a place where they could not only live but also work, so in a sense, it was also a design laboratory. Soon after the preliminary design was complete, Charles Eames attended an exhibition of the work of Mies van der Rohe at the Museum of Modern Art in New York City. He was already aware of the work of Mies van der Rohe. In 1929, he had visited Europe with the express intention of visiting all of the major buildings of the architects of the Modern Movement, which along with Mies van der Rohe included Le Corbusier, Walter Gropius, and Henry Van de Velde. According to Ray Eames, this trip to New York in 1947 had a formative impact on her husband. The materials for their house had already been delivered to the site, including the steel. But Charles decided to adapt them to a new plan, feeling that the existing bridge house was too similar to a sketch that he had seen in the Museum of Modern Art exhibition.

The new design of the Eames house, which appeared in the May 1949 issue of *Arts and Architecture* magazine, was completely different from the first scheme. In the original rectangular one, the living portion of the house had been extended like the long leg of an "L" from the studio portion and was placed perpendicular to a steep slope to the north. In the second it was pulled back in line with the studio, so that they both formed a linear wall against the embankment separated by a patio between them. This change simplified the plan in one respect, but complicated it in another. The change required the construction of a long retaining wall that had only been necessary as part of the studio in the first plan. This now was extended to run along the entire length of the hill, effectively becoming the majority of the ground floor wall on that side of the house. The second major impact that this change in orientation had was that it affected the view toward the Pacific, which was one of the major reasons behind placing the living portion of the house perpendicular to the slope on the northern side of the site in the first place. Another consequence was that the Entenza House, Case Study House No. 9, was now completely visible from the Eames House above it. To provide privacy, the Eameses planted a row of Eucalyptus trees along the fronts of both the house and the studio as a way of providing privacy and shade. Now that the Eucalyptus trees

Eames House.   © Tim Street-Portwer / Esto

have grown, they have become an integral part of the front of the house. In each case, in both the first bridge house scheme and the second linear one, the residences have been divided into a series of equal bays. The living portion of the house, as it now exists, has eight bays with an additional one added to the western end to support an open overhang, which provides shade on that side of the house. The central courtyard between the living and working portions of the house is four bays wide and the studio has five bays. The steel frame that has been used to construct these bays is minimal. The "I" columns are only 4 inches wide and 12 inches deep, and they support open web steel joists that have been used for roof support. Exposed corrugated metal decking has been used as a ceiling throughout the house and studio.

The Eames House, which was one of the first projects built in the Case Study House Program, compellingly fulfills the original intentions of its founder John Entenza in that it is the image of a prefabricated, standardized steel residence using all of the latest industrialized products and materials in its construction. In addition to the concrete used for the extended retaining wall, the steel used for the columns, joists, and roof deck, and the glass used for the windows, the Eameses also applied Celotex insulation board on plywood, Cemesto, asbestos, and pylon, which is a translucent laminate similar to fiberglass. Descriptions written by the architect-owners after the house was completed clearly express their intention to provide a stark contrast with nature rather than using materials that would bring the house into harmony with it. Although the relationship to nature is not created by a use of telluric materials, there is a more subtle intention at work here.

A Film Used as a Metaphor for the House Charles and Ray Eames produced many films during their long collaboration, and one of these is called *House After Five Years of Living*. It becomes clear after watching this film, which has no narration, that the intention of the architects was to use the house as a device for refracting its natural context, using it as a *camera obscura* through which to view the microcosm of the world around them. A great deal of the film is dedicated to patterns and the shifting range of colors coming through the long horizontal window frames. It also focuses on distant views through the Eucalyptus trees to the Pacific Ocean. The film is relatively short, being only a little over ten minutes long and includes images photographed by the Eameses between 1949 and 1955. The impression it leaves is one of segmental and fragmentary views rather than that of a continuous narrative. This technique is echoed in the house itself. For example, there are several seemingly randomly placed panels on the exterior wall of the front elevation. These are painted in primary colors of red, yellow, and blue, and there are some white panels included as well. They contribute to this refracted scheme by blocking views in some sections and emphasizing or framing other views through the transparent glass windows around and between them. This technique is reminiscent of that used in traditional Japanese houses in which selected views are framed by translucent rice paper screens beside them. In each case, a staccato impression is conveyed to the viewer, which heightens a sense of connection with nature.

The entry sequence into the house begins at the driveway. After parking, a pathway leads to the main entrance of the residential part of the house, which is 1,500 square feet in area. There is a spiral stairway, which is the only way to get up to the first floor, directly opposite the entrance, which immediately underscores the mechanistic impression that the house conveys. It appears to be like a vertical steel sculpture made up of steel beams welded onto a central pipe column with plywood treads. The dining room, kitchen, and utility zone is located to the right of the main entrance with a view out to the central courtyard, which divides the living area of the house from the studio and office. There is a similar service zone in the office across the way, which echoes the one in the house. By grouping the service cores of both the house and the studio along opposite edges of the court, it was possible to set up open spaces on either side of the servant spaces. These open spaces are the major volumes of both the house and the studio, and in each case are double height; the bedroom and bath are located in a mezzanine above the service core in the house. In the original design, the central core was originally shown to have a steel arcade on the open side opposite to the retaining wall. Windows on the retaining wall side in both the house and the studio must, by necessity, be high on the wall with their bottom edges resting on the concrete.

This contrapuntal treatment of space is amplified by the position of the windows, which are used like apertures. This recalls Charles Eames's intense interest in photography and cameras. The windows are placed in deliberate conjunction with or opposition to others across the main space of both the house and the studio. This deliberate visual game is not immediately evident and becomes apparent only after repeated visits to the house. Their film *House After Five Years of Living* is a clue to the architect's intention to emphasize the impact of the diurnal cycle of the sun as it moves diagonally across the extended length of the residence by capturing and projecting as much light and shadow as possible into the interior.

The Machine in the Garden Is Humanized One of the most important legacies of the Eames House is the impact that it had in its own time as well as on subsequent generations of young architects from all over the world who have visited it. It was intended to be a prototype of a concept that Le Corbusier had called "The House as a Machine for Living." In many ways, it is a paradigm for it. For the Eameses, however, their work was an important part of their lifestyle, and the studio part of this house was the epicenter of their professional life at the beginning of their residency in Pacific Palisades. The studio was able to accommodate their needs as a home office, but they decided to move this part of their activity to 910 Washington Boulevard in Venice, California, in 1958 when the Herman Miller Furniture Company vacated that space. Both the house and the studio during the time between the completion of construction and the relocation of their home office in 1958 were like a living museum in which the various collections accumulated during their private and professional lives were on constant display. Unlike the Purist and Minimalist interiors of the Modernist houses designed by leading architects of that movement in both Europe and America, the Eames House is not only a screen on which the natural environment around it is reflected but also an exhibition space. By layering over the mechanistic aesthetic of the early Rationalistic phase of the Modern Movement, with their own penchant for exhibition, the Eameses provided a new model of a personalized house that stood in sharp contrast to the sterile images seen elsewhere. It demonstrated to other architects at the time, and to others since, that it was possible to follow the principles of Modernism without depriving people of their right to express themselves.

Mies van der Rohe, whom Charles Eames had admired so much, and who was the catalyst for the final configuration of the house, is the opposite example of this position. His Farnsworth House in Plano, Illinois, which he completed soon after arriving in America, is almost monastic in its carefully prescribed restrictiveness. This house was designed for a single woman who simply wanted the quiet retreat of countryside. What Mies van der Rohe provided was a long linear glass and steel pavilion elevated above its site on steel columns both to solve the problem of potential flooding from a nearby stream and, more importantly, to convey the unmistakable image of a detachment from nature. As part of his commission, Mies van der Rohe requested that he be able to advise the client on the selection of the furniture that would be used in the house. The majority of the pieces selected were of his own design, which is famously spare. His theory of interior design was derived almost directly from that developed by Adolph Loos, who proposed that the exterior shell of a house should be an anonymous mask, but that the interior should be made of luxurious materials to provide comfort for the inhabitants and to elevate their mood. Mies van der Rohe refined this theory, utilizing luxurious materials to offset the severe restraint of the furniture he designed. He followed this pattern in the Farnsworth House, which is a testimony to his single-minded adherence to high modern theory. Whether or not this suited the needs of the client does not seem to have been a factor in this case.

A Singular Achievement While Charles Eames famously adhered to this idea of using luxurious materials in his furniture designs, most notably in his well-known armchair and footrest combination, he certainly did not ascribe to the same attitude about Minimalism throughout the interior of the house that he and Ray shared. After Case Study House No. 8 was finished, Charles and Ray Eames had an opportunity to design a house for the Hollywood director Billy Wilder as well as another that was intended to be a prototype that would be produced by a major corporation located in Anaheim, California, called the "Kwikset House." They approached these two projects in the same way that they had conceived the design of their own house, as a prefabricated exercise that could be built quickly from components that were readily available. They did, however, introduce plywood in a more consistent way in both laminated beams and roof sections. Both projects were not realized, and as a result the Eames redirected their focus toward industrial

and furniture design as well as the production of films and exhibitions.

For this reason, the Eames House, or Case Study No. 8, is a singular example of their design genius and as such it is even more significant in the history of contemporary architecture.

Charles and Henry Greene: The Gamble House

As the Arts and Crafts Movement became more well established in the United Kingdom at the end of the nineteenth century, several American entrepreneurs, such as Gustav Stickley and Charles Eastlake, started cooperatives that were similar to those that William Morris had founded in Hammersmith and Oxford. These were primarily intended for the production of furniture and interior fittings for residential use. It remained to architects, such as Frank Lloyd Wright in the Midwest and Charles and Henry Greene on the West Coast, to formulate an American version of the Arts and Crafts ethic, and they completely assimilated the ideals of their British counterparts, such as Charles Rennie Mackintosh, C. A. Voysey, and Norman Shaw. The early work of Wright, for example, has uncanny similarity to that of Mackintosh even though it is not believed that the two men ever

Charles and Henry Greene designed many Arts and Crafts homes throughout California, but the Gamble and Blacker Houses are considered their best. *Source:* James Steele

95

met. Each of them also shared a deep admiration of and affinity for the Japanese aesthetic that had just become known to the outside world when each of these architects were starting out, because of an American naval mission led by Admiral Perry that sailed into Yokohama Harbor in the mid-1860s and demanded that the Tokugawa Shogunate open that country up to trade with the West. Japanese sensibilities, which stressed a reverence for the environment and the judicious use of natural materials in a handcrafted architecture that was at one with its surroundings, fit well with Arts and Crafts principles of human involvement in the production process. Charles Robert Ashbee, who had been instrumental in institutionalizing Morris's idealistic position into the Guild of Handicraft, which was based in the Cotswolds and which was the first formalization of the Arts and Crafts identity, visited America in the late 1800s. He later wrote that he found Frank Lloyd Wright and the Greene brothers to be among those who were most clearly dedicated to Arts and Crafts ideals, and even ranked the Greenes higher than Wright in their attention to detail.[73]

Charles and Henry Greene were born in Ohio and both attended the Manual Training School at Washington University. Their curriculum included wood- and metalworking and machine tool making, and through the director of the school, they were introduced to the writings of John Ruskin. They went on to attend the Massachusetts Institute of Technology before opening up their own firm in Pasadena, California, in 1894. It took some time for them to develop their own distinctive approach to the British Arts and Crafts model, adapted to a Japanese aesthetic as well as the benign environment of California. In the interim, publications such as *The Craftsman* by Gustav Stickley were awakening American interest in this direction, and prefabricated kits of parts for houses, referred to as bungalows, began to appear in the catalogs of mail order companies such as Sears and Roebuck, among others. The bungalow-type house, which is described in detail elsewhere in this set, was perfectly attuned to the semitropical climate of California, having been adapted from a colonial residence that was used by the British in India and Southeast Asia, in response to the high level of heat and humidity there. Ironically, the colonial bungalow named after an indigenous Indian housing type called a *bangla* did not transplant well in England because of climatic differences. But it was firmly established in the public consciousness with exotic locales and escapism and was translated into a house called a cottage in Britain, usually associated with holiday accommodation. The defining elements of the bungalow as it evolved in its colonial adaptation are a raised ground floor to allow air to circulate through a crawl space underneath a wide front porch, which sometimes also extended around the sides and back as the conversion of the colonial verandah, wide, overhanging eaves to protect the porch and the windows from sun, a limitation to one story, or the addition of a sizable attic at most, and a fairly open but modest floor plan typically divided between public spaces, such as the entry, living room, dining room, and kitchen to one side and the private areas, including the bedrooms and bathrooms, to the other.

The Bungalow Embodied Arts and Crafts Ideals The bungalow proved to be a commercial success in the period between the turn of the century and the beginning of World War I because it captured the popular imagination as the embodiment of the anti-Industrial Arts and Crafts ethic of handicraft. This image belied its mass-produced origins, but even though it was standardized and prefabricated each of the craftspeople involved in its construction did have some leeway in how each house was built and was able to contribute his or her own personal skills to it. Mass production made the bungalow inexpensive and an attractive choice for property developers, especially in and around Los Angeles, which was attracting new residents from the middle of America and growing so rapidly at this time.

Greene and Greene Perfected the Bungalow Charles and Henry Greene essentially refined the bungalow, upgrading it from a home for the masses to a country retreat for the rich by dramatically increasing its plot size and scale, as well as the extent and the quality of the craftsmanship in it. Between 1907 and 1909 they produced seven of these highly sophisticated bungalows, all involving handcrafted parts custom-made in their own workshops. This period of frenetic activity pushed the limits of their own ability to oversee and control the quality of production. It also led them to increase their costs to the point where they priced themselves out of even the privileged market that they operated in.

The Gamble and Blacker Houses A house that the Greene brothers designed and built for David B. Gamble and his family in Pasadena, in the spring of 1908, is generally considered to be one of the best examples of their rarefied version of the California bungalow. It was designed and built at exactly the same time as another similar residence nearby for Mr. and Mrs. Robert R. Blacker, with which it invites careful comparison. David Gamble and his wife, Mary, originated from Cincinnati, Ohio, where David was involved in the family company, Proctor and Gamble. They had come to know Pasadena fairly well after spending the winter there for several years and bought land on Westmoreland Place near North Orange Grove Boulevard in 1907. They commissioned the Greene brothers to design their house and, after working through three distinctly different concepts, went into working drawings that were submitted for approval by the local building department on March 9, 1908.[74] Work on the interiors of the Blacker house started little more than a month later. Both houses were substantially complete in September of that year.

The Blacker House, which occupies a 5-1/2-acre site, was positioned near the entrance to an exclusive subdivision that was being developed at that time. Robert Blacker had originally commissioned Myron Hunt and Elmer Grey as his architects, but dismissed them following the San Francisco earthquake on April 18, 1906, because they were unable to satisfactorily describe how their design would survive a similar event. The Greenes, in a characteristically empathetic move, relocated the house to the northeast corner of its site, near the intersection of Hillcrest and Wentworth Avenues, creating an elongated L-shaped scheme, with each leg of the "L" running parallel to one of these streets. This left the majority of the property, behind the house, open for landscaping, and they had a small lake dug; to the east, they brought an entry in from the intersection to a circular driveway leading under a *porte cochere*, which had an extension parallel to Wentworth Avenue to a garage and caretaker's cottage beyond. This 12,000 square foot house was the largest the Greene brothers had ever designed, and yet their sensitive positioning of the house along the slight ridge that they created along the northern edge of the site

Blacker House.   © Wayne Andrews / Esto

made it possible to make it seem to nestle into and become one with the land. The slope provided by this gentle shaping of the landscape made it possible to expose a lower story on the south side, near the lake, so that the house seems to gradually emerge from the ground. A brick foundation, which acts as a base for the wood-framed shingle-clad structure above, contributes to this impression, as do the wide, overhanging eaves of the roof.

The first Gamble House design was based on this approach, with separate wings protecting a higher knoll near the middle of the site.[75] The second scheme was straight, but set at an angle to Westmoreland Place to facilitate cross ventilation. In their third scheme, the architecture made the house parallel to the street. It is zoned on entry into a wide, dark hall that extends from the front of the house to the back, into hallway, stair, living room, and office to the right, and dining room and kitchen to the left on the ground floor. Paid live-in help was typical in the wealthier households of prewar America, and the Greenes positioned the dining room to be a buffer between the activity in the kitchen and pantry and family and guests waiting in the living room while meals were prepared. There was also a secondary circulation system, almost hidden from public view, for employee use only. This division on either side of a wide central hall continues on the first floor with the bedrooms and bathrooms for Mr. and Mrs. Gamble on one side, and a suite for Mrs. Gamble's sister, Julia Huggins, as well as a guest room and bath on the other. Wide porches on the upper level of the house, covered only with gently sloping roofs, were intended for sleeping out in the open air during the summer.

A Total Work of Art The Gamble House, like all other Greene and Greene houses, was approached as a complete artistic statement, with much of the carpentry and craft, including doorways, windows, stairs, furniture, lighting, and other fittings, produced in the architects' own workshop. The front door and main stairway of this house are especially noteworthy as examples of their skill, with wooden dowels, rather than nails, being used in a construction technique similar to that used in traditional Japanese building.

Julia Morgan: Hearst Castle

Hearst Castle, or more accurately *La Cuesta Encantada* or the "Enchanted Hill," was designed for press baron William Randolph Hearst by San Francisco architect Julia Morgan right after the end of World War II, but it still remained unfurnished at the time of Hearst's death in 1951 at the age of 88. When the project started, Hearst was 56 years old and Julia Morgan was 47. Each was then at the height of his/her powers. Hearst was born in San Francisco and was an only child. His parents, George and Phoebe Hearst, had been patrons of talented Bay Area architects, such as Bernard Maybeck, who had designed for them a country estate on the McCloud River near Mount Shasta, in northern California, called Wyntoon. It is described elsewhere in this volume. Like *La Cuesta Encantada*, Wyntoon was an overscaled fantasy based on the romanticized style of another age. George Hearst had become wealthy in the California silver mines in 1859, and he increased the money he had made there by investing in other mining operations as well as in real estate. Some of the land he bought had previously been part of the Mexican *rancho* holdings in California, including the haciendas of San Simeon, Piedra Blanca, and Santa Rosa.[76] When he was young, William Randolph and his mother made the Grand Tour of Europe, and her love of art, and collecting it, later inspired her son to do the same.

Hearst attended Harvard, and during breaks he liked to stay at the San Simeon ranch, as well as at Wyntoon. After George Hearst died, Phoebe became involved in philanthropy, and the University of California at Berkeley was a frequent beneficiary of her wealth. It was through this connection that she met Julia Morgan, who received a degree in civil engineering at Berkeley in 1894 and was working with Bernard Maybeck while he was designing Wyntoon. She was the first woman to be accepted into the *Ecole des Beaux Arts* in Paris and enrolled there in 1898, after several restrictions to her admission, which was breaking with precedent, were overcome. She graduated in 1902 as the first woman, and one of the first Americans, to do so. Phoebe Hearst commissioned Morgan to design a hacienda-style house for her at Pleasanton. Morgan also became heavily involved in commissions for women's colleges, sororities, and clubs.[77]

William Randolph Hearst did not complete his studies at Harvard, becoming an editor at the San Francisco *Examiner*, instead, at the age of 23. He invested family money into what was then a moribund newspaper, using techniques similar to those used by Rupert Murdoch, such as sensationalism and an appeal to popular taste, to turn the paper around. He succeeded and then went on to create a publishing empire by buying up newspapers in many major cities throughout the United

States. He either started or bought many popular magazines as well, so that by 1913 his empire was well established. He then ventured into film, establishing Cosmopolitan Productions in the early 1920s. He moved this production company to Los Angeles in 1924 and joined it with Metro-Goldwyn-Mayer. At its height, Hearst's media empire included 29 newspapers, 15 magazines, 8 radio stations, and 4 film companies, leading to his being immortalized as the evil press baron in *Citizen Kane*, played by Orson Welles.

San Simeon George Hearst started purchasing land in the Santa Lucia Mountains near the California coast, halfway between Los Angeles and San Francisco as early as 1891, building a ranch on 85,000 acres, near the site where Hearst Castle now stands. William Randolph also visited this ranch many times as a boy. The young Hearst received the ranch as a bequest in his mother's will, and he decided to build another house on a 1,465 feet high mountain nearby called Camp Hill.[78]

And so in 1918 with a history of a love of architecture inherited from his mother, a connection to the Bay Area School and Julia Morgan, an existing connection to the Spanish Mediterranean tradition through his father's real estate holdings, and multistory warehouses in New York and California full of art and architectural artifacts, such as the entire contents of a castle in Scotland, William Randolph Hearst decided to embark on a residential adventure that would occupy both him and his architect, Julia Morgan, for the rest of his life.

He started by visiting Morgan's office in San Francisco and going through many scrapbooks showing different historical styles that she had there. The thought that architectural history was simply a repository of different styles that could be selected out of source books and mixed and matched at will, with a little Spanish here, a little Gothic there, and a touch of Italian Renaissance in between, was one of the reasons why the Modern Movement abandoned the idea of historical reference altogether. Morgan's willingness and eagerness to entertain such an eclectic historical palette undoubtedly derived from her experience at the *Ecole des Beaux Arts*, where precedents from all historical periods were entertained interchangeably, and the pedagogical emphasis was on uncovering the typological lesson behind each precedent, and if it was appropriate and the architect decided to use it, it should be executed in a way that was faithful to the original. Hearst had originally wanted a bungalow on the property and it is not clear how that simple request escalated into a megalomaniacal domestic extravaganza on par with Nero's Golden House in Rome or Versailles.

The Spanish Mediterranean tradition that eventually inspired both client and architect to embark on a hacienda-like mansion on Camp Hill, instead of a simple bungalow, at least has strong roots in the history of California, through Mexican homesteads in the region. The *haciendas* that were built there, following the model of those built in Mexico itself, which are discussed in detail in Volume II of this set, were organized around a large house, or *casa grande*, where the owner and his family lived. This was separated from the rest of its dependencies by a series of courtyards, and the entire complex was surrounded by a wall. The only other building that came close to the scale of the *casa grande* in the *hacienda* was the chapel. The Churrigueresque style, which the Spanish evolved in the Americas, is characterized by ornate doorways, surrounds, window frames, cornices, and towers contrasted against plain exterior walls for maximum impact. The Pan-California International Exposition, which had been planned by architect Bertram Goodhue in San Diego in 1915, had popularized the Spanish Colonial, Churrigueresque, and Spanish Mission style, adding impetus to Hearst's decision to use it as the basis for the residence he wanted Julia Morgan to design for Camp Hill. Hearst had seen and admired the Cathedral of Santa Maria la Mayor in Ronda, Spain, which he saw in one of Morgan's source books and later went to visit when he traveled to Seville.

The Church and the Steeple The bell tower at the Cathedral of Santa Maria la Mayor in Ronda is a clear reminder of the Islamic presence in that region for hundreds of years, since many churches were converted to mosques during that time and single minarets were added to them. The minaret was used by a *muezzin* who sang out the call to prayer to the faithful from the top at each of the five prescribed prayer times during the day. In other cases, mosques and their minarets were adapted after the *Reconquista* of Muslim territory in Spain to become Christian cathedrals, and the minarets were converted to bell towers. The bell tower of Santa Maria la Mayor has a classic tripartite minaret shape, telescoping upward from a high square tower that occupies more than half of its height, to an octagonal center with high arched openings on each of its eight sides, and then capped with a smaller ornate cornice that is like an octagonal band, with pointed spires at each juncture, making it look like a crown. Morgan adapted this bell tower, using a pair of them to flank the central doorway to Hearst's main house or *Casa Grande* at *La Cuesta Encantada*. In this case then, the chapel, which was always the second largest building in the Mexican *hacienda*, next to the *Casa Grande*, has become the *Casa Grande*, and the subject of veneration is Hearst himself

A Village of Its Own Julia Morgan created a very skillful site plan that occupies the entire top of Camp Hill, following the natural contours and using them and the orientation toward the Pacific Ocean, which is less than a mile away, to best advantage. In addition to the *Casa Grande*, there are three guesthouses, creating a courtyard called the Main Terrace by circling around behind the large house. With similar romantic allusion these are called *Casa del Mar* (House of the Sea), *Casa del Monte* (House of the Mountains), and *Casa del Sol* (House of the Sun). A fourth guesthouse was planned to be located between *Casa del Monte* and the *Casa Grande*, but it was never completed. Hearst loved to have guests visit him at *La Cuesta Encantada*, and the guest list of those who did during the time that he lived there reads like a "Who's Who" of Hollywood, of Washington, D.C., as well as of foreign dignitaries during the height of Hearst's power.

The plan of the *Casa Grande* itself has an unfortunate and obviously unintentional resemblance to a lobster, spread out on a kitchen counter. The main entrance with its two flanking towers is located at the tail end and a long hallway connected it to the main part of the house, which is a U-shaped part, like the head and the claws at the other end, where a rear courtyard is located. Hearst and Morgan had also planned a "Great Hall" on this portion of the site that would have closed off the "U," enclosed the second courtyard, and eliminated the crustacean analogy, but Hearst had finally overspent and nearly went bankrupt until World War II and the accompanying need for news and newsreels that went with it rescued him.

Hearst had his own study called the "Gothic Suite" on the third floor, which occupied the entire level. It includes a sitting room, study, and bedroom and is accessible by several sets of stairs as well as by an elevator. Hearst liked to greet his guests in the "Assembly Room" on the first floor, above the main entrance, where the two towers are joined together into one long rectangular space, for pre-dinner drinks, before leading them into the "Refectory" or dining room directly above the main hall on the entrance level for dinner. There is also a theatre on this level where guests might gather after dinner to watch a movie. Hearst reportedly arranged for an exclusive advanced screening of *Gone With the Wind* here for his friends.[79] During the day they could amuse themselves by choosing between two swimming pools: the outdoor Neptune Pool or the indoor Roman version in its own recreation building sited at an angle to the main house and some distance away from it. They could also visit Hearst's private zoo, which included lions, tigers, leopards, panthers, cheetahs, bears, elephants, monkeys, and rare birds.[80]

An Architect's Nightmare Julia Morgan had a thriving architectural practice in place when she accepted the commission to design *La Cuesta Encantada*. Because of her busy schedule, she typically went down to the site on a Friday night and remained there over the weekend, returning to San Francisco on Monday morning. During the time it was in construction the area was initially inaccessible, and heavy construction materials including the cement and the reinforcing bars for the concrete, from which a majority of the substructure of houses is made, had to be transported by ship. The project, which involved a small army of laborers that varied from 50 to 150 a day, lasted more than 20 years. Hearst had not only collected works of art during his extensive travels but historical furniture, fixtures, and entire period ensembles as well, described by one source as "the contents of Hamilton castle in Scotland, an entire Spanish cloister, 50 entire Gothic rooms, enormous carved ceilings, paneling by the roomful, staircases, doorways, windows, fireplaces, mantels and corbels," and the list goes on to include every kind of furniture, furnishing, and interior design object imaginable.[81] Morgan had to design a specific space to accommodate each of these items, surveying each of them in the process. Hearst was also a perfectionist, constantly changing his mind about decisions he and Morgan had already made, frequently doing so after a space was already complete. He was also often slow to pay the workers and suppliers, and with such a complicated construction schedule to maintain, one lapse caused by lack of payment created a chain reaction of delay.[82] Because of the lack of accommodation, the plan was to complete one of the guesthouses first, and for Morgan to use that as a construction office and living quarters during her weekend trips to the site. California does get cold and wet during the winter, especially at elevations as high as Camp Hill, which is also subject to high winds from both the mountains and the Pacific Ocean. *Casa del Mar* was the residence of choice to be used as a headquarters, but Morgan had to use it even before it was enclosed.[83] Hearst himself said that the house should be made more livable and if it was not the houses would have to be renamed: "Pneumonia House, Diphtheria House and Influenza Bungalow."

Her patience against such daunting odds paid off, and Hearst's fantasy is now a reality. After his financial troubles eased, in 1943 Hearst returned to his mountaintop retreat and wanted Morgan to resume work on the parts of the plan, like the Great Hall, that were still unfinished. But she had retired and offered to have her assistant complete the work. A heart condition and his physician's orders forced Hearst to leave the hill for the last time in 1947, and he died four years later.

Irving Gill: The Dodge House and Horatio West Court, Los Angeles

The conventional wisdom is that Modernism in the United States started in California, with the construction of the second Lovell House, designed by Richard Neutra, in 1927. Frank Lloyd Wright was active in that city at the time, but it would be several years before his scheme for Fallingwater, which is the ultimate *riposte* to European Modernists such as Walter Gropius and Le Corbusier, was to be built near Pittsburgh in the early 1930s. During the time Wright was in Los Angeles, he was still wrestling with the issue of the place of tradition in an architecture that would accurately reflect the Industrial Age. The so-called "textile block" houses that he produced during that period, which are made of preformed concrete panels inserted into a steel reinforcing bar frame, were his attempt at reconciling the use of concrete with handwork, in the Arts and Crafts sense, since the blocks or panels were perforated in various ways and formed in a mold.

Rudolph Schindler, who was one of Wright's most gifted disciples and Neutra's childhood friend, was too steeped in German Romanticism to really qualify as an arch Modernist, even though his political views undoubtedly were aligned with a large number of the most prominent members of that movement. The Greene brothers were purely Arts and Crafts advocates, and although it is possible to make a strong case for that sensibility being the foundation of Modernists principles, as Peter Davey has managed to do with great skill and pervasiveness, the Gamble and Blacker Houses in Pasadena, as well as other residential projects that this creative and prolific duo have left behind in California, are a long way from the minimalist language of the Weissenhofseidlung, discussed elsewhere here.

Irving Gill Only the work of Irving Gill, whose career crested well before the second Lovell house was even conceived, deserves consideration as being one of the first examples of true proto-Modernism in the region of Southern California. There are a remarkable series of overlaps between his early career and that of Frank Lloyd Wright. Each architect worked for Joseph Silsbee in Chicago, although not at the same time. Silsbee's practice was primarily focused on large single-family residential projects for wealthy clients in suburban Chicago, and he was

Horatio West Court.   Courtesy of Andrew B. Hurvitz; Flickr

103

known as a slick, sophisticated salesman with a distinctive, historically based style. Frank Lloyd Wright moved to the office of Adler and Sullivan in 1887, and was well established there as chief draftsman by the time Irving Gill also joined the firm four years later. Gill was supervised by Wright, and together they worked on Louis Sullivan's convention-breaking Transportation Building, which was a centerpiece of an otherwise exclusively Classical World's Columbian Exposition.

The Move to San Diego Irving Gill did not thrive in Chicago, as Wright did, and in 1893 he decided to move to San Diego in search of a better physical and psychological climate in which to pursue his career.[84] When Gill arrived on the West Coast, things were just starting to happen. San Diego was well situated for growth, since it has a major port, and the California Southern Railroad, linking it to the East Coast of America, was completed in 1885. At the time he arrived, the local population was little more than 20,000 but would soon start to grow. Boosterism, which was intended to attract people from all across the United States to both San Diego and Los Angeles, would soon be at its height, and the housing market, and industrial growth, was about to explode. Boosters, in the form of local Chambers of Commerce, promoted an exotic image of Southern California as the land of Spanish missions, orange trees, swaying palms, and ocean breezes. A novel called *Ramona*, by Helen Hunt Jackson, which appeared in 1884 and used the *Casa de Estudillo* as a backdrop, became enormously popular in America and directed national attention to the region.

Irving Gill, as a partner in his new firm of Hebbard and Gill, started to prosper, being primarily involved in residential design in and around San Diego during the last decade of the nineteenth century. The first portland cement plant was built in Pennsylvania in 1875, and Gill started on his own quest to reconcile past and present by attempting to simplify the Mission tradition of the region and render it in concrete, to make it modern. He was inspired by historical examples of the style locally, such as the San Diego Mission, which had been restored soon after he arrived in the region.[85] His direction, to express regional history in a stripped down, concrete language, was set.

Rejection To celebrate the opening of the Panama Canal, and to use the strategic location of the city as the first port that ships would encounter after leaving it as a marketing strategy to help the local economy, San Diego boosters decided to hold an event that would promote civic history. Irving Gill seemed to be the local choice to direct what was billed as the Panama California Exposition of 1915 to be held in Balboa Park. Bertram Goodhue was selected instead, however, because he favored a more ornate version of the Mission style, which had become a popular symbol of the area, based on Spanish Baroque. Gill was considered to be too modern.[86]

The Dodge House This displacement indicates that the general perception of Irving Gill was one of an architect who did not fit in. He encouraged that image by experimenting with new ways to build with concrete, which was his material of choice, such as the tilt-up slab method. This technique was not entirely new, but was considered untested, even when Rudolph Schindler and Clyde Chace used it to build their house on Kings Road in Los Angeles in 1922. The idea behind tilt-slab construction, at least in the beginning, was to eliminate the need for expensive formwork by using a shallow depression in the ground dug as deep as the thickness of the slab needed, placing the wet concrete in it, and then hoisting or "tilting" it up onto a grade beam or the top of a foundation wall after it had dried. Gill hoped to make concrete as commonplace as stone construction by using such expedients, to lower its cost and make it easier to use.[87]

One of the largest and most effective applications of his principles took place in Los Angeles in 1915, after his rejection by the Panama California Exposition had prompted him to look further north for support. During this period just after the beginning of the First World War, the bungalow was beginning to become increasingly popular as the choice for people moving into the region, and for the developers and real estate speculators who courted them. The bungalow, because of its origins in the British colonial enterprise in India, became associated with exotic locales and a leisurely life in the tropics, which was especially appealing to refugees from the snowy cold winters of the Midwest. Gill had his work cut out for him in trying to introduce another option to a public that was then being bombarded by such images in the press, in pattern books, and by agents trying to sell them property. Gill, like other notable architects of the time, such as Wright, found his major source of support among wealthy independently minded patrons, who were above the stylistic fray and liked the idea of promoting something new and different. A rich industrialist named Walter Dodge and his wife, Winnie, who had made their fortune in the Midwest in patent medicines and had come to Los Angeles to retire, were such clients.[88]

Gill responded by giving them what many regard as his best residential design, which was uncharacteristically expansive for an architect known for compact plans. The Dodge House, like many important buildings in the region, has unfortunately been torn down, but when complete, it stretched horizontally across its lushly planted site like a palace. The 6,500 square foot house started at a *porte cochere* facing the street followed by a compartmentalized entrance foyer placed slightly off-axis with a garden court, visible through a large window and a pair of French doors on its opposite side. This foyer, with an L-shaped stair leading up to a second floor, was in the midst of a larger, more public wing, with a living room and game room on its western edge. Each of these had fireplaces on the external, western wall, increasing their sense of formality. A dining room on the east side of the entry served as a transition space through a kitchen and breakfast room, into a bedroom wing that extended out across the property, and was oriented to take best advantage of natural light from both the north and the south. Three of the four bedrooms in this wing are located along the south wall for this reason, and this orientation, along with the view out over the generously landscaped manicured lawn, must have made waking up in one of them a pleasant experience. To provide a sense of privacy for the largest bedroom in this sequence, which was adjacent to the breakfast room, Gil extended an arcaded wall out from the main entry block, wrapped it around these rooms as if to shield them from view, and placed an open patio between the wall and the house.

The Dodge house had massive 8-inch thick concrete walls, and all of the windows and door frames, as well as the window mullions themselves, were made of steel. The main street-facing arch of the *porte cochere*, as well as the smaller arches of the screening wall around the breakfast room and its adjacent bathroom, contrasted with the rectilinear windows used on the rest of the house, seeming to be an intentional attempt by Gill to remind everyone of his commitment to regionalism.

In 1919, Gill designed the Horatio West Court in the Ocean Park district of Santa Monica, which has survived. It consists of four freestanding two-story units clustered around shared courtyards and surrounded by an enclosure that also extends upward to become the external wall of each unit as it passes them. The Horatio West Court units are unlike the Dodge house in that they are compact and vertical rather than opulently horizontal, conveying an impression of strength and privacy. Arches are also used in this complex as a way to separate the personal territory of each house and to demarcate points of entrance.

Influence Irving Gill was clearly a visionary, ahead of his time in his insistence on using new materials and technologies in his contemporary interpretation of a popular regional historical style. Richard Neutra, who would finally receive recognition as a leader of the Modern Movement in Southern California in a more accepting time, recognized Gill in his book *Amerika*, published in Germany in 1930, and also paid homage to him in his own designs, such as his Strathmore Apartments in Los Angeles, built in 1937, which is clearly inspired by his inventive predecessor.[89]

Rudolph Schindler: The How House

James Eads How, the client for what is arguably one of the best houses that Rudolph Schindler ever designed, was a complicated and unconventional man. He was the scion of a wealthy family and had a great deal to live up to, but chose to do just the opposite. His father, James Buchanan Eads, the son of the Colonel Thomas Clark and Ann Eads of St. Louis, Missouri, was a paradigmatic American inventor in the best tradition of the Wright Brothers or Thomas Alva Edison, a self-educated engineer who began his career as a clerk aboard the steamship *Knickerbocker.*

He invented a diving bell to assist in the recovery of the vessel and its contents when it sank in the Mississippi in 1839. This led to the formation of a highly profitable salvage company that he ran until the outbreak of the Civil War in the spring of 1861. He consequently proposed plans for an ironclad gunboat to the attorney general of the United States, which was approved by President Abraham Lincoln's Cabinet. Seven ships built to his design were instrumental in the eventual defeat of Confederate naval forces, but by 1864 he was completely exhausted from overwork and, following the advice of his doctor, he retired.

The Eads House on Compton Hill overlooked the Mississippi, and he was aware of the need for a bridge over the river, owing to the westward expansion of the railroad after the Civil War. Railroad cargo was then being unloaded in East St. Louis, loaded onto ferries for the trip across the river, and then loaded onto a second train on the other side. Eads's active mind recognized the opportunity presented by this situation and, in spite of bitter infighting, he entered the fray, becoming engineer in chief in 1867. His plan for the St. Louis Bridge was approved, and excavation on the abutments began in the same year. His highly controversial scheme for an arch bridge contradicted the contemporary preference for heavy truss sections

Rudolf Schindler has only recently become more well known by a wider audience of admirers who have come to appreciate his unique approach to space and form.   *Source:* Julius Schulman

and medium spans; the public supported Eads and the engineering establishment uniformly opposed him.

Against formidable odds, Eads saw the project through, leading to Congressional approval and complete construction of the 158.5 meters span, which was 70 meters longer than any previous arch bridge. In addition to many other innovations, such as the first use of a steel superstructure in a bridge in the United States, the east abutment—which is 41.5 meters below the mean low watermark—is still the deepest pneumatic caisson foundation in the world, inspiring the Roebling design of the Brooklyn Bridge that followed it. Andrew Carnegie, who was a business partner with one of Eads's engineering advisors on the St. Louis Bridge, described its designer as "an original genius minus scientific knowledge to guide his erratic ideas of thing mechanical." In spite of his lack of formal education, James B. Eads had a significant impact on both the course of American history and engineering theory though his designs.

Because a definitive biography of James Buchanan Eads has yet to be written, subsequent details of both himself and his family remain sketchy, but his son surfaced in the media soon after the turn of the century when he graduated from Harvard Medical School. James attempted to donate his million dollar inheritance to the National Socialist Party, but was prevented from doing so by a court order brought by his relatives. He closely identified with the poor and the homeless and started riding freight cars in trains, eventually crossing every state in America, possibly also traversing the bridge that his famous father had built. Like nearly 60,000 of these homeless, he also gravitated to Chicago just before World War I and organized the International Brotherhood Association where free lodging and meals were on offer. This Association was different from similar organizations run by religious institutions, where food and a bed came at the cost of attempted conversion. Eads also offered alcohol, which some believe resulted in his pseudonym since, unlike the Salvation Army, he knew "how" to treat hobos, who took cold comfort from the religious service required before soup and clean sheets would be dispensed elsewhere.[90] Eads How, along with a group of other men including Irving St. John Tucker, then opened Hobo College on Congress Street in Chicago in 1913, which graduated its first class of 100 four years later. Their diplomas read in part:

> Be it known to all the world that a hobo has been a student at the Hobo College, in a desire to get an education, and build a world that will be free of unemployment, poverty, war, prostitution, ignorance and injustice.[91]

The circumstances that brought Dr. James Eads How to Los Angeles in the early 1920s are still as unclear as his motives for commissioning Rudolph Schindler to design a detached house for himself and his family in the Silver Lake section of the city in 1925, especially considering his strongly held political views against wealth and privilege. At the time it was commissioned, Schindler had only recently arrived in the city himself, and a brief review of the events directly preceding his arrival is pertinent to the way in which he approached the design as well as its realization. Schindler was a product of the Otto Wagner Studio at the Imperial Academy of Fine Arts in Vienna, moving from there to Chicago to work as a draftsman in the office of Ottenheimer, Stern, and Reichert in 1914. Four years later, he was able to secure a position with Frank Lloyd Wright at his Oak Park studio.

In 1920, Schindler went to Taliesin with his wife, Sophie, whom he had met and married in Chicago. He was overwhelmed by the natural beauty of Wisconsin, in the heartland of America, as well as by Wright's conception of living in harmony with the environment. As an extension of the separate yet equal status accorded to living and working in Oak Park, Taliesin blended them together even more, which appealed to Schindler's personal worldview that was rooted in the German Romantic movement. This view was based in the idea of sacrifice for idealistic goals, and the relentless pursuit of perfection through work. Historian Kathryn Smith has touched upon the significance of the timing of Schindler's arrival in America, in terms of the perpetuation of that view here, rather than the darker Nietzschean antithesis that soon followed. It is important to remember that Schindler left Austria and never returned. His departure was only a few months before the beginning of World War I, 1914. His timing was coincidental, not intentional, and he did not arrive in America as a refugee. But the fact that he did not experience the war in the same way as other Modernist architects of his generation did mean that he was able to retain a part of the Romantic tradition, which was destroyed by the violence of the conflict for others. He remained an idealist, still unconvinced of the need for technological predominance.[92]

This important historical coincidence partially explains Schindler's disdain for the functionalists whom he characterized as the enemies of the artistic basis of architecture, and his wish to be excluded from the International style in general.

His position on the meaning of Modernism was philosophically more closely related to the views put forward to Otto Wagner in *Moderne Architektur* in 1896. This included a theoretical marriage between the classical lineage of the *Schinkel-schulen* and the pragmatic necessity of recognizing the advantages of the new materials made available by industrialization. His concept of the relationship between architecture and nature was correspondingly different from that of the Modernists, as was his notion of space, which was such a loaded word for the entire movement. Schindler is vehement and passionately eloquent on this subject in his writing, referring to a revelation that he had while sitting in a stone cottage in the Austrian countryside, shortly before his departure to the United States. "A sudden realization of the meaning of space in architecture came to me," he said. The house had

> Heavy walls built of the stone of the mountain . . . in feeling and material and nothing, but an artificial reproduction of one of the many caverns of the mountainside. I saw that essentially all architecture of the past, whether Egyptian or Roman, was nothing but the work of a sculptor dealing with abstract forms.

Later, after going through the doorway, he said, "I looked up into the sunny sky. Here I saw the real medium of architecture space. A new medium as far as human history goes." [93]

Soon after their arrival in Taliesin, Schindler and his wife moved on to Los Angeles in late November 1920. Frank Lloyd Wright had asked him to take over as the project manager on the Barnsdall House, which was then under construction. Wright's commission for the Imperial Hotel in Tokyo was requiring more of his time and presence in Japan, and Aline Barnsdall was becoming increasingly agitated by his absence. Mounting costs far above Wright's original estimate contributed to her anger. Wright's hunch that Schindler's charm would placate his nervous client was correct, and through most of 1921 Schindler oversaw construction.

Wright's design approach on Olive Hill corresponds completely with Schindler's view of the need for a continuous flow of space interchange between inside and outside. The central courtyard of the Barnsdall house was the embodiment of the freedom that the idea of architectural space had come to represent to him. One year after arriving in Los Angeles, the Schindlers bought land of their own on Kings Road in Hollywood, with the intention of building "a cooperative dwelling" on it with their friends Clyde and Marian Chace. This was to become the testing ground for Schindler, the opportunity to implement the growing stock of ideas he had been nurturing since his years with Otto Wagner.

Schindler's Kings Road House as a Model As the repository of his principles, as well as the studio in which he was to design the How House that immediately followed it, the Kings Road house serves as a point of departure for the analysis of Schindler's How House in Silver Lake and a valid basis for comparison because of the evolution of ideas it engendered. Inspired by Schindler's recent experience in Wisconsin, as well as a camping trip to Yosemite and the Grand Canyon in the fall of 1921, the Kings Road house was minimal and casual, reaching out to the rectilinear site. It is a double square, 30.5 meters wide by 61 meters long, with three L-shaped arms radiating out in a spiral from a fireplace at the core. Two of these three angled arms were designated as living areas, given over to the Schindlers and the Chaces, respectively, with each bracketing a patio garden that is shielded by that arm. The third "L" was reserved for services, such as the kitchen, laundry, and garage, as well as a guest room, with the tacit understanding that each member of the "cooperative" would share in the cooking, cleaning, and washing up. Each wing was designed to be self-contained, with each leg of each "L" assigned to one person, and the bathrooms located at the juncture. Beds were placed in "sleeping baskets" on the roof, located separately above each wing and positioned adroitly for maximum privacy, with canvas curtains for inclement weather. The final and perhaps most important innovation was the relationship that Schindler introduced between each wing and the garden that it surrounded, establishing an equal balance between inside and outside space. Fireplaces, which anchored the end of each "L" turned to face the outside as well, confirming the architect's view of the garden as an external room, the ideal embodiment of his romantic notion of nature.

The Kings Road house invites comparisons with an early brick country house design of Ludwig Mies van der Rohe, executed the year after the design of Schindler's home. The critical difference was the thin glass line that separates the internal and external worlds that Mies claims to have united in the "free flow of space" he attempted. Schindler described California as a paradise on earth, and it seemed sacrilegious to him to place even the thinnest glass barrier between this Eden and the new architecture he wanted to create, especially in a house he was designing for himself. Sliding wood and canvas panels, reminiscent of Japanese *shoji* screens, provide the only closure between the bilateral gardens and the sheltered rooms facing onto them, and these are placed deep inside an intermediary zone that intentionally blurs the modernistic distinction between outside and inside. These screens extend the connection with nature that Schindler had seen at both Taliesin and Hollyhock House, as does the successive depression of the ground plane as it recedes from the foundation of the house. The effect is immediate and startling to western sensibilities, a sense of freedom and connection where a line of demarcation is normally found, and spaces inside that seem to levitate. Close inspection reveals that the reason for this impression is a radically different structural system promoted by the architect as the "Schindler Frame" without much media or popular success after the Kings Road house was completed.

Schindler decided to make a major change in the conventional wood platform system by cutting off all studs throughout the house at door height to create a continuous visual and structural horizontal line. With this startling departure from construction norms, Schindler was refining the *Raumplan* or "Plan of Volumes" initiated by Adolf Loos, which was to be misunderstood by key proponents of the Modern Movement, such as Le Corbusier. There are obvious surface comparisons between Loos's residential projects, although few in number, which were executed between 1900 and the beginning of World War I, and Le Corbusier's more publicized attempts, such as the Maison Citrohan of 1920, the Pessac Housing estate of 1926, and the Villa de Monzie in Garches of 1927. While Le Corbusier affected the stripped down, unornamental surfaces that Loos proposed and polemically defended in his influential tract "Ornament and Crime," he concentrated primarily on the columnar structure on which floor plates were supported, rather than the more intricate concept of Loosian space.

By contrast, in his *Raumplan*, which few, except Schindler, truly grasped and appreciated, Loos attempted to redefine traditional concepts of space without shattering them completely. He sought historical continuity with classical precedents reinforced by Schinkel, Semper, and others in combination with a frank recognition of the undeniable changes taking place in the capacity of building materials. His architecture was one of walls interacting in the third dimension, using the same floor slabs that Le Corbusier pierced with columns in his *Dom-i-no* system as basis for his "five points" and the grid they began with. By shifting volumes up and down, and penetrating them with deep openings rather than strip windows, Loos infused internal space with layered interrelationships that plans alone fail to convey. His houses seem to be based on conventional room arrangements at first sight. A proper study of a Loos house design requires numerous planer cuts, not only at the standard position above the floor, but every few meters after that, to suitably describe the spaces

At a time when Loos, who had a significant impression on Schindler, made these determinations, Vienna was an unparalleled crucible of exploration into the bifurcations that Modernism was causing in contemporary life. These were occurring in all the arts, through the work of Mahler and Schoenberg in music, by Munch, Klimt, and Kokoschka in art, and through Freud in psychology. The reasons behind the concentration on what was to be a central issue in the century to follow, specifically in this place at this time, have yet to be completely determined, but the implications for architecture were profound. Loos's description of a house was that it "doesn't have anything to tell the exterior, instead all its richness must be manifest in the interior." [94]

Beatriz Colomina has perceptively identified Loos's insight as

the need for a mask. To be uprooted Loos believed, there was nothing to be ashamed of, it was part of the modern condition. The silence that he prescribed is no more than the recognition of our schizophrenia; the inside has nothing to tell the outside because our intimate being has split from our social being. We are divided between what we think and what we do. Loos had realized that modern life was preceding on two irreconcilable levels, the one of our experience as individuals, the other of our existence as society. [95]

Loos believed that the interior, protected by the limiting walls that defined these various levels between existence and experience, is the repository of culture, in the sense that the distillation of the best of a society takes place there. The inside of a home is the one hope for retaining, interpreting, and translating identity, and the exterior represents the intractable process that threatens it.

Channeling Loos in the How House While this realization rendered Loos a virtual exile in his own city because he designed houses with blank façades, the underlying conditions that prompted it made Schindler a real exile in Los Angeles, since it is a city that has come to symbolize modern displacement. The dichotomy Schindler tried to reconcile in the How House, as a direct extension of its expression in his own Kings Road residence, was how to respect Loos's implicit recognition.

He wanted to do so while still allowing his own enthusiasm for what he had found in California to be expressed freely. Los Angeles is certainly not Vienna, and many other expatriates, such as Reyner Banham, Berthod Brecht, and Theodor Adorno, have been initially liberated there. Inevitably, however, *ennui* sets in, and the temporal land of the lotus eaters takes its toll. Schindler's discipline, in retrospect, seems to have lasted longer than most, due to the structural and spatial system he established, which found its prime expression in the How House.

In the How House Schindler made maximum use of the steeply sloping hillside site, designing it to appear to be only one story high, with a raised central part, when seen from the street. It actually has a second level made possible by retaining walls that are visible only on a private approach to the garage, and especially from the ravine below.

Using a technique reminiscent of Frank Lloyd Wright, Schindler deliberately made the entry tight, with one doorway leading straight into Dr. How's study, giving him the separate entrance he requested. Another entrance, further over to the right, goes past a stairway to the lower level, giving access to the living room itself. From that vantage point, the Wrightian maneuver of offering up a breathtaking view in distinct contrast to the previous experience of a restricted and frequently dark entry, is replicated, but highly refined. It lifts this house to an entirely different level of experience. This is achieved by a sophisticated layering of space and plane in both the horizontal and vertical dimensions by modular proportioning. An overview of the plans shows them to be symmetrical, in the central section, if not in the kitchen and entrance appendages, with a diagonal axis running through the living room and outdoor patio portions of the house. This, along with clerestory light provided by the roof raised above an upper gallery, helps to convey a prismatic impression, of primarily glass walls moving inward below the mezzanine, and outward above it, refracting light and amplifying space in a powerfully dynamic way. The symmetry of the How House, as past owner and Schindler scholar Lionel March explains, is "Not the conventional symmetry of classicism. This is an example of the transformation of classical symmetry (orthogonal bilateral) to another kind of symmetry (diagonal bilateral)." [96] March has further explained that Schindler has built Classicism anew, transforming the tradition in ways that Loos and Wagner might have appreciated. At one level the How living room mimics Loos. What Wagner and Loos thought about in Vienna happened in Los Angeles with Schindler.

The primary vehicle in this transfer is the proportional system that Schindler adopted. He used a 1.2 meter module as a basic unit. This choice is related to human use. Schindler used the Vitruvian ideal of human height at 1.8 meters as one-and-a-half units, the industrial standards of door height at 2 meters as one-and-two-thirds units, and a room height of 2.4 meters as two units. He felt that this unit system contained all the necessary dimensions for building within it, subdividing it into one-quarter (30.5 centimeters), one-third (40.6 centimeters), and one-half (61 centimeters) to provide a unit system that an architect can easily remember without resorting to fractional calculations that have no human connection. The How House is laid out on a 1.2 meter grid. Vertical dimensions are given in a measurement above sea level, the low point being 178.6 meters. There is a vertical drop of 6.1 meters from the front to the back of the house, which becomes evident inside from the position of a square light well that also mitigates between inside and outside space, or by going down the stair to the lower level. Where the entry level is glass and wood refracting transparency and light, with the only impressions of solidity being concrete in the fireplace core in the kitchen and dining area, or in the study, the lower level is just the opposite, which is appropriate to its function as a private zone. The bedrooms and one bath are located here, including one for a housekeeper located near the hall entrance to the garage.

Consequently, the central spatial experience of the house is forward and upward, from the living room across the patio toward the mountains and valley in the distance. This is the first "outlook" that Schindler mentions in his own description. The second impression is in the opposite direction of the diagonal axis, toward the raised garden terrace that separates the house from the street. This was intended to be Schindler's recognition of the "outdoor life" similar to that experimentally introduced at Kings Road. This experience, at such a condensed scale, remains intellectually and emotionally memorable not only because of the architect's sensitivity in siting the house but also because of the infinitely varied, integral geometries he introduces. Schindler's realization of a spatial system of planes, which are transparent and refractory as well as protective and solid, is a vindication of Loos's insight about walls. But, it has been expanded here in ways that are consistent with the optimism that was once endemic to Los Angeles. Instead of adopting bilateral symmetry that is static, his proportional system is dynamic, transforming Loos's *Raumplan* into a medium that is far more appropriate to a positive view of the future. In that way it is a microcosm of the American aspirations that Los Angeles once represented.

Pierre Koenig Case Study Houses No. 21 and No. 22

Case Study House No. 21 by Pierre Koenig was commissioned in 1957 and was completed two years later. It was built for Walter and Mary Bailey on a level lot in the Hollywood Hills above Los Angeles. Koenig had only recently graduated from the University of Southern California School of Architecture in 1952, which he attended on the GI Bill after serving in World War II. He was precocious, having designed and built a steel and glass house for himself while still in school. It brought him national attention and caused consternation among his instructors, who were not yet sympathetic to his choice of materials.

A Visionary Ally Koenig's deliberate affinity for an industrial palette integrated with prefabricated interior components brought him to the attention of John Entenza, who had acquired a moribund regional magazine named *California Art and Architecture* in the mid-1940s. He revamped it, dropping the state name to give a wider appeal, so that he might use it to proselytize for Modernism. Entenza and Koenig were both men in a hurry, driven by a vision that encompassed nothing less than revolutionizing the way Americans lived. Entenza intended to do this through a brilliantly conceived initiative he called the Case Study House Program. It was a win-win idea in which potential clients who were amenable to living in a modern house were matched up with architects who shared the ideals of the Modern Movement and were eager to design one with little or no compensation except for the recognition they would receive in print. Entenza offered contractors, material suppliers, and manufacturers a similar incentive. As a result, he was able to present 36 houses in *Arts and Architecture* magazine over a period of nearly two decades. A few of the designs were never realized, but the impact their publication had was incalculable.

A Historical Coincidence The full extent of Pierre Koenig's achievement becomes apparent only when viewed against the background of the dramatic developments taking place in America at that time. Modernism had only recently been introduced into the country by messianic émigrés Walter Gropius and Ludwig Mies van der Rohe. Gropius had relocated from Germany to become chairman of the Graduate School of Design at Harvard in 1937, and he remained there until 1952. His house in Lincoln, Massachusetts, is discussed elsewhere here. During that time he completely revamped the curriculum to conform to a more ahistorical, antithetical educational model based in Modernist theory. His compatriot, Mies van der Rohe, accepted an equally influential post at the Armour Institute, later IIT, in Illinois in 1938, remaining until 1958. He had a parallel influence on IIT graduates of that time, and there is no question that Gropius and Mies van der Rohe subsequently redirected the course of American architecture.

The Basis of Modernism It is important to remember, relative to Koenig's Case Study House No. 21, that the Modernist credo that Gropius, Mies van der Rohe, and other disciples brought with them to America was heavily freighted with nationalistic implications. It had a clear social agenda, initially formulated in the mid-nineteenth century, as both a patriotic and an economically motivated response to the technological advances made by other European nations at that time. It was specifically instigated by the manufacturing prowess of the United Kingdom in the nineteenth century and a competitive desire to surpass it. A powerful faction in the German government believed that this would best be achieved by emulating the principles of the Arts and Crafts Movement, which they had concluded to be responsible for British manufacturing success. German envoy Herman Muthesius maintained that Arts and Crafts architects such as Charles Rennie Mackintosh had synthesized the reflexive and humanistic ethos of the movement. This ethos was formulated in response to the social ills caused by rapid industrialization, by Victorian intellectuals such as A. W. N. Pugin, Thomas Carlyle, John Ruskin, and William Morris. They maintained that the physiological well-being of the worker was paramount and that to ensure it handcraft must play a central part in the production process, so that the laborer would not be made redundant.

Gropius, along with Muthesius and others, was instrumental in launching an institutional prototype called the Werkbund in Germany just prior to World War I to test the efficacy of applying Arts and Crafts principles to industrial production. This demonstrates a national will to excel, to be systematically implemented through education, so that eventually every citizen would either be involved in some aspect of industrial design or become knowledgeable enough to be an informed consumer.

The architecture that Gropius conceived to house the Werkbund was symbolically anonymous, deliberately free of any historical clues that might relate to style. The moralistic implications inherent in the Arts and Crafts position became more crystallized in this iteration; their transformation into Modernist principles involved metaphorical neutrality to erase signs of social status. Rather than being fondly regarded as a tangible record of cultural tradition, historical style was disdainfully seen as the irrefutable evidence of the exploitation of the poor by the rich, since, Modernists argued, only the upper class could afford to build durable monuments that would survive the ravages of time and remain as a historical record of the past.

Industrial materials were believed to offer a neutral means of architectural expression, appropriate for a bright, new egalitarian future that would be free of stratified economic associations. Telluric materials, such as timber, brick, and stone were shunned because they were reminders of the past. Glass was singled out as being especially symbolic of the Modernist ideal of equality and social well-being because of its transparency.

Immediately after World War I, in which both Gropius and Mies van der Rohe fought, the Werkbund experiment was reconfigured into the Bauhaus, which was first based in Weimar in 1919 and then moved to Dessau. Walter Gropius was its founder and first director, and his mission, now more focused than before the war, was to use this institution as an engine with which to help rebuild his defeated nation through industrial development and design excellence. As he said in its first catalog: "Together let us desire, conceive and create a new structure of the future, which will embrace architecture and sculpture and painting in one unity and which will one day rise toward heaven from the hands of a million workers like the crystal symbols of a new faith."

The Appeal of Minimalism, Without Ideology The structure Gropius was referring to, of course, was political, and modern architecture was to be the phalanx in the epic struggle to build it. This ideological implication was not readily apparent to many of the American architects who so readily adopted the physical aspect of Modernism, however, or to the students who were faced with a new educational doctrine that quickly replaced existing *Beaux Arts* curricula. Many were attracted to the freedom that Modernism represented. Its minimal simplicity was a welcome relief from prewar social conventions and the traditional architectural forms and materials that represented and sustained them. The cataclysmic events that returning veterans, like Pierre Koenig, had witnessed abroad and the sacrifice, anxiety, deprivation, and tragedy experienced by those who had remained behind fed a national desire for change.

Those who fought in the war, for better or worse, were also exposed to new cultures, quite different from their own. They returned to America with a broader, less parochial worldview. In retrospect, the seismic shift in social patterns that followed was inevitable. It included major technological advances prompted by wartime necessity, greater mobility due to better automobiles and the new interstate highway system of the Eisenhower years. This time is now viewed by many as the most optimistic period in American history, and the height of its international prestige. Industrialization made possible an expanding middle class and the end of the prewar prevalence of domestic help. One result was a mass migration away from the city to the suburbs and a more casual lifestyle.

A New Way of Living Recognizing the vast social changes that were taking place, suburban developers like William Levitt, Joseph Eichler, Henry Wright, and Clarence S. Stein provided single-family houses with attached garages. These

115

were centrally positioned on small lots to allow a sizable lawn in front and yard behind, where children could play and be easily supervised from the kitchen. Without domestic help, and before women's liberation, the kitchen became the domain of the housewife, and manufacturers clambered to provide the labor-saving devices necessary to make her life easier. Levittown, built in 1947, was vaguely based on an easily recognizable historical style and was still divided into rooms with clearly designated functions in mind, as in the past.

Like these suburban developers, John Entenza also had the foresight to predict the pent-up demographic demand of the baby boomer generation for a new and different kind of housing. But, unlike them, his goal was to use the most advanced industrial processes and the latest technological developments and material available to provide housing at a price everyone could afford. He envisioned the residential equivalent of the Model T Ford.

A Legend among Legends Entenza and the architects he enlisted to help him realize this goal are now legends, but Pierre Koenig is among those who arguably understood the mission behind the Case Study House Program best. This is because he was able to resolve many of the ideas that were only partially explored by others before him and to bring them to realization in a new medium and a more fully resolved way. Many of the other Case Study contributors, for example, designed wood frame houses. While they may have included many design innovations and have used new materials and appliances, they did not do so in a comprehensive way that would allow their houses to become prototypes, suitable for production. Many others also employed skillful site planning strategies, but these also were not systematically thought through. Pierre Koenig implemented a series of generic siting principles that could be replicated elsewhere, if local microclimatic conditions were taken into account.

History, of course, is never as simple as the previous discussion about Modernism implies. There was a much simpler earlier homegrown variant in the United States that developed as part of the race, primarily between architects and engineers in New York and Chicago, to find a practical way to fireproof cast iron and steel at the end of the nineteenth century. It started with the modular building systems by James Bogardus in Manhattan in the 1840s and evolved through William Le Baron Jenney's steel frame First and Second Leiter Buildings in Chicago between 1879 and 1891. It then culminated in the Reliance Building by Burnham and Root in 1895 and the Carson Pirie Scott Department Store by Louis Sullivan in 1899. These Midwestern achievements are the basis of the Chicago School, which also produced Sullivan's apprentice and protégé, Frank Lloyd Wright. His Fallingwater near Pittsburgh, Pennsylvania, completed in 1934, just before the arrival of the Bauhaus missionaries, is generally considered the apotheosis of the early phase of modern architecture in America. Richard Neutra, however, is credited with designing the first modern steel house in the nation for Philip and Jean Lovell in Los Angeles in the same year.

Modernism but Not Necessarily Modernist As Case Study House No. 21 clearly demonstrates, Pierre Koenig personified this earlier American spirit. He was the essence of the Yankee "can do" inventor, working diligently away in his home office to devise ever more efficient steel joints to lower the cost and increase the likelihood of the production of a prototype house, eventually reducing them to only two. He wanted to produce a desirable and marketable alternative to the generic suburban house that was then spreading out around American cities by showing what could be done on a far less conventional site. Instead of the predictable approach of placing the house and its attached garage across the middle of the lot to create a front and backyard, he extended an open carport perpendicular to the main rectangular residence to create an L-shaped plan. Rather than focusing on curb appeal as the developers in suburbia did, Koenig's pragmatic move puts the convenience of his client first.

It recognizes the important role that the automobile was beginning to play in American, and especially Angeleno, culture. It also provided the Baileys with a protective open arcade to shield them from the sun or rain and lead them from their car to the main entrance. This arrangement also shows off the front elevation of the house to good advantage, against the backdrop of the surrounding mountains, but it is a private, not a public, view.

The message that this opening move sends is that it is people and not image alone that matters to this designer. This sets him apart from Modernist architects, who were trying to attract converts through form. This message is reinforced repeatedly from that point on, showing comfort and convenience to be his first priority. The *porte cochere* leads directly into the kitchen, which is treated as the center of domestic activity as it is in suburban house plans at that time, but here it is far more open, with virtually no separation between it and the living area except a kitchen counter with high cabinets supported with an open steel frame. A central service core, which includes two bathrooms, a mechanical room, and a small open courtyard, separates this more public side of the house from the bedroom and office side. This again shows preference for the owners' needs by giving them privacy. Koenig's approach here stands in stark contrast to that taken by Mies van der Rohe in the Farnsworth house in Plano, Illinois, in 1950, in which the sensibilities of its single female owner were subordinated to the architect's desire for transparency, or the Glass House of his American follower, Philip Johnson, in New Canaan, Connecticut, which preceded it in 1948, and is equally open to outside view.

Reality versus Fantasy In contrast to this abstract approach, the space planning of the Bailey House shows a heightened awareness of a new modern lifestyle in which social rules have irrevocably changed, but in which basic requirements of common human decency remain intact. It goes beyond Modernism, which for all of its professed concern about social good and the welfare of the worker, finally failed to demonstrate a real understanding of peoples' needs. Modernists seemed to prefer to determine what they should be, to conform to the ideal world that they imagined, rather than what they really were.

Modernism was called the International style because it was intended to work everywhere, regardless of climate, culture, or topography. When Ian McHarg came forward with the notion that architecture should respond to its specific environmental context instead, Modernists considered him an iconoclast. McHarg's book *Design with Nature* was released at the same time the Bailey house was being designed, and Pierre Koenig is in the same contrarian category. Case Study House No. 21 is testimony to his belief that technology is an extension of human intellect rather than a replacement for it. He believed architecture should reconnect us to our surroundings rather than separate us from them behind fixed sheets of glass with nature on display at a distance. Koenig was far ahead of his time in his sensitive approach to integration with the environment, and contemporary advocates of ecological architecture have a great deal to learn from him.

British historian Reyner Banham, in his classic study of Los Angeles architecture famously referred to the Case Study House Program as "the Style that Nearly..." because it failed to achieve its mission of revolutionizing house construction in the United States. Recent publications related to the design professions indicate that the time for prefabrication has now arrived, and it is in the forefront of the public consciousness. "The Style that Nearly" is now the style of preference and Koenig was way ahead of that curve too. His vision of prefabricated, mass-produced houses that can be available to all, it now seems, will finally become a reality.

Case Study House No. 22 Three years after the Bailey commission, Pierre Koenig received a second opportunity to design another Case Study house for the Stahl family high in the Hollywood Hills. Case Study House No. 22 in tandem with the Eames House, which was Case Study No. 8, has come to epitomize the goals that John Entenza established for the program when he established it, just before the end of the Second World War. It also represents the boundless optimism and belief in progress in postwar America that seemed to have concentrated in Los Angeles. The West Coast was the symbol of the future, unfettered by the restrictions of an extended national history, and Case Study House No. 22 was especially evocative of that spirit. By 1960, when the house was realized, the emphasis of the Case Study House Program had shifted even more decisively toward the principle of creating an industrial prototype that would solve the problem of housing shortages brought on by the postwar baby boom. This idea had admittedly been present from the beginning as the mechanistic image of the Eames House proves, but other participants in the program, such as Conrad Buff and Donald Hensman, had emphasized timber construction in their submissions rather than steel. This friendly competition, between those like Eames and Koenig, as well as Edward Killingsworth and Raphael Soriano, who believed that residential development should be mechanized in steel and standardized to approximate the assembly line production of automobiles, and others like Buff and Hensman, who felt this process should be tempered by the use of natural materials to cater to popular sensibilities, tilted in favor of the machine when Case Study No. 22 was finished.

A Breathtaking View Koenig was faced with the challenge of what might euphemistically be called an unbuildable site. He made a virtue of necessity by creating an L-shaped plan with its outward edge facing the street and a pool in the protected inward part of the right angle. One leg of the "L" cantilevers out over a portion of the cliff, making it seem like the living area in that portion is suspended out in space. By using this kind of plan, Koenig made it possible for the inhabitants to have an unobstructed, 270 degree view of Los Angeles in the valley far below, with its lights twinkling like stars in the seemingly infinite horizon. By the 1960s, when the house appeared, the freeway system that started to encircle the city as part of the Interstate Highway System promoted by President Eisenhower in the late 1950s was beginning to generate the smog for which Los Angeles has now become infamous. With actual stars no longer visible in the sky because of a perpetual blanket of haze, the electric lights that now replace them have become a perfect symbol of the replacement of nature by technology that Case Study House No. 22 also represents.

Pierre Koenig used massive concrete floor beams and 300 millimeter deep steel beams on a 6 meter grid, topped with exposed corrugated steel decking for the roof, as well as floor to ceiling glass panels both to deal with the difficult topography of the site and to create a minimal, mechanistic design vocabulary. The combination of a relatively solid side of the house facing the street and a glazed side providing unobstructed views out over the pool to the city in the distance emphasizes the feeling of delight and surprise one feels when entering the house. There are two bedrooms and two bathrooms, as well as a kitchen, dining room, and living room inside, but because of the minimal amount of structure, and the liberal use of glass, there is no impression of compressed space. The roof extends out past the wall line to create a shaded sitting area around the pool, as well as for the area of the living room at the edge of the cliff.

John Lautner: The Sheats House, Los Angeles

Generations of young people in America were inspired by the example of Frank Lloyd Wright to become architects, and John Lautner was one of them. Many, like Lautner, were drawn to the cult of individuality that Wright personified and actively encouraged. This emphasis on personality was typical of the architects in the Modern Movement as well, who could hardly be accused of being shy, but Wright added a new dimension, of disdain and pride, to this egotistical tendency. He feigned indifference to the New Architecture that was beginning to emerge in Europe at the turn of the century, but privately held it in contempt, thinking it to be devoid of any connection to nature or human emotion. He was proud, instead, of the American tradition of freedom and individuality protected by the Bill of Rights. So, there was a defiant aspect to his attitude, running as an unspoken, but consistent, theme through each of his many projects.

John Lautner as Wrightian Disciple John Lautner was born in Marquette, Michigan, in 1911, and grew up in the North Woods along the shore of Lake Superior. Both of his parents taught at Marquette University, prior to its becoming North Michigan University, which Lautner also attended, graduating with a Bachelor of Arts and a major in English. His mother, Viola, brought the autobiography of Frank Lloyd Wright to Lautner's attention soon after it was published in 1932, and he decided to attend Taliesin West, which is Wright's architectural school in Scottsdale, Arizona. This school was, and still remains, unconventional. At the time that Lautner attended in the mid-1930s, it was entirely focused on the personality of its founder. Wright had just come to the forefront of public consciousness once again because of the stunning success of his design of a house in southwestern Pennsylvania for the Kauffman family in Pittsburgh called Fallingwater. It represented Wright's clear response to the rational abstraction favored by Modernists, such as Le Corbusier, because, rather than being detached and aloof from nature as the Swiss-French architect's well-known Villa Savoye was, Fallingwater was literally fused to its hillside site, connected to a huge boulder on a cliff so that it could hover effortlessly over a raging stream below it. The two approaches could hardly

John Lautner was a student of American master Frank Lloyd Wright, and the influence of his teacher is evident in the way that this architect integrates his houses with their sites.

be more dissimilar, and in that difference lies the story of one of the most epic issues revolving around Modernism, with important implications for the Lautner design being discussed here.

Expressionism In 1933, the same year that Fallingwater made the cover of *Time* magazine, the *Congrès Internationaux d'Architecture Moderne*, or CIAM, was holding its fourth meeting on the *Patris II*, a boat sailing from Marseilles to Athens. The International Congress for Modern Architecture had been founded in La Sarraz, Switzerland, in 1928, as an offshoot of an international competition held in Geneva to design the Palace of the League of Nations there. The competition jury was equally split between Modernists and non-Modernists, and the outcome served as a catalyst for the foundation of the CIAM, for the good of "social progress." [97] In its statutes, the Congress was described as being dedicated to the "representation of the modern architecture idea." In its first and subsequent meetings, the Congress focused on "The dwelling," constantly discussing the theme of "A Modern Form of Habitation." [98] There are many familiar names on the CIAM membership role, from every country in the developed world at that time, including Gerrit Rietveld and Cornelius van Eesteren from Holland, Gino Pollini and Piero Bottoni from Italy, Jose Luis Sert from Spain, Richard Neutra from America, and Alvar Aalto from Finland. But Le Corbusier is the most consistent and obviously galvanizing presence. His major preoccupation at the time that he helped establish the Congress, along with Helene de Mandrot, Siegfried Gideon, and Walter Gropius, was economic and political issues rather than historical styles, primarily related to the rationalization and standardization of the means of production. [99]

From this international platform, Le Corbusier basically declared war on other competing schools of thought, such as those that might propose a subjective, rather than an objective, approach to design, defined as *Sachlichkeit* at the time. In spite of its association with disciplined judgment, *Sachlichkeit* implied that irrational criteria could coexist beside, or even outweigh, empirical data in the design process and was therefore unscientific. Through his own national heritage, Le Corbusier belonged to the French Rationalist tradition, beginning with the Enlightenment, and so he adhered closely to it. Any subjective approach to design was considered to be flawed by emotionalism. Through his influence, and the rising power of the CIAM, Le Corbusier almost single-handedly marginalized Expressionistic tendencies in the Modern Movement, which were just as strong as the Rationalistic Purist point of view that he promoted.

Frank Lloyd Wright, on the other hand, was guided as much by emotion as he was by reason in his work, often responding intuitively to a particular site condition, as he did at Fallingwater. His inspiration there was to cantilever the entire house above a rushing stream. His trust in his own intuitive powers extended to his inherent love of and empathy with nature. He wrote extensively about his search for an organic architecture that was at one with the environment, in which natural and industrial materials played an equal role. This was certainly the case at Fallingwater, where he balanced his use of local stone, which makes up all of the vertical parts of the house, with reinforced concrete. It was used on the horizontal, structural decks because of the extensive cantilevers involved. Wright categorized his own personal struggle, which was by extension the same one that bedeviled the entire Arts and Crafts Movement, as "Art Against the Machine." Art, in this equation, meant spontaneous creativity, handicraft, and the introduction of intuitive, human intervention into the production process, which was "the machine."

A Dedicated Group of Followers In addition to John Lautner, Frank Lloyd Wright had many other followers, such as Bart Prince and Bruce Goff, who shared in his belief in the need for an organic alternative to mechanization and prefabrication. They also tried to balance the use of natural materials with industrially produced alternatives. Bruce Goff, for example, in his somewhat notorious Bavinger House, which is also discussed in this volume, used local stone for its spiraling core, but steel cables for the roof of what is essentially a sophisticated tent.

The Sheats House by John Lautner All of this is an introduction to what must certainly be one of the most extraordinary houses of contemporary times: the Sheats-Goldstein House by John Lautner in Los Angeles, California. It was originally built for Mr. and Mrs. Paul Sheats in 1963 and was subsequently remodeled for James Goldstein in 1989.

After serving his apprenticeship at Taliesin West, John Lautner moved to Los Angeles to establish his office during World War II. He remembered that the garish sprawl of the city was repulsive to him. Work was difficult to find during that time, and the best he could do in the mid-1940s was to become the architect for a franchise called Googie's Coffee Shop in Los Angeles. He introduced a design language of steeply pitched roofs, large expanses of sheet glass, and high ceilings that has subsequently been used to define an entire genre in that city that continued on throughout the postwar period. "Googie architecture" now connotes Lautner's daring structural approach, as well as his bold use of open space, but is also a bit pejorative, since it was at odds with the Modernist principles that started to have such a strong influence in America, and particularly in Los Angeles, at that time.

Because of the proselytizing power of publisher John Entenza through his widely read *Arts and Architecture* magazine, as well as the CIAM connection made by local architect Richard Neutra, Modernism had gained a solid foothold in Southern California by the time that Lautner arrived. The University of Southern California School of Architecture, which was founded in 1924 by the local chapter of the American Institute of Architects, had many iconoclasts on its faculty who were leaders in the new movement. They looked down on Lautner because the Taliesin Fellowship did not have an accredited degree at that time and because his "Googie" style was not consistent with the production-based rules that Modernism had established.

Lautner, on the other hand, had contempt for what he called "facilities" buildings based on Functionalism alone, calling instead for a "free, beautiful, architecture for individuals, for people, to daily increase the joy of life," as well as houses that were "alive, fresh, exhilarating, yet solid and enduring." [100]

The Sheats House Mr. and Mrs. Sheats asked for a rather large residence with six bedrooms and six bathrooms for themselves, their parents, their children, and a maid, in addition to a guest room, office space, living and dining room, and a kitchen. The site is located on a steep slope above Beverly Hills, with a clear view out and down over Century City below. The plan of the house is simplicity itself, as an elongated "X" stretched out along the edge of the slope, so that the edge of one of the triangles that is formed by the "X" projects out over the edge of the cliff. Lautner used one of the cross bars of this stretched "X" as a circulation spine leading from a garage in one of the triangles to the living room and fireplace where the legs cross, and finally to a stairway down to the master bedroom suite, tucked under the pool deck. It is under a projecting, cantilevered corner to take advantage of a dip in the topography there. Lautner compounded this fairly simple geometry, however, by placing a second high angled roof, shaped like a parallelogram and made out of triangular concrete coffers, at an angle to the high side of the slope, above the living area and part of the swimming pool at the heart of the house. Because of the long spans involved, this high angled concrete canopy has a deep edge beam and massive buttress supports where it meets the ground. The family and guest bedrooms, other than the master bedroom suite, are all located in the first half of the "X," near the garage and the entrance, separated from the living area by the intersection in the middle. The ceiling in this area is low and faced with wood planks, so that the overall impression is elemental and angular. The space beneath the high-coffered parallelogram has been variously described as primeval and cave-like, and the complete openness around the perimeter, with immediate views out to the wooded slope next to the house, contributes to this feeling. Lautner had originally intended that there be no enclosure along the perimeter at all, with just an air curtain providing warmth during the winter. But large silicone jointed glass sheets have since been added. These are virtually invisible, so the sense of being under a huge sheltering canopy remains. Lautner had 750 glasses inserted into holes cut through the slab, between the triangular coffers, that flood the living room with rays of light during the day, in a contemporary rendition of the *omriyyad* used in the dome of a Turkish *hammam*. The floors in the public spaces are covered with carpeting, and Lautner also designed all of the furniture. Its sharp angles and concrete and glass palette matches the rest of the house, so that it contributes to a sense of continuity and unity. Strategically placed lighting along the slope and the water areas, combined with the openness of the edges and massive scale of the supporting structure, also blur the lines of demarcation between inside and outside. Even though Lautner has predominantly used concrete and glass in this house, this connection to nature clearly reveals his allegiance to his mentor, Frank Lloyd Wright.

Eric Moss: The Lawson-Westen House

Eric Owen Moss has primarily been involved in partnership with Frederick Norton Smith in the regeneration of a large portion of Culver City, California, in an area located south of the Santa Monica Freeway, west of Los Angeles. Frederick Smith inherited a great deal of land there, and he has been redeveloping a series of movie studios that were located on it into office spaces primarily for people involved in recording, entertainment, and IT industries. The number of renovations that Smith and Moss have been involved in to date have encouraged Smith to name this area Conjunctive Points in reference to the idea of a new prototype of urban development. Smith has even negotiated the air rights for the zone over the railroad running through the area so that he and Moss could design an elevated conglomeration, which they called Spar City. This has left little time or opportunity for Eric Moss to design private residences, so when he does take on such a project, the results are invariably exciting and novel. In the projects he has done in Culver City with Frederick Smith, he has primarily focused on creating internalized environments, which allow employees who are primarily using computer technologies to do so in comfortable surroundings. In those designs, however, the final clients were often unknown to him because these were speculative office projects and may change hands many times after construction. He has, however, used each opportunity to make an insightful commentary about some aspect of the urban condition in Los Angeles, in his correct assumption that architects will increasingly be involved in designing and building in the urban environment in the future. In the early part of the twenty-first century, approximately 60 percent of the world's population live in cities but as the century progresses that percentage will climb dramatically. Moss has been one of the few architects to understand this sea change that is now underway and to tackle the difficult problem of how to cope with the residue of the industrial past. In the Samitaur Building, for example, which is part of the Conjunctive Points complex, he has seized the opportunity of the right of way running through the site for a road that was located there to use the building as a prototype for one that might be built over a freeway. There are differences in scale, since the road beneath the Samitaur Building is much narrower than the freeway, but the comparison is valid. Moss has used massive structural elements to support a linear building above it, which could conceivably be extruded outward at each end to run along the length of a freeway. In the Stealth Building nearby, he tackles the problem of the brownfield site. Frederick Smith and Moss discovered the condition of the site when excavation was begun and they undertook the necessary clean-up precautions. The Stealth Building hovers lightly above this site on thin metal columns as a symbolic gesture of the previous condition of the ground. And there are many more examples of Moss's use of this opportunity to build in Conjunctive Points using buildings as pedagogical models for others to follow.

Commentary on the Contemporary Condition It should come as no surprise, then, that when he does take on a residential commission, Moss uses each chance as a way of making a similar commentary on contemporary life. He is not the first architect to do so in Southern California. Greene and Greene in their design of the Gamble House in Pasadena, which is described elsewhere here, used the commission as a way of making a commentary on the influence that Japan was then having on American architecture as well as the impact that the influence would have on a new and more casual way of life that was more sensitively attuned to nature. Frank Lloyd Wright in the various houses he did in the region expanded on this theme by focusing on the balance between industrial development and the environment that he felt was an essential issue of the time in which the houses were built. Rudolph Schindler, who was a disciple of Wright, was also concerned about the conflict between industrialization and nature. The house he built for himself on Kings Road in Los Angeles is a cogent commentary on the need to avoid it since it is as much interior as exterior in the living spaces that are provided in it. The Case Study House Program that was instituted by John Entenza and lasted from the end of World War II up through the mid-1960s was also an attempt to try to revolutionize the involvement of industry into the area of residential development as a paragon for the future.

Eric Moss as a Prophet of Change One of Eric Moss's first forays into the grand tradition of innovation in the residential area is the Petal House, which he designed in 1982. It is located in West Los Angeles in a typical suburban neighborhood, and Moss decided to use the house as a commentary on this context to challenge conventional ideas of what a home should look like. There has been a great deal of controversy surrounding the role that architects should have taken in the housing boom that followed World War II. Many believe that they abdicated their responsibility in becoming involved in that market because of hesitations about the moral compromises that would be involved in something that was basically a commercial activity. Moss's use of the same materials and forms on the houses surrounding the site of his projects to provoke debate about this lost opportunity is a central part of this design.

Lawson-Westen House The Lawson-Westen House commission, which followed that of the Petal House, offered Moss an opportunity to continue his intention of social commentary. This larger project was begun in 1988 and is located on a long and narrow flat site on Westgate Avenue between Sunset Boulevard and San Vincente on the north and south and Barrington Avenue and Bundy Avenue on the east and west sides. This area is one of the wealthier neighborhoods in Los Angeles. The clients in this instance took an active part in formulating the program for their house. A series of letters between the clients and the architect were transformed into a list of the functional requirements needed. These letters and the notes and sketches that they inspired can now be read as a progressive design process in which Moss translated the clients' wishes into reality. In their letters, the clients referred to houses they had owned in the past and the parts of those houses that they wanted to replicate. They were especially interested in the vertical scale of the rooms and the need for large spaces. They requested a living room with a high ceiling and skylights that would let in natural light. In the architect's hand this became a central soaring space that is the most prominent part of the scheme of open spaces instead of a group of smaller ones. The challenge in designing such a space is to balance the request for openness and height with the need to feel comfortable and to provide intimate scale. The clients had an extensive art collection and loved listening to music, as well as cooking and entertaining a large number of people. This led Moss to connect the large living area with a high ceiling to an open kitchen that serves a dining room nearby.

In their written comments to the architect about the relationship they wished to have between the inside and outside of the house, they specifically referred to the Glass House by Philip Johnson in New Canaan, Connecticut. This initially seemed to be an incongruous example because the Glass House is located in the middle of an enormous heavily wooded site and is able to maintain its privacy only because of its seclusion. The site for the Lawson-Westen House is 70 feet wide by 180 feet long and so is much more restricted in area than Johnson's property in New Canaan. To reconcile the difference between the two projects, Moss adopted the idea of a "Garden Home in the middle of a city." In initial sketches there is a notion of a layered house consisting of circular forms made out of glass in the interior surrounded by solid bearing walls to provide privacy with a garden in between. The extensive use of glass in the inner walls was reduced in the final design, but by mid-November of 1988 Moss had arrived at this basic organizational element as the basis for his design. As finally realized, this initial idea resulted in a rectangular house running parallel to the lawn at the northern boundary of the site and being closer to Westgate Avenue on the east. By pulling the house toward one corner of the rectangle, Moss was able to provide as much garden as possible in the rest of the site. He also used a circle with a 30-foot diameter, which intersects the rectangular plan as the fulcrum for the entire layout. This circle contains the kitchen, and the rest of the structure appears to be walls that spin out from it.

The main entrance is different for both the owners and the guests. For guests there is a heavy gate in the middle of a concrete block wall that greets them at the Westgate Avenue entrance. Once the gate is open, they walk along the southeast edge of the house protected by an overhanging part of a guest bedroom wing to a front door that is about one-quarter of the way down the side of the building. Moss delights in reinventing conventional elements of his houses such as doors and windows and in making them works of art in their own right. This front door is no exception. It consists of two large glass panels, which meet at a right angle with thick strips of wood at the base and then at doorknob level. These continue at head height and wrap around the corner as well. These are connected by equally thick vertical members, which provide structural stability and have heavy black metal hinges at the intersections between the horizontal and vertical pieces. The door opens inward toward the corner after which guests or visitors step into a relatively small vestibule area. From this entrance vestibule, they discover a circular space that is the highlight of the plan. It is gradually revealed through a sequence of experiences rather than all at once. This allows the architect to develop a series of views, which build the anticipation of those entering the house as they move into it. The owners, on the other hand, have a second, more private entrance from the garage, which they access through a double gate in the same concrete block wall at the boundary of the site. Once they enter their two-car garage, a second door leads them into a series of rooms that contain functional elements such as the laundry room and storage areas as well as a back stair to the upper level. As the architect himself describes the duality of the entrance experience,

> There is a split in the house between limited and limitless, known and unknown. I tried very hard to build that into the experience of the building . . . You could consider the front door as experimental in a small way; its combining pieces of wood door and glass door give you aspects of both; it gives you something else. The door is not a Venturi joke, it raises the possibility that things can be understood in a different way.[101]

The entire front elevation of the house, however, *is* very much a continuation of a Venturi joke. When Robert Venturi designed a house for his mother in Chestnut Hill in the early 1960s, he made a point of using windows on the exterior wall facing the street as symbols that would send subliminal messages about the changing role of the house in the life of the American family. He deliberately intended that the windows on that elevation read as holes in the wall rather than the strip window that was so much a part of the Le Corbusier dogma. As Venturi said, "In modern architecture, the ideal was not a hole in the wall which negated the integrity of the wall, but an interruption of wall, and absence of wall which promoted flowing space and abrogated enclosed space." [102]

Venturi went to great pains to design a window that would represent the traditional windows of the past using horizontal and vertical dividers in the middle of the square frame and to divide it into four equal glass panes. He oversized this one major square window to emphasize this point of difference with the modern movement. Other devices used on the front elevation of the Vanna Venturi House continue this iconoclastic approach toward references to the changing state of architectural principles at that time. These include a large-scale gable front, split at the apex, as well as a wide vertical mass that appears to be a chimney between them and a dado that runs horizontally along the entire length of the house that aligns with the central cross bar of the square window. In retrospect, what Venturi was doing was creating the profile of a child's drawing of a house complete with gable roof, chimney, and welcoming doorway. By splitting the gable in half, he was making a comment on the growing insecurity then felt by the American family and the rising divorce rate in the United States that started two decades after the end of World War II. He was continuing this illusion by placing a dado, which is typically used on the walls on the inside of the house to prevent them from being damaged by chairs, which might otherwise hit the wall. The dado was especially important before the advent of plasterboard and drywall, which is fairly easy to repair if it is damaged. Plaster walls that preceded the invention of drywall were much more difficult to repair. By placing the dado on the outside of his mother's house, Robert Venturi was literally turning it inside out. The symbols he uses, then, of the oversized window divided to look like a traditional "hole in the wall," the split gable, the faux oversized chimney, and the dado, all send a subliminal image of the diminution of the core element of the American dream.

Eric Moss in the front elevation of the Lawson-Westen House continues this dialogue about the changing nature of the nuclear family. There are two Venturi style windows on that elevation, the first on the right-hand side provides light into the bedroom at that end of the house and the second is a partial version of the first placed at an angle to the left in a wall that is in front of the first one. This entire elevation is cast in concrete with a different surface treatment than the steel trow-eled stucco used on the rest of the house. This front wall is detailed to appear almost like a portal frame, which has a one-dimensional feel to it. This dual win-dow treatment in which the second partial opening appears to crank away from the first at an angle, combined with the harshness of the concrete portal frame, and the heaviness of the other walls in the house and the hard rusticated texture of the boundary wall as well as the metal gates leading through it, all combine to convey a sense of insecurity and agoraphobia. The message the architect seems to be sending is similar to one put forward by the Los Angeles–based author Mike Davis, in his book *Ecology of Fear*, that regardless of how accurate the perception of public insecurity is, that perception prevails in Los Angeles.

Once visitors can negotiate this graphic description of the state of public realm of Los Angeles today and enter the house, they are aware of a beautiful inner world, which stands in stark contrast to the hard carapace outside. In many ways, this approach is similar to the one that Moss consistently uses in his renovations and reinventions of the office buildings he designs in Culver City for Frederick Smith in which the inner world is treated in a much different way than the exterior.

The kitchen of the Lawson-Westen House, which is circumscribed in a circle that bisects the southern wall, comes into view after entering the two-story living room. The kitchen is a home chef's dream with more than ample counter space and preparation area. It has direct access to the dining room, which is on the northern side of the house on direct axis with it. It is only separated from the kitchen by a pair of doors to make serving easier. This large circular kitchen acknowledges the tendency in many contemporary houses for guests to gather in this space while dinner is being prepared, since it is almost equal in floor area to the living room diagonal to it. This space has a cone-shaped roof, which is the sec-ond most prominent feature of the exterior of the house after the disjunctive organization of the front elevation. A fireplace in the living room contributes to a welcoming sense of domesticity in this space. It is made of steel and soars up for the full two stories of the living room wall, being as much a sculptural object as a functioning fireplace. It is yet another example of Moss's love of reinventing con-ventional elements. Here he was assisted by metal worker Tom Farrage, who also contributed all of the other innovative metal work in the house. This metallic theme is first announced by the wide galvanized sheet metal gates on the Westgate edge of the property that separates the walkway to the house from the street. It continues in the truss-like struts that diagonally brace the end of a glulam beam that supports the vaulted living room roof. It continues inside in the structural frame of the bifurcated drum that spirals upward from the circular kitchen that is really the social center of the house. This conical tower was originally intended to be made of cast-in-place concrete but in its final form is framed with metal and wood and has two large concentric rings of steel. The first of these is 6 inches deep and the second is 3 inches wider. Together, these form the top of the cone. Parts of these rings are exposed in both the inside and outside of the house, as are portions of the metal columns that support them. This metallic language continues Moss's use of deep steel sections that span across these columns and also act as bracing struts. Diamond plate steel is used as flooring in some portions of the house as well as on the upper reaches of the stairs, and this along with the pipe railings that are used throughout the house all combined to convey an impression of toughness. There is a sense of concealed energy trying to burst through other surfaces that are conventionally covered with gypsum wallboard.

The Carceri d' Invenzione by Piranesi In a previous analysis of this house written in 1995, I compared the impression conveyed by the metal work and the effect that has upon the circular spaces of the house to the drawings of the Renaissance artist Piranesi. This is especially true in the case of the encircling stair that spirals upward inside the cone-shaped space above the kitchen. When walking up the stairway there are many different perspectives in all directions that evoke comparisons with images in Piranesi's drawings, although these may not have been intended by the architect. One of the most obvious comparisons is a series that the artist produced in 1760 called *Carceri d' Invenzione* or imaginary prisons. This prison series was not intended for wide distribution and consists of only 14 sketches in which the artist uses illusion, multiple perspectives, and dramatic lighting to experiment with new forms of architectural expression. Piranesi deliberately distorts optical conventions to increase visual excitement, which paradoxically results in both pleasant and unpleasant sensations. The artist challenges the newly developing science of perspective that was being constructed during the Renaissance in Italy when he was producing this series. By doing so, he offered a new way of seeing that was not continued until the Cubist period in nineteenth-century France. Moss, like Piranesi in this *Carceri* series, seems to be launching an attack on the restrictions imposed by convention. In each case, the weapons used are unexpected monumentality and excessive scale, sharp contrast between light and dark, theatricality, and the malevolent image of a metallic structure expressed in flying bridges, precarious galleries, and staircases that extend into space without seeming to end.

The stair leading to the first floor juts out slightly into the living room to give a subtle clue of its location along the inside wall of the circular kitchen form. One side of the stair conforms exactly to the curved wall, while the outside rail is straight. It is also treated as a sculptural element rising upward in a series of switchbacks that lead to a corridor above. This corridor that runs along the southeastern wall of the house, is actually a balcony above the living room and joins the master bedroom at the back of the site to two other bedrooms in the front. The intention of this split is to give privacy to the master bedroom, which has a curving wall at the back of the space. The bedroom is part of the extensive master suite at the end of the bridge that spans across the two-story-high living room space. This suite is a private world that is wrapped in the arm of the long sweeping western wall of the house against which a custom-made double bed with a large wooden headboard is located. The curve of the wall puts the bed on a direct axis with the fireplace, which is notched into the wall of the central cone opposite to it. This fireplace has a built-in wood storage bin located next to it. The roof of the bedroom angles up sharply from the curving wall behind the bed, making it seem almost like a tent, and a long clerestory window located at the juncture of this angled roof and the curved bedroom wall supports this impression. This long window continues from the bedroom to the master bathroom as a source of daylight and moonlight to both. This custom-made clerestory window is typical of the kind of fenestration that Moss uses throughout this house, including the highly symbolic translation of the Venturi window that he has designed facing the street. He typically uses conventional stock and redesigns it in unusual combinations to create these retranslations of window forms. This is obvious in the long clerestory window he uses in the bedroom as well as three windows that bend around the upper edge of the central cone of the house. Moss prefers to use natural light as a way to extenuate changes in dimension from vertical to horizontal. Placing windows at strategic locations as a way of emphasizing the three dimensionality of the space and to break down conventional ideas about joints between walls, ceilings, and roofs. In the Lawson-Westen House, the challenge that the architect set out for himself was to balance areas of large scale and the need to provide a sense of intimacy, and the natural light provided by these windows is one of the means he has used to do this. He has clearly distinguished between natural light that comes through the wall from that which comes through the ceiling.

There is a stairway leading from the master bedroom down to a jacuzzi, which is on an outside deck attached to the cylinder of the kitchen and positioned in such a way that it has complete privacy. There is a spiral staircase attached to the balcony on which the jacuzzi sits that then allows the owners to go down to the garden below without going through the entire length of the house to get outside.

The Significance of the Lawson-Westen House For the reasons just described, as well as many others, the Lawson-Westen House is one of the most unconventional residences during the contemporary period in American architecture. But its significance goes beyond its mere unconventionality. It continues in its attempt to extend the social commentary started by Robert Venturi nearly three decades before, described here. These two houses, the Vanna Venturi house in Chestnut Hill, Pennsylvania, and the Lawson-Westen House in Los Angeles, are 30 years and 2,000 miles apart; however, they both provide a profound commentary on the change that has taken place in the idea of "home" in America. The Vanna Venturi house was built at a time in which the belief in progress and moral certitude had just ended in the United States. The postwar period from 1946 until the early 1960s has been widely described as a time of happiness, economic prosperity, and unquestioned power in America. Those happy years were followed by a series of tragic events that came in rapid succession. These included race riots, nuclear confrontation in Cuba, the assassination of President John F. Kennedy, the Vietnam War, humiliation in Iran, and a difficult shift from an industrial economy to the information-based society. These events and many others have led to a questioning of authority and the institutions that support them, including government, the courts, the church, and corporations. The sociological changes that started in the late 1950s and increased during the following decades can be traced through this lack of trust in institutions as well as the painful transfer from an industrial to an information economy. These have led to the reduction in the middle class, a widening gap between the rich and poor, decreasing salaries, and diminished expectations. Additional symptoms of this change have been a radical change in the idea of what a family is, accompanied by increasingly larger divorce rates.

Moss has courageously chosen to update the commentary on these fundamental changes in a house that exaggerates them even further.

Bernard Maybeck: Wyntoon

Born in Greenwich Village, New York City, in 1862, Bernard Maybeck was the son of German émigrés who had arrived in America little more than a decade earlier. His father was a cabinetmaker and Bernard became his apprentice, learning mechanical drawing, geometry, and an appreciation of the rewards to be derived from a painstaking attention to details. Travel to France in 1881, on business related to his work with his father, brought him into contact with the *Ecole des Beaux Arts*. His subsequent interest in the school led to his entering and passing the difficult entrance examination the following year. Lectures by Henry Lemmonier on Gothic architecture, the free classicism of his tutor Jules-Louis Andre, the legacy of structural determinism left by Viollet-le-Duc, and exhaustive surveys of French and German Romanesque and Gothic churches all had a lasting influence on Maybeck and may be traced in varying degrees in all of the work that he later produced.

After arriving back in New York in 1884, Maybeck joined several other recent graduates from the *Ecole* in establishing an architectural practice, but his unpretentious emphasis on pragmatic craftsmanship, rather than on establishing the social connections necessary to thrive in Manhattan, prompted him to move west in 1889 to Kansas City to seek a more substantial basis for his career. Friends made there, in turn, encouraged him to move on to California, and he traveled to San Francisco in November 1890.

San Francisco was in the midst of a building boom, a frontier city growing rapidly as a result of new railroad connections to the Midwest and the frenzy created by the gold rush. He and his wife settled in Oakland, and he found work with the Charles M. Plum Company as a designer of custom-made furniture and interiors, before an offer from A. Page Brown made it possible for him to focus on architecture once again in the following year.

His subsequent involvement in the design of an entry for the World's Columbian Exposition in 1893 led to his being sent to Chicago to supervise construction of the "California Building" that his firm had submitted. Its eclectic display of quasi-Spanish elements was similar to those used on the Ponce de Leon Hotel in St. Augustine, Florida, which he had worked on shortly after leaving the *Ecole*. Like a surprising number of other influential architects of the time, such as Louis Sullivan, Adolf Loos, and Frank Lloyd Wright, Maybeck was greatly impressed by the Columbia Exposition, which Daniel Burnham had intended to use as a platform from which to launch Classicism as the ideal civil and national style. Maybeck's Palace of Fine Arts, for the Panama-Pacific International Exposition that followed in San Francisco in 1913, shows the extent to which he was influenced by his brief stay in Chicago and by the argument that Burnham had put forward, rather than by the exceptions to Classicism, such as the *Ho-o-den* Temple, which were sought out by Wright and Sullivan.

Shortly after returning from Chicago, Maybeck moved to Berkeley to a neighborhood close to the University of California, which in 1892 was surrounded by oak forests and green fields. His proximity to the university and the social contacts he made there led to his appointment as a graphic arts instructor in 1894. This course developed over time into a full architectural curriculum. He was also appointed director of the Architectural Section of the Mark Hopkins Institute of Art in 1893, and these two initiatives, along with his increasing involvement in the university community, encouraged the architect, who was then 33 years old, to begin private practice.

A remodeled one-story cottage at Grove and Berryman Streets in Berkeley, which Maybeck extended in 1892, served as his studio, and shortly afterwards he received his first major commission referred to him by the university president, Martin Kellogg. The client, Phoebe Hearst, wanted to erect a memorial to her late husband, George Hearst, on the campus and responded enthusiastically to the preliminary scheme that Maybeck presented.

This meeting of Hearst and Maybeck was also instrumental in putting Maybeck in charge of administering and establishing a competition for a master plan for the future growth of the University of California. A reception hall was also to be designed by Maybeck in which Mrs. Hearst could participate in the formal ceremonies related to the competition.

Early in 1897 Maybeck traveled to Europe to enlist international entrants, especially at the *Ecole des Beaux Arts*, and to interview possible jurors, such as Norman Shaw, whom he and his wife visited in Hampstead.

There are intriguing similarities between Shaw's Holy Trinity Church on Latimer Road in West London, completed in 1886, and Maybeck's final design for what is now known as Hearst Hall. Primarily this is apparent in the form of the central vaulted nave, but rather than using steel girders to frame the steeply pitched painted arches of the Hall, as Shaw had done, Maybeck has used laminated wooden girders, making the angle of the sides steeper to avoid the cross ties seen in Holy Trinity Church.

Possible parallels between these two buildings continue, as Maybeck also visited Robert Sandilands, a classmate at the *Ecole*, in Glasgow, at the same time that Queen's Cross Church by Charles Rennie Mackintosh was being built. This has a nave that was also undoubtedly derived from Shaw's Holy Trinity Church. Shaw appears to have been Maybeck's main connection to the English Arts and Crafts Movement, but unlike its more progressive practitioners, such as Mackintosh, who sought a synthesis between industrial materials and craftsmanship in order to derive a contemporary architecture based in tradition, Maybeck adopted a reductive stance, similar to that of William Morris, best described in lectures such as "Art and the Beauty of Life" delivered to the Birmingham Society of Arts in 1880, "Gothic Architecture," printed by Kelmscott Press in 1893, and "Art and Industry in the Fourteenth Century," in which Morris extolled the virtues of handicraft, particularly as practiced in the Middle Ages.

Bernard Maybeck House.   Photo by Allan R. Ferguson. © Allan R. Ferguson; Flickr

Maybeck's medievalism is patently apparent in his second project for Phoebe Hearst, a residence that was executed after his return to California, called Wyntoon. This fanciful castle, rendered in lava rock, rubble stone, and local timber with a green glazed tile roof, displays many of the same eccentricities that can be found in country houses of the same period, such as Cragside and Grim's Dyke, by Norman Shaw, and also has affinities with estates designed by H. H. Richardson in both massiveness of scale and in attempting to blend with rugged and natural surroundings.

The 67,000 acres deep in the forest must have resonated with Maybeck because of his German background and its similarity to Bavaria. He created a five-story high tower for the main part of the house, made out of reinforced concrete faced with local stone, which is connected by an angled hall to a second portion next to it. The house burned down in 1929, after Phoebe Hearst had died, and Julia Morgan, who had been a protégée of Maybeck's and had been the first woman, and one of few Americans, to graduate from the *Ecole des Beaux Arts* in Paris, was commissioned to replace it. Rather than a fanciful, castle-like house, Morgan decided on the theme of a Bavarian village instead, breaking the single volume down into three separate parts.

William Randolph Hearst had also commissioned Julia Morgan to design another house for him near another family property called San Simeon, near the Pacific Ocean, halfway between Los Angeles and San Francisco, called *La Cuesta Encantada*, or the Enchanted Hill. It is a stylized *hacienda* in a quasi-Churrigueresque style, influenced by the Mission style architecture that was made popular at the beginning of the First World War by the Panama-California

Exposition held in San Diego in 1915, which was planned by Bertram Goodhue. Between 1937 and 1942, Hearst nearly went bankrupt, and he moved from San Simeon to the new Wyntoon as an economy measure. But it was too isolated for him and he returned to the Enchanted Hill as soon as the hunger for newspapers during the war years helped his finances to improve.

Richard Neutra: The Lovell Health, VDL Research, and Kaufmann Palm Springs Houses

Richard Neutra was born in Vienna, Austria, in 1892, and attended the Vienna Technical University along with Rudolph Schindler, who was to become his close friend. Schindler emigrated to America prior to World War I, while Neutra stayed behind, leaving in 1933. This gap was to create a crucial difference in the world-view of each architect, with Schindler retaining a more romantic attitude toward technological developments at that time, and Neutra being more rationalistic because he had witnessed the devastation that technology could also cause.

Schindler had apprenticed with Frank Lloyd Wright in Wisconsin, and he had also been instrumental in bringing the young Austrian architect to Los Angeles to assist in overseeing the construction of the Barnsdall house in the early 1920s. Schindler and his wife, Sophie Gibling, along with another couple, built a house on Kings Road in West Los Angeles that was to subsequently serve as the model for the Case Study House architects of the post–World War II period. After the Chaces moved out of the house, Richard Neutra and his family joined the Schindlers there, until he could get established in the city. Schindler had designed a house for Philip and Leah Lovell in Newport Beach, California, that was unlike any of his other projects in several important ways. Philip Lovell, who was a physician from New York City, had relocated to Los Angeles along with his wife in search of a healthier lifestyle and became well known in the region because of articles he wrote on fitness for the *Los Angeles Times*.

Schindler's Newport Beach house is made of a series of reinforced concrete portal frames lined up parallel to the beach, so that the first floor slab where all the living functions were located, as well as the flat roof that they support, is perpendicular to the ocean and the view toward it. The structure, which effectively lifts the main portion of the house above street level to provide those inside with a better view, and to allow parking beneath, is massive. But the actual interior area that it supports is relatively small and introspective for a couple who liked to live large, wearing as few clothes as possible to get maximum benefit from what were then thought to be the health-giving rays of the sun.

When the Lovells chose to build a second home in the Hollywood Hills of West Los Angeles, they turned to Richard Neutra instead, who took an entirely different approach in his design. The personal story behind the Lovell's decision to change architects and the strain that this caused on the Schindler-Neutra friendship reads like an architectural soap opera, but the important thing, in this instance, is that Richard Neutra produced a masterpiece for the Lovells that has been called the first truly modern house in America. It was completed in 1929.

The Lovell House in Los Angeles Commonly referred to as the Health House because of Lovell's reputation as a fitness guru, the Neutra-designed residence in North Hollywood is framed entirely in light gauge steel, with each piece prefabricated in a factory. The thin vertical columns are left exposed where necessary to also serve as dividers for the windows and are located with center-to-center distances that allow for the use of standard steel frames. The walls are made of concrete hosed onto metal mesh and trowelled smooth, which later became a technique also used to build swimming pools. The house is three stories high, with projecting decks that have high solid parapet railings to prevent neighbors from seeing the Lovells while they were sunbathing. Using innovative structural techniques, Neutra was able to make various parts of the façade, facing the downhill side of the steep slope on which it is built, appear to float in space.

The main entrance to the Lovell Health House is on the top floor, where the bedrooms are also located, to take maximum advantage of city views to the south and Griffith Park in the opposite direction. A large stairway leads down to the main living, sitting, and dining areas, which flow seamlessly into one another.

The VDL Research House By 1931, Neutra and his family were living in Los Angeles, with a house and office in the Echo Park section of Silver Lake. He had by then earned an international reputation, on his way to becoming well established on the strength of the Lovell Health House project.

The Lovell Health House also helped establish Richard Neutra's international reputation as an avant-garde Modernist, even though it was the source of a great deal of controversy locally. After completing the Jardinette Apartment complex soon afterward, he received a visit from a Dutch industrialist named Cornelius Van der Leeuw, who was impressed by Neutra's accomplishments and wanted to become his patron. At the time, Neutra and his family were living in a small rented house and office in the Echo Park section of Silver Lake, and Van der Leeuw offered to loan Neutra enough money to build more spacious quarters. Neutra was reluctant to request too much money, and so asked for only $3,000. He found a 60-foot wide by 70-foot long building site near the Silver Lake Reservoir and started designing what he referred to as the Van der Leeuw, or VDL, Research House in 1931. Including the cost of land, it ended up totaling $8,000, and Neutra raised the additional money from private sources.[103]

In typical Modernist fashion, Neutra felt obliged to use this opportunity for the greater good of society rather than just the welfare of his own family. He imagined the house as a living laboratory in which to test the latest materials and technological innovations available, as a prototype for the future. Because of the restricted size of the site and the need to take advantage of possible views toward the reservoir and San Gabriel Mountains to the north, Neutra chose to build as close to the site lines as he could and to go up to two stories high, with a basement, to maximize space. He located his studio office on the ground floor and the more private family area on the second, as well as a "solarium" on the roof.

Because of cost restrictions, Neutra was forced to use wood rather than steel as a structural material, choosing the balloon-frame method for efficiency. In the early days of American carpentry, when forests were being cut for the first time and trees were tall and straight, timber framing ran vertically all the way from the ground floor slab to the roof, with floor joists hung from the inside of these tall external members. With the onset of clear cutting and less long timber, external walls now support each floor, which is called a platform frame. Rather than running up the entire side of the house as the balloon-frame timbers did, timbers only go as far as the underside of the floor they support with new timbers added on top of the floor or platform to support the next one. By using the balloon frame, Neutra was opting for the most efficient solution to the problem as well as paying homage to a time-honored carpentry tradition, but did not necessarily select the most realistic approach. He used 4-inch by 4-inch wood posts that were laid out on a module that would allow them to accommodate standard industrial sash.

The research component of the VDL House divides into three distinct categories. The first of these is what Richard Neutra referred to as "biorealism," which he characterized as the physiological and psychological responses that a person has to the natural environment and the subsequent ways in which those reactions can be recorded and translated into architectural form. The second category, which is closely related to the first and is a logical extension of it, is Gestalt theory, which was just becoming known at the time Neutra was designing his Silver Lake house. This theory stresses the importance of being open to the immediacy of experience. Neutra hoped to combine biorealism and Gestalt theory to alter people's perception of reality, especially in situations where it was necessary to make spaces seem larger, as was the case in the VDL House. The third category of research involved finding ways to more closely integrate interior and exterior space to connect architecture to the outdoors. For Neutra, as for Schindler, there are inevitable comparisons between the closed, urban world they had come from in Vienna, with its cold, dark winters, and the nearly paradisiacal climate of Los Angeles, where spending a great deal of time outside is not only possible but preferable. Neutra used reflection, transparency, and water to accentuate this experience.

Water, Glass, and Mirrors Neutra used a design strategy based on reflection, transparency, and water to achieve these goals at the VDL House, positioning mirrors, water, and glass walls in strategic locations to increase a sense of spaciousness and to alter perceptions of depth. Doors were transformed into windows and glass windows were expanded to become entire walls. One of these glass walls faces into an open courtyard in the center of the house, and another has been used as the entire side of the living room on the second floor, which looks out onto a sleeping terrace, blurring the line between inside and outside space. The original VDL House burned down, but was rebuilt as VDL II in 1966 with a substantial assist from Richard Neutra's son Dion, who is also an architect.

The Kaufmann House in Palm Springs Edgar Kaufmann, who was the client who commissioned Frank Lloyd Wright to design Fallingwater in Ohiopyle, Pennsylvania, turned to Richard Neutra to design a winter residence near Palm Springs in 1946. This was surprising at the time, and still seems so in retrospect, given the positive public response to Wright's masterpiece near Pittsburgh, and its critical historical role as a counterpoint to European Modernism at the time it was built. And so it happened that the same man who had designed the second house for a client of his best friend did the same with one of the most important patrons of his mentor and previous supporter, Frank Lloyd Wright. The Kaufmann House near Palm Springs is entirely different in character from either Fallingwater or Taliesin West, however. Perhaps the mercantile entrepreneur from

Pittsburgh had had enough of organic architecture, after the completion of the daring structural experiment at Bear Run more than a decade earlier.

A Modernist Pueblo In 1927, prior to his arrival in the United States, Richard Neutra had written a book entitled *Wie Bout Amerika*, in which he admiringly described the ingenuity of the Anasazi, who built the pueblos in New Mexico and Arizona. He especially praised their sensitive use of masonry, rooftop terraces, and climactic awareness. Neutra tried to replicate their design intelligence in steel and glass, as well as wood and sandstone, without the use of air conditioning, in one of the hottest and most arid regions in America. He used a floor plan that looks something like a pinwheel, similar to a concept that Wright often used in his early work. This ensured the privacy and cross ventilation of the rooms at the end of each of the legs, and flat roofs with long overhangs provided the glass walls with shade. Kaufmann had intended that he and his family and their guests would use the house only during the winter, when the heat, which can reach 120 degrees Fahrenheit in the summer, abated.

Neutra's design did not include air conditioning, but it did incorporate radiant heating in the floors for the wintertime. Different owners, throughout the years, added closets, air conditioning units, and ventilation pipes that cluttered the roof, destroying the clean lines of the design. The flooring was changed and the overall square footage of the residence changed from 3,200 to 5,100 square feet.

Brent and Beth Harris had seen a classic picture by famous architectural photographer Julius Shulman and said that, at first, they barely recognized the house as it had appeared in the photograph. After buying the residence in 1992, they decided to restore it back to the original Neutra design.

They commissioned the Santa Monica–based architectural firm Marmol and Radziner, who had restored Neutra's 1950 Kun House in the Hollywood Hills, to bring the house back to its past glory. The architects used original materials to convert the house to year-round use. It had been altered to such an extent that the biggest challenge was to find out what it was like when built in 1947. Ron Radziner and Leo Marmol found the original drawings in the UCLA Research Library Special Collections Branch. Their investigation extended to interviews with Albert Frey, the architect who designed the house next door to Kaufmann's. Julius Shulman's photographs provided key clues about exterior surface materials, but the most interesting discovery was that the house became an archaeological dig as walls were torn down and wall color names were discovered between the plaster and paint.[104] Neutra had used innovative materials in his design. A mixture of plaster was used to cover the walls, which allow the flecks to reflect sunlight and reduce heat gain. Marmol and Radzinger followed Neutra's intent and located the mineral that matched. They reproduced the recipe and devised a technique for application. The cabinet woodwork was replicated with precision and matched perfectly. New insulation techniques were also used to make the house more durable and prevent water damage in shower areas.

One of the biggest challenges the architects faced was the integration of a cooling and heating system that would not clutter the spaces or destroy the clean exterior profile of the house. The amount of crawl space was limited, so the architects had to devise a way to not aesthetically disrupt space. They concealed vents and ductwork in built-in furniture. In addition to a new air conditioning and heating system, new drains were hidden inside the flat roof. The architect's skill and perseverance paid off, since the house now appears to be just as Neutra intended it.

The Pugh Scarpa Residence, Venice, California

In spite of its relatively brief history, compared to other American counterparts and certainly to many European cities, Los Angeles does have many well-established architectural traditions. Many of these are a result of the multiethnic background of the region and its distinctive climate as well as a steady stream of perceptive visitors, who have each interpreted these factors in his own way. Frank Lloyd Wright, for example, was probably inspired by the numerous Spanish missions in Southern California, which led him to use a central courtyard in the Hollyhock House, which was his first commission in the region. This, in turn, may have influenced his follower, Rudolph Schindler, to elaborate on the central courtyard concept in the design of his own house on Kings Road soon afterward. Rather than concentrating the open space in the middle of the residence, however, he refined it by breaking it down into pieces of green area that each relate directly to interior spaces. In an obvious gesture to Japanese traditional architecture, Schindler used sliding canvas panels that allow interior and exterior space to be joined whenever possible, which is quite often in sunny Los Angeles, with an *engawa*-like ledge mitigating between the two.

Since the Hollyhock and Schindler Kings Road houses were completed, however, many new building regulations have been passed that have presented more complex challenges to an architect's creativity. These require design professionals to be fully aware of a plethora of laws related to use, materials that can be used in a given area, setbacks, and height restrictions, among many other considerations, before they even begin to develop a working concept for their project. Familiarity with and skillful manipulation of these building codes and zoning regulations can mean success, but the opposite can mean misery. A renovation of an existing house poses even more problems for an architect, but one of the best solutions to emerge in a long time in Los Angeles, on a number of levels, has been achieved by the husband and wife team of Angela Brooks and Lawrence Scarpa, based in Venice, California. They bought a single-story 650 square foot, 1920s stucco bungalow in 1997 with the intention of living in it until they designed a modern enhancement to it. The 41-foot by 100-foot property is called a "through-lot" because it spans between Woodlawn and Boccaccio Avenues, and it allowed them some latitude in repositioning various parts of the renovation to take better advantage of sunlight, provide a better entrance and parking, and generally add the square footage they needed. They flipped the front elevation, which had been on the northern side of the site, to the south, which gave it much better solar exposure, and built an L-shaped second floor, with one of its equal legs crossing the short dimension of the site at approximately the middle. This effectively divided the project into a formal open, public courtyard garden in the front, to the north, and the covered private side of the house behind it, to the south. The courtyard, which has a variegated water feature stretched out along its western edge, is in the best tradition of Wright and Schindler and their Japanese precepts in its direct connection to the main living space, which opens up to it through sliding glass panels that fold into pockets.

These glass doors are not the standard issue hardware store variety of a pair of rectangular glass panels in thin aluminum frames that slide past each other in a recessed track, but a highly sophisticated, frameless wall of thin glass strips that run from the floor to the soffit of a balcony above and are completely transparent. This removes any sense of division between the garden and the living room adjacent to it. The feeling of complete transparency that this slick, streamlined wall sets up continues throughout the remainder of the house, in which the conventional lines between the interior and the exterior are blurred.

The Umbrella House, Reinvented Angela Brooks and Lawrence Scarpa were inspired by the Umbrella House, designed by architect Paul Rudolph in Lido Shores, near Sarasota, Florida, in 1953. Rudolph, who is perhaps best known for the hyperformal and excessively brutal late Modernist language of the Art and Architecture Building, completed between 1958 and 1964 at Yale University in New Haven, Connecticut, is not usually associated with environmental sensitivity, but the Umbrella House demonstrates his awareness of a difference in regional contexts. This may not seem to be that significant, now that critical regionalism is something of a commonplace among architects, but in 1953 there was a different expectation in place, of using technology, such as air conditioning, to solve the problem of heat gain and humidity in such conditions. This first Umbrella House is undoubtedly still a part of the International style because the main part of it is glass, and Rudolph did rely on air conditioning to cool it. But the glazed portion of the residence is covered by a second, pergola-like shade structure above it, held up by a thin steel structure of columns of beams. The pergola has a rectangular opening in it to allow natural light to shine unhindered into the garden court in front of the house, but otherwise covers the entire site.

It was not until six years later that Louis Kahn proposed a similar second roof solution to the problem of overheating in a U.S. Consulate that he designed for Luanda, Angola, reiterating a growing awareness of the environment that was soon to emerge full-blown in the ecological movement, characterized by leaders such as Barry Commoner and Ian McHarg in the late 1960s and early 1970s.

Brooks and Scarpa have taken that sensibility to an entirely new level by using a canopy rather than a higher louvered pergola as Rudolph did. This is significant because of the rather lackluster three decades, with a jump-start after the oil shocks of 1973 and 1976, that lost momentum as oil prices leveled out. The conventional wisdom among the uninformed in the design professions has been that photovoltaic technology is too expensive for practical application, but Brooks and Scarpa did more thorough research and discovered that there are really options in that field, with varying levels of cost and effectiveness to choose from. These are crystalline, polycrystalline, and amorphous cells. The last of these, more accurately referred to as thin film amorphous silicone solar technology, involves putting a thin layer of silicone on a suitable surface, such as glass, in an assembly line process in which labor costs have been greatly reduced. One of the many advantages that this system has other than the crystalline and polycrystalline options is that it can replace part of the building envelope, rather than simply being added to it, reducing costs even further. The first two options also lose effectiveness over time as direct sunlight causes them to deteriorate. But, amorphous silicone is less efficient in converting solar rays to electrical power, requiring more area of exposure to produce an equivalent amount of output. These results led the architect owners to use the panels as both a canopy roof and a second wall on the western side of the house. This led to a different profile than that of the original Umbrella House in Florida. While the Rudolph covering seems to float above the glass house like a thin steel cloud, the silicone scrimmed glass panels above the Brooks and Scarpa version in California is in a tighter horizontal formation, but then folds over the side as a shield against the hot afternoon sun. Rather than being supported by equal ranks of tall thin square steel columns that Paul Rudolph used, the Venice-based architects have chosen to use a series of wide, vertical tilt-up concrete panels that seem to spiral around the house, with the flat side presented to the entrance, in the first entrance, and only the edge of the second one, extended into an entire wall on the east side, as the second. The syncopation that this sets up is continued in a minor note by two metal-sheathed pylons that extend up from the first floor to the silicone-sheathed umbrella above, with the flat side of one facing forward and the second one next to it, turned at a right angle to its left. This interplay between concrete and metal, combined with the seamless wall of glass in front of the living room, create an image of Modernist materials used in delicate balance, creating a dynamic composition that is in harmony with natural forces, rather than in competition with them. The cold-rolled steel facing used as a surface material for the smaller vertical members is recycled, and the tilt-up system used for their concrete equivalents requires much less wood formwork than conventional poured-in-place systems.

The choice of this tilt-up construction system was probably also dictated by financial logic, since pouring concrete in shallow depressions dug out of the site and lined with reinforcing bars that then become the form eliminates all the vertical framing, including plywood and two by four or six supports necessary to hold the wet concrete placed in them by a crane-held hose.

Recalling a California Classic The choice of a concrete tilt-up procedure by Brooks and Scarpa also evokes memories of Rudolph Schindler's Kings Road house, mentioned earlier here in reference to the similar use of an inside-outside sense of continuity in each of these houses. Schindler chose the tilt-up slab system for similar economic reasons, since he and his wife had borrowed the money to build from his wife's parents and they were on an extremely tight budget. But, as in the Brooks and Scarpa house, it also conformed well with an overall minimalist ethos and a desire to be as efficient in the use of available resources as possible. Because of these overlaps, the Brooks Scarpa house is now part of a well-established, but increasingly ignored, regional tradition of sensitivity to nature, indoor-outdoor living, and technological innovation.

A. Quincy Jones

Archibald Quincy Jones came from the heartland of America. He was born in Kansas City, Missouri, in 1913 and attended the University of Washington in Seattle, where he received a Bachelor of Architecture degree in 1936. He is now closely associated with the progressive phase of the Modern Movement in Los Angeles from the end of World War II until the late 1970s, but his values and beliefs were as mainstream as those of his hero, Frank Lloyd Wright. Although he never worked for Wright as other important Los Angeles Modernists such as Rudolph Schindler and Richard Neutra had, he assimilated the transcendental philosophy of his protean American mentor.

Consistent Principles A. Quincy Jones channeled Wright's principles into an approach to design that sustained him throughout his abbreviated career, until his death in Los Angeles in 1979. These began with a love of his country and the democratic ideals it represents, made legible in unrestricted floor plans and innovative structures that celebrate individuality and freedom of expression. They continue in his nearly spiritual reverence for the Earth, since he sought to have his buildings interact with and take shelter in the site they were built on, letting the shape of the ground, rather than functional requirements alone, dictate his generation in California since they, with the exception of Schindler, were more concerned with internal, rather than external, space.

Although Wright was in his fifties when the Depression struck, rather than his teens as Jones was, this catastrophe imbued each with an immutable sense of social responsibility, making people and their needs the most important part of their work. For Jones this meant using new industrial processes for the greater good, rather than being suspicious of them. He wanted to provide an attainable common denominator that would make the American dream of owning a single-family home possible for all.

While Jones's early projects in Los Angeles have obvious Wrightian precedents, such as the bold cantilever and patterned concrete piers of his Mutual Housing Association Site Office in 1948, or the central roman brick hearth and horizontal shiplap siding used in the first Nordlinger House in 1949, the two architects part company over the issue of what Wright almost derisively referred to as "the Machine," or the manufacturing of materials. With his Romantic, Arts and Crafts background, Wright considered industrial production to be a threat to human ingenuity and integrity, rather than a source of liberation and prosperity. Jones eagerly anticipated and adapted new materials and systems, using them in startlingly innovative ways.

Esther McCoy, who was one of the first to document the dramatic changes taking place in California, described this difference more succinctly by saying: "Architects who matured in the 30's were dedicated to the ideal of architecture as a social art. Wright was dandy, but the true path was through standardization." [105]

Seizing an Opportunity A. Quincy Jones helped to reinvent the American residential typology to accommodate the extensive social changes that took place after the war, such as the shift from hired help to a housewife-centered domestic universe before feminism took hold. This resulted in a formal transformation from a double to a single story to make housework easier and an open kitchen with clear views to all parts of the house and garden so children could be supervised.

The Interstate Highway System of the Eisenhower era opened up just as the Pacific Electric Rail or "Red Car" line had reached the limit of its effectiveness. The Pasadena Parkway, which was built in 1939, was followed in quick succession by a network of freeways that were not as picturesque or contextually sensitive. Federal, state, and local laws passed in favor of the automobile pushed the urban edge of Los Angeles out in all directions beyond the first tiers of suburbs around the downtown core, creating an unprecedented demand for new housing.

Frank Lloyd Wright had anticipated this growth in his Broadacre City Plan of 1936, but in spite of his example, modernists reacted in a disdainful way to the opportunities that this second suburban revolution offered. They were put off by the fact that "the merchant builders" such as William Levitt and Joseph Eichler, who had already seized the initiative, seemed to be driven by economic rather than idealistic motives and felt that the market would corrupt their ideals. In retrospect, this willful abdication was misguided and cost the profession dearly by alienating it from the popular audience it once sought.

Jones, on the other hand, saw no such conflict of values, believing that the principles he had evolved in his custom designed single-family homes would be adopted more quickly if they were implemented at a large scale. After organizing the Mutual Housing Association with Whitney S. Smith and Edgardo Contini in 1946, which involved the cooperative development of 500 lots in the Santa Monica mountains, scaled down to eight different types built on 100 lots, Jones designed an exhibition house for local developer H. C. Hvistendahl, which received an AIA First Honor Award as "Builders House of the Year" in 1950 and was published in *Architectural Forum* magazine. This brought Jones to the attention of Joseph L. Eichler, who was recognized as the builder of the "subdivision of the year" in the same issue.

A Quiet Domestic Revolution Jones and Emmons subsequently collaborated with Eichler in redefining how the family in postwar America could live, proposing new ideas that transformed the tract house into a more personal custom residence. Jones did a close analysis of the generic developer product, introducing quality whenever possible in ways that did not drastically alter the bottom line. Jones and Emmons introduced the notion of complete living, including community centers, parks, and pools that made a new neighborhood model more feasible. Through incremental improvements, such as the addition of a second bathroom, a breakfast "bar'" that allowed the family to share meals at the heart of the house, and a gable roof to introduce more light into the interior, as well as by using a marginally higher grade of materials, the architect and the developer converted a commodity into a domestic paragon.

In the more than 5,000 homes they designed and built together from their first meeting in 1950 until 1974, Jones, Emmons, and Eichler followed a set of consistent principles that allow for flexibility and efficient construction, such as the post and beam system, modules based on material sizes, and mass production that made small luxuries, such as fireplaces, plate glass windows, and sliding glass doors possible. This approach, which Jones referred to as "a controlled business process," is clearly evident in the Eichler Steel House X-100, built in San Mateo in 1956, intended as a prototype that would revolutionize future developments, because it could be largely fabricated and included built-in furniture. The project was discontinued when the price of steel soared during the Korean War, but it typifies Jones's innovative approach to new structural possibilities.

A Green Pioneer Jones has been referred to as a pioneer of "green" architecture. His advocacy of higher density subdivision design at the beginning of the suburban revolution to protect the land from sprawl alone justifies this title. The community centers that he promoted in them, which included recreation halls, swimming pools, social clubs, nursery schools, day care facilities, and green common areas, anticipated and even promoted the social changes that would soon alter the gender profile of the American economy and are consistent with the collective rather than singular ideals of sustainable design.

His entry into the Case Study House Program in 1961 is also a good example of his environmental sensibilities. It was audacious and would still be considered so if it were proposed today.

The Case Study Experiment The Case Study House Program as conceived by John Entenza was consistent with the high-risk, experimental attitude of the time as a collaborative endeavor that benefited all concerned. He bought a moribund magazine, *California Arts and Architecture*, and dropped the state name to give it wider appeal as a way to proselytize for modernism across the country. Entenza understood the burgeoning postwar need for housing and a more casual lifestyle and believed he could fulfill this desire. He bought a 5-acre parcel in Pacific Palisades and identified several young architects who shared his point of view to design houses for it, for no fee, including one for himself. He also made arrangements with contractors and furniture and material suppliers to participate at reduced cost, all in return for having their names mentioned when the houses were opened up for public visits and published in his magazine.

Public response to the first six homes that were built surprised everyone, as 368,554 visitors experienced what Esther McCoy has described as "mirrors of an age in which emerging pragmatism veiled Rooseveltian idealism." [106] Encouraged by this positive reaction and convinced that America was ready to embrace a more modern, mass-produced version of the suburban tract house, Entenza expanded the program.

Venturing outside the single-family market into the more complicated arena of development, he initiated the Triad project by Killingsworth, Brady, and Smith in 1960 in La Jolla. The positive public response that it received encouraged him to invite Jones and his partner, Frederick E. Emmons, to adapt one of the 260 homes they were then designing for Joseph Eichler on a 148-acre site near Chatsworth in the San Fernando Valley as Case Study House No. 24. The scheme that Entenza received differed radically from earlier entries because it was mostly underground, with only an extended *porte cochere* projecting out to announce its existence. It was intended as a model home that would be repeated throughout the development. It was T-shaped, with the cross bar ending in open pergolas on each side that rested on retaining walls that made the subterranean scheme possible, and included a symmetrical pair of perimeter courtyards that let light inside.[107]

Case Study House No. 24 is arguably the most extreme example of Jones's commitment to the integration of nature and architecture; the unusual design received Planning Commission approval but was rejected by the City Council Committee on Zoning on the basis that the communal green space it made possible could not be properly maintained.

There are many other instances of his commitment to the synthesis of building site, however, at a variety of scales, beginning with Palm Springs Tennis Club and Town and Country Restaurant designed in 1947–1948 in collaboration with Paul Williams, the Griffith Park Girls Camp of 1949 with Whitney R. Smith, Warner Brothers Records in Burbank in 1975, and the Annenberg School for Communications at the University of Southern California in 1976.

Frank Gehry: The Schnabel Residence

Frank Gehry is perhaps best known today for his pyrotechnical design approach in public institutions such as the Guggenheim Museum in Bilbao, Spain, or the Disney Concert Hall in Los Angeles. But he started his career with a series of private houses in which he experimented with and developed his unique architectural language. These private houses are primarily located in and around Los Angeles, beginning with his own house, which he designed in Santa Monica in the early 1970s. In that first instance, he added to an existing bungalow using a series of disjunctive forms, which are attached to it as a way of exploring the potentials of commonplace materials not normally used in house design at that time. Gehry is a graduate of the University of Southern California School of Architecture, but he associated in the early part of his career just as easily with artists as architects. He identified with the fledgling art movement in Los Angeles in the early 1950s but also had a special affinity for the work of the Russian Constructivists. The Constructivists were a politically based art movement that arose in the Soviet Union soon after the Revolution that only lasted until the rise of the Soviet Realism at

The Schnabel Residence, which is on the west side of Los Angeles, is one of the last in a series of private houses designed by Frank Gehry, who soon afterward started to focus on larger public projects. *Source:* James Steele

the beginning of the reign of Joseph Stalin. Constructivism was based on the idea of finding a new means of artistic expression to adequately conform to the political shift from Capitalism to Socialism, combined with the rise of industrialization that Russia then needed in order to progress. The dilemma that Constructivism faced was how to express the technological ethic of industrialization without mimicking the images that had been produced by Capitalist countries that had done so previously. To do this, the Constructivists questioned every precept and principle that existed at the time, in an attempt to find new ways of creating form. One of its most extreme positions, it included a proposal by artist and architect Kasimir Malevich, who believed that in order to create a new Socialist architecture, it was necessary to first imagine the absence of gravity to arrive at conceptual purity. He then believed that gravity could be factored back in the engineering equation as judiciously as possible to arrive at a different constructed solution that would differentiate this new architecture from its Capitalist predecessor. This direction is called Suprematism. Theoretically, it shares a great deal with Rationalism in that each position is based on the possibility of perfection and the necessity to avoid the compromises that are imposed by real world conditions. Constructivism differs from Rationalism, however, in its political basis for a utopian solution. Many Constructivist artists preferred to use commonplace materials and found objects in their art as a symbol of their allegiance to an egalitarian society or, alternatively, as a commentary on the wastefulness of consumerism.

The Schnabel House After designing his own house, which caused a great deal of controversy and even violent reaction when it was completed, Gehry went on to design other residences that were equally unorthodox. One of these, for the Norton family, is located on the boardwalk in Venice, California. It remains a prominent part of the scene in that eccentric neighborhood even though it now has been surrounded by other houses that are equally unorthodox. The Norton House is divided into two parts, separated by a central courtyard. It has an entrance directly from the boardwalk, or more accurately, asphalt track, which runs parallel to the beach. Mr. Norton was once a lifeguard, and to recall his youth Frank Gehry designed an office for him at the front of the property that looks like a large lifeguard stand. From this high perch, Mr. Norton can look out over the beach and reminisce about days gone by. Below the assimilated lifeguard stand, which is supported by a huge square steel column, there is a one-story apartment clad in blue tiles that are intended to mirror the color that people wish the Pacific Ocean would be. This apartment has an off-the-shelf pair of patio doors that lead out to a small patio between it and the front wall. It has a shade structure running horizontally above the door, which is modeled after a Japanese temple gate, in recognition of the fact that Japan is directly across the Pacific Ocean from the house, about 5,000 miles away. A cactus is located on the opposite side of the front elevation from the lifeguard stand to counterbalance it and add yet another exotic image to this cluster of symbols. The main house is placed at the back of the rectangular site and is hardly visible from the boardwalk in the front to give it more privacy. This assemblage is typical of Gehry's early habit, prior to the latest stage of his career, of creating what may be described as small villages composed of separate elements. In the Norton House, those elements are visually distinct and symbolically divided as well. The Norton House is in the middle of a series of houses in which the architect explored this idea of clustering various elements around a site. This exploration culminated in his design of the Schnabel House in 1987.

The Schnabel House is located in Brentwood on the west side of Los Angeles, north of Sunset Boulevard near the Pacific Ocean. The houses in this wealthy neighborhood run the gamut from Italianate palazzos to Tudor mansions. Gehry's response to this eclectic context was to pull the house back from the front of the 100-foot by 250-foot lot and to create a world of his own. The Schnabels bought the lot in 1986, just before Rockwell Schnabel left to become the U.S. ambassador to Finland. Even though the family knew that the posting would last for three years, they decided to have their first meeting with Frank Gehry to discuss the preliminary design of the house. Marna Schnabel is also trained as an architect, and, like Gehry, graduated from the University of Southern California School of Architecture. They all agreed on a design that would allow as much open space on the site as possible, and Gehry once again began imagining the house as being a series of small pavilions located around a village green.

Memories of Finland While the Schnabels were in Finland, Gehry was asked to give a lecture in Helsinki and decided to visit the family while he was there. During that time, they were invited to dinner at the home of a famous publisher on Lake Hvittrask. While they were there, they walked around the lake at sunset; the wind was rustling through the birch trees on the shore and creating small waves on the water. They all decided at that time that this would be something that they would like to recreate in Los Angeles, and so the basic ingredients of the house were set by the time the Schnabels returned to America. These components were the idea of separate pavilions dispersed on the long and narrow sloping site with the most public of these being at the main street called Carmelina Avenue. The most private of these, such as the master bedroom, were envisioned as being at the far end on the site. The second of these was the desire to recreate in some small way the romantic image of the lake that they all visited in Finland. Gehry managed all of this with his usual deceptive ease in a composition that, in less talented hands, would be extremely difficult to achieve.

There are basically five parts to the Schnabel house, beginning with the garage with the maid's quarters above, which is the first of these located nearest to the street. This is connected to an L-shaped kitchen and living room wing by a narrow, covered arcade. This arcade ends at one leg of the "L," which runs parallel to the property line on the northern edge of the site, and contains the kitchen, family room, and a small study as well as a stairway leading up to the bedrooms of the two Schnabel daughters. The second leg of this "L," which projects perpendicular to the first, crosses the site at approximately its midpoint, dividing it into two separate courtyards. The first of these courtyards is more public since it is between this wing and the street. The second courtyard is more private because it is protected by the angle of this wing and the kitchen wing from which it projects and faces the downhill side of the site, which is in the back. The second wing is roughly cruciform and focuses on a living and dining area in the middle with a library at its far end. It has a pair of doors leading out to the private courtyard. This entire L-shaped complex makes up the second main body of the house.

The third piece, located to the side of the front public courtyard, is almost a perfect square in shape and is intended to be a private office for both Rockwell and Marna Schnabel. It has a fireplace in one corner and its roof is inspired by the dome of the Griffith Observatory, which is a major landmark in Los Angeles. Marna Schnabel suggested that Gehry consider interpreting the Griffith Observatory dome here, and the clients tell an amusing story about its construction. The interior of the dome is faced with drywall, and the contractors who built it had to use long ladders to reach the top and inner sides of the dome. Making drywall conform to a smooth curve is a real art, involving a complicated process of wetting the thin drywall panels and then spackling them before painting them. Such a curved space, however, induces what is known as a Ganz effect, in which someone in the middle of a domed space like this loses his sense of orientation, so the contractors were constantly falling off the ladders. This office is the third element of the house.

The fourth main part is another nearly square piece perched precariously on top of an intentionally created cliff-like edge. This is actually a concrete retaining wall that demarcates the upper part of the site from its downhill end. This fourth component is the bedroom of the Schnabel's son, Evan, and has a serrated roof made up of monitor-like skylights. This bedroom, which terminates the private courtyard, is visually connected to the domed office in the more public courtyard in the front of the site by a long, narrow lap pool, which mitigates between them. The change in level made possible by the retaining wall that crosses the entire width of the site on its lower end was utilized by Gehry as an opportunity to place a home gymnasium under the private courtyard part of the house at that edge. This gymnasium has a corridor running along its entire outer edge, which provides access to a series of workout rooms and a sauna, which is another reminder of the Schnabel's trip to Finland.

The architect made ingenious use of the downhill back end of the site by designing a reflecting pool that occupies most of it. This reflecting pool is polygonal and is only 9 inches deep because of local codes that would have required a protective fence around it if it had been deeper. To avoid this restriction, Gehry made it shallow, but used a blue surface at the bottom to make it appear to be deeper than it is. There is a stairway leading down from the kitchen wing to this level, which is approximately 10 feet lower than the main courtyard levels above. The Schnabel's master bedroom is located above this reflecting pool at the lower level. It is placed at an angle from the house above and clad in metal panels, with windows facing out in each direction for light. It has a metal parasol roof of the same material suspended above it, supported by a series of diagonal braces and a pair of intersecting beams in a cruciform shape that hold up the roof. This shades the skylight on the roof below. The windows are shielded from public view by a series of freestanding vertical shafts that are clad in a darker brown metal. These are strategically placed around the perimeter of the master bedroom block to prevent any possibility of the neighbors seeing into the space. These vertical elements are of various heights and profiles, appearing like silent sentinels positioned around this romantic bower. The reflecting pool and the master bedroom, which seems to float upon it, are most obviously inspired by the evening walk around Lake Hvittrask in Finland that the architect and the Schnabels shared. The boat-like appearance of the master bedroom suite in which the parasol roof may be read as a sail of a ship and the angular form of the base can also be imagined as a prow offer a clue that the reflecting pool may have been imagined as a harbor by the architect as well.

The serrated roof of Evan's bedroom resembles many of the factories in postindustrial cities throughout America. The cruciform shape of the living room and library wing that projects out from the kitchen to divide the property into two separate courtyard-like squares has obvious religious references, which might allow it to be construed as a church-like form. These three images taken together suggest a New England village, with the church taking pride of place on the village square and an industrial building overlooking a harbor where fishing boats are moored. This image is consistent with Frank Gehry's pattern, which is most evident at the time this house was built, of creating small cities within a city. The reason for this miniaturization may have come from the fact that Los Angeles really has no city center, and so to make up for that, Gehry feels he has to create his own context.

Los Angeles, like every other city in the United States, started around the kernel of a civic center where the pueblo was once located. It grew from that beginning in the way that other cities have grown and seemed poised to become a metropolis on the West Coast that was the equivalent of its urban alter egos to the East Coast. But, with the advent of the automobile, a critical juncture was taken in an administrative decision to give priority to highways and freeways and to neglect a fledgling railway system, which at that point in the city's history was one of the best mass transit systems in the nation. With the abandonment of the railway system and the priority given to the automobile, the center of Los Angeles was atomized, as freeways spread outwards from the center like the tentacles of an octopus. In the post–World War II era, these were extended even farther to the north and south, creating suburban sprawl that continues to expand today. This has led to Los Angeles being described as many cities in search of a center and, depending on the source, these many cities number from seven to nine. Prior to his alienation from the Los Angeles scene, due to circumstances surrounding delays in the construction of the Walt Disney Concert Hall that were not his fault, Frank Gehry was considered an oracle who had his finger in the heart of the city. No wonder, then, that Gehry's reading of how to respond to the rootless condition of Los Angeles would result in his creation of contexts that are self-sufficient in their own right. The Schnabel house is the most evocative of all of these villages in miniature.

Not as Random as It First Appears In order to convey the impression that the house gives to a guest who visits it for the first time, it is necessary to begin at the front gate, which opens in from Carmelina Avenue at the southwestern end of the site. The Schnabel family park in a garage located farther to the west of this gate and have secure entry along an arcade leading to the kitchen wing, but the gateway is the customary way for guests to enter. After coming inside, the house appears to be almost random, a habitable sculpture garden with no obvious reason for the positioning for each of its parts on the long narrow site. That first reaction is soon replaced, however, by the awareness of the delicate balance between each of the pieces of the composition that are judiciously placed so that each is neither too close nor too far away from the others. The straight pathway provided for visitors is paved in a cream-colored California sandstone. This leads past the domed office element described earlier toward the cruciform church-like element, which divides the site in two. The living room, dining room, and library are located here. The path leads past an olive grove and a lawn of uncut Bermuda grass on the right-hand side. This lawn also has several small palms and succulents on the left-hand side of the pathway.

Olive trees were once unusual in Los Angeles until they were introduced in Barnsdall Park in the early 1900s. In their native habitat, olive trees grow randomly. But on Olive Hill in Barnsdall Park, they were planted in rows. By emulating that here in a much smaller scale installation, Frank Gehry is also showing his awareness of the role that Frank Lloyd Wright played in the history of Los Angeles architecture. In his early work, Gehry revealed an obvious debt to Wright's contribution to the city, and this small olive grove is a more subtle testimony to it. The copper panels that clad the living and dining area, which is the central part of the house, match the grey-green color of the olive trees.

The living wing is a complex building—while the idea of attaching several box-like forms at angles to the central hall may seem simple, the spatial experience that this arrangement creates is far more intricate. Gehry skillfully uses level changes and compartmentalization to essentially create five rooms inside of one. The living area, which is in the center of the cruciform building, is the primary spatial experience. The interior of this entire wing is finished in gypsum board, which is painted white to reflect the brilliant light that is typical of this neighborhood only 7 miles away from the Pacific Ocean. There are exposed pine beams and a plywood roof, which are a reminder of Gehry's habit of using commonplace materials in an uncommon way. Gehry uses glass doors opposite the front door into the living room, to give a sense of transparency to the space and to direct the view of a person entering into the room through it and onward to the end of the site. He also uses windows high up in the space that let natural light flood into it during the day. The contrast of white walls and natural wood in the ceilings adds to the richness and texture of the shadows. The living room wing, which has an access that is oriented roughly east and west, is a prism that refracts the light in unexpected and beautiful ways. This symmetrical nave-like access sets up a certain formal arrangement in the space reflected by the arrangement of the furniture in it. Marna Schnabel personally designed an ensemble of leather club chairs for this area, which underscore its formality. There is a square tower with a window on each side, with another cube positioned askew above it to mark the importance of this central space. By shear coincidence, or carefully calculated planning, there is a palm tree on the southern end of the axis through the living room that can be seen by the high skylight window on that side, providing a memorable reminder of Southern California. This tower has an even more pragmatic purpose as well, since warmer air rises up through it by convection and can escape at the top, reducing the need for air conditioning.

Environmentally Challenged In the 20 years since the Schnabel house was built, however, the sustainable movement has taken center stage as an architectural direction. Gehry's work as a whole raises important issues about the need to balance aesthetic issues with environmental concerns. Arranging each part of the Schnabel house in a separate pavilion has made it necessary to increase the mechanical services to reach each one of them, raising the amount of energy required to do so.

Separate pavilions also heat up and cool down faster than one single house would. So environmental advantages such as the stack effect, created by the tall tower above the living room, are offset by the fragmentation of the house into six different parts, and the individual systems that this then has required to heat and cool them.

Gehry's skill, however, in providing a sense of continuity within this fragmented plan is paramount. In the cruciform living block, for example, the dining room is adjacent to the kitchen in the service wing that connects to it and is raised several steps above the living room in the middle. This small gesture of a level change makes all the difference in giving this space a quality of its own. On the other side of the living room there is a fireplace nook that makes up the southern arm of the cross; it has a group of banquettes next to and across from the fireplace that make it a very intimate and comfortable place to sit. This room is several steps below the living room, which also make it seem quite separate from it. This sequential progression from the kitchen into the dining room, then down several steps into the living room, and then down several more steps to the fireplace area provides continuity and also a sense of separation, which is very difficult to achieve. The kitchen, family room, and study wing, which are perpendicular to this cruciform living portion of the house, extends along the northern edge of the property. It is a continuation of the more private circulation spine that begins at the garage near the street, and has a maid's quarters above it. This wing is the more private equivalent of the entertaining center of the house that is focused around the living room. The kitchen in this linear portion of the house has a U-shaped counter component, which is positioned in such a way to facilitate service into the dining room while not presenting an obstacle to the family room located next to it. This family room is designed to encourage a more casual relaxing atmosphere, which becomes the heart of the private portion of the house. It is the epicenter of activity for this busy family of five. Marna Schnabel's office and studio, which is a counterpoint to her husband's office of roughly equal size that is covered with a dome and located near the front of the site, is located directly next to the family room. It can be shut off with pocket doors when seclusion is necessary to separate it from activity in the family room. It has a built-in desk to increase the amount of open space and this faces the reflecting pool and master bedroom with its elegant canopy roof, to the east. The office is also located near a straight run stair, which leads up to the bedrooms of Mary Darrin and Christy Schnabel, and another stair that leads down to the master bedroom below. The family room in the center of this long rectangular hall-like wing has three pairs of doors that open up to the second, more secluded open courtyard on the site and is also multistory, giving it a sense of spaciousness and connection to nature. A bridge-like corridor that appears like a balcony above it connects the bedrooms of each of the daughters located at either end of this long rectangular wing.

SOUTH AMERICA: BRAZIL

Oscar Niemeyer: The Canoas and Strick Houses

Oscar Niemeyer, who celebrated his centenary on December 15, 2007, and won the Pritzker Prize in Architecture in 1988, is the leading proponent of the Modern

Movement in South America, and specifically in Brazil where a majority of his work is located. He still practices, working out of his studio in Rio de Janeiro. The Canoas House that he designed there in 1953 has been referred to as the Brazilian equivalent of Fallingwater by Frank Lloyd Wright or the Villa Savoye by Le Corbusier, as a masterpiece that captures the essence of its time as well as the spirit of the nation in which it was built.

Throughout his long career, Niemeyer has consistently adhered to the Modernist ideal of the architect as protean form-giver, as well as the belief that architecture should express the highest technological achievements of its time. He differs, however, in his poetic and naturalistic use of those forms, which reflect the rich context in which he works. This sets him apart from purely pragmatic Modernists, such as Walter Gropius, who viewed architecture as a means to an end, of bringing about social equality through minimal, rational, replicable, and typically rectilinear strategies. This does not mean that Niemeyer's politics do not include the desire for social reform, but rather that the sensual forms he prefers are not universally applicable.

The Canoas House The Canoas House, which Niemeyer designed for himself in 1953, with the assistance of landscape architect Roberto Burle Marx, is named for the street on which it is located in the Sao Conrado district of Rio de Janeiro. At first glance, the house seems to be simplicity itself, as a wing-shaped roof made of a flat slab of concrete that hovers over the glass-enclosed living area beneath it as if by magic, seeming to protect it without any visible means of support. The approaches to each of the other Modern masterpieces to which it is frequently compared, such as Fallingwater in Pennsylvania and the Villa Savoye outside of Paris, are each predicated on the automobile. But, one first sees the Canoas House on foot, after leaving the car at a gated fence along the street at the top of a hill far above it and walking down a winding pathway through the jungle toward it. Fallingwater is at the end of a narrow road that winds down the slope of the valley in which it is located, crossing a bridge over Bear Run, before ending under a concrete pergola that connects the house to another hill, rising on the opposite side of the gulch created by the rushing stream. The Villa Savoye, in Poissy-sur-Seine near Paris, was also intended by its architect to be fully accessible by car and to be appreciated in a 360 degree spiraling approach around it, before the automobile pulled under the house and parked near the front door. By stopping cars at the gate and forcing people to walk down a ramp from there to the house, Niemeyer has added another layer of sensory discovery to what Le Corbusier termed the *"promenade architecturale."* [108] The Canoas House is surrounded by tropical jungle, and so the simple act of clearing a space in the dense foliage, placing a huge boulder and free-form shallow pool there, and integrating a pavilion-like single-story house with a flat sculptural concrete roof with them, is much more profound than a more complex architectural strategy would have been. The three elements symbolize their elemental equivalents: the granite boulder represents the Serrado Mar Mountains that loom above the house nearby, the pool is the sea, and the roof is a canopy of trees, hinting at the shelter that they provide.[109]

But the house is not as simple as it first appears, since it also has a lower cut into the side of the cliff, which is oriented toward a view of the sea. A stair running

The Canoas House. © Arcaid / Alamy

alongside the boulder leads down to this level, adding the symbolic natural element of a cave to those of the mountain, forest pond, and tree-like canopy mentioned above when seen from the clearing; the concrete roof only appears to be a single curving horizontal white line. Since the cylindrical black steel columns that support it are inset and dispersed around its perimeter as randomly as the trees in the jungle-like surrounding, they seem to visually disappear. The roof overhangs the line of the glass enclosure, shading it and further blurring the line of demarcation between nature and human-made space.

The Strick House Nearly ten years after Niemeyer completed his own house in the mountains above Rio, he was commissioned to design another for Joseph and Anne Strick in Santa Monica, California. Strick was a film director who had visited Brasilia and wanted the architect to solve the problem of a difficult site next to a steep bluff overlooking the Santa Monica Mountains in the distance.[110] The Stricks' wish was complicated by the fact that they had never met the architect and that Niemeyer was not allowed into the United States at that time because of his political affiliation. Niemeyer, however, was fascinated by the prospect of having his first project built in North America and was undaunted by the inconvenience of being unable to visit the site. The first conceptual proposal he presented to the Stricks was remarkably like his own house on Canoas road, with a slightly more angular flat concrete roof replacing the curving one he had built for himself in Rio. In that first proposal, he pulled the house, which curls in a fetal-like "U" around a pool and open courtyard in its midst, away from a main road toward the edge of the steep bluff at the far end of the site. He then carved a second lower level, reminiscent of the subterranean floor of his own house, into the face of the bluff, facing stunning views of the mountain. This lower level eliminated the need for a second story, which would have destroyed the purity of the flat concrete roof.

Red Tape Unfortunately, local building codes prohibited the lower story, and so Neimeyer graciously provided an alternative scheme, with a far more rectilinear form than he is usually associated with, to satisfy legal requirements. The new design is T-shaped, with the crossbar of the "T" spanning the entire length of the site along its right-hand property line when facing the house from the street. The stem on the "T" crosses it at midsite, dividing the rectilinear plot into a somewhat public forecourt near the street and a private backyard facing the Santa Monica Mountains and Canyon below. With his typical restraint, Niemeyer kept the palette of materials simple, restricting it to a brick wall running along the entire forecourt side of the crossbar of the "T" on the sideline of the site, and laminated wooden beams spaced on a short module supporting the roof of the stem of the "T" running across the middle of the lot, at a higher level. This diagram made the allocation of functions inside the house equally simple, since private areas like the bedrooms, bathrooms, and study fit naturally into the wing running parallel to the side of the site, with a solid brick wall protecting them from the large and more public living space placed perpendicular to them. The kitchen, which is located at the intersection between the two, reflects the more public role that this space was beginning to assume in the postwar period in America, as does the open dining room beside it. A walkway, leading directly from the street, follows the brick wall to the front door, which is placed slightly off-axis to the right of the centerline of the pavement, as if to deflect the imaginary line of force that it transmits. It opens directly into the living room at the center of the transecting part of the house in the stem of the "T," perpendicular to the private part, which is separated from it by the brick wall. This is logistically the focal point of the house, and this entire wing, which has a 14-foot high ceiling, is also the dominant spatial zone of the entire dwelling. The wall facing east, toward the forecourt and then the street is only partially glazed, but its linear west-facing complement is entirely composed of floor-to-ceiling glass panels that provide a completely unhindered view of the pool deck and the mountains beyond. Both the lower private wing and this higher living, dining, and study wing, along with the large area of glass on the walls and the hardwood floors give this space a fragile, brittle, and almost inhospitable feeling that is at odds with the protective, humanely scaled nurturing and elemental aspects of the Canoas house that preceded it. This may be due to the difficulty that Niemeyer had in communicating with the Stricks, combined with his inability to visit the site, as well as being forced to change his scheme from an initial concept that conformed almost exactly to the Canoas model to a more rectilinear direction. What the Strick House does demonstrate, however, is Niemeyer's exceptional ability to work within the more minimal linear language of the Modern Movement when circumstances dictated that he do so, when he was prevented from following the more organic direction he preferred.

Hassan Fathy House Hassan Fathy was an Egyptian architect who sought to discover a truly authentic architectural identity for his country. To do so, he researched historical typologies, focusing on the Medieval core of Cairo to do so. He also investigated preexisting sources of information, such as the surveys carried out by French archaeologists during the Napoleonic expedition that resulted in the book series called *The Description of Egypt.* To the typologies he discovered in this way, he added Nubian techniques of building in mud brick. *Source:* James Steele

The Airport House   The Airport House is one of more than a dozen residences that have been custom designed for a development called the Great Wall Commune located near the Badaling section of the wall. Architects were commissioned to showcase the rising talent of Asian design, and each took a different approach to his or her own project. The idea behind the Airport House is one of "terminals" attached to a circulation spine, with each "terminal" being allocated to a different living space.   *Source:* James Steele

Cheong Fatt Tze Mansion In the mid-1800s a wealthy Chinese merchant named Cheong Fatt Tze built a mansion in the Georgetown section of Penang Island, which is now one of the 13 states of Malaysia. He had worked his way up from being a day laborer and coulee on the docks there when he came from Fukian province in China, as a young boy. His house, known locally as the "Blue Mansion" because of its distinctive hue, is eclectic, combining traditional techniques such as a central courtyard with the latest and best construction materials available in Europe at the time it was built. *Source:* James Steele

The Salinger House Kuala Lumpur–based architect Jimmy C. S. Lim has created a contemporary translation of the traditional Malaysian house, for Rudin Salinger and his wife, on a site that was once part of a rubber plantation, south of the old capital city. He had introduced exciting new elements into the historical model, making it fresh and yet still comfortably familiar. *Source:* James Steele

Hvittrask   While they were still students, Armas Lindgren, Herman Gesellius, and Eliel Saarinen formed a successful partnership that led to their commission to design Finland's pavilion at the 1900 World Exposition held in Paris. They jointly bought a large property on a hillside overlooking Lake Hvittrask, about an hour's drive from Helsinki; with the idea of building a living and working compound for themselves and their families there. This compound was inspired by a wave of nationalism sweeping through the country at the time, mixed with other influences, such as the work of the American architect H. H. Richardson, as well as the British Arts and Crafts Movement.   *Source:* James Steele

Chiswick   The Arts and Crafts Movement favored the Gothic Revival style because of its allusions to a more egalitarian and less secular time. The "battle of the styles" between advocates of Gothicism and their Classical counterparts was loaded with moralistic overtones. Norman Shaw, who designed the houses in Turnham Green Terrace, chose to stay above the fray by introducing the Queen Anne Style, rendered in red brick, which provides a sense of uniformity.   *Source: James Steele*

Suliaman House Abdel Wahed El-Wakil, who is one of the foremost disciples of the late Egyptian architect Hassan Fathy, has translated the traditional vertical Jeddah tower house into a horizontal equivalent on an open site. This house, which is really a palace, is one block from the Red Sea and includes many of the same typological elements that Fathy introduced as historical ties to his culture. © Christopher Little/AGA Khan Trust for Culture

Villa Hvittrask Villa Hvittrask, 1903, by Armas Lindgren, Herman Gesellius, and Eliel Saarinen. It served as a communal house and studio for these three architects until a personal issue broke the team up. It is located on a hillside overlooking the White Lake several hours from Helsinki Finland and is a good example of the Finnish Arts and Crafts style. © Rolf Richardson/Alamy

Joseph Strick never lived in this house, since he and his wife separated before construction was complete. Anne lived there and raised the children in it, putting it up for sale in 2003. A local developer tried to tear it down, but Michael and Gabrielle Boyd bought it in 2004, and have restored it as closely as possible to Niemeyer's original intention.

COLOMBIA

A Contemporary Hacienda in Colombia, Casa Puente
Rogelio Salmona

The colonial tradition is as well established in Colombia as it is elsewhere in Central and South America. That period, which was called the *Nuevo Reino de Granada*, or the New Kingdom of Granada, ended in 1830, with a hiatus until the Republic of Colombia was founded in 1886.[111] As in other Latin America countries, such as Mexico and Brazil, which share in that tradition, there were large *haciendas* and land holdings or *latifundio* throughout the land, where geography permitted, before huge coffee plantations came to dominate the economy. That shared heritage includes a similar layering of the social class structure, beginning with the Spanish colonial overload at the top, followed by the landlord, then the sharecropper and/or peasant farmer.[112]

A Simple Life The *haciendas* of the colonial period reflected the infrastructural economic and production systems themselves, which were rudimentary in the extreme. The *hacienda*, which centered around farming and the raising of cattle, were self-sufficient bastions in the jungle that relied upon agents at a point of sale to move their products. Farming techniques were crude and yields were relatively low. The *haciendas* here, as in other colonized parts of Central and South America, were made up of a *casa grande*, or main house, a bunkhouse or living quarters for the farm or ranch hands, barns for the horses, equipment sheds, and pens for the cattle when needed, as well as a small chapel, all arranged within a walled compound. Walls of the houses, service buildings, and enclosures were typically adobe, and the grounds were usually shaded by nature trees and interspersed with open court-yards of various sizes at strategic points to effectively separate public and private areas, ensure the integrity of the landlord and his family, and promote cross ventilation throughout the entire *hacienda* complex.

A civil war, followed by rapid industrialization, slowly destroyed that way of life, as laborers who went into the army never returned and train tracks, built to serve special interests, carved the various *latifundio* up into smaller pieces.[113] The *haciendas* had tended to be clustered on the Cundinamarca and Boyacá Plains, as well as in the Cauca Valley, because those were the areas where it was easiest to farm and raise and herd cattle. There were other zones, to be sure, such as the Magdalena, Casanare, Huila, and Tolima Prairies, but the first group had more impressive *haciendas*.

These farms did differ somewhat from those in other Latin American regions in that the landlord often did not live in the *casa grande*, but in the nearest urban area, only visiting the *hacienda* occasionally to make sure that the foreman had everything under control and that production was going smoothly.

This pattern is reminiscent of that followed in colonial Egypt, where landlords in the Delta region would often build "resthouses" on their huge estates, but these would remain empty until they visited. Transport there was easier than in Colombia, however, where landlords remained in the cities such as Rio Negro or Santa Fe and went to their *haciendas* rather infrequently, due to the difficulty involved in reaching them.[114]

King Coffee Coffee, for which Colombia is perhaps best known to the rest of the world today, only started to gain a substantial place in the national economy in the mid-1800s, and only in the higher and cooler regions of Caldas and Antioquia. Coffee had come to Colombia from Africa, through Brazil, where it had an equally profound impact on what had previously been an agrarian and cattle-based economy. The outside demand that Brazil created for the product paved the way for Colombia.

The coffee estates, however, are quite different in form and design from the agrarian *hacienda*. They are more formal and are built of more industrialized imported materials, due to the easier access to markets in the United States and Europe during this later period.

The Power of Memory In spite of the fact that many of the old colonial *haciendas* have been destroyed, and the political and social system they represent has a bitter taste for many, there is still a great deal of nostalgia for these houses in Colombia. Rogelio Salmona, who died at age 78 on October 4, 2007, designed several houses in his long career that are reminiscent of the intention of the *hacienda*, without copying its style literally. Salmona, who was born in Paris in 1929, came with his parents to Colombia when he was 2 years old. He apprenticed with Le Corbusier in Paris for many years as a young man, before coming back to set up his own practice in Bogotá. The majority of his work, which ranges in scope from small single-family homes to large institutional projects, is located near that city.

Bogotá is located at the southernmost end of the same high plateau of Cundinamarca and Boyacá, in central Colombia, where the majority of the old *haciendas* were built, because it has a temperate climate. Salmona was inspired not only by their rich legacy but also by the North African, Islamic, and Iberian sources behind it, mixed with the Pre-Colombian heritage of the area before the Spanish arrived. The informal organizational planning principles on which the *hacienda* is based, as well as its plain exterior appearance in stark contrast to ornately decorated interiors, strategic use of courtyards, gardens, and water, come straight from Islamic precedents, which were brought into Spain from North Africa and transplanted there over several centuries of occupation, prior to the *Reconquista*.

Salmona adopted all of these techniques, translating adobe into brick, which is also telluric, but more durable and acceptable to a contemporary client base. Of the many houses he completed in the Sabana during his career, the *Casa Puente*, which is in Suba and was realized in 1975, is one of the most typical. It also demonstrates the strong influence that Le Corbusier had on his Colombian apprentice, since it has a strong processional line of entry. It is also made entirely of brick, with several courtyards reflecting a quote from a Mayan Codex that Salmona kept on the wall of his office. It reads: "When I enter my home, I enter the earth and when I leave my house I ascend to heaven." [115]

2

Africa

EGYPT

Abdel Wahed El-Wakil: The Halawa, Chourbaggy, and Hydra Houses

Abdel Wahed El-Wakil's Halawa House in Agamy, Egypt, was completed in 1975. While a trained eye can determine several basic relationships from the plan, which divides public and private spaces with a square central courtyard, the play of forms that results from the massing of these spaces does not become evident without deeper study. In acknowledgment of this richness, this house was awarded an Aga Khan Award for Architecture in 1980, because, in the words of the jury,

> it represents a dedicated search for identity with traditional forms. The courtyard plan, the use of domes, vaults, and arches, the articulation of space, and the sensitive use of light, combine to produce a house that fully satisfies contemporary needs. This imaginative handling of a traditional vocabulary is also enhanced by the consistent use of traditional methods of construction and the careful attention to details and craftsmanship.[1]

This award marked the beginning of worldwide recognition for the architect, as well as the end of his training with his mentor Hassan Fathy, and so can be identified as the first of several landmark commissions in the first major cycle of his career.

The house is not only a final homage to El-Wakil's teacher, Hassan Fathy, but also to Fathy's master mason, Aladdin Moustafa, whom El-Wakil had helped and insisted should receive a portion of the award. This was a sign of his key role in making Fathy's architecture possible, and the lack of official recognition of that partnership in the past. In describing his determination to include Moustafa, the architect is fond of telling a story about a major university in the United States that had once contacted Fathy about the possibility of organizing an exhibition of his work, which at the time would have been one of the first of its kind. Fathy was, as always, extremely hesitant to part with his drawings, but was persuaded to do so by El-Wakil, who saw the potential for international appreciation that this exhibit held. When Fathy insisted that travel arrangements also be extended to include Aladdin Moustafa, the university was hesitant and then offered a token allowance that was so ridiculously meager as to be insulting. While Fathy eventually consented to send some material, he refused to attend the exhibition because of his vivid memories of this incident as well as his own debt to the teachings of this mason. El-Wakil persisted in recognizing him in an article for *Domus Magazine*, in which Moustafa made the cover. In that issue his true contribution was put into perspective because it emphasized El-Wakil's focus on traditional wisdom and officially considered for the first time the possibility of an autonomous Muslim architecture without the associated issues of separation. The notion put forward in that issue, of a contemporary version of Islamic architecture that might arise out of Fathy's and El-Wakil's example has now come true. While there has been a sense of continuity in both materiality and in traditional methods of construction, the Halawa House demonstrated how these consistent elements can be adapted to a contemporary way of life. The lesson of the Halawa House is the timelessness of vernacular architecture, in spite of the changes that take place in social values over time.

In the traditional life view, time is seen as a cyclical continuum, naturally marked by night and day, birth and death, and the changing of the seasons. This is central to an appreciation of the difference between El-Wakil's architecture and the latest fashion of the moment. Fathy himself constantly reminded his followers that a true, socially related architecture such as the Sultan Hassan Mosque takes more than one generation to develop. He saw himself as only a single link in a long chain, stretching backward to the beginning of his own culture. In the majority of cases, the most characteristic constructs of that culture have emerged as an expression of the people themselves, without any architect taking the credit for them. They are also part of nature rather than alien to it. As El-Wakil has described the appeal of traditional architecture as being versatile and durable, as well as humane, it also has a spirit of place and has been adapted over time to comply with specific human needs. It was built by the community and has always incorporated existential needs, including heritage and mythology as well as comfort. "In addition to seeing architecture as a functional art," he has said, "the traditional builders also treated it as a significant art reflecting human faith and a concrete image of our metaphysical aspirations." [2]

In such architecture ego has no place, and in recognizing Aladdin Moustafa's part in the Halawa House, which exhibits all of these attributes at their best, El-Wakil has acknowledged the importance of transferring knowledge. This transcends the mason himself, regardless of his contribution, which was considerable in many ways.

The Chourbaggy House In another project, for his uncle, Abdel Wahed El-Wakil accepted a self-imposed challenge to apply the social and environmental lessons that were used by Hassan Fathy. He converted them into a prototype for an urban setting in order to silence those who have criticized his mentors' principle as never having been applied in this way. The idea for such a prototype came about as a result of the client's purchase of a row of long, narrow plots of land that had been in an agricultural zone near Cairo. These were quickly being converted to housing because of pressure of a rapidly growing population. Rather than combining all of these thin, rectilinear plots into one, and building a large villa on a single piece of land, both client and architect agreed that it would serve a greater social purpose and make better economic sense to build a prototype terrace house, to be followed by others of similar design in the future. The architect set out to prove, as one observer has noted, "that a modern Egyptian house traditionally inspired could be built economically, comfortably using conventional reinforced concrete under urban conditions." [3]

Because of these parameters, the Chourbaggy residence now looks rather strange, like a townhouse without a town, but will change as the inexorable growth of Cairo continues. The fate of Fathy's clients who have ignored this possibility, such as Hamid Said in Marg, who had the opportunity to put acreage around his small mud brick studio when it was first built in 1943 and refused to do so, is proof enough of the wisdom of El-Wakil's tactic here. In the best Cairene tradition, which can be clearly seen in the medieval part of the city in examples such as the *Beit Souheimi, Beit Gamal-adin Dahabi*, and *Beit Sennari*, this house presents a plain face to the street with *mushrabiyya* screens that are smaller on the lower story for privacy and wider at the top for view, being the most prominent feature. As is also the case in those older examples there is a *"magaz,"* or indirect entry from the front door, which leads onto a set of stairs and into an open courtyard before coming to the offset door to the interior of the house itself. True to past examples, this courtyard also has a *"mastaba"* or bench along the wall, which has historically been used by the doorman or *"bawab"* to rest on while he guarded the inner sanctum, but is here conceived of as a place to sit and talk to those not known to the family. The *mastaba* also provides a convenient way of squaring off the court in order to more easily design a paved tile floor for it, which is hexagonal and surrounds a small fountain. Two doors lead out of this court, with the least obvious one giving convenient access to the kitchen, and the more prominent of the two leading into a reception room. This is organized as a *Qa'a* in which to greet and entertain guests, with one *iwan* provided with built-in seating, and the other used as the stairway to the upper floors of the house. Contrary to the traditional arrangement, there is also another grouping of built-in seating in the *Qa'a*, which is placed between the central *Dorga'a*, and the court from which it is divided by an open *mushrabiyya* screen. A *shuksheikha* of sorts also covers the *Dorga'a*, which is a double-high space, but it is a false cupola, built beneath the thick concrete roof slab, and not open to the sky to allow heated air to escape by convection, as *shuksheikha* were in the past. This *Qa'a* also opens onto an additional sitting area and then finally onto a garden. The view of the fields beyond this view, in fact, is the primary force behind the form of these two sitting rooms, as well as the U-shaped built-in seating in front of the courtyard itself, with a continuous shaft of space being seen to connect inside and outside in the ground floor plan. Two groupings of *"Sabra"* doors, which when open leave no obstacle between the reception areas and the exterior make this connection possible. The stair in the second *Qa'a iwan* leads to the first floor, which has three bedrooms and each has an en suite bath for added privacy. A hallway, which runs the width of the house and connects each of the bedrooms with the stair, passes between the *Qa'a* and the court with *mushrabiyya* screens provided for a secluded view into each space below. This device was also commonly used in the past as can be seen in the *Beit Kritleyya* where the women of the house habitually sat in window seats above the *Qa'a* to secretly watch the men discussing business and drinking tea. A light well, which is used to pull the windows of the two largest bedrooms away from the exterior wall, adds additional insulation from the rising noise level in Cairo, and anticipates the future role that this house will play as a model urban residence. Regardless of several compromises, the architect obviously met his own challenge, and the result is a contemporary expression of traditional residential typologies.

House in Hydra, Greece It is ironic that one of Hassan Fathy's most talented disciples should be given a commission to design a house in Greece, which had such a profound effect upon the master himself. While Fathy is not known to have built anything on any of the Greek Islands, his travels there while a member of the Doxiadis organization between 1957 and 1962 had a visible impact on his later work. Fathy did design a house for Marion Carr in Liopessi near Athens, which was never built. In it he shows a facility equal to that of El-Wakil for the assimilation of a local vernacular style, as well as a different way of life. Hydra, like most Greek fishing villages, totally revolves around the life of its port, and yet its topography, which tightly juxtaposes mountains to close, curved proximity with the shoreline, gives this house a special clustered character, similar to the village, which has a visual unity and identity that is even greater than other Greek islands. The bowl-shaped form of the town, as it rises up from the water on both sides of the mountains, puts almost every house in it on view when it is seen from the water. This unity is even evident while walking along the quay, where most of the social life in Hydra takes place. Steep stairways lead up the mountainside to small plazas that then feed into the narrow pedestrian streets that serve the houses. The plot allocated for the El-Wakil design, which is about halfway up the mountainside, is approximately 13 meters wide and 25 meters long with a 7 meter drop across its width. The foundations and the primitive means of transport, which is still limited mainly to mules, discouraged costly excavations and any thought of leveling the site to make design easier.

In Tune with Its Site As a consequence, the design conforms to existing contours, and this makes optimum use of the land available by making the house plan conform to the irregularities of the site. With typical thoroughness the architect spent a great deal of time researching the traditional architecture of the island, in order to make this house blend in with those around it. His concern was to retain the unity of the architectural panorama seen from the quay. The main gate to the house, which was commissioned by Julius Nezer in 1978, was placed on the lowest corner of the steeply sloping lot and was, as the architect has described it, "intended to be seen as a welcoming hand reaching out to newcomers arriving after an exhausting climb from the harbor below."[4]

After this restful welcome, the ascent continues through a stepped passageway, which leads up to a terrace that also includes a swimming pool. While this may seem a bit redundant on a Greek island, the beaches on Hydra are especially rocky with difficult access to the water, making a pool of this sort desirable for comfort as well as privacy. There are two bedrooms at this terrace level, as well as a small living room and porch that have all been provided for guests in order to ensure the necessary degree of seclusion. From this terrace another flight of stone steps, which are carved into the landscaped slope of the hill, lead up to the upper terrace of the main floor above.

The main living room is based on the form of the traditional fisherman's houses on the island and opens directly onto the surrounding terrace in a way that is typical of the Mediterranean preference for an indoor-outdoor continuity of space. The master bedroom, along with the children's bedroom makes up a house within a house, and while this wing is connected by a passageway it is totally self-contained around its own courtyard, which overlooks the Bay of Hydra. The living room has been positioned in such a way that visitors can be kept to a terrace of their own without disturbing the privacy of others when large groups are being entertained. A kitchen, which is adjacent to the living room, also opens onto the terrace, as well as an outdoor barbeque that can be used in conjunction with the ovens inside, making entertainment here a joy rather than a drudge. An *au pair* suite with its own entrance from the uphill side of the house completes this upper level, utilizing the elongated character of the site to its fullest.

The result of all these considerations is a scheme that capitalizes on difficult site conditions rather than being defeated by them, in the creation of a series of stepped terraces that provide openness and privacy where each is required. This has been achieved by working with rather than against the natural and the man-made environment of Hydra, and by accepting the particular lifestyle that exists there. In the process, the architect has produced what he feels is a microcosmic image of Hydra with water terraces and stepped gardens representing the bay, dockside, and mountains that are the essence of the island.

The Suliaman Palace, Jeddah, K.S.A. In his design for the Suliaman Palace, El-Wakil has not only overcome the twin challenges of a large and relatively flat site, but has also successfully turned them to his advantage. To fully understand how this has been done and the subsequent importance of these residences as a prototype for others in this region, it is first necessary to recall that until relatively recently Jeddah where the palace is located was a walled city confined to a few square miles of area along the coast of the Red Sea. For reasons of efficiency, as well as privacy, the houses within this walled area were organized within a vertical tower, typically using three main divisions of space. Ground level, which was much more accessible to the public, was usually reserved for rooms associated with service and storage, as well as an official reception room for guests. The second and third floors of these tower houses were set aside for the family, with the topmost floor being the most private of all. Because of the compact nature of these residential quarters and the proximity of the houses inside them, *mushrabiyya* screens or *roshan*, as they are called in Jeddah, were an essential addition to the windows of each house as was a central courtyard that also provided privacy.

After the city wall was demolished and Jeddah began to expand after World War II, the restraints that had faced house builders in the past became redundant. Detached villas sprung up on individual lots as quickly as civic services could be extended to them. El-Wakil's concept for this particular residence was to make a contemporary version of the traditional Arab house in Jeddah. He believes tradition is dynamic and is open to change, and that the architect must maintain continuity within change by being aware of constants and reinterpreting them in a new context. As he says, "This interaction between what is constant and what is change brought on by newly arising situations results in new formal entities."[5]

The Suliaman Palace is located in new Jeddah, which is reclaimed desert area to the north of the older city and is mainly used for housing. There are no narrow streets as there are in the old city, and building sites are isolated by wide avenues to allow for cars. The Palace is different from older houses in being on an individual site. As a visible symbol of these new conditions, the Suliaman Palace extends horizontally from the middle of its triangular site, with long elevations toward the north and south to take maximum advantage of the best light and views toward the Red Sea. It is formally defined by the different functions in it. These include the public area, the semipublic and totally private sleeping quarters, and service wing. The house has a southern elevation that is over 70 meters in length. This profile was imposed by the site, which is an extended triangle. El-Wakil also wanted to provide maximum views of the Red Sea. He used a standard square module of 6 feet, or 180 centimeters, throughout the design as an ordering device. This module helped to bring order to what would otherwise be a confusing array of forms and a variety of dimensions. This would have been difficult to build, due to its size. He also used a dominant axis to give order to the plan.

As originally conceived, the sequence of spaces along this axis begins with a small courtyard that acts as one part of a *magaz* leading to the main entrance of the house itself. A large *majlis*, or *salamlik*, which is located on one side of this court upon entrance, is organized in the shape of a "U" with its open end facing the court, and it has a continuous banquette running along three walls in the fashion of a traditional male reception room. Of these three walls, the one to the south facing the door is dominant. It has a large ornately carved wooden panel running from the back of the banquette to the ceiling to designate it as a place of honor for the sheikh himself, with windows looking out to the gardens and the sea beyond flanking it on both sides. The walls of the two sides of the "U" also have smaller carved wooden panels, which alternate with solid vertical bands of brick and plaster wall. Antique *Bedu* rifles from the sheikh's extensive collections of weapons, hanging muzzle down in these white bonds, are a vivid reminder of the bands of tribal fealty that he still commands.

Sometime after the construction of the house had already begun, the client decided that there was a need for several guest rooms, and, in spite of the generous size of the site, the placement of the foundations and linear increasingly private character of the concept dictated that these be located near the entrance courtyard as well. Because of municipal setback requirements, the proximity of the site line to the guest wing dictated that it be deflected from the main axis. With characteristic optimism, the architect also looked upon this unexpected turn of events as an opportunity rather than a difficulty. He used the apparent conflict between the space required and the area remaining to the advantage of the design. To some the result may be reminiscent of the kind of juxtaposition and transformation that takes place in the Fatimid and Mamluk complexes in medieval Cairo. Three examples are the *madrasa* of Al Salih Najm al Din Ayyub, the *madrasa* and mausoleum of

Amir Sanjar al Jawli, and the *khangah* and mosque of Amir Shaykhu. Such examples were definitely in the architect's mind as he went about solving this problem. As he says:

> As the space for this added wing was confined within the existing internal vehicle drive-ways use was made of an old design technique; aligning the elevation walls with the streets and disposing of the rooms inside accordingly filling in spaces where necessary. This solution was often used in the old irregular street patterns and especially in Mosques where the buildings were aligned with the street whilst prayer space was directed toward *Makkah*.[6]

The resulting addition, which represents one of the few examples of such complexity in El-Wakil's residential work, serves to augment the entry court and *samalik* across the drive and to act as a visual hinge generating the extended fugal of movement of spaces that extend horizontally from it. As such, it both begins and ends the linear form of the house, paradoxically giving it more animation than it could otherwise have had.

The towering *Qa'a*, which is the highest volume in this extended elevation, is reached through a long, exquisitely tiled hallway that joins the public zones of the Palace. A subtle shift in zoning, from the grouping of the *majlis*, to an inner sanctum reserved for close friends, is marked by level as well as scale with three semicircular steps leading up into the high, square space. This change of level, which is repeated in an even more exaggerated way between the semiprivate and private zones is far from accidental, as can be seen in an early rendering, in which a tripartile garden, rendered in the fashion of Hassan Fathy's pharaonically inspired gouaches, clearly indicates these horizontal break points and an increasing sense of closure where they occur. The dining room, the kitchen, and the party wing that is perpendicular to it further confirms the purpose of this zone, meant for entertaining important guests, relatives, and close friends. The family quarters located across an open courtyard from this middle zone terminates the line and is really a self-contained atrium house in its own right. A wooden cupola, inspired by one of similar formed design for the Monesterli residence in Cairo by Hassan Fathy signifies the fragile character of this grouping as compared to the *Qa'a* across the court casting delicate shadows on the white walls of the bedroom arcades below. This sense of playfulness continues in the central fountain of the atrium itself, which is updated here into a plunge connected by a covered passageway to the swimming pool beyond.

Through such innovation, El-Wakil has shown the possibility inherent in the traditional typologies of the past, and these four houses each represent a different contemporary condition in which they have been implemented.

Hassan Fathy

Hassan Fathy was born in the Delta region of Egypt, far from the bustle of Cairo and Alexandria. His family owned an agricultural estate, and he recalled that some of his earliest and fondest memories were those of his interaction with the laborers on the farm with whom he seemed to have an affinity. When the time came to go to university, he naturally chose agriculture as a major, and both he and his family

Dar al Islam, Abiquiu, New Mexico, Hassan Fathy.   *Source:* Laura McAlpine; Flickr

were disappointed to find that he had no aptitude for it. He also liked music, knew how to play the piano and the violin, and drew well. Because of his artistic sensibilities, he decided to enroll in architectural school; the prospects for financial survival seemed better in that area than they would be as a musician or an artist.

A Classic **Beaux Arts** *Education* He attended Cairo University; since Egypt at that time was under colonial rule, his instructors were British. The curriculum followed the *Beaux Arts* conventions, and so was based on Classical Greek and Roman precedents. This meant that Modernism, which had just begun to emerge when he was a student in the early 1920s, was officially excluded from his educational experience. But, he was aware of it nonetheless, and as soon as he graduated, in the early 1920s, he started to explore the same formal language then being promoted by Modernist leaders such as Walter Gropius, Ludwig Mies Van der Rohe, and Le Corbusier. This early phase of his career included a project that was never built for a villa for Hosni Omar, intended for a site in Giza on the outskirts of Cairo near the pyramids. It is starkly modern in style, with flat roofs, white stucco walls, and severe steel industrial windows. It was designed in 1930 in collaboration with Ahmed Omar, who was related to the client. The Villa Hosni Omar was the first of several Modernist designs that Fathy completed at this time. Another of these was the Sada Al-Barreya Villa, designed for a site in Fomm Al-Khalig. This villa design pragmatically linked a living area for the owner with two additional rental units. Each of these, while joined, are perfectly self-contained with separate internal stairs that make the two-story plan feasible. While this is again a Modernist plan, there is a vestigial central court in it that is used to provide privacy for the owner, giving evidence of the kind of spatial organization that proved to be so characteristic of the work that Fathy was to do in the future.

Several other Modernist exercises followed, such as the Azmi Bey Adel Malek and El Beyli Villas, designed in 1934. But soon afterward, in 1937, Fathy made a distinct change of direction in a house he did for Mrs. Isabel Garvice. It has several traditional elements that were new to his work, which in addition to a more clearly defined and intentionally placed central courtyard and separation of public and private spaces, included a *máqaad*, which is a covered second story balcony open to the courtyard where the family would gather for an evening meal, and *mushrabiyya* screens, used to protect the privacy of the female occupants of a house in the past, on an otherwise blank exterior wall. This house, revealingly named "Dar al Islam," or the "world of Islam" on the architect's drawings, is a benchmark in Fathy's development, but is still tentative and uninformed in its execution.

Part of a Nationalist Movement About this same time, in the period just before the Second World War, Fathy became a member of a group of artists, writers, musicians, and architects who were using their individual talents and media to express their dissatisfaction with colonial occupation and the government that enabled it. Naguib Mahfouz, for example, who won a Nobel Peace Prize for literature for his stories of a typical neighborhood in Cairo, was writing thinly veiled allegories about times during the Pharaonic period when Egyptians had overthrown and expelled foreign invaders. Others, such as the artist and poet Hamid Said, who became Fathy's close friend and an important client, were really expressing their belief in Egyptian traditional values.

For Fathy, an intention to find a true indigenous architecture language that could replace one that imposed Western values on his country was his way of responding to colonial rule and contributing to this effort. He worked on a series of projects using this new language, which he was starting to learn by studying documents such as *The Description of Egypt*, in the Institute Francaise Archaeologique Oriental (IFAO) in Cairo, and by surveying old homes in the medieval quarter such as the Beit Gamal-adin Dahabi and the Beit Souheimi. When he had completed several of them at a conceptual stage, he held an exhibition that showcased his new style in Mansouria, on the outskirts of Cairo, in 1938.

Some of the projects included a villa for Taher al-Omari Bey, which was intended for a site in the Fayum at Sedmant al Gabal, which has a long linear plan, centered around a *qa'a*, or reception room of the kind found in the houses built in the twelfth, thirteenth, and fourteenth centuries in the medieval quarter of Cairo.

In 1941, Fathy was commissioned to design a farm for the Royal Society of Agriculture, and this project was critical as a beginning point in his search for an inexpensive alternative to more expensive ways of construction involving imported steel and cement. These materials were in short supply at any rate, due to the war. He made several attempts to build domes and vaults in this project, following the formal language that he had unveiled at Mansouria, but they all collapsed.

His brother, Aly, who lived in Luxor, suggested that Fathy visit the Nubian villages near Aswan, since the masons that built them used an ancient method of construction that eliminated the need for centering or internal supports of any kind, and just required the use of mud brick.

Traditional Nubian Wisdom Fathy went to several Nubian villages and studied the traditional method that they used. It started with a standard wall, made of mud brick. A mason then inscribed a parabolic arch on that wall in mud mortar and laid up a first course of brick on it, with the bricks near the ground being wider than those near the crown, so that a compressive thrust was set up into the wall and down to the ground. Each subsequent course of bricks on the vault was scored by the mason's fingers before the brick dried to create grooves that would allow that course to adhere to the next. The vault was built, constantly moving the base out, slightly further than the crown, until the entire space was covered. A dome could be built in the same way by using this same process in a 360 degree turn.

Ezbet Al-Bazry In 1942, Hassan Fathy tested this system of Nubian mud brick vault and dome construction, using the spatial typologies such as the central courtyard, *qa'a*, and *máqaad* that he had discovered in his research at the IFAO and the medieval quarter of Cairo, by constructing a small house at Ezbet Al-Bazry. It was built beside a canal running between Cairo and Maadi, and was intended to prove to the Red Crescent Society that was sponsoring the experiment that this kind of construction could be used to replace 25 houses that had been destroyed by a flood shortly beforehand. The prototype had a *qa'a*, or reception room for guests, as well as a dining room, kitchen, large sleeping area, and bathroom. Each of these spaces was covered with a dome and was grouped around a central court. Fathy was convinced that the Red Crescent Society would choose to replace the ruined houses with his prototype when they saw how comfortable it was and how inexpensive it was to build, and he was disappointed when they chose a more expensive concrete design proposed by a local builder. This was his first encounter with what he would later describe as the "contractor establishment" in Egypt, which was later to intentionally undermine his theories because they saw his work as a low-cost threat to their business. He was later to describe this experience in detail in a book he wrote in the 1960s called *Architecture for the People*, which was later published in 1973 as *Architecture for the Poor*, in a chapter entitled "Iblis in Ambush," referring to *Iblis*, the name given to the devil in the Quran.

Undeterred, Fathy then went on to build a series of houses in his new style. This was for the El-Razek family, and it was built in 1941. In it, Fathy established a sequence of formal reception spaces, related to the clients' need to entertain guests quite frequently, and this is set up along a north-south axis. In contrast to this line, he also established a counteraxis for all of the private family spaces, and at that intersection of these two axis, he placed a series of courtyards that relate directly to each grouping.

Hamid Said His friend Hamid Said, who was also part of the group of young artists, musicians, writers, and architects that Fathy had joined because they shared his belief in the need to establish an indigenous Egyptians means of expression in the arts, asked Fathy to design and build a house for him using the new elements the architect had developed.

The Hamid Said House, which is in Marg, was begun in 1942, and was built in two phases. The first began with a large vaulted loggia, or *iwan*, which was intended as the main entrance as well as a sitting area from which Said could look out on the lush green countryside, since this area was once an oasis. It also included a domed studio space with another attached *iwan* for sleeping. The second phase, built three years later, provided Said with a dining room, kitchen, and larger bathroom wing, and is linked to the first phase by an articulated gallery leading to a larger studio that was built across the central court. This courtyard later became the meeting place for the Society of Art and Life, which was founded by Hamid Said to promote indigenous Egyptian art.

MOROCCO

Charles Boccara: The Abtan House, Marrakesh

Charles Boccara was born in Tunisia in 1940 and was raised in Morocco. He was trained as an architect at the *Ecole des Beaux Arts* in Paris, just before that legendary program was discontinued in the late 1960s. His thesis project was located in Fez, and after graduation he returned to Morocco in 1970. He apprenticed with E. Azagury in Casablanca before establishing his own office in Marrakesh. Soon afterward in December 1979, King Hassan II expressed his support of the preservation of the traditional architecture of Morocco, and of the perpetuation of its values in its contemporary as a way of protecting family values as well. This led to royal sponsorship of an extremely important publication of an enormous two-volume set of books entitled *Le Maroc et l'Artisanat*, by Andre Paccard in 1980. This anthology of the Moroccan building craft consolidated and reiterated the unique position of this nation as a valuable repository of traditional construction skills at all levels, throughout the Islamic world. As one example of this, Moroccan craftsmen were brought in to do the final detailing, including the exquisitely ornate plaster work that only they know how to do, throughout the interior of the Ministry of Foreign Affairs in Riyadh when it was completed in 1987.

Charles Boccara, then had access to a remarkably well established and protected heritage of traditional craftwork extending back for hundreds of years to draw from in his own work, as well as the official mandate of the Moroccan government to follow well-established historical prototypes in doing so. One example of his skill and sensitivity in doing so is the Abtan House.[7]

The Abtan house, which was completed in 1984, is located on the outskirts of Marrakesh. It continues the grand tradition of the garden in Islamic architecture, and updates it by adding other components to it. The site is an irregularly shaped extended polygon that pushed out into a triangle on the east. Boccara has used this irregularity to its best advantage by creating a main axis along the elongated north-south line, placing the main residence at the far end of the entry on the north, and a cross-axis from east to west with a guesthouse occupying the triangular piece on the east. The design challenge then was to tie these two disparate parts together, which Boccara does by establishing two allies that radiate outward from the guest-house toward the main axis, each being at an angle that is parallel to the legs of the triangular site lines at that part of the relatively small property.

The Islamic Garden The landscaped garden is a well-established tradition throughout the Islamic world. This partly derives from the idea of paradise, or *al-firdous*, mentioned in the Quran, where a judgment day will take place in the presence of "a crowd of those of yore, and a few of the latter day," who will be served by "eternal youths and large eyed maidens."[8] The Garden of Paradise described in the Quran was also divided in two, with each one being shaded by trees and irrigated by fountains. One was for dates and the other was for pomegranates. This

165

encouraged a landscaping tradition based on three key ingredients of shade trees, which could be of various kinds, water, and flowers. One of the earliest expressions of the Islamic garden occurred in Persia, in the tenth century, as well as during the Mughal Dynasty in India. Each of these was carefully detailed in miniature paintings which were popular at the time. These typically show gardens that were divided into sections by water channels, or lines with fountains located at their intersections, or a pavilion. Four channels were commonly used in Persian gardens, perhaps because, as one historian has explained, "of the cosmological idea that the universe was divided into quarters by four great rivers, an ancient belief suggested also by the Old Testament description of Eden." [9]

As the Islamic garden developed, these three essential elements were refined to also include more ornate pavilions, such as the *chabutra*, which was raised and open, with a railing around it, or a *baldaquin*, which was a tent-like canopy. These pavilions also became more elaborate extending up to more than one story. The water lines also changed, becoming wider or larger pools. But in recognition of the source of Islam, in the desert of Arabia, and the predominance of a hot arid climate where most of the gardens were located, the preference was for fountains that sprayed rather than gushed, like a waterfall, reflecting both the preciousness of water in the desert and the physical phenomenon that a mist of water can actually perfume the air in an arid climate, as well as cool it more effectively.

Symbolism Was Important The kinds of trees used in the Islamic garden also began to proliferate, as depicted in Persian miniatures based on certain symbolic associations. Cypress symbolized death, while plum and almond trees represented life. In Pharaonic Egypt, the Sycamore tree was associated with Osiris and rebirth since, according to the myth, his wife, Isis, finally found the coffin in which he was entombed and set afloat down the Nile, held aloft in the branches of the quick-growing sycamore tree, which had grown up around it when it ran aground. Palm trees were introduced from Arabia, fulfilling part of the bisected image of *al-firdous* provided in the Quran, and were the source for dates. Shade trees that were indigenous to the region where the garden evolved were added, such as poplars and sweet myrtle. Fruit trees, such as pomegranates, fulfilled the second half of the Quranic image of paradise. [10]

The evaluation of this early phase culminated in the Menghal Garden of Shalimar in Kashmir perfected by the Emperor Jahangir, who also built the Taj Mahal in memory of his wife, Mamtaz. Shalimar was built on four levels, with each terrace dedicated to different kinds of trees and flowers and having its own pavilion. A waterfall runs through the four terraces connecting them.

This garden tradition then spreads across North Africa to Morocco, and then into Spain, producing examples such as the Alcazar in Seville and those within the Alhambra in Granada. The two most famous of these gardens are the Court of the Myrtles and the Courtyard of the Lions, which each have arcades that feature the high Moorish arches that curve like a horseshoe and have become closely associated with this region, as well as the fairly flat, tile-covered pitched roof of the symmetrically placed pavilions into which the waterlines of the Courtyard of the Lions terminate.

Continuing a Proud Heritage Charles Boccara continues this proud garden tradition in the Abtan House, which is as much an extended pavilion as a residence. The long, narrow house, which runs across the bottom of its site along an east-west axis is symmetrically divided into three sections, the first of these is aligned with the front entrance, is linked to it by a waterline that stops short of the main entrance, and is separated from it by a one-story vestibule with rectangular pools of water flanking the entry corridor inside. This is a traditional local typology, called a *riad*, or enclosed garden. This leads to the double-height reception hall with the focal point of the residence, which is square in plan, and twice as high as it is wide. Its roof is the same form as those of the pavilions of the Courtyard of the Lions at the Alhambra, a triangular tile-covered hip roof that evokes the Moorish tradition that moved from this part of North Africa into Spain and was firmly established there over many centuries. The arches in the colonnades around the reception hall are also reminiscent of the horseshoe-shaped *vouissions* found in the arcades of the Alhambra.

There is a garden behind the main reception hall that is the classic model of the paradise gardens of early Islam since it is divided into four quadrants by waterlines on each axis, with a fountain in the middle. The central reception pavilion of the house is symmetrically flanked on each side by equally sized living pavilions. These also have a two-story space as their focal point, but in this case the floor of each is given over to a pool, setting up a studied solid and void counterpoint across the entire front elevation of the house. Water penetrates it on the first axis of the three parallel lines used in front of the house, then is stopped short of the main entrance in the second, and then penetrates it again in the third.

The guesthouse is presented in the site plan in much the same way that a pavilion would have been located in one of the classic pleasure gardens of the past, keeping intact the illusion of timelessness that Boccara creates.

3

Asia and Australia

AUSTRALIA

Glenn Murcutt: The Magney House

In the 1970s, historian Kenneth Frampton helped to popularize the term "Critical Regionalism," to draw attention to a variant of Modernism that took context, environment, and local heritage into consideration. In retrospect, this seems a bit inconsequential and even unnecessary, but it does give some indication of the hold that this movement had over the architectural profession at an international scale. The list of practitioners, both alive and dead, that may be grouped under the title of "Critical Regionalist," however, is still surprisingly short. Hassan Fathy comes to mind, as do Geoffrey Bawa, Balkrishna Doshi, Sedad Hakki Eldern, Abdel Wahed El-Wakil, Rasem Badran, Sam Mockbee, Kengo Kuma, Jimmy Lim, and Glenn Murcutt. What each of these architects share is an intense interest in their own national culture and identity, as well as its vernacular tradition. They have respect and admiration for the social and environmental efficacy of that heritage, and seek to perpetuate, but not literally copy it. They believe it has lessons to teach us about how to survive, and coexist, in various natural settings of a range of extremities, and have collectively attempted to learn from the past, rather than dismissing it as redundant and irrelevant.

In some cases, such as that of Glenn Murcutt, the link to Modernism has been retained, making him one of the best examples of what Kenneth Frampton meant when he spoke of a Critical Regionalist. The term is meant to convey an abiding belief in the benefits of science when applied to architecture, overlaid with the equally determined intention that technology should be used in ways that make it adapt to vernacular, collective wisdom.

The Magney House The Magney House, in New South Wales, is one of the clearest examples of Murcutt's belief in such adaptation. It is on the South Coast, at Bingie Point, near Moruya, which is more than 250 kilometers from Sydney. The clients had been drawn over the years to the site, which is near the ocean, as a place to camp, eventually buying a 33-hectare property on a slope overlooking the water, which circles around the point in front of it. The family wanted the house to replicate the tent that they used to camp in, rather than being a heavy structure, since it was intended as a vacation home and not a permanent residence. There have been several other notable examples of campsites that have become houses, with varying degrees of permanency as a result. Fallingwater, at Bear Run, Pennsylvania, by Frank Lloyd Wright, was built on a property where the Kaufman family used to camp. They would drive down from Pittsburgh for the weekend to stay in a cabin at the top of a hill overlooking the valley and mountain stream where the famous house now stands.

In that case, Wright gave them much more house than they had expected, but once they saw his concept they changed their mind, spending more time there after it was finished. The house is made of stone and reinforced concrete, inextricably connected to its hillside site. Another memorable example of a campsite that has been converted into a residence is the Kings Road House of Rudolph and Pauline Schindler, built in Los Angeles in 1922. This is a less literal case, since the young couple wanted to replicate an experience they had in Yellowstone while camping there earlier. The house that Schindler designed, of light wood frame, sliding canvas screens, and glass, with concrete used only for interior and exterior fireplaces and kitchen counter tops, feels impermanent, but has been preserved because of its landmark status as a model for the California courtyard house that followed. Schindler combined a series of L-shaped wings that are used to protect individual courtyards related to each of the living spaces, and the couple originally slept in a canvas-covered loft on the roof to replicate the feeling that they had of sleeping under the stars at Yosemite.

Glenn Murcutt has taken an approach very different from either of these, since his long linear scheme is neither permanent, like Fallingwater, nor protective, like Schindler's residence on Kings Road. The clients expressed the wish to connect with the elements, and this house certainly fulfills that request, seeming to be nothing more than a covered platform from which to watch the sea and the sky and the changing of the weather. Murcutt backed the house into the slope and opened it up toward the north and the view. This is a necessary reversal of the ideal *feng-shui* position of having a mountain or a slope behind the house to deflect the north wind and having water to the south.

The *parti* of the house is very simply a dotted line connected by a continuous, gently curving roof that opens up toward the front, and slopes toward the back, with a gutter in the middle to deal with the rain. One part of the line is for the adults, the second part is for the children, and a break in between is used as communal space and an entrance. The line is also zoned, with a long, thin service bar running the length of the house at the back, separated by a corridor that is parallel to it from the "served" rooms in the front.

Murcutt has used a 5.6-meter bay as an organizing device for the one-story high building. The corrugated metal roof, which recalls the use of this material on barns and sheds throughout the Australian outback, is kept thin and braced by struts against updraft. The gently curved roof appears to have been spontaneously designed, but it was not since it is curved to relate to the angle of the sun in the summer and the winter. The goal was to use it to block the heat of the high summer sun while allowing the warming rays of the lower winter sun to come in. The curve on the south side, over the service zone in the back, was also configured to protect against the high winds coming off the top of the hill. Louvered blinds behind glass walls can be adjusted to protect from the sun when necessary, or to be opened for a view to the Pacific whenever possible. Fixed glass on the upper range, just below the roof, is louver-free, because it is shaded by the roof overhang.

Le Corbusier once described a house as "a machine for living," and the Magney House has a machine-like quality to it. This comes from its logical modular construction, highly crafted materials, precision engineering, and minimalism. Yet the difference here, relative to the earlier discussion about Critical Regionalism, is that it is integral to its time and place, with a clearly defined connection to its vernacular legacy.

CHINA

The Great Wall Commune

The Great Wall Commune is a group of 11 houses and a clubhouse, commissioned by Zhang Xin, each designed by a different Asian architect. The project was conceived by SOHO China Ltd., a development company run by husband and wife team Zhang Xin and Pan Shiyi, and represents a $24 million investment. The site is located near the Badaling section of the wall, which attracts many tourists because it is one of the best preserved and most well-restored parts of this phenomenal movement. Each of the architects for the Commune were especially selected by Zhang Xin and Yung-Ho Chang, who is a professor at Beijing University, from Asian countries including China, Japan, Singapore, and Taiwan in order to help generate an Asian identity in the next generation of emerging designers. The architects were asked to experiment. The intention in organizing the residential equivalent of an art collection in an open museum beside the Great Wall is to inspire young Asian architects and artists to develop their talent. It was inaugurated in 2002, only 24 years after Chinese leader Deng Xio Peng opened that country up to capitalism. Prior to 1978, Chinese architects typically worked in government offices or bureaus in collective organizations that discouraged individual initiative or identification with the design of a specific building. The houses are placed throughout the 8 square kilometer site and are connected by a winding access road that snakes up into the mountain pass on which they are located. The barren hills in which they are placed create a dramatic backdrop for the houses, which have each been designed with a different theme in mind, as follows.

The Suitcase House Architect Gary Chang from Hong Kong proposed a solution to the perennial problems of storage and clutter in a house by designing one that acts like a suitcase. Compartments, organized in what the architect has called "stacking strata," allow everything in the house to be kept out of sight when not in use.[1] The bottom "strata" contains all domestic equipment and is also the level where the household help live. The top strata contains a series of partitions that collapse into the floor and can be raised to subdivide the long, narrow rectangular house into different sections as desired. The skin of the house is also stratified into layers, made of folding panels that cover the entire side, which can be moved to

The Airport House is one of a group of contemporary homes that comprise the Great Wall Commune, near the phenomenal structure in China from which they take their name.   *Source:* James Steele

create various patterns of openings. A middle stratum has been conceived as a *piano nobile* for living.

The structure of the house is essentially a steel box beam that cantilevers out over a concrete base on all four sides. This base houses the mechanical equipment. This long, narrow box beam allows the house to project out over the Nangou Valley wall on which the house is sited on one end, to take advantage of the view toward the Great Wall, and to use a north-south orientation to reduce solar exposure. The architect has named the 374 square meters residence the House of Wood; the middle, the House of Wind; and the bottom, the House of Stone.

The Furniture House The second house, by Japanese architect Shigeru Ban, is a contemporary translation of the traditional Chinese *hutong*, based around a courtyard in a square compound. Ban was also inspired by the rebirth of the furniture industry in China, and this, in addition to a furniture system he has been working on for several years, was behind his selection of the theme: He based the construction module on the standard sizes used in the contemporary Chinese furniture industry, and during his research found that bamboo plywood was used for concrete formwork and that it is stronger than veneer plywood used in Japan. He laminated bamboo strips onto plywood to create laminated veneer lumber that became the construction system of the 333 square meters house. Each of the rooms around the central courtyard are different inside, but share a floor designed like the deck of a yacht to convey a sense of luxury.

The See and Seen House The third entry was the See and Seen House by architect Cui Kai from China. This designer addressed the issue of how to interact with projects around him to retain a sense of privacy while still being a good neighbor. The name he chose also reflects the need to preserve a sense of identity, while still being one part of what is essentially a series.

The Distorted Courtyard House Rocco Yim, who is based in Hong Kong, also chose the theme of the traditional courtyard, as Shigeru Ban did, and at 481 square meters it is substantially larger than that of his Japanese counterpart. Yim has introduced an interesting twist, however, in deciding to "distort" the vernacular prototype both to provide good views of the wall and to fit the house to the hilly terrain of the Shuiguan Mountains foothills. Yim was also interested in the effect that contemporary life has had on past ideas about privacy, making the idea of distortion symbolically as well as physically relevant. This house, like the others in the collection, is intended for rental by guests on holiday so that the way it will be used is far different from the way a family occupied a courtyard dwelling in the past.

The Split House Chinese architect Yung Ho Chang responded to the poetic notion of *Shan*, or mountain, and *Shui*, or water, as the beginning idea for his design. To accommodate both, he split this house into two parts so a stream running down the side of the mountain and through the site could pass through the middle, under an entrance with a glass floor, so the water can remain visible. By introducing a natural element into the center of the house, he intended to blur conventional distinctions between exterior and interior and the natural and human-made environment. He also approached it as a prototype that could be joined together on another site, if conditions permitted. He took a rather unconventional approach to materials, as well as using rammed earth combined with a wooden frame. Rammed earth or *terre pisè* has been used in China since the Prehistoric Period, and has been found in archaeological digs dating from the Shang Dynasty. Earth has the environmental advantage of leveling out temperature swings during the diurnal cycle, which can be extreme in this region.

The Twins Kay Ngee Tan, from Singapore, was also inspired by a poetic image from China's past, but in his case, it was the landscape-painting tradition, which focused on the improbably vertical limestone karsts found in Guilin. He saw a parallel between the Shuiguan Mountains and these paintings, and intended for his design to blend into its surroundings. To do this, he chose local stone as the predominant material, and then decided to break down the scale of his residence by dividing it into two L-shaped parts. One contains the main living areas, and the other is positioned next to a steep cliff in this part of the valley, is placed at a 45 degree angle to the first, and holds the dining room, kitchen, bedrooms, and baths. There is a secluded courtyard between them, with a series of stepped wooden decks that connect the main living levels with the landscape. A stone pathway leads to the main entrance, located between the "twins."

The Shared House Kanika R'kul, from Thailand, decided to concentrate on expressing the difference between the rugged character of the site and the lack of exposure to nature that is typical in the city, where a majority of the guests would be coming from. Rather than being inward and protective as urban houses are, he wanted this experience to be different, so that those in this rural equivalent could share the open surroundings, breathe clean air, see "a clear sky full of stars," and participate in other things that are now rare in all urban areas in China.

The Cantilever House The Suitcase House, described earlier, has a cantilevered structure, but it is secondary to its basic concept of putting the detritus of daily life in storage, out of view. This Cantilever House, by Chinese architect Antonio Ochoa, however, uses the structural device as its main idea, to create a platform from which to look out and down to the Great Wall, the mountains, and the valley floor. It has a commanding location, nearly halfway up the steeply banked road that links all the projects together. Ochoa, following Le Corbusier in all but his rejection of the grid and its subsequent "freedoms" of plan, elevation, and strip window, does appropriate the idea of a *promenade architectural* from the Modernist master and the roof garden as its termination point. This *promenade* leads up naturally from the sloping path that approaches the flat-roofed, orthogonal, box-like building jutting out above it, into a telescoping monumental stair beneath it that leads up to a hidden entrance. The roof garden is treated, in the architect's words, as a "*belvedere.*"

The Bamboo Wall Rather than concentrating entirely on the character of the site, as the majority of the other designers who were selected to contribute projects to the Great Wall Commune decided to do, Japanese architect Kengo Kuma chose to make a commentary on the historical relationship between his nation and that of his client. This is a fundamental, symbolic decision that strikes at the heart of the choice by Zhang Xin and Pan Shiyi to promote Asian identity in their selection process on two levels. The first is the issue of the reality of Asia itself, which is really a western construct, implying a unity when no such conformity exists. The second issue is the relationship between China and Japan, which has not always been smooth, especially during the period just before World War II. As Thai architect Sumet Jumsai once said, "The only thing that Asian nations have in common is the monsoon, bamboo and rice." Rather than being uniform, however, bamboo comes in many shapes and sizes. While both China and Japan have bamboo, there has been an active trade in it between the two nations because of this difference. Kuma chose to use it in his house design as a gesture of sharing. His idea of also using the metaphor of the wall has the same intent, echoing the Great Wall nearby. In his original concept sketch, Kuma reveals it very clearly, because it shows a wavy base line, representing the undulating terrain throughout the project site with a series of straight vertical lines running across it. These are longer or shorter on the bottom as necessary to deal with differences in topography, but are all of the same height, implying the seemingly endless continuity of the Great Wall itself.

Kengo Kuma stands alone, among the top international group that he belongs to, in his expressed wish to create architecture that is transparent to the point of immateriality and has a light footprint and impact on the earth. He favored the concept of a form that implies continuity such as a wall made of light bamboo rather than a single object building for the same reason. At 716 square meters in area, this house is one of the largest in the entire series, but because of this lightness, it does not seem to be.

The Forest Home Kuma's fellow countryman Nobuaki Furuya selected an equally evocative but less potentially polemical metaphor in his design. He was inspired by a dream that Italian sculptor Alberto Giacometti had described, of seeing a ball of light shining in a dark forest, and thought of people coming to the wild

Great Wall Commune site from all over the world in this way as a communion of spirits.

The Airport House Chinese architect Chien Hsueh-Yi approached the design of the last of these 11 guest residences as a series of pavilions that are each designated to serve a different function, attached to a common service spine, like terminals at an airport. This led him to use the linear service zone as a retaining wall, backing it against a slope at the back of the site, and to connect the house to the main road with a curving driveway, across the gently rolling site. There are, finally, three "terminals" on living spaces that project out at different angles from the spine, relegated to living room, kitchen, and dining room functions, while the stone service bar behind them also acts as an internal "street," or concourse-like circulation pathway, that joins them all together.

The Commune Club The clients also commissioned Seung H-Sang, from South Korea, to design a "Commune Club," to provide shared facilities for the guests renting these 11 houses, as well as management offices and a reception area. The facilities include two different restaurants, a swimming pool, and several shops. The main material used for the Club is Corten steel, which provided maximum contrast with the trees and rocky terrain around it. As the steel rusts, however, it will increasingly blend in with its rugged setting.

JAPAN

Tadao Ando: The Koshino, Nakayama, and 4 X 4 Houses

Tadao Ando is a self-taught Japanese architect who has been inspired by proto-Modernists such as Le Corbusier and Louis Kahn. He served as an apprentice in a traditional carpenter shop near Osaka and was a professional boxer for a short time before setting out on a journey of self-discovery that led him to be an architect. His time as a boxer left him with the belief that life involves struggle and that to survive and succeed, one must be physically and mentally tough.[2] This philosophy has served him well in his chosen profession, in which these two attributes are certainly important. Ando shares with Le Corbusier and Louis Kahn what historian Kenneth Frampton has described as a "virtually religious conviction about the spiritual calling and capacity of architecture and its critical potential for the revitalization of society and life."[3]

This belief in the regenerative power of his art is especially poignant in Japan, where a majority of Ando's buildings are located, because of the chaotic soullessness that has characterized Japanese urbanism since the end of the American occupation in the mid-1950s. That lack of order is even more surprising in a nation that prides itself on its affinity with nature and the beauty of its traditional architecture and especially its houses. Whether they are rural *minka* farms or more formal *shoin*, these vernacular residences are invariably in complete harmony with their natural settings. This is also because they are built of local material, such as wood and stone, which accentuate their close relationship with their context.

Tadao Ando continually strives to recapture the sense of place that traditional dwellings in Japan consistently convey. But, paradoxically, he does so with untraditional materials, such as concrete. This may seem strange, but after understanding his motives more completely, it becomes clear that his work exemplifies the essential attributes of *Shinto*. This is an animistic religion, unique to Japan, which is based on the idea of a sacred life force, or *kami*, that exists in both the animate and inanimate elements of nature. Ando has managed to combine the quest for spatial spirituality, typical of the early Modernists, with the idea of a life embodied in all materials that comes from his own ancient heritage.

Concrete Comes Alive In Ando's hands, concrete is transformed from an inert, industrial material, into beautiful walls with silken surfaces that provide the perfect foil for sunlight, shadow, and the sky. He uses it in minimal geometric configurations that emphasize the contrast between its nontelluric essence and the natural context around it. The order that he imposes on nature with these Cartesian systems heightens our awareness and appreciation of each. To achieve this, Ando has investigated concrete construction, in his goal to make the material seem to come alive. He has done this by interrogating and altering each of the steps involved in building a concrete wall. First of all, he uses a stiffer mix to give it a denser consistency. Second, he carefully controls the spacing of the steel reinforcing bars inside it. Third, he specifies a more thorough vibration of the mix, once it is placed inside the forms, which also makes the surface of the wall smoother. Fourth, he has carpenters handcraft these forms, and uses tightly grained wood for the face boards, instead of a generic brand of plywood. He even assigns two separate teams of carpenters to build the forms at this stage so that there is a sense of competition, and at least one of them will approximate perfection.[4]

Ando has described his intention as an attempt to create "architecture which brings new energy and life through constant dialogue with and the collision of contextural elements." He says he seeks to compose "purified spaces defined by light." [5]

The Koshino, Nakayama, and 4 X 4 Houses Three examples of Ando's approach that span the range of his career, in the chronological order of their completion, are the Koshino, Nakayama, and 4 X 4 Houses.

The Koshino House, which he completed from 1979 to 1981, is located in the foothills of Mount Rokko, in Kobe, at the edge of a national park. It was designed for fashion designer Hiroko Koshino, for the upscale neighborhood of Ashiya, located there. The original house was based on the concept of two parallel bars, and a semicircular addition was placed next to them in 1984. The house illustrates Ando's idea of contrasting concrete against a natural background because of the lush, forested landscape beside the house. One of the bars is private, with bedroom and bathroom functions located there, while the second is more public, with living, dining, and kitchen inside. In the public part, Ando has held the flat roof slightly away from the concrete wall, which lets the sunlight cascade down its side. The roof is supported by two thick crossbeams, which divide the rectilinear roof into three equal square bays. The light coming through the rift between the roof and the wall also casts deep, diagonal shadows from these beams, which open from wall to wall, and this angle constantly changes as the sun moves, marking the passage of time as they do so.

There is a courtyard between the parallel, bar-like wings, with steps that allow it to conform to the sloping site. Ando designed this is as an outdoor living room, to be used when weather permits, and this reinforces the idea of connecting to nature, which is so important in his work.

The Nakayama House The Nakayama House, which is located in Suzaku on the border between the Prectures of Kyoto and Nara, was completed between 1983 and 1985, at the same time as the Koshino House addition. The *parti* is similar to that of the Kobe house in that it is also based on the idea of two parallel, rectangular forms, but rather than being separated by a courtyard as they are in the Koshino House, they are divided by a wall. This is due to the restrictions caused by a long, narrow, urban site, which Ando accepted as a challenge. The house is two stories high, divided into a built bar and a second, unbuilt volume of equal width and length that is its walled, open courtyard. This division between living spaces in one volume, separated by a wall along their longitudinal east-west axis from an open courtyard, sets up a tense spatial dialectic, and Ando says that "this relationship, of the house to the courtyard is central to the entire composition."[6] A second wall, running along the site line on the east, acts as a guide to the entrance, located on the side of the house, in a gap between the two. This gap is 20 percent as wide as the combined house and courtyard, based on the module that Ando has used to divide the site along its north-south axis. All that is visible, on approaching the house across an empty open court in front of it, is the blank two-story concrete wall joining the living bar and its twin courtyard. The finish of this wall is typical of the level of excellence that Ando has consistently achieved in the use of this material. It serves as a dramatic screen or background for the shadows that are cast on it by several tall trees placed at the edge of the small, open, entry courtyard. There are only three long, narrow, vertical slots, which are cut into this two-story high wall, along its eastern edge on the right-hand side of the entry court as one approaches, which are placed there to offer a hint of the long-walled inner courtyard beyond.

The entrance leads into a short L-shaped hallway, past a kitchen and dining space, into the living room at the end of the long rectangular volume. Sliding glass doors along its entire length can be opened to allow it to be joined to the courtyard beside it, essentially doubling its size. The parallel courtyard, which is like an open-air alter ego of the house beside it, has no plants or trees or water in it, just a flat concrete floor, and stark enveloping walls that are as high as the living component of the house itself. This starkly minimal, almost monastic, Zen-like space is a microcosm of Ando's aesthetic, intended to heighten one's awareness of nature, rather than destroy it. All that is visible from inside the house is the concrete wall surrounding the open courtyard, the trees above the wall, and the sky above them. He has said,

> the problem I set for myself in the design was to see how rich an imagery could be created by means of natural elements such as sunlight and wind operating on these spaces. I wondered if it would not be possible to create sublime architectural spaces, paradoxically through an exhaustive concern for the conditions of materials, and to transform hard materials in something that appeared soft.[7]

The 4 X 4 House The 4 X 4 House was built soon after the Kobe earthquake in 1995, near the Akashi Kaikyo Bridge connecting Kobe with Awaji Island. Ando had access to the extremely small 65 square meters site, with an allowable building

External view of 4 X 4 House.   Courtesy of Leo DiLeo, France; Flickr

footprint of only 23 square meters, and thought of an unorthodox way of finding a client for a house there. He advertised in a popular periodical that he would design one for whoever provided the most interesting response to his question of why they would want to live in such a restricted space. The answer he chose came from a young bachelor with architectural training who simply drew a cartoon of himself sliding down a board from the top of a tower into the bay below.

Ando's design is characteristically deceptively simple. It is a four-story high square plan tower with a scissor stair taking up one-third of its volume, divided into an entry and bathroom on the first floor, a bedroom on the second, a study on the third, and a living room, dining room, and kitchen on the fourth at the top. To accommodate the additional area needed to accommodate these extra functions and to maximize the potential of a view, the volume at the top shifts one meter south and east, toward the water, adding an L-shaped piece of space, and more square footage as it does so. The visual effect of this offset is that the top floor is presented as a cube, with one whole side of glass equally divided into four square panes, facing the water, displaced from the centerline of the tower that supports it. This glass wall ensures that the living and dining areas are constantly full of light, and at night the light inside this cube makes the tower look like a lighthouse from the bridge and the water.

The Ushida Findlay Partnership: Soft and Hairy House

Ushida Findlay is an architectural firm that is based in Tokyo, made up of husband and wife team Kathryn Findlay and Eisaku Ushida. Findlay, who attended the Architectural Association in London, was greatly influenced by Peter Cook, of Archigram and Plug-in City fame. In his own work and in his teaching, Cook has always tried to challenge established conventions and has drawn inspiration from popular culture in making iconoclastic attacks on the status quo. The Archigram group, of which he was a part, for example, focused on the city rather than individual buildings and proposed solutions to urban overcrowding and Wright that seemed outrageous when they were put forward in the 1960s, but are gradually appearing to be extremely visionary now. In spite of the fact that their proposals were entirely graphic, they were delivered in a Pop Art style, and they never actually had anything built, they had an enormous impact on several generations of young, mostly British architects.

Findlay went to Japan after leaving the AA to do postgraduate research at the University of Tokyo, while also working in the office of Arata Isozaki. She met Eisaku Ushida there, who had also worked in Britain previously. They are now married and have a family. Findlay claims that the partnership has resulted in a "duality that gives us perspective through distance, which is quadrupled with familiarity. Knowledge from one culture provides a fresh approach to the designs we execute in the other country." [8]

The Soft and Hairy House After testing the objectivity that this duality provided them in several unorthodox projects such as the Truss Wall House, which explores the structure potential of replicating an exoskeleton, they were contacted by a young Japanese couple who wanted to build a house near Tsukuba, in Ibaraki Prefecture. Because of overcrowding in Tokyo, the Japanese government has adopted a satellite city policy in an attempt to decentralize the services provided by the capital and distribute the population more evenly throughout the country. Tsukuba is one of these new centers, and it received attention in architectural terms with the new Civic Center that was built there in 1988 to announce its higher status, designed by Arata Isozaki. Isozaki used that opportunity to make a commentary on the social and urban conditions that this disbursement policy is causing by clustering the various buildings of the Center, such as the offices, shops, and a hotel that are usually associated with complexes of this sort, around a sunken, elliptical plaza. In addition, he deliberately used historical references, such as Michelangelo's plaza at the Campidoglio in Rome and Charles Moore's Piazza d'Italia in New Orleans, and eroded the edges of them to convey the sense of an empty, decaying middle. By replicating and then erasing recognizable precedents of an urban public realm, and then sinking it below ground level, Isozaki tried to symbolize the plight of such instant cities as Tsukuba, which have not had the benefit of a long period of evolution, which others, like Kyoto, have had. This has left them with a soulless, empty feeling, as contemporary versions of an urban wasteland.

As development of quickly constructed, contractor designed and built structures continues to cover the flat *ibaragi*, or flat rice fields, of the Prefecture that takes their name, this chaotic human-made landscape continues to metastasize. This, along with the brief given to the architects by their young clients, was the point of departure that Ushida Findlay used in designing this house. The clients, who are architectural journalists, were fascinated by a prophecy that the Spanish artist Salvador Dali made about the architecture of the future, saying it could be "soft and hairy." [9] They wanted to explore the possibility of creating such a house for themselves and felt that Ushida and Findlay were the architects who could best help them realize their fantasy. They wanted to use surreal devices to free themselves from the predictable banality being propagated around them. This desire dovetailed nicely with the architect's wish to make a commentary on the state of urban development in Japan, similar to that made by Isozaki in Tsukuba, but at the micoscale of the house.

Social Order, Urban Disorder Kathryn Findlay has verbalized that intention quite eloquently when she said,

> In Japan, the promise of the future obliterates any meaningful ties with its rich cultural history. In the West, society is unruly, but its cities are ordered, while in Japan, it is the reverse. Chaotic cities, free from aesthetic planning control, are inhabited by a population controlled by a rigid social order. [10]

Ushida and Findlay started with the idea of reproduction, inspired by a photograph that their clients had given them of the young husband and wife lying on the floor of their previous house, curled toward their baby, who was placed between them. They translated this photograph quite literally into a plan in which two opposing walls, which form the external perimeter of the residence, meet on its northern edge, and each curls inward to form a spiral that represents the heads of the mother and father. The front door is located in the gap between these circular, stylized heads, which each contain a "den." An egg-shaped form, presumably coming out of the part symbolizing the mother, projects into an open central courtyard and contains the bathroom. This egg is distinctly different in appearance from the rest of the one-story reinforced concrete and granite/Gunite house in that it is intensely dark blue in color, nubby in texture, and covered with small portholes that let in light. One larger porthole at the tip of the egg allows a direct view out from and into the Jacuzzi-style bathtub to and from the central courtyard. There is a uniformly wide cornice, starting at the continual 8 feet height used for the doors, surrounding the open courtyard, which is more than a meter deep, creating a parapet for a garden that covers the entire, flat roof of the house. A stairway, running along the southwest edge of the court, opposite the front door, provides access up to this planted surface, which represents the "hairy" part of the house. The egg is tucked underneath the soffit of the continuous cornice, with its wider arching bottom effectively providing a separation between an anteroom located just beyond the front door to its left and the master bedroom. The other spaces that are distributed in continuing series around the court are a living room in the northwest, which has a built-in, inflatable, amphitheater-like sofa in that corner as seating, a gallery-style kitchen, and a large playroom. There is a back entrance directly next to an uncovered, two-car off-street parking area, with several steps leading up from that concrete apron onto a long, narrow walkway that leads past the playroom. This is the less formal entrance that the couple uses everyday, with access to and from it through the kitchen.

An Edible Roof Because of its verdant covering, the Soft and Hairy House has been cited as a model of sustainability and ecological sensitivity. It is true that the green roof cuts down on energy use, and it does include herbs and edible greens in addition to the local grasses and larger bushes and trees that grow there, making the owners partially self-sufficient, since they save a few trips to the grocery store. The use of a courtyard typology may also be said to contribute to this claim of environmental credibility, but that argument really misses one of the main points behind the design. The house is intended as a reflection upon the character of the built and unbuilt landscape around it, in addition to its role as a three-dimensional representation of a Surrealist painting. The predominant impression that the greenery on the roof gives is one of continuity with the underdeveloped plots around the house. After some time living in it, the young owners have also told the architects that entering the house is like experiencing a utopian version of the constructed monotony outside. In a sense, inside and outside are reversed, which is suitably surreal. But, the claim of sustainability is also questionable because this is a single-family house, mostly made of reinforced concrete.

Life Imitates Art Imitates Life The planting on top may be the hairy part of the house, but where is its soft equivalent? This virtually unseen component, which is integral to the experiential impression of each of the spaces, is a pleated, tent-like, canvas ceiling that runs around the entire tube-like interior, with the exception of the kitchen. In the corner, above the inflatable mini-amphitheater of the living room and above each of the cranial dens, the pleating turns into a complete circle, creating the impression of a sultan's palindrome of the type that would be used as the ceiling of a battle tent. In their search, carried out prior to design, the architects encountered the writings of Bachelard, who discusses the symbolic, and "psycho-geographical" aspects of space and has attempted to empirically measure human reaction to different kinds of interior, three-dimensional experiences. There were also many other precedents, such as *Association Sens Espace* established in Paris by Hervé Baley in 1969, to explore the connection between environmental deprivation and psychological disorders, in an effort to reverse that dehumanizing process.[11] *Sens Espace* also advocates "soft, flexible, morphogenic" architecture to facilitate the reintroduction of biomorphic unity.[12] Other, previous attempts to achieve this same goal include the "Endless House" by Frederick Kiesler, in the 1960s, and the Casa Mila and Casa Batlló by Antonio Gaudi, described elsewhere here.

Neither the Kiesler nor Gaudi examples, however, are soft and hairy; they are just organic, rather than being based on orthogonal spaces. As such, the Ushida-Findlay house is part of the Expressionistic tradition in contemporary architecture, based solidly in the desire to allow subjective feelings to predominate over a rational, objective approach in an effort to establish continuity between the human body and the built spaces around it. The fluidity of those spaces not only recalls the biological form and functions of the human body, but also reproduces the psycho-sensorial landscape of the subconscious.

Shigeru Ban: The Picture Window House

The Picture Window House is located in Shizwoka, Japan, near Tokyo. It was completed in 2002 and is one of a series of houses by Shigeru Ban in which the well-known Japanese architect has explored the ways in which the envelope or skin of a building can be manipulated to create a better relationship to the natural environment. This idea was the driving force behind the Picture Window House. It is located on a gently sloping site that overlooks the Pacific Ocean, making the need for an external connection to maximize the view one of the most important considerations. Ban decided to use the side of the house facing the ocean as an unobstructed frame for this view, requiring a creative structural solution to do so. The house is two stories high, with a long and narrow rectilinear configuration. Ban has supported the second floor by using two 60-feet long trusses, creating a columnless 8 feet high by 65 feet long opening facing the ocean.

The concept is essentially based on the use of two parallel 10 feet deep trusses, supported at each end by equally wide, cross-braced, truss-like legs, to create a completely column-free middle, open in both the front and the back. One potential problem with this very straightforward Craig Elwood-like box beam solution is that the long parallel walls of the second floor have the diagonal cross braces of the trusses running along the entire length, blocking the view. Ban has solved this potential conflict by conceptualizing the second floor as a private zone where the bedrooms are located, with their privacy protected by a floor-to-ceiling louvered screen that runs along the entire oceanside elevation, which also blurs the issue of obstruction of the view by the cross bracing. The wide legs at each end of the pair of trusses also provide areas for subsidiary uses, the category that Louis Kahn referred to as "servant spaces" in his own work. The first floor of the house has been kept as open as possible and is treated as one large space divided by a freestanding kitchen counter and a stairway to the second floor. This minimal approach to the interior accentuates the direct reference to the ocean and the horizon in the distance. The second floor has four bedrooms, which are each also oriented to the view. Subsidiary spaces, such as an entrance vestibule, study storage rooms, and bathrooms, have been treated like saddlebags attached to each end of the rectilinear plan on each level to keep the center of the house as open as possible. The stairway is made of thin metal treads and rails, using as little material as possible, and no risers, to make it seem to float in the central space. The wide legs at each end of the two trusses make this possible.

The minimal approach and singular vision of the architect of the Picture Window House, related to a confrontation with nature, make it tempting to compare it to several of the houses designed by Ban's fellow countryman, Tadao Ando. There are obvious similarities in these areas, but the one major difference, of course, is the palette of materials that each architect uses and the reasons behind their use. Ando prefers concrete, because it is essentially antithetical to nature and he finds beauty in this paradox. By contrasting the delicate, living ecological context in which he places his houses with the harsh unnatural material he uses to make them, Ando heightens the experience of appreciation. His minimal interiors and judicious use of natural light do the same. Shigeru Ban, on the other hand, characterizes himself as an architect who is at the forefront of the battle for sustainability, using environmentally friendly materials whenever possible. He first gained international recognition through his creative use of paper tubes as structural components in projects of various types and sizes. He was inspired by the stability of a commercially available product called a Sonotube, which is a pressed paper cylinder that comes in an incremental series of diameters that is used as a form for a round concrete column. A circular cage of reinforcing bars is slipped into the tube, which is braced to stand vertically, and after the concrete is placed in it and has been allowed to cure for the required time, the paper Sonotube is stripped off by cutting and uncoiling it. Ban has used the tubes on their own, without the concrete inside, by connecting them with metal wires or fasteners. One of his most memorable projects is a "paper" church, built entirely of these tubes.

The deep steel trusses that were a necessity to support the goal of an unobstructed view in the Picture Window house are obviously not as sustainable as the use of paper tubes, but the environmental impact of the use of steel here is somewhat mitigated by the reduced amount of material that the clean span makes possible, as well as the natural ventilation that it provides, since both the front and back of the house is entirely open on the ground floor. This clear span also reduces the amount of energy needed to heat and cool it during the year, in a region in which summers are hot and humid and winters can be bone-chillingly cold.

Ando and Ban also share an interest in updating the traditional elements of Japanese houses, such as the *engawa*. This has historically been used as a narrow porch beyond the demising line that separates the interior from the interior in which people can sit and enjoy a garden view, or see beyond the confines of that landscaped enclosure to the forests or mountains beyond. The *engawa* is usually a few steps lower than the interior, but not yet at the level of the garden, and so it is truly an intermediate space that mitigates between the human-made and the natural world. There are many contemporary equivalents of such a space in Ando's houses and Ban's Picture Window House has one as well. This runs the entire length of the oceanfront side of the house and is roughly as wide as its traditional counterpart.

MALAYSIA

The Cheong Fatt Tze Mansion

Cheong Fatt Tze came from Fukian, China, to Penang as a young man and labored as a coulee on the docks at the main port of the island at Georgetown.[13] He rose up through the ranks of the stevedores, and after saving his wages for some years became a merchant. He grew wealthier and in the late 1880s built a house on Leith Street that is one of the finest examples of a Chinese Courtyard style house outside that country. It took him over 20 years, until 1904, to complete it because he insisted on using only the best craftspeople and materials available for its construction. He brought masters of various crafts techniques to Penang from China, such as experts in the art of using pieces of varicolored broken glazed pottery for the decoration of the gable ends of the roof. He also imported Art Nouveau–inspired stained glass windows from Europe, geometric floor tiles, which were then in vogue in the most stylish Victorian homes in England, from the principle tile works in Stoke-on-Trent, and cast iron railings from Glasgow, Scotland.[14]

A House with Many Rooms and Wives The house, which has a large-scale rectangular section aligned with, but set back from, Leith Street, also has several wings, containing 38 rooms in all, five courtyards covered with massive granite pavers, seven staircases, including several elegant spiral examples, and 220 windows. The eclectic character of the house, which is a result of the mixture of Asian and

European styles, building techniques, and materials, is also the main reason for its charm. Dependencies, including the houses for the staff, were built in the same style in a row house configuration on the other side of Leith Street.[15]

One of the most beautiful artifacts in the house is a gold-leafed wooden screen that separates the front reception hall from the first major central courtyard in the midst of the family section beyond. Cast iron columns support an upper level balcony that surrounds this courtyard, and several of the spiral stairs also have composite risers and treads that were cast in one piece, with cast iron railings.

This central courtyard serves an important environmental function in helping to keep the house cool by promoting natural ventilation. Cooler outside air, provided by the prevailing breeze from the water, little more than two blocks away, is drawn in across the front lawn and in through the windows and front doors, which are left open during the hottest time of the daily convection. As the air heats up in the wide expanse of the square, open courtyard, it rises, keeping the cycle going. The courtyard is also several feet below the level of the ground floor, so that drains, or sluices, cut into the middle of each of its four sides, direct rainwater, which is considerable in this tropical region, into channels and pipes placed below the floor. These run in a complex network beneath each of the rooms on the ground floor of the house to cool them off during the humid aftermath of each storm.

Cooler temperatures were certainly important in a household in which there were a number of women competing for the position of lady of the house, since Cheong Fatt Tze had several wives as well as a number of concubines that were constantly vying for attention.

Feng Shui *Feng shui*, which translates roughly as "wind and water" in Chinese and amounts to a form of geomancy, was a major determinant in all of the choices made in the design of this mansion. These relate to the relationship between the primary and secondary courtyards, in order to amplify the benefits of cross ventilation to the entire house. But *feng shui* relates to more than just physiological phenomenon, involving beliefs that border on superstition as well. This may be based in the origins of the practice, which were solidly based on common sense decisions about beneficial orientation, which then shifted to the desire to use it to increase the good fortune of the family living in a particular house. It has now evolved into a mixture of sound environmental strategies and siting decisions based on beliefs about the best direction to face to receive wealth, or at least not to lose it.[16]

The Blue Mansion The Cheong Fatt Tze house is known locally as "the blue mansion" because of the vivid hue of its exterior walls. This color is so powerful that it hardly seems possible that it is original, and yet the present owners, who have extensively restored the house over the past several decades, found it as the final color under many other different ones that were layered over it in the past. Architects Laurence and Lillian Lo, who bought the house in the late 1980s, found it in a dilapidated state, with many different people occupying every room, including the central hall. The wooden screen had been removed and sold, and there were motorcycles parked in the courtyard as well. The couple has done a remarkable job in bringing the house back to its original state, in what has clearly been a labor of love.[17]

One apocryphal story that deserves retelling, among many others about the eccentric millionaire businessman who lived a quiet adventurous life, is an incident related to his lifelong dream to sail on a cruise liner to America. When he was wealthy enough to be able to afford the price of a round trip ticket for himself and his entourage, he was refused passage because he was Chinese.[18] He then bought the cruise line and fired those responsible for the prejudicial decision before setting sail for New York. Among the many photographs of Cheong Fatt Tze and his family that now hang in a room used as a library in the mansion, there are two that are especially memorable. One of those is of the tycoon dressed in top hat and tails, with his many wives and concubines around him, ready to leave for his transatlantic voyage. The second is of his seventh wife, who apparently ruled the household with an iron hand. Her piercing eyes seem to follow you, no matter where you move in the room.[19]

Ken Yeang: Roof Roof House

Ken Yeang was born in Penang, on the west coast of Malaysia, in 1948. He attended both the Architectural Association in London and Cambridge University in that city in Britain before studying for his doctorate at the University of Pennsylvania. His area of emphasis, not surprisingly, is ecological design, because each of these institutions, especially at the time he attended them, had particularly strong areas of emphasis on the subject. While he was at the Architectural Association, Maxwell Fry and Jane Drew were working on their landmark book on tropical architecture, which remains the standard text in the field. The reputation of the Environmental Division of Cambridge University continues to build from strength to strength, and while Yeang was at the University of Pennsylvania, Ian McHarg was also just completing *Design with Nature*, which revolutionized the way that architects and landscape architects viewed their interventions into the environment. The publication of McHarg's book coincided with the first Earth Day in June 1970, becoming a handbook for all those who were actively involved in the ecological awakening that took place at that time.

The Advent of Sustainability Ken Yeang, then, had the best training in ecological design that was available to him at the time of his professional education, just prior to the rising interest in sustainability, which is so prevalent in all the design disciplines.

Yeang returned to Malaysia after leaving Philadelphia to open his own firm in partnership with T. R. Hamzah, in Kuala Lumpur. Soon afterward he designed and built a house near his office for his growing family that bears testimony to his personal design principles. It was completed in 1984 when Yeang was 36 years old.

The Roof Roof House The Yeang house is commonly referred to as the Roof Roof House because of a distinctive curving canopy that stretches across a second, enclosing roof below it. This name is a double *entendre* of sorts as well because in Bahasa, which is the local language of the Malays, plurality is expressed by repeating a word rather than ending it with "s," so that books, for example, are *buku-buku*.

Yeang uses three passive strategies to ameliorate the hot, humid microclimate in which the house is situated, in addition to the canopy roof, which provides shade for the second enclosure, and so reduces heat again through the surface that gets the majority of the solar exposure during the day, including a veranda, a wind tower, and a fountain.[20]

The Black and White Bungalows of Singapore as a part of the bungalow typology, described elsewhere here, are equally effective in dealing with an even hotter and more humid equatorial climate of that city-state to the south of Kuala Lumpur. The second louvered canopy of the Roof Roof House, as well as numerous open air decks and balconies on both the lower roof and first floor below it, serves a similar purpose to that of the verandah of the colonial bungalow, of providing a shade structure that induces air movement across the decks and up through the openings in them, through a chimney effect that begins at the core of the house on the ground floor. This effect overlaps the second concept of the wind tower, which is associated more with the Gulf States, such as Bahrain, than it is with Malaysia. The principle of the wind tower, described elsewhere here, is to capture the high laminar flow of the prevailing breeze and to direct it into the main living space. People in the hot, humid regions of the world in the past planned their houses according to diurnal zoning, in which they occupied the most climactically suitable area of the residence at the time of the day that it was at peak performance, with functions of the various rooms following suit, rather than remaining in one space during the diurnal cycle. A more succinct way of describing the difference between the living patterns of people in the past and those today is that in traditional societies people moved from room to room as the day progressed. Today people remain stationary in the living room, family room, or whatever the main space of the house is, while the mechanical equipment that keeps the house warm or cool is the only thing that moves.

In the case of the wind tower, the air that it brings into the house begins to rise by convection as it heats up, moving up through the openings in the decks mentioned earlier, and this is how the overlay with the verandah effect takes place. Wind towers in the Gulf States, as well as Saudi Arabia and Egypt, were typically also paired up with a water source, called a *salsabil*, placed at the base of the tower, to cool the breeze as it entered the room. Environmental testing laboratories, such as those at Cambridge University, are now experimenting with misting devices to produce a contemporary version of this interaction between air and water, but Ken Yeang has used a swimming pool to replicate the process in a way that is appropriate to his fun-loving nature.

The house is divided into living, dining, and kitchen functions on the first floor, along with large and small bedrooms that each have an en suite bathroom connected by a spiral stair to a second level above. This upper floor, which is organized around a small open, central atrium, has an additional three bedrooms and two baths, including a south-facing master bedroom suite presumably positioned to take maximum advantage of good *feng shui* and *chi*.

The house is modest in size, with each room being of minimal scale. Outdoor decks, however, nearly double the livable square footage of the residence, concurrent with Yeang's general belief that the relatively benign climate of Malaysia can support an indoor-outdoor lifestyle at all but the hottest times of the day.

Jimmy C. S. Lim: The Salinger House

The Salinger House, by Jimmy Lim, is located on the fringe of what used to be a rubber plantation about one hour south by car from Kuala Lumpur, Malaysia, and was built in 1992. It was commissioned by Rudin Salinger, the brother of Pierre Salinger who was well-known as the press secretary during the Kennedy administration, and his wife, Monica. Rudin Salinger, who converted to Islam, and his wife wanted a traditional Malay house, and Lim decided to translate that venerable vernacular standard into a contemporary equivalent. He wanted to provide the clients with all of the environmental advantages of the traditional Malay house, but to add necessary modern convenience as well.

To achieve this double objective, Lim enlisted the help of a master carpenter from the area named Ibrahim bin Adam to help him. Adam was one of the last remaining craftsmen in the area who knew how to build a Malay house in the traditional way, with no metal connectors, such as nails or screws, of any kind. The process of design and construction took more than six years, mostly because of the difficulty that both the architect and the builder had in obtaining the wood they wanted and in precutting the wood into the components they wanted, to be assembled on the site. In the past the material most commonly used to build a house of this kind was either ironwood or chengal because of their resistance to rot and infestation by termites, but due to increasingly stringent regulations that safeguard rain forest hardwoods in Malaysia, these species have become very scarce and expensive. Lim was able to find three chengal trees that were available from the state park service, and Adam assured the architect that they were big enough to provide all of the timber necessary to build the house. This gives some idea of both the size of these trees and the efficiency of the builder in cutting the pieces he needs from them. Ironwood and chengal are each so dense that they sink when put in water. They also grow very slowly and are very heavy, and one 25-feet column in the Salinger house weighs one ton.

When the time came to buy the trees, the architect, along with Ibrahim bin Adam and several members of his crew, went to the state forest and selected them personally. They were delivered to the bottom of the site, which is located on a slight rise, and the builders worked with them there since they were too heavy to move. Adam was constrained by several disabilities, since he is blind in one eye and lost his right hand in a fishing accident, yet was still able to precisely measure each piece of wood and to make the intricate cuts required to join them without metal fasteners. These joints are similar to those used in the construction of the traditional Japanese house. One of them, called a *tebuk pasak*, is a mortise and tenon joint, involving the making of a slot through one piece of wood and a shaped projection that extends beyond this slot, with a hole in the end of it, on another, so that the two pieces can be joined by a peg.

Two Adjoining Triangles Jimmy Lim changed the conventional, linear, and inherently additive organization of the traditional Malay house in this instance, using a plan form that resembles two conjoined triangles. The larger of these, which is enclosed by timber walls for privacy, has the living area on the first level and a kitchen raised by columns above the ground, joined by a stairway to the bedroom and bathroom above. Strip windows have been placed in the wood slotted

187

walls where necessary to provide light and air, and these are shaded by wide roof overhangs. The smaller triangle contains the dining area, on a veranda or deck adjoining the kitchen, which is partially shaded by its sown angular pitched roof. These roofs are covered in handmade tiles, produced by packing clay from the site into a frame-like open mold and then putting the wet tiles out in the sun to dry. The tiles, which are straight on three sides and pointed on the fourth downslope edge, have one curled edge opposite the pointed end that wraps around a horizontal roof purloin below it. This eliminates the need to nail the tiles down, since they overlap like the feathers on a bird, and their weight holds each successive layer down. This vernacular system is impressive, considering the fact that Malaysia is subject to monsoon strength rains and wind. The clay also allows the roof and the spaces it covers to breathe, ventilating the house vertically as it does so. The house has a hexagonal masonry core, unlike its traditional counterpart, which contains the entrance, a small foyer, a toilet, and the main stairway. This stair links the living room, inside dining area, kitchen, and guest bedrooms on the raised first floor with the master bedroom, dressing room, and study on the second, and also provides an air shaft for an additional source of vertical ventilation in the process. The house has a contemporary equivalent of the *anjung*, which plays such an important part in the social life of its traditional Malay equivalent. This room, which straddles the public/private division that is critical in this society, is partially inside and partially out; it is meant for receiving visitors and guests as well as serving as a social space for the family. In the informal postoccupancy evaluation made by the architect, he found that the house performs very well environmentally, with the stairwell having the most stable temperature readings and being the coolest area over a 24-hour period, and the *anjung* having the most pronounced temperature swings, being slightly cooler than the outside temperature during the day and cool at night.

Similarities and Differences The key similarities between the Salinger House and its traditional Malaysian predecessor then are that each was made by hand, with no machinery or machine-made parts being used. They are each made of tropical hardwood to resist rot and termites. They are raised on stilts to allow for natural ventilation and to prevent rats and reptiles from getting in. There is a similar use of precut, standardized timbers put together with intricate joinery, carving, and symbolic forms. The Salinger House, like the Malay house, is also oriented toward Makkah.

The differences between the traditional house and this contemporary translation are formal. The Salinger House is triangular, while the traditional Malay house is always rectilinear. Lim also incorporated electricity, running water, masonry, and a second story. He did not follow the vernacular pattern of emphasizing the importance of different parts of the house by raising or lowering adjacent sections. He also did not use premade, carved, wooden wall panels that are typically inserted between vertical columns.

A Difficult Task It is very challenging for an architect to attempt to translate traditional residential conventions into a relevant and meaningful contemporary equivalent. It takes sensitivity, extensive knowledge of the precedent involved, and a willingness to both follow and confront conventions. In his design of the

Salinger House, Lim has provided a model for others to follow. He has been inspired by the book *Tropical Architecture*, by Jane Drew and Maxwell Fry, which begs to be updated and yet provides the most comprehensive attempt yet published at defining what it means to build in these environmentally extreme parts of the world. Jimmy Cheok Siang Lim is one of the few architects in that region to convincingly demonstrate that he understands the difficult climactic parameters he is faced with, and he has poetically referred to them as "the rites of the tropics." The rites of the tropics, in his view, are the recognition of the colors of nature, the play of light and darkness that one experiences in the rain forest, the feel and sound of rain, rivers, and streams, the feel of intense heat and the way it radiates from the ground, especially after a storm, and the mystery of things that cannot be seen but only felt. In his travels throughout Southeast Asia, he was particularly impressed by the way the Balinese view nature. They see it as being sacred, to be revered and not treated with disrespect. He observed that water is given special status in Bali, as a source of life. He describes the destruction of the rain forest throughout his region as being criminal, drawing parallels between chain saws that can cut down a tree that is several hundred years old in a few minutes and a lethal weapon, like a gun. This profound respect for the natural environment lies behind his approach to the design of the Salinger House and his decision to use chengal in its construction. Before he did so, he made sure the trees were replaceable.

Abdul Harris Othman: Serandah House

Almost every child wants to build a tree house, although very few have the opportunity to do so. There is an almost primeval appeal in being high above the ground, in the middle of a natural canopy of leaves, in a somewhat secret place away from the prying eyes of parents. That desire, of course, passes as we get older and social conventions increase their inexorable hold on us, but two architects in Malaysia, Abdul Harris Othman and his wife, Liza, have managed to renew this childhood dream and realize it in mid-career. Their adult version of this fantasy is located in Ipoh, which is several hours drive away from Kuala Lumpur, to the north. It is located at the crest of a steep slope, which allowed them to locate a more conventional part of the house, made of concrete, block, and stucco coating, on the flat part of the site at the top. The solid part, facing the driveway, takes the form of a tower, which is thick and wide at the base and tapers up gradually to an open lookout covered by a pent roof at the top. This tower seems to stand like a sentinel, guarding the far more fragile wooden component of the residence that hovers above the heavily forested slope below it. It serves the double purpose of entrance and mechanical and stair tower.

A Deliberate Departure Abdul Harris and his partner made a deliberate decision to create a new prototype for tropical residential architecture here that differed markedly from a current trend toward Balinese or Thai inspired typologies, or other regional directions initiated by designers such as Ken Yeang or Jimmy Lim, each described elsewhere here. The Othmans sought to discover, or rediscover, a truly Malaysian expression, rather than an imported one, no matter how seductive the lure of traditional Balinese or Thai houses might be. Contemporary interpretations of historical artifacts from these countries, as well as other crafts, are flooding the market in Malaysia, and while they are primarily intended for tourists, they are difficult for Malaysians to ignore since they seem to be everywhere.

The Bidayuh Tribal House The Othmans turned to the Bidayuh house, built by a tribe in the state of Sarawak, for inspiration, avoiding the other stereotype of the traditional Malay house in the process. The reason for this may be the similarity of this type to Balinese and Thai houses, which all fall into the Australasian category of residence that is typified by being raised above the ground on columns to avoid flooding, reptiles, rats, and insects, a flexible floor plan that is multifunctional rather than space specific, and an all-encompassing nipped or gambrel roof. The Malay house, like its Balinese and Thai counterparts, is based on modular measurements derived from the anthropomorphic equivalents, and built of precut hardwood members that make its construction fast.

The Bidayuh house, on the other hand, is very similar to the Japanese Jomon dwelling; its foundation is a round pit, about 4 to 6 feet deep, covered by a thatched roof supported by angled rafters that meet at a peak, giving it a conical appearance. Unlike the Jomon house, however, the Bidayuh cone has flaps along its lower edge, near ground level, that can be opened to allow for cross ventilation during the hottest time of the day and closed during the torrential rainstorms that are typical in this region.

The architects felt that a complete conical roof would not allow them the sense of freedom that they wanted, and so have used only a segment of it, which relies upon the concrete and masonry tower for support at the ridge point. They have not eliminated traditional Malay influence entirely, however, using it to provide a sense of openness and lightness in the way that the various platforms that act as floor levels are framed underneath the segmented Bidayuh-style covering above. The main roof girders radiate from the tower and angle down and over these open platforms, which are supported by wooden columns anchored to small concrete foundations dug into the steep slope below.

This provides both a structural and a visual duality in the house, created by the solid vertical tower and sloping, light framed floors attached to it, intentionally expressing a delicate balance between opposing forces to achieve harmony. In less skillful hands this architectural equivalent of Yin and Yang may not have been as successful, but it certainly is in this case.

There are other parts of the traditional Malay house that have also been assimilated in this design, such as the *para* or kitchen, which *is* completely open, and aligned with the dining area located next to the edge of the middle platform and its railing. Abdul Harris describes the feeling of living here as like being in a tree house, because "you can feel the breeze, hear the leaves rustling, birds chirping and animals moving along the ground at night."[21]

SCDA: Heeren Street House, Malaka

Soo K. Chan was born in Penang, Malaysia. He received a bachelor's degree from Washington University, followed by a master's degree in architecture from Yale in 1987. He founded Soo Chan Design Associates (SCDA) in Singapore in 1995, and since that time he and his firm have been at the forefront of a quiet revolution that is transforming the architecture of Southeast Asia. Since achieving independence, Singapore has been a remarkable success story in its region, but its stability and progress has left a legacy of conformity. With a new administration, however, the prosperous city-state began to open up and be more receptive to different stylistic directions in residential design, as it became more confident of its image. In the category of the single-family house, which is a bit of a luxury on a tiny island nation on which land is at a premium and tower blocks are the norm, this revolution is most visible in a shift from the predictable and somewhat conventional language of thick bearing walls, defended on the basis of the social tradition of privacy, covered by steeply pitched clay tile roofs, deemed necessary because of the heavy rains that are typical in this region.

A New Architectural Language Soo K. Chan and his firm have been among a small group of architects who have been challenging that stereotype. SCDA is modest in size, but has an impressive list of projects in many other countries besides Singapore to its credit. In each of these, the signature of the firm has been a sensitive response to the particular constraints of each unique context and an unexpected way of solving design problems, with innovative approaches for each one. Their work is characterized by transparency, rather than the mute solidity that has been typical of residential architecture in the past. They also prefer flat, rather than pitched, roofs; expressive structure; a judicious mix of materials, textures, and colors; and a preference for natural light. Sunlight has understandably been viewed with suspicion in the climactic zone on the equator, where Singapore is located. But SCDA has shown an acute awareness that a little bit of it goes a long way in this region, so that a sliver of glass at the top of a wall, which washes it with light during the day without appreciably raising the heat level in the house, or deep overhangs used to shade glass window walls are among their strategies for providing natural light to the interior. They also pay attention to landscaping, including the use of water, in their residential work. This area of design has been sorely neglected in contemporary residential design in general, but this has been especially true in Asia, which is sad in a region with such a variety of proud landscaping traditions. While the Japanese strand of that complex history does not pertain to Singapore, it does have Chinese and Indian presentation in a diverse population that also includes many Malays. Water has played a key role in both the Chinese and Indian gardens in the past, and SCDA has typically used it as a line of demarcation between the public realm and the privacy beyond the entrance to each house.

The Heeren Street Shophouse The unique approach to each project that typifies SCDA's style is clearly evident in a house they have designed in Malacca, which is located halfway up the Straits of the same name, on the west coast of Malaysia. Malacca was the first major settlement in Malaysia, and it was founded by Javanese Prince Parameswara to take advantage of its strategic location at the narrowest point along the only shipping route from Japan, China, and Southeast Asia to India and the West. This Malay city was subsequently conquered and occupied by the Portuguese, who were then replaced by the Dutch and then the British, before being returned to Malaysia after independence in 1957. There is still vigorous debate about whether or not the British actually colonized Malaysia, with the consensus being that it was *de facto*, if not *de jine*. The main mechanism of what was effectively their colonial enterprise was the establishment of three Straits Settlements along the west coast of Malaysia, which were Penang, Malacca, and

Singapore. Penang, which is the northernmost of these, was established after Malacca, followed by Singapore. Partially because of an assessment of the harbor capacity and potential for future growth by Sir Stanford Raffles, British attention slowly shifted toward Singapore, which remains one of the largest ports in Southeast Asia today. Although they retained Straits Settlement status until independence was declared, which included the granting of British passports to those who were born there, Penang and Malacca faded in importance over time. This demolition accelerated in Malacca as its river began to silt up and landfill continued to move its coastline seaward.

All of the Straits Settlements share a traditional residential typology, called a shophouse, discussed in detail elsewhere in this series. This type of house is found throughout Asia and Southeast Asia, in the cities and villages that served the aquatic version of the Silk Route that started in Japan, Beijing, and Shanghai and extended south along the coast of China to Taiwan, then down to Hoi Am, in Vietnam, followed by Penang, Malacca, and Singapore. The route then turned northwest, toward India and Arabia, where European merchants traded for the goods on these ships.

The Shophouse Although the basic unit changes slightly in each place, according to local conditions, the shophouse typology consistently demonstrates a live-work environment in which trading takes place on the ground floor, with delivery of goods from either the main street in the front or a back alley, storage of goods is allocated to a mezzanine and attic, and living space is confined to the second floor. These houses are typically long and narrow, and are lined up along the street, with thick masonry party walls separating them from each other. In some cases they have a central open courtyard that helps to regulate internal temperatures by inducing cross ventilation, since air that enters through the street side, which is open during the day for over-the-counter sales, is then drawn into the courtyard and moves upward due to convection. Sir Stanford Raffles added a refinement called the 5-foot way, or *Kakilima* in Bahasa, which is a 5-foot wide covered arcade that joins the houses together and is raised about 8 inches above the level of the street. This provides shade and also protects pedestrians from the torrential rains that are typical throughout this region. It also accelerates the flow of cooler air from the street through the front of the house to the courtyard and the living area above.

The Heeren Street Shophouse The shophouses in Malacca are concentrated in the center of the old city. They are primarily owned by Malaysians of Chinese descent, or mixed Chinese and Malay background, which is called *Peranakan* in the local dialect. This is because the British administration encouraged this ethnic group to be merchants during the Colonial Period and displaced earlier occupants of Portuguese descent from this district to the outer ring of the city to facilitate trade in the central zone. Heeren Street, which is named after the Dutch associations of the street that preceded British rule, was once one of the most prestigious thoroughfares in the old city, but as Malacca fortunes declined its elegant shophouses also started to deteriorate. This process has been hastened by a practice of boarding up vacant or abandoned shophouses and using them as meeting places for swallows, who fly in and out through several openings cut into the roof. The swallows' nests, used for birds' nest soup, bring high prices on the market, but to make the houses more appealing to the swallows, rain gutters are redirected into the interior to make it damp. This destroys the structural timbers and erodes the mortar that holds the side walls together, making it nearly impossible to restore such a house, even if someone wanted to.

A client from Singapore who wanted a second weekend home in Malacca bought a shophouse on Heeren Street and asked Soo K. Chan to convert it. He and his firm adopted a typically novel approach to the problem by gutting the existing roof and floors, leaving only the 5-foot way, front, back, and side walls intact. They have then built a second, smaller house inside the ruin of the old house, using its walls to screen the new house from view from the street. This creates an unexpected surprise for those who visit the house for the first time, because it completely reverses conventional expectations of exterior and interior, solid and void. In this instance, the inner wall of the preexisting house becomes the compound boundary of the new one. Chan has left the inner face of the old shophouse unfurnished, to further sharpen the contrast between it and the sleek, new modern residence inside it. This house has four rooms reduced down to the essentials of kitchen, dining room, office space, sleeping area, and bathrooms. It also has a long narrow pool that runs from the front of the old house, under the raised floor of the new one. This symbolically and physically joins the two, visually easing the historical transition between them.

4

Europe and the Western Mediterranean

AUSTRIA

Adolf Loos: The Villa Scheu, Vienna

Adolf Loos remains a shadowy figure in the recent history of architecture in spite of the profound influence he has had upon it. A steadily increasing amount of research on his life and work has begun to redress this imbalance, but he remains something of an enigma to many. He concentrated mainly on residential design, in which he had a particular interest. The topic of the house played both an empirical and a symbolic role in the development of his highly individualized theory of the contemporary condition and the way that people should cope with it. The general lack of appreciation for his contribution derives, in large part, from the dichotomies that he intentionally embraced, related to the ambivalence of the period and city he inhabited.

Adolf Loos was born in Brno, Czechoslovakia, in 1870, in the midst of what was then the Austro-Hungarian Empire. After enrolling and withdrawing from a succession of educational programs that were related to architecture or engineering in one way or another that eventually gave him sufficient credentials to practice, Loos decided to take some time out to travel. Instead of making the conventional Grand Tour that was typical among young artists and architects of his generation, he decided to travel throughout the United States instead, supporting himself by working a variety of odd jobs in several large cities as he did so.[1]

Like Frank Lloyd Wright, Loos also visited the World's Columbia Exposition that was held in Chicago in 1896, before an extensive tour of New York City on his way back to Vienna that same year. The time that Loos spent in America changed him, making him believe that he lived in a closed, intolerant, and highly stratified society. He started to write critical articles about it in newspapers and journals, contrasting what he characterized as a Viennese tendency for pessimism, negativity, and small-mindedness with the progressive, positive can-do spirit he

Tristan Tzara House.   © Wayne Andrews / Estol

had encountered in America. He quickly gained a reputation as a contrarian and a dissident, which he seemed to both relish and encourage.

Fin de Siecle Vienna At the time of his return to Austria, Vienna was in the midst of a whirlwind of creativity in all of the arts and sciences, including architecture. Otto Wagner and disciples, such as Josef Hoffmann and Josef Maria Olbrich, were each searching for new ways in which they could resolve perceived dichotomies between tradition and modernity, attempting to retain several meaningful aspects of historicism and to strengthen cultural continuity, while embracing new materials and technologies. Wagner's design of the Viennese Central Post Office, the *Postparkasse*, is a clear example of this since it combines Classical motifs and strategies with engineering advances that are avant-garde even by today's standards. These include freestanding aluminum stanchions that are strategically placed around the main hall to deliver hot air during the winter and air conditioning during the summer. These are placed slightly above head height, to deliver the air in the most energy-efficient way possible, so that additional power would not be needed to move it down from the ceiling, where it is usually delivered, resulting in a temperature rise or drop in the process, depending on the season. This concept of task delivery has also been used more recently, in large projects such as the King Khaled International Airport in Riyadh, designed by Hellmuth Obata and Kassabaum, in 1988, and was advertised as an engineering breakthrough at that time. The *Postparkasse*, however, was built in 1901. The use of aluminum, as well as air conditioning, was also very advanced for its time.

In addition to such bold strides in architecture, there were equally audacious advances in art, music, theatre, and psychology, making the critiques that Loos was launching at the time seem all the more outrageous and unfounded.

Das Andere, or The Other While he may have been on somewhat shaky ground in castigating such a progressive milieu for being backward, his most profound contribution, which still seems staggeringly insightful in retrospect, is his theory of external anonymity and internal luxury in a house in the face of a hostile urban condition. In the wake of the first Industrial Revolution as in the second taking place in the developing world at the moment, there was an unprecedented migration from rural areas to the cities to find work, and Loos himself is an example of that trend. The painting called *The Scream* by Edvard Munch captures the *angst* that this painful expulsion from a rural Eden caused, showing a monad, representing everyone, seeming to be alone on a bridge, even though surrounded by other people. Loos fastened on this phenomenon of being thrust from a rural community in which everyone knew each other and helped or hindered each other for good or ill, into the enforced anonymity of urban life as a member of the "lonely crowd." As an architectural response to it, he put forward the idea that stylistic responses on the outside of a house made no sense, since the communal recognition of the status that such gestures supported no longer made any sense. Classical, Tudor, or other external styles, then could and should be replaced, in Loos's view, with a black façade, free of decoration or historical associations, which might convey ancestral lineage or economic status rendered irrelevant by relocation.

On the other hand, by way of compensation, he also proposed that the interior of the house for the new urban nomad be as luxurious, comforting, and personalized as possible, as the ultimate retreat from the dehumanizing indignities suffered outside its protective walls. Rather than agreeing with the Arts and Crafts notion, popularized by William Morris, that the interior of a house should contain "nothing you do not think to be beautiful or know to be useful" as a gesture of solidarity with the working class, Loos lined it with unctuous layers of leather, rare hardwoods, fine woolens, rare marble, silver, chrome, and glass, to make it a protective haven of precious identity.

The Raumplan Loos also introduced into this bifurcated equation the idea of the *Raumplan*, which translates roughly as "the spatial implications of a plan."[2] In his design methodology, he carefully considered the volumetric impression made by a sequence of spaces, as well as the size of their perimeter; as a consequence of the ability of new materials and technological advances to provide longer spans and more wide open spaces in the house, he approached each design problem as a three-dimensional challenge involving interlocking voids joined by staircases, and he often used mezzanines or half-levels in his sections: He typically placed the more pragmatic spaces, at a time when families still hired live-in household help, at the lowest level, in the typical "upstairs-downstairs" division that was commonly found in middle, upper-middle, and upper class houses of the time, on the ground floor, or in a basement. He then subdivided the remaining household functions into day and night or public and private spaces and combined each on its own separate floor accordingly. There is usually also provision for the living quarters of the servants on the top floor.

Consistent with his idea of everyone having a social persona as well as a private domestic one, he approached the design of the entrance as a transitional zone between the two. It typically has a washroom or bathroom in it to cleanse away the cares and dirt brought in from the outside.

The Villa Scheu Of all of Loos's house designs, the Villa Scheu, which was completed just before the war in 1913 that would bring his world crashing down, is the most prophetic of the external severity that would soon become the norm in Modern architecture. It is sited parallel to a main street, rather than perpendicular to it, like a row house, organized in a series of three distinct volumes that step upward in regular progression from the entrance, which is raised up one level above the street. When looking at the house from the front, these levels march upward from left to right, and there is a stairway leading up from a gated entrance along the street to a small entrance hall with an adjoining bathroom. An outdoor terrace opens out from this hall toward a garden in the back, reiterating Loos's consistent distinction between the public and private worlds experienced by each person, between civilization and nature, which the garden represents in this case. This outdoor, covered terrace is one of the largest spaces on the ground floor, and it has its own stairway, leading back down to ground level.

After this ritualistic gesture of purification, by both washing and viewing the natural world in miniature, there is a second, more compressed passage with three doors offering entrance into a sitting room to the left on the garden side, a dining room straight ahead, and a kitchen to the right. A music room and a library, as well as the main stair leading up from the sitting room complete the ground floor plan. This spatial arrangement perfectly describes the social conventions of a family at this economic level in pre–World War I Vienna, with a series of rooms organized primarily for socializing and entertaining, greatly assisted by the availability of household help. After being met in the foyer, guests would be led into the sitting room while a meal was being prepared in the kitchen, on the other side of the house. They and their hosts would then move to the dining room, in the middle, and after dinner they would all retire to the music room for entertainment, passing beneath the highest run of the central stair in the process.

The stair leads up to the second floor, where the children's bedrooms and bathroom are located as well as the maids' quarters, to be close to them. The first step back of the volume of the house designates this level and serves as a terrace for it as well. The master bedroom and bath area is located at the topmost, third level, with its own equally spacious setback terrace. This is adjacent to an interior counterpart, designated as a "winter garden," which is full of light and would have been a welcome retreat during the cold Viennese winters. Loos was way ahead of his time in his minimalistic architectural language, which would not surface again until Le Corbusier's work in the 1920s.

BELGIUM

Josef Hoffmann: The Palais Stoclet, Brussels

The Palais Stoclet, by Josef Hoffmann, has only recently been analyzed in any detail by historian Eduard F. Sekler, in 1985.[3] Yet, even now, it remains something of a mystery because of both its scope and the timing of its construction, as well as the architect's allegiances outside of his own contemporary circle. Any attempt to shed some light on the significance of this extraordinary house might best start with a brief discussion of those allegiances, since they are central to both its final form and content; and help them place it in context.

Fierce Competition In the decades just before the end of the nineteenth century there was intense competition for market share taking place between the rapidly industrializing nations of the world, involving Britain and Germany in particular. Some historians believe that this was one of the most important factors behind the First World War as a testing ground of tech-

External view of the Palais Stoclet.   Courtesy of Amy Hood; Flickr

nology, but what is uncontestable is that a struggle for national industrial dominance characterized the end of this era. The Great Exhibition, held in London in 1851, may reliably be used as the beginning of this rush, since it marks the point at which the British government felt confident enough in its own manufacturing superiority to invite other nations to display their wares in the Crystal Palace in Hyde Park. In this instance, and in several that followed, such as in Paris and Philadelphia, German goods suffered by comparison, consistently getting low marks from the judges and bad reviews in the press. To correct this disparity, which had enormous economic implications for the country, Germany made a concerted effort to catch up with and surpass the British. This included a sophisticated attempt at industrial espionage under the guise of diplomatic and artistic exchange. In one instance, Hermann Muthesius and his wife, Anna, were sent to London as cultural attachés, with the real intention of discovering the secrets behind British manufacturing skill. During this period, Muthesius wrote *Das Englishe Haus* (*The English House*), which is based on the premise that one major goal of British industrial production is to make things for domestic consumption, and that if Germany could comprehend inventory and duplicate each of the manufactured items in the typical English house, it could surpass its rival. But Muthesius went further than that in his book by identifying the Arts and Crafts Movement and Charles Rennie Mackintosh, in particular, as stylistic exemplars to be followed. He personally sought out Mackintosh and befriended him. As a result of his research, Josef Hoffmann followed Muthesius, and also made the same pilgrimage to Glasgow to meet the Scottish icon of English-Free Architecture, as the British themselves were then referring to the legacy of A. W. N. Pugin, John Ruskin, and William Morris.

A Tragic Figure There are several conflicting opinions about why Mackintosh did not receive the recognition at home that many of those from abroad, like Muthesius and Hoffmann so openly offered him. Some attribute it to the fact that Mackintosh came from a working class background rather than the upper-middle class, as Ruskin, Morris, and a majority of other Arts and Crafts architects did. Others believe it was because of his Scottish background, since Glasgow was considered to be provincial by those in London. Still others feel that Mackintosh was his own worst enemy, habitually engaging in behavior that alienated him from the clients that others won away from him. Wherever the truth lies, Mackintosh certainly was the prophet without honor in his own land. One particularly tragic circumstance of this neglect, with direct relevance to the Palais Stoclet, was a competition that Mackintosh and his wife, Margaret Macdonald, entered for a House for an Art Lover in 1901. Their submission, which was disqualified because one of the required drawings was missing, depicted a long, linear building running parallel to a main street next to it from which it is separated by a high fence. The competition program described what was essentially a residential gallery, or museum, syncopated by social spaces such as a main entry and reception hall, a music room, and a dining room, which were all predicated upon the main purpose of the exhibition of art. A wealthy entrepreneur in Glasgow named Graham Roxborough has subsequently built the Art Lovers House in Bellahouston Park in the center of that city, based on the plans that Mackintosh and Macdonald did complete.

There can never be any doubt that the Mackintosh and Macdonald scheme for the *Haus fer Ein Kunstfreundes* influenced what is widely considered to be Josef Hoffmann's most important work: the Palais Stoclet in Brussels, of 1905.

On one of his many trips to visit Mackintosh in Glasgow, reciprocated when the Scottish architect and his wife came to Vienna on several occasions to exhibit their work there, Hoffmann recalled that Mackintosh advised him to found a workshop that would finally fulfill William Morris's dream of producing beautiful handcrafted goods for the home at an affordable price. This ideal was rooted in the Arts and Crafts aspiration of alleviating the burden of the working class by making finely crafted objects available to them that would be aesthetically uplifting. Hoffmann responded by founding the *Weiner Werkstätte*, which translates roughly into the "Vienna Working Cooperative," or "Workshop," based on the same idea. The problem that he faced, just as William Morris did before him, was that he could not keep his production costs low enough to justify sales below the upper-middle range of the market, putting these products out of the reach of the people they were intended for.

Good Architecture Requires a Good Client The clients for Hoffmann's masterwork were Adolphe and Suzanne Stoclet. The Stoclet family had made their fortune in banking, in operations related to trade with the Congo in Africa, which was under Belgian colonial control at that time. Mrs. Stoclet was the daughter of a French art dealer named Arthur Stevens, and her uncle, Alfred, was a well-known painter. Adolphe Stoclet had been based in Vienna for some time before coming to Brussels, and so had become familiar with the work of the *Weiner Werkstätte* while he was there.[4] They officially met Hoffmann while on a stroll through the wealthy district of Brussels called the *Hohe Warte*. They saw a new house under construction and came into the garden to have a look at it. It belonged to Carl Moll, who invited them to meet the designer, Josef Hoffmann, later that afternoon.

As in the House for an Art Lover that inspired it, the house that Hoffmann designed for Adolphe and Suzanne Stoclet was primarily intended to be a gallery or museum in which to display the vast collection of art and sculpture that they had amassed. More than that, however, it was also conceived as a *salon*, in which new talent in each of the arts could have an outlet for discovery, as well as a creative laboratory in which the architect could test out new ideas and collaborate with artists in fulfilling them.

Hoffmann was a student of the influential Viennese architect Otto Wagner who, because of his social and academic connections, played an important role in formulating the aesthetic direction of that time. In his book *Modern Architecture*, Wagner argues that only the latest materials, technologies, and construction methods should be used in contemporary construction to set it apart from the past. Yet, he still attempted to accommodate historical precedents in his work, especially from the Classical past that the Viennese associated so closely with. In projects such as the Church of Steinhof and the *Postsparkasse* in Vienna, Wagner attempted to bridge this apparent dichotomy by making sure to mix traditional materials, such as marble, with new ones, such as aluminum, and to clearly show the difference. In the *Postsparkasse* building or Vienna Postal Savings Bank of 1904, for example, this resulted in marble slabs used as veneer on a concrete substructure, and connected to it with intentionally visible aluminum bolts.

The Palais Stoclet In the Stoclet house, Hoffmann transformed this declaration of honesty in the use of materials into a flat, two-dimensional image, in which the marble slabs used as a surface are joined by half round metal strips. The windows on both the elongated elevation along the Avenue de Tervueren, in front, and the garden façade facing the garden in the back are designed to be flush with the marble surface, and this, along with the decision to have them protrude through the cornice line of the slightly gabled metal roof, as dormers at the top, gives the house the overall appearance of unmitigated flatness.

Also in keeping with the spirit of the Art Lovers House, the ground floor rooms of the Palais Stoclet are given over to public, ceremonial functions. The conceptual device that Hoffmann uses to do this, is counterpoint, juxtaposing the large spaces that are allocated to each of the functions located there, such as the main reception hall and gallery, as well as the dining room and the music room and theater at a cross axis to the main one running parallel to the Avenue de Tervueren. A long, thin pergola extends from the fenced wall along the sidewalk to the front door, which once acted as an exact symmetrical cross axis to the long street-front elevation of the house, but was moved to the right in the last permutation of the plan to make way for an apse at the end of the great hall in the middle. The result is an indirect, bent entrance, reminiscent of those used in medieval Islamic houses in Cairo or Spain and the shift from a compartmentalized sequence of increasingly large, nearly square entry spaces into the vast expanse of the two-story-high great hall, is elegantly done. The attention to detail and sensory overload caused by a surfeit of materials, patterns, colors, surfaces, and spatial experiences that characterize the interior of this house begin here. The walls of the entrance vestibule are faced in green marble and have niches filled with vases that hold golden branches. The entry floor has alternating white and black stone pavers. There is a mosaic by Leopold Fortsner inset into a stucco ceiling. Turning left from the entrance vestibule and then right, one comes into the two-story-high great hall, which is the main space of the house. Its walls are clad in yellowish Paonazzo marble, with gold flecks and veins, contrasting with the light grey Belgian marble that wraps the thin, square, seven-meters-high forest of columns that fill the space. The railing of the mezzanine that wraps around and overlooks the hall is made of solid white panels. Dark marble pedestals placed through the hall showcase the Stoclets' collection of Classical, Greek, and Roman as well as Byzantine sculpture. Josef Hoffmann designed a carpet for the floor of the hall as well as the Macassar wood and suede sofa and chairs, and all the lighting fixtures, among everything else.[5]

A Musical Plan The contrapunctual flipping of the main space along the elongated axis from the music room, which projects into the garden at the back on the far left of the entry, to the great hall, with its fountain-filled apse pointing to the street in the front, in the middle, to the dining room, behind the entrance vestibule, which again projects toward the rear, sets up a musical rhythm that is very appropriate to the artistic purpose to which the house was dedicated. After the great hall, the dining room is the second most important room in this carefully choreographed sequence, most fully representing the spirit of artistic collaboration that both the clients and the architect wanted to achieve. The walls of the long, narrow room step back in three stages from the floor to ceiling, with base cabinets running along the entire length of the wall at the bottom. There is a space between the top of these cabinets and the bottom of a mosaic frieze by Gustav Klimt set into walls of Paonazzo marble that clad the entire room. Seklar has interpreted the mosaic as being composed so that "the two figural elements occur in proximity to the window," so that one sees them last after entering the room at the other end. This, he believes, is intended to hold the friezes together as a "total composition" as one enters the room from the great hall, so that one "sees first the Dancer (Expectation) and then the Pair of Lovers (Fulfillment)" displayed in "a garden of art and love, a garden that, unlike the real garden in front of the windows, would never wither."[6] Klimt was only one of a series of artists who contributed their skills to the house, including Moser, Czeschka, Metzner, Minne, Khnopff, and Forstner, as previously mentioned.[7]

FINLAND

Hvittrask, Lindgren, Gesellius, and Saarinen

Finland has been in the orbit of its two most powerful neighbors, Sweden and Russia, for most of its history, and has only recently achieved independence from foreign rule. It became a Grand Duchy of the Russian Empire in 1809 and at first had relative autonomy in that relationship, before Tsar Nicholas II started to take measures to restrict Finnish freedom that became more aggressive as the century progressed.[8] These actions prompted a patriotic response from all those in the arts, including architects in a movement that is now referred to as Finnish National Romanticism. Artists, such as Axel Gallen, writers, poets, and musicians, such as Jean Sibelius, tried to solidify Finnish identity in the face of autocratic rule, and focused on the idea of a homeland as a way of projecting a collective spirit and independent tradition. In 1835 an amateur historian named Elias Lönnrot, who was actually a physician, compiled all of the written and oral evidence of possible origins into the *Kalevala*, which served the same purpose of unification that other, similar documents have for various cultures in the past. Lönnrot directed attention to an area on the border between Finland and Russia, called Karelia, which stretched from the White Sea to the Gulf of Finland, as the national homeland, and the historical birthplace of the Finnish people.

The Log Cabin as a Patriotic Symbol Architect Lars Sonck built a log cabin in the Karelian style, on one of the Aland Islands between Finland and Sweden. It had ornate detailing on the exterior molding around the windows and the door, as well as an ornamented ridge beam, and drew the attention of three young students of the Polytechnic Institute of Helsinki, which he had also attended several years before they did. Herman Gesellius, Armas Lindgren, and Eliel Saarinen, whom Sonck had impressed, decided to start their own firm before they had even graduated, and in 1898 they completed a house project called Villa Wuorio, similar to that of their mentor.[9]

As some indication of the status in Finland and of the talent that this young trio of prodigies had at that time, they were selected to design the national pavilion that would represent their country in the Paris Exposition of 1900, just as Edwin Lutyens had done for Britain. By the time of Lutyens's selection, he was already in mid-career and well established as an architect, doing country houses for the British upper-middle class and aristocracy with his partner Gertrude Jekyll. The opportunity to participate in the Paris Exposition, which happened only after a strategic public relations campaign on his part, launched his career into orbit.

A Magical Hillside One year after the Exhibition, Gesellius, Lindgren, and Saarinen found a property on a hillside overlooking Lake Vitträsk, near the town of Kirkkonummi, south of Helsinki.[10] They decided to build a shared housing and studio complex there because of the isolation of the site, the beauty of the surrounding forest, and the view out over the lake.

Among the three, Saarinen was especially knowledgeable about international trends in architecture, judging from the diversity of topics found in his library at Hvittrask.[11] Among these were books on the Arts and Crafts Movement in Britain and the work of Henry Hobson Richardson in the United States, which was just gaining popularity as the trio started to design their creative retreat. In spite of an attempt to arrive at a culturally pure style, there are strains of each of these influences in the final scheme that these architects produced.[12] These emerge in various ways, primarily related to the massiveness of the scale used in the complex, the use of rough, local materials, and the detailing uniformly employed throughout.

Each of the three architects had originally intended to have a residence within the walled compound as well as to share a common studio space. After entering the compound through a gated wall, from a road that winds its way through the dense woods, each of these distinct units becomes distinct, one each side of a central courtyard. The house of Herman Gesellius, who was a bachelor at the time that construction started at Hvittrask, is located on the left side of the court, when looking into it from the entrance gate. It was the first building built and is more primitive in appearance than the rest. It was completed in the late summer of 1902, and Saarinen and his family lived on the top floor while their own house and that of the Lindgren family, as well as the joint studio, were being built on the other side of the courtyard at the edge of the hillside facing the lake. This part of the compound extends from the gate wall on the north in a line toward the two-story Saarinen house at the southern end of the cliff. The studio portion, which originally had a tower, was in the center, dividing the Lindgren residence from that of the Saarinens. A stone stairway leads down the hillside to the lake, far below, and it is easy to imagine the three partners and their entourage spending long, languorous summer afternoons and evenings by the water's edge.

When seen from this hillside stair, the combination Lindgren-Saarinen houses and the joint studio of the three partners seem to fuse seamlessly with its cliff-like site. This is because the architects have used local granite for the basement and foundation of this part of the complex, which changes to wood frame covered with shingles above that level. This tendency to use local materials in their rough state recalls the same strategy used by British Arts and Crafts architects such as C. A. Voysey and Edwin Lutyens, as well as H. H. Richardson, in America. The Arts and Crafts references continue throughout the interior of the larger residential and studio wing, in areas such as the Saarinen master bedroom, which has white furniture in the best Mackintosh and McDonald manner.[13] The difference lies in the delicacy and consistency of the detailing, which is not as skillful and self-assured in this room, or throughout the rest of the complex.

The common thread between Hvittrask and the Arts and Crafts aesthetic, in spite of this difference of execution and consistency of vision, is the idea of the total work of art, in which the house and everything in it is designed by one hand. The Saarinen house has a great deal of built-in furniture, the most memorable of which is a series of green leather couches, which establish a feeling of domesticity in the living room, and the freestanding tile stoves, which augment the fireplaces in many of the rooms, becoming sculptural objects in their own right. Dark wood floors and heavy timbered exposed beam ceilings in addition to the built-in cabinets and couches make the social areas of this house seem heavy and stolid, but a line of windows in the living room, with a uniform sill height that aligns with the top of the leather settees, lightens the mood during the day.

Brief Occupancy In retrospect, it should have been obvious that regardless of how close their friendship was, it would be difficult for three architects with such strong egos to remain together in such isolated surroundings for very long. This is especially true, considering that two of the partners were married and one of them was single, setting up the same uncomfortable dynamic as a young male coming of age in a pride of lions. The first obvious signs of divisiveness occurred in 1904, only two years after the partners and their families occupied Hvittrask, when Eliel Saarinen entered and won a competition to design the Helsinki Railway Station on his own. While the reasons for his decision to exclude his partners is not known, subsequent events suggest that it may have been done out of spite.

Trouble in Paradise In the same year that he won this prestigious competition, for what remains one of the largest and most visible public buildings in Helsinki, Saarinen divorced his wife, Mathilda Gylden, who then married Herman Gesellius. Saarinen then married Gesellius's sister Louise, who was known as Loja.[14] Armas Lindgren left Hvittrask at about the same time, selling his share to the other two partners and moving back to Helsinki. In spite of the obvious tension that then existed between the two couples that remained, Gesellius left his log cabin across the courtyard, and he and his new wife moved into the house that Lindgren had vacated, next to Eliel Saarinen and Loja. They built a wall between them to make their separation easier, which later, in 1922, kept a fire from spreading to the Saarinen's house, and saved it. Saarinen and Gesellius dissolved their professional partnership in 1907, but Gesellius and Mathilda continued to live in their section of the Hvittrask complex until Gesellius's death in 1916. Ownership of the entire estate then passed to the Saarinen family and remained with them until they sold it in 1949. The government of Finland acquired it in 1981 and has restored it, with the exception of much of the furniture, which was auctioned in 1968. It is now run as a museum.

Alvar Aalto: Villa Mairea

By the time that Alvar Aalto was commissioned to design a house for Maire and Harry Gullichsen, in Noormarkku, Finland, in 1938, he was already a well-established architect with a growing international reputation as a leading Modernist. The most prestigious design he completed prior to the Villa Mairea was a Tuberculosis Sanatorium in Pairnis, Finland, which he finalized in 1933. Aalto had won a competition to design this hospital in 1928 because of his revolutionary holistic approach to the connection between architecture and health, by giving patients as much exposure as possible to light and sun, to help cure them. To do so, his plan is broken into clearly defined fragments to provide maximum external exposure. The seven-story patients' wing is a long narrow linear building, with rooms and an adjacent open porch on each floor on one side and the corridor on the other, to allow as much time outside as possible when weather permitted.

Aalto's approach to the design of the Pairnio Sanatorium is indicative of the humanistic values that set him apart from a majority of other Modernists at the time. He was cognizant of the necessity of connecting people to the natural environment, and of bringing context into his architecture as much as possible.

The Villa Mairea Maire and Harry Gullichsen were close friends of Alvar and Aino Aalto, and shared a love of art and good design.[15] Harry Gullichsen was the general director of the Ahlstrom Company, and Maire was a wealthy heiress of the family that had founded the firm. They gave the architect a free hand in the design, which they hoped would be unconventional, and they certainly got their wish.

Aalto and his wife had built a home for themselves near Helsinki two years before receiving the commission for the Villa Mairea, and in spite of the difference

External view of Villa Mairea.   *Source:* Rafael Rybczynski; Flickr

in scale and scope between the two houses, there are some obvious similarities. These lend weight to the conclusion that Aalto was working out several ideas that remained constant in his work. In his own house, as in the Villa Mairea, these are the necessity of having continuity between interior and exterior space, typically through the use of a courtyard, the primacy of natural rather than industrial materials, the combination of a living and working environment, but the separation of those functions into public and private zones, and the judicious use of light, air, and scale.

The L-shaped plan of the house he built for himself and his wife Aino, which lends itself well to these principles because the inner angle of the "L" creates a natural inner courtyard and outside living space, as well as being an obvious diagram for the separation of working and relaxing, or private and public space within the home. In the Gullichsen house in Noormarkku, this nascent "L" actually transforms into a "U" wrapped around the north side of a courtyard to protect it from the cold winds coming from that direction. The house has been placed in a clearing in the middle of a forest, and Aalto underscores this wooded context by using clusters of thin round columns, wrapped together with rope in some cases, throughout the interior to recall the trees outside. The main stairway, which leads from an expansive, open living room to Maire's studio and the master bed and bathroom wing above, has a screen of these randomly clustered tree-like poles on either side of it, making it seem like the entrance to a magical kingdom hidden behind a forest glade. The "U" of this plan is really an "L" with a turf-covered sauna at the end of one leg that turns inward. It is next to a free-form plunge pool, making it possible to follow the Finnish tradition of moving back and forth from the hot sauna to the cold water in the pool as part of the sauna ritual.

Aalto never visited Japan, but was influenced by the traditional architecture of that country. There are echoes of the Katsura Palace throughout the Villa Mairea, even though climactic extremes did not allow Aalto to use the *engawas* or the long, narrow viewing porches that are used throughout the *shoin* of the Emperor's rest house in Kyoto. These come from the horizontality of the Gullichsen house and its sensitive interaction with its site. From some angles, when seen from the outside, the Villa Mairea has an almost identical relationship to its adjacent body of water as well, in spite of the fact that its pool is much smaller than the artificial lake in front of the Japanese equivalent.

Japanese *shoin* architecture was based on the concept of *MA*, which came from the tea house tradition established by Sen-no-Rikyu for the Shogun Hideyoshi Toyotomi. While the character for the word "*MA*" translates literally as "space," it has other, more complex, esoteric connotations. The most essential of all of these is a space-time relationship related to perfection symbolized in the tea house as a rudimentary structure made from materials found close by to shelter friends meeting to celebrate a peaceful moment in time together. The durability of this shelter was not as important as its ability to contribute to a feeling of togetherness. In fact, the aspect of impermanence was as important as its intimacy and naturalistic source. As the *shoin* typology developed, however, a certain amount of formality was also layered over what became known as the *sukiya* style of casual dwellings, which seem to have been randomly built of the natural materials that were readily at hand, such as wood, rice straw, and clay, even though this apparent randomness was carefully considered.

The Villa Mairea also has this feeling of having been built of found materials, but this is skillfully layered beneath a formal exterior in many places. The two conditions of formality and studied randomness coexist in delicate balance, with the long, narrow white band of the second floor elevation, which acts as a visual datum above and behind the partially enclosed, partially open courtyard at the front of the house, serving as a compositional foil for the free-form elements faced in vertical wooden strips that project out from it.

This is a *shoin*-like house for Finnish aristocracy, with just enough *sukiya* to remind everyone of their solidarity with the common people. Its college-like appearance is no accident, since Aalto tried diligently to have the house convey a sense of immediacy, mixed with permanence that matches its inner mixture of spaces intended for both work and play, business and relaxation, public and private use. He actually stopped the construction of the first iteration of his design soon after it started because he was not happy with this balance, and he redesigned part of the house at that point.

Maire Gullichsen's Studio The most obvious manifestation of this interplay between formal and casual, or rational and spontaneous, or industrial and natural, is the studio that Aalto designed especially for Maire Gullichsen on the second floor, at the far end of the southern leg of the "L." It is curved, and overhangs the living room on the ground floor below. It is also faced in vertical wooden strips that contrast sharply with the stark, white flat surface of the upstairs hallway leading to it.

Aalto's allegiance to the Modern Movement, in this early stage of its evolution, is clear in his expressed wish that the Villa Mairea serve as a prototype for others in the new egalitarian society that he and his clients hoped it would inspire in the future.[16] But it is more difficult to imagine how this custom-designed mansion in the forest could be converted to public use than the Villa Savoye could be, for example. While he did use concrete, steel, and glass in its construction, there is an equal amount of dark timber, brick, tile, wooden ceilings and screens, and hemp used as a counterpoint, and this transforms it into a highly individualized masterwork.

Details This individuality is evident in the spatial experience that Aalto has carefully orchestrated in his plan beginning at the front entrance on the outer, northeastern side of the "L." It leads directly into a spacious living and dining area that is reminiscent of a Wrightian interior, completely devoid of walls or partitions, so that the space seems at one with the exterior courtyard in the angle of the "L" beyond. This openness is countered by a service wing, containing the kitchen, as well as an office and service functions, that is in the other leg of the "L" on the ground floor, offering functional support to the first.

There are few structural supports in this wide open area, but those that Aalto had used are each treated individually as metaphorical representations of trees. One is finished in black lacquer. Others are wrapped with thin, vertical wooden slats. These and the thin wooden slats used on the ceiling made this seem to be a finely crafted symbolic landscape, which is the architectonic equivalent of the forest and carefully protected field on the other side of the glass walls and doors that enclose it.

FRANCE

Pierre Chareau: *Maison de Verre*

The *Maison de Verre*, or Glass House, was designed by Pierre Chareau in 1931. It is located on the Left Bank of the Seine in Paris, behind a traditional eighteenth-century townhouse that faces onto the Rue Saint-Guillaume, and is separated from it by a nearly square cobblestone courtyard. Every house has a history, but that of the Glass House almost defies description. The architect, for example, only had this house and another small artist's studio completed before dying, largely forgotten and unknown in New York almost 20 years after the Glass House was finished. His clients for the Glass House in Paris, Dr. Jean Dalsace and his wife, Anna, were prominent members of the Jewish community there when the Second World War started, as were Pierre Chareau and his wife, Dottie, so they were equally threatened when the Germans occupied France. The Dalsace family joined the Resistance and were forced to constantly keep on the move throughout the country. Pierre Chareau and his wife left for America before the Germans arrived, by way of Marseilles and then Morocco.[17] The Dalsace's were no strangers to German persecution since Anna's family, the Bernheims, had been displaced from Alsace Lorraine in 1871 at the end of the Franco-Prussian War. After they settled in Paris,

Pierre Chareau's wife, Dottie, who was British, was hired by the Bernheims to teach Anna English, which eventually led to a friendship being established between the two couples and the commissioning of the house on Rue Saint-Guillaume.[18]

Pierre Chareau was born in Paris in 1883 and was educated at the *Ecole des Beaux Arts*. He started his career with an apprenticeship at British furniture maker Waring and Gillow in 1918. They had a Paris office and also branched out into theatre design, being responsible for several small theatres throughout the city, such as the Gaité, the Vaudeville, the *Ambigu*, and the Renaissance.[19] Chareau was one of the founding members of the *Union des Artistes Moderne* in 1929 and, in spite of his Classical *Ecole des Beaux Arts* training, was interested more in industrial design than space planning. He shared the Gallic tradition of *ingenier* with other notable French architects such as Auguste Perret and Jean Prouvé. While the Crystal Palace Exhibition Hall by Joseph Paxton, which was built in Hyde Park in 1851, is generally remembered as the building that inaugurated the Industrial Age, the *Gallerie des Machines* by engineers Dutert and Contamin, which followed it soon afterward in Paris, was actually more technologically innovative, with a mezzanine viewing platform that moved on rails above the vast hall. This allowed observers an unobstructed view of the mechanical marvels on display on the exhibition floor below.

Like Prouvé, Chareau was as much an inventor as an architect. His Glass House is like a technological jewel box, filled with the latest innovations of the time, such as a new type of glass block that had just come on the market several months before he received the commission to design the house. He was also one of the first to use a recently invented type of rubber floor matting, with a raised circular pattern that increased traction that is now widely found in industrial interiors. It was then unknown, and his use of duraluminum in the bathrooms was also among many other novel and unusual applications. As if to underscore Chareau's egalitarianism and love of invention, a bronze plaque on the side of the house reads, "Pierre Chareau 1931; Coll-Bijvoet; Fers-Dalbert." Chareau had been assisted by Bernard Bijvoet, and the metal work throughout the majority of the house was done by a blacksmith named Bernard Dalbert. Bijvoet had just completed another collaboration with Dutch architect Johannes Duiker on the Zonnestraal Sanatorium in Hilversum, which was completed in 1928. It clearly reflects Duiker's affiliation with Constructivist principles that were then being formulated in Russia at the same time, related to the clear formal description of the way a building functioned. Constructivism, which was a state-sanctioned movement that had a short but incandescent life span in post-Revolutionary Russia before being replaced by Stalinism Realism, was based on the premise that the Communist ethic required a different noncapitalistic architecture, made in a new way. Ironically, however, the mechanistic image that the Constructivists proposed as an alternative was also inspired by the industrial-capitalistic model.

Forced to accommodate a neighbor who would not sell to the Dalsace family, Chareau fit the Glass House into a narrow site and under an existing house and yet managed to retain a traditional Parisian *Hotel Particular* typology of a central courtyard. This courtyard, which is slightly skewed by the adjacent properties, is part of a sequence that Chareau carefully orchestrated, beginning at a pair of gates leading into a long, narrow walkway from the Rue Saint-Guillaume and ending in the *pièce de résistance* of the house, which is a soaring grand salon on the second floor overhanging the main entrance from the courtyard below.

A Processional DNA Jean Dalsace was a gynecologist, and Chareau reserved the ground floor for his professional office. So a second challenge, after that of how to deal with the constricted site, was the problem of how to deal with the separation between the public and private zones of the house. Chareau managed this by setting up a clear circulation path that guides patients into the office suite on the one hand and family, friends, visitors, and guests up to the main living space on the first floor on the other. A patient, entering through the double doors at the end of the courtyard, would go straight ahead along a short corridor to the office at the back of the ground floor, facing onto a garden at the rear. Dr. Dalsace used a stair in that area as a shortcut to his living quarters upstairs. The examination area is in an open space, made flexible by a field of steel I-beam columns in the best Corbusien grid and free-plan tradition, divided by curving, straight, and angled partition walls into examination rooms, as well as a surgery near the center. What makes the plan of this ground floor so exceptional, in addition to its main characteristic of being able to effortlessly separate public and private circulation through the strategic interlocking arrangement of divergent corridors and sliding doors, is the extent to which Chareau utilizes the free-plan ideal. Enclosure is difficult to distinguish from circulation space, open from closed, and hall from room in what amounts to an opus to the non-load-bearing wall.

For this reason and a multitude of others, the Glass House is unique, unlike any other house before or since. Every inch of it was custom designed by Chareau, Bijovet, and Dalbert, on the spot, as construction progressed. This aspect of particularity begins to become clear when one approaches the house from across the small courtyard in front of it. There are two permanent metal ladders placed wide apart at some distance away from the front wall to serve as masts for movable light fixtures that can be moved up or down at will to create different angles or intensities of illumination in the main salon on the first floor at night. These klieg lights reinforced Chareau's main intention of encouraging visitors and guests to move through the ground floor when the pocket door was opened. This allowed them access into the inner sanctum, and they then had to turn back through a curved glass door that would have been left open to invite them upstairs. The lights, shining through the glass wall of the front façade, would have provided an additional, unmistakable clue that they should come upstairs, as would the music from the piano in the upstairs *salon*. It was just as much an architectural fixture as the steel columns that soar up like industrial imitations of trees at various places in this elegant, soaring two-story space. Guests to the house at the height of its social activity, prior to the German invasion of France, recall the host and hostess standing at the top of the stairs, with the golden glow of the light coming through the glass lens of the front wall behind them and piano music in the background as being a magical image. The upper *salon* was intended to live up to its name as a place to entertain, to have *soirees* that would include the intellectual elite of Paris. The furniture looks out of place because it came from the Bernheim family, as a gift for Anna.[20] In addition to the piano, these pieces, which are each masterpieces of Art Deco design, include divans of various sizes and side chairs, with small tables for putting down glasses. These are located strategically between them and were clustered to allow for different conversation groups to form or for the entire group to talk to each other.

The stair leading up to the first floor contributes to the sense of floating in air that guests must have felt as they moved effortlessly upward toward the light above. It has steel treads coated in the same rubber matting used on a majority of the floors throughout the house, but no risers, so that the steps, which are supported by two substantial steel girders that run diagonally from the ground to the first floor, seem to hover, without being subjected to the rules of gravity. The handrailing is also unusual, since it is much lower than most and splays slightly outward, as if to say that it is there to catch someone if he or she falls, but it really is not necessary to use it, since that would be *déclassé*.

The movable klieg lights on their twin steel ladders serve a second purpose, beyond the purely functional one of turning night into day, or at least a modulated version of it, in that they literally convert the *salon* into a stage on which the *glitterati* of the time could perform. The *salon* has a mezzanine running across part of the back wall that serves as a balcony for the sleeping level, with private bedrooms and bathrooms behind it. It also has a floor-to-ceiling bookcase covering the third inner wall on the opposite side of the glass façade. The books, which are accessible by yet another handcrafted metal object unlike most ladders, create a pattern of their own on that two-story high wall, with their varicolored spines angled this way and that. Their titles reveal the full intellectual breadth of the owners, far afield of the medical topics that one would expect to find there.

This wall of books, along with an easel, a piano, the random pieces of Art Deco furniture, the macassar wood inserts on the balcony railing, and various potted plants placed here and there seem incongruous at first, but eventually become an indelible part of the quasi-futuristic, quasi-retrograde image that makes the *Maison de Verre* so unforgettable. The spatial concept of the house, then, is one of a contemporary version of an eighteenth-century Parisian *hotel particular*, with work and storage space on the ground floor, the *piano nobile* for receiving visitors and guests on the first, and the private quarters for the family on the second.[21] One can only imagine what an evening spent in the *salon* there must have been like, with soft, filtered light shining in through the glass lens of the front façade, someone playing the piano, clusters of sitting and standing people having animated conversations about politics, art, architecture, the theatre, and recent books. The Surrealist painters were particularly favored guests, including Miró, Tanguy, Cocteau, Paul Eluard, Aragon and Max Jacob.[22] The house itself has often been compared to a three-dimensional, habitable piece of Surrealistic art, as a collage of the kinds of found objects that Marcel Duchamp would use in his mechanistic constructions. This was the thesis of one of the first, and certainly the most insightful, articles written about the *Maison de Verre* by Kenneth Frampton. He has compared it to Duchamp's 1923 piece *Large Glass; The Bride Laid Bare by Her Bachelors, Even*.[23]

The Congress Internationale d'Architecture Moderne The first meeting of the *Congress Internationale d'Architecture Moderne* (CIAM) was convened in Saaritz, Switzerland, in the mid-1920s. The formulation of this powerful organization and its ultimate impact on Modern architecture was profoundly important because it established the principles of the movement for the next three decades. Its authority remained unchallenged until the Team Ten Group, which included Aldo Van Eyck and Alison and Peter Smithson, humanized its basic tenets in the late 1950s. The dominant figure in the CIAM was the Swiss-French architect Le Corbusier, who directed it toward an *über*-rational path, devoid of the possibility of subjectivity and spontaneity. He specifically targeted a position labeled Expressionism. By emphasizing a scientific approach to architecture and urban planning that he and C.I.A.M members believed to be most consistent with the spirit of the industrial age, and the objective, empirical, analytical, and typological methodology that accompanies it, this group marginalized those who believed in a subjective alternative, or at least a more balanced, left and right brain approach to design.

In a historic photograph taken of the architects, urban planners, and theoreticians that attended the first C.I.A.M Conference, Le Corbusier is in the center of the group, but is almost enveloped in the shadow of a deep stone doorway. He is unmistakable nonetheless, his striking features and signature round glasses, which he had custom-made for himself, making him stand out. He is an almost sinister, partially hidden presence amidst a number of people whose names are now synonymous with the early, heroic phase of Modernism. Pierre Chareau is clearly visible at the periphery of the group, which is appropriate given the fact that he is known to have been something of a solitary genius, as well as a loner. His inclusion in this photograph is significant because it indicates where his sympathies remained. This is in spite of the fact that his name was virtually excluded from all of the mainstream histories of the Modern Movement written after the dust from the revolutionary moves that it made in its first and most radical phase had settled.

His tendency to remain aloof from the fray continued after he and his wife emigrated to the United States, at a time when other famous Modernists, such as Walter Gropius, Ludwig Mies Van der Rohe, and Marcel Breuer, had also relocated there. Unlike each of them, he did not open an office in America, avoided academia and politics, and except for several close friends, such as Leo Castelli and Ileana Sonnaband, he and his wife kept to themselves. In an interview about the architectural opportunity that was lost by not having Chareau involved in design projects in the later part of his career, Philip Johnson, who was the *doyenne* of Modernists in post–World War II America simply stated, "He was never really *around*."[24] Through the few friends that the couple did permit themselves, they started to socialize with people who had summer houses in the Hamptons, on Long Island, including art patron Jane Bowles. Through Bowles, Chareau met American abstract expressionist Robert Motherwell. He agreed to allow the French architect to design a house for him in exchange for letting Chareau build a modest residence for himself on the four-acre property Motherwell had bought in East Hampton in 1945. Motherwell had a limited budget and Charaeu suggested that they look into the possibility of using a Quonset hut to stay within it.[25] Quonset huts are semicircular prefabricated corrugated metal units developed by the CB's during WWII that would be airlifted and dropped in any location as an emergency shelter. Motherwell and Chareau bought two of them, for a grand total of $3,000, which Chareau combined into one long house. He added a partial upper level for a sleeping loft accessible by a steep stair at one end supported by a series of off-the-shelf round steel lally columns. Chareau cut long slits into the sides of the hut to insert a 36-feet long strip of casement windows that Chareau retrieved from a dismantled greenhouse he had found to provide light and ventilation and designed an integral system of cloth blinds that could be rolled up or down to control light and heat.

To counter the sense of a thin metal wall, Chareau also added a three-feet deep cabinet below the sill of the windows where they occurred and up to the bottom of the mezzanine level where they did not appear, facing them with louvered metal panels that give the interior an aesthetic that was reminiscent of the *Maison de Verre*.

To gain the interior height necessary for the loft space, which was not envisioned by the Navy engineers who designed the Quonset hut, Chareau excavated the site to create a floor level that was several feet below grade, and then contained the wall that was built to retain the earth on each long side up several more feet to act as the foundation for the bottom edge of the arch. The arched ends of the Quonset hut had custom-made fixed windows divided by steel mullions and a glass door that Motherwell replaced with a wooden one. The few walls that he used to divide spaces inside the house were made out of smooth plywood. There was also a fireplace. The ground floor was paved in brick, and, to save money, the upper, mezzanine level was covered with sections of oak trees pressed into concrete because Motherwell could not afford tile. The house has subsequently been torn down, which is a loss for American architectural heritage.

The Legacy of the Glass House The Villa Savoye, which is generally considered to be one of the most significant buildings of the Modern Movement in the twentieth century, was designed and built after the Glass House, and Chareau and his clients liked to speculate that they had an impact on Le Corbusier's groundbreaking design. But, the two houses are quite different in several essential ways. While Le Corbusier envisoned the Villa Savoye as a replicable prototype, the Maison de Verre is the paradigmatic *gesamtskunstwerk*, or total work of art, a custom-made celebration of mechanization and the new materials made possible by the Industrial Revolution. It is unique to its context and also replicates a traditional Parisian housing typology, being a contemporary translation of the *hotel particular* that evolved in that city in response to the residential requirements of the nobility during the *ancien régime*. It also has political overtones, in its references to Russian Constructivism and all that is implied

The *Maison de Verre* had had a quiet, but profound, influence on several important architects, such as Richard Rogers, whose own work reflects the impact that this house had upon him.

Le Corbusier: The Villa Savoye

Though Le Corbusier is remembered as a protean modernist, his architecture also shows great sensitivity to context and an interest in more earthy forms of building. He was born in 1887 to a French-speaking Swiss family, Le Corbusier (originally Charles Edouard Jeanneret-Gris) and is the most influential architect of the Modern Movement. He trained as a watch engraver, but he decided to study architecture when he was 19, and almost immediately began to work on local commissions. These show a strong Arts and Crafts influence. He then moved to Paris, where he served his apprenticeship with Auguste Perret. His mentor pioneered the use of *beton armeé*, or concrete reinforced with steel, and this was to remain

Le Corbusier's preference for the rest of his life. In 1910 he studied trends in German architecture, and around the time of his *Voyage d'Orient*, a tour of the French colonial holdings at that time, was deeply impressed by Ruskin's *Seven Lamps of Architecture*. He died in 1965.

The Villa Savoye Le Corbusier is generally associated in the public consciousness with the machine aesthetic of Purism that he introduced soon after the First World War. The Villa Savoye in Poissy, near Paris, completed in 1929, is the apotheosis of that philosophy, a constructed demonstration of the "Five Points" that he used as a shorthand list to describe the opportunities made available to architects by the Industrial Revolution. High-strength steel, he argued, dictated a switch from the masonry bearing wall to the columnar frame, predicting the first and most important of his points—the grid—from which all others follow. The grid made it possible to have a free plan (the second point), since structural loads are no longer carried by partitioning walls. The third and fourth points: a free elevation, or external skin, and long horizontal strip windows (rather than small rectangular openings punched out a bearing wall) logically follow since internal columns (rather than continuous masonry exterior bearing walls) carry the load of the roof. And this roof, which is the fifth point, can become a garden to replace the land on which this new, lightweight trabeated structure is raised. From this he developed his own reinforced concrete post-and-slab system, which he named *Dom-i-no* because of the resemblance of the pattern of the columns on plan to the numerical designations on the game pieces of that name.

Two Opposing Views of the World, Expressed in Architecture In spite of Le Corbusier's determined advocacy of the *Dom-i-no* idea, perfected through many built examples prior to final fruition in the Villa Savoye, it is, initially, difficult to reconcile his development of an alternative bearing wall system called the *Monol:* he was, after all, possessed of an exceptional, visionary grasp of the potential of the new materials made available at the end of the nineteenth century, making him the leader of the Modern Movement. When viewed against the political and intellectual climate of post–First World War France, however, this second system begins to make sense as a complement to rather than a contradiction of his trabeated theory. This less abstract, more humane and environmentally sensitive, direction adds richness and depth to the enormous contribution of this singular figure, revealing him to be even more complicated than commonly believed.

Le Corbusier proposed a variant of the *Dom-i-no*, or "Citrohan," system to the French government as a solution to the housing crisis following the 1914–1918 war. It was initially conceived as a panel system connected by metal channels that could easily be transported and erected as framework to be filled with concrete made with crushed stone aggregate from the area in which the houses were built. The roof was a slightly curved or vaulted corrugated steel sheet, also covered with a thin layer of concrete; the long, narrow houses were intended to be parallel and to share walls for additional support. The *Dom-i-no* and *Monol* systems of 1919 then were structurally antithetical, but each was the result of a search for an easily replicable standard. Each alternative was subsequently explored, the *Dom-i-no* approach most notably in the early to mid-1920s, in the Esprit Nouveau Pavilion at the "Arts Decoratifs" Exposition in Paris (1925), the Ozenfant House in Paris (1922), the

Fruges garden city in Pessac, near Bordeaux (1925), two houses in the Weissenhof-seidlung in Stuttgart (1927), the La Roche/Jeanneret house in Paris (1923), and the Villa Stein in Garches (1927), prior to its culminating statement in the Villa Savoye in Poissy (1929).[26]

The radical futuristic images of the projects of Le Corbusier's "White Period" epitomized by the Villa Savoye have fixated public perception to the point that the *Monol* has not been given the consideration as the counterpoint it was intended to be. He described the *Dom-i-no* approach as "a strong objectivity of forms, under the intense light of a Mediterranean sun: male architecture," and the *Monol* as "limitless subjectivity rising against a clouded sky, a female architecture." Following its appearance in 1919, the *Monol* system did not surface again in a significant way until it was used in a small, stone, sod-covered "Maison de weekend" in Saint-Cloud (a suburb of Paris) in 1933—it appeared in a village cooperative five years later, then in a residential complex in Cherchell, North Africa (1942), a house in Sainte-Baume, La Tourade (1945), the Roq and Rob Housing Project in Cap Martin (1949), the Fueter House in Constance, Switzerland (1950), and the Maisons Jaoul in 1952, before its *denouement* in the Sarabhai house in Ahmedabad, India, in 1955. The Sarabhai house may be considered to be the equivalent of the Villa Savoye, the final evolution of an idea—in this case, the *Monol* concept.

Rational and Irrational Alternatives These two alternatives—the light, frame, modular system of reinforced columns and beams that culminated in the Villa Savoye and its massive, vaulted bearing wall alter ego, finally realized in Ahmedabed—represent more than the tectonic equivalent of a balance of x and y chromosomes, however, being instead a consistent search for elemental types by a committed rationalist. Over and above the political and social motivation of finding a practical and inexpensive solution to the postwar housing shortage, Le Corbusier was also motivated by the intellectual debate taking place in the early part of the twentieth century, centered in the art world, being carried out in the café society of Paris. He explored his formal and spatial innovations in a variety of media, in addition to conventional architectural means, much as his ground-breaking contemporary Pablo Picasso did in his art.

Back to Basics In a broader sense, the typological experimentation represented by Le Corbusier's frame and bearing wall antipodes is best understood against the background of the aesthetic revolution initiated by Cézanne and then expanded by Picasso, culminating in the *Demoiselles d'Avignon* in 1907. The advent of Cubism that had a relatively short life span, ending with the First World War, was symptomatic of the disaffection that Picasso, following Cézanne, and a small group of *avant-garde* artists felt with conventional, perspectival methods of describing reality, as well as with the social system that such a singular view of the world represented. At the time of this breakthrough the Marxist critiques of capitalism, as well as its Arts and Crafts equivalent as a riposte to industrialization, were still fresh issues. The appeal of a simpler pre-Industrial world had been eloquently evoked by William Morris and John Ruskin as well as by Dante Gabriel Rossetti, the leader of the Pre-Raphaelite movement, but Cézanne, Gaugin, and Picasso wanted to go back further, in search of the "noble savage" described by Rousseau, and found inspiration in tribal art such as that exhibited in the Museé d'Ethnographie du Trocadéro, which opened in 1882. Rousseau also provides the link with the rationalist traditions of which Le Corbusier is a part, since his writing distills the dissatisfaction of Enlightenment *philosophes* with the excesses of the *ancien régime*, much as Abbé Laugier did in his *Essai sur l'architecture*, in which the concept of the "Primitive Hut" is introduced.

The paradigm shift prompted by tribal or primitive art has been described as being from the perceptual to the conceptual: of using simple forms and symbolism as a critical "instrument," a lens through which to examine a preconceived worldview. Primitivism is defined as "deriving its energies from differences and their cancellation, creating a charged division by recognizing the significance of that which is distinctly *other*. It does not view this *other* as inferior, only different seeing purity and virtue in simplicity, in contrast to the perceived artifice and superficiality of civilized society." [27] Primitivism is also based on the idea "of a beginning or original condition, and the irreducible foundation of a thing or experience, referring to that which is most deeply innate within oneself."

As one of a handful of buildings that are considered to be the most important structures of the twentieth century, the Villa Savoye has had its share of analysis, but it somehow seems to resist explanation, literally and figuratively rising above all attempts to ground it in reality. Why is it so important, and why is it also so elusive?

"Les Heures Claire" The Villa Savoye, or *Les Heures Claire* as it was named by its owners, is important because it represents the synthesis of the initial stage of development of a designer who is inarguably the most important architect of his

Villa Savoye exterior.   Courtesy of Sandra Draskovic; Flickr

time, against whom all other Modernists are now measured. The Villa Savoye is located in Poissy, in the Yvelines region of France, about 30 kilometers west of Paris. It is situated at the top of a slightly rounded hill, with a view of the river Seine in the distance. This hill, which is like an inverted bowl surrounded by trees, gives the house an added sense of presence, making it appear to be like a temple in its own sacred enclosure with a vast convex lawn stretching out in all directions to the tree line around the site. This location in the center of the site also objectifies the house, making it seem to be placed on a pedestal. It also encourages a sense of progression, and actually initiates it, beginning at the entrance through the tree line. Le Corbusier visualized the approach to the house as being made by automobile as shown by the intentional lifting of it on columns, or *piloti*, to allow the car to drive underneath it, up to the front door. In this sense, the house is raised up to become a large *porte cochere* and the car was intended to spiral around the house in a constantly narrowing arc before arrival.

The columns make the house seem to float, which, along with its siting at the crown of the hill, contributes to its sense of detachment from nature, which was certainly intentional. It seems ethereal, rather than real, but the aura of perfection is also deliberately compromised by a series of discrepancies.

Deliberate Ambiguities The first of these is the geometry of the house. It looks square, when seen from a distance, but is actually rectangular. The perfection of the square is also compromised on the inside by a long ramp that is placed off-axis, bisecting the plan into two unequal parts. The ramp is also a key element in the theme of procession, which in turn is a key ingredient in Le Corbusier's intention of revealing the spaces within the house slowly, and of having the roof garden, which is the fifth of his five points, and the breathtaking view that it provides out to the 360 degree circle of trees in the distance be the last impression.

This optical illusion of what is apparently a perfect square, being revealed as a compromise, leads to the second ambiguity, which is symmetry. The appearance of the house as a contemporary version of a classical Greek temple implies the same symmetry that is associated with that historical image, but the dark enclosed area of the ground floor, below what appears to be the square volume above it, is pulled toward the back or underside of the house, setting up an asymmetrical dynamic that continues with the displacement of the ramp inside. This symmetrical/asymmetrical dichotomy is also played out in the four elevations, since the front is symmetrical and each of the sides are not.

The elevations then are the third ambiguity, since each one of the four is different from the rest. This also stems from the expectation that the approach to the house by automobile would involve a spiral path around it, in which each elevation would be revealed in turn, before entering under the house and moving to the front door. The elevations also hint at tropism toward both the sun path, at a diagonal from the lower right to the upper left-hand corner of the almost square enclosure, as well as the view to the Seine, toward the upper left, or northwest corner.

The fourth ambiguity is the use of mass and space. The long horizontal voids, corresponding to the strip window as another one of Le Corbusier's five points, are glazed on the front elevation and open on the others, making the enclosing wall of the upper *piano nobile* seem like a screen in some places and a more conventional, and formal, window wall on approach. This selection degree of enclosure also helped the architect control the amount of sunlight that he allowed into the interior. This leads to the play of light and shadow in the house that is the last dichotomy and that led the owners to name it "Les Heures Claires," which refers to the long shadows that are typical just before sunset.

Interacting with Nature Roq and Rob, an apartment-hotel project intended for a steeply sloping site on the Côte d'Azur but never realized, is a good example of Le Corbusier's intention to use the *Monol* model as a synthesis of vernacular forms and the latest construction technology. The units, which stretch out in horizontal ranks along the hillside, on either side of a central, open access stair, are based on a pre-fabricated modular 89 inch (226 centimeter) cube that the architect called *le brevet*. Each unit is composed of three cubes in a row, perpendicular to the hillside. The vaulted roofs, which are reminiscent of sketches Le Corbusier had made of houses he had seen in desert villages in North Africa, were intended to be curved corrugated aluminum sheeting supporting a thin concrete layer covered with earth sown with grass. Portions of the modular grid would have been left open to create an irregular checkerboard pattern of courtyards stepping up the hill. Hellenistic Priene is an obvious historical precedent and the organizational principles are very similar in each case. Horizontal terracing is used in both to adapt to the sheer, cliff-side site as is a central stepping spine, and public plazas carved out of a dense, honeycomb pattern of houses, allowing light and air to penetrate into the midst of the lightly structured, cellular structure of the community.[28]

The defining feature of the Roq and Rob project is structural thinness to the point of frailty and a relentless modular regularity, compared to the relative weight of the earth on the roof. The challenge that this dichotomy presents to previously held images of barrel-vaulted, bearing-wall buildings, is deliberate. The long, narrow interior of the units, with interlocking upper level balconies, recall those of the *Unité d'habitation* in Marseilles, also proposed as a mass-produced solution to postwar housing shortages, but the most obvious difference between the Cap Martin and Marseilles proposals is lightness, airiness and a much more humane relationship to, and connectedness with, the environment in the Roq and Rob project. The *Unité d'habitation* almost single-handedly launched the New Brutalist movement and the tower blocks that are arguably its grim inheritance. It is particularly regrettable that Roq and Rob was never realized to provide a more human alternative.

Maisons Jaoul In 1952, Le Corbusier did build a weightier version of the Cap d'Antibes community at Neuilly-sur-Seine using a different modular interval. The Jaoul houses on the rue de Longchamp lack the wire-frame thinness of the Roq and Rob structures, having rough concrete piers, beams, and vaults, with brick infill and colored glazed tiles pressed into the underside of the vaults, which are exposed as the ceiling of the interior spaces. The beams, which are the end of an enormous vaulted concrete roof, are scaled to support the exposed brick walls on top of them, and so are lateral members taking the thrust of the tiled arches and longitudinal bond beams at the same time. An interwoven arrangement of form-work on the exposed outer edge of these beams creates a basket weave pattern that intentionally offsets their massiveness and visually defrays their critical structure role as the containing frame that holds everything up. This is one of many small

Maisons Jaoul exterior view.   Courtesy of Philippe de Chabot; Flickr

but revealing details that show Le Corbusier's innate understanding of structural forces. Like the Roq and Rob experiment, the Jaoul houses also have sod and grass roofs, but in this instance concrete seems more suitable for the heavy loads that the earth transmits.

The Sarabhai House in Ahmedabad Le Corbusier's intellectual search for a historical, environmental, and technological synthesis as well as a balancing of the polarities in his own personality as revealed in his paintings, sketchbooks, and diaries came to fruition in Ahmedabad, India, in a house designed for Mrs. Manoerama Sarabhai, in 1952. Having been commissioned by Nehru to design the capital city of Chandigarh in East Punjab soon after independence in 1947, Le Corbusier began a series of biannual trips to India, which he was contractually obliged to make. Sketchbooks from these trips, like those he religiously kept from all his travels, reveal a number of important impressions of sites he visited, beginning with the capital complex in New Delhi by Sir Edwin Lutyens and the Jantar Mantar astronomical observatory built by Maharajah Jai Singh in the older section of that city. These initial images were followed in quick succession by those of the *Diwan-i-Am* inside the Red Fort in Delhi, the Mughal city of Fathipur Sikri, the Palace at Sarkej, near Ahmedabad, and especially the pillared pavilion near the palace mosque, and the step well in that city, among other sites.

Balkrishna Doshi, who worked in Le Corbusier's Paris office for five years in the early 1950s, was heavily involved in both the planning and construction of the capital city of Chandigarh. Born in Gujarat and based in Ahmedabad, he was a natural guide to these critical historical monuments and a source of information about them. Ahmedabad was destined to play an important role as a manufacturing center in newly independent India, because of its well-established textile industry, and was a fertile source of commissions for Le Corbusier because of the wealthy Jain families—the owners of the textile mills—who lived there. Through Doshi, he soon met members of the four leading mill-owning families, Kasturbhai Lalbhai, Chinubhai Chimanbhai, Surottam Hutheesing, and Gautam Sarabhai, all of whom supported the growth of cultural and educational institutions in Ahmedabad. They saw the opportunity of having buildings designed by this world famous architect as a rare chance to enhance their city, and acted decisively to engage him. The optimism and syncretism of Le Corbusier and his prospective clients overlapped to a remarkable degree, both he and they wanted to preserve the rich traditions of the region and advance them with the most up-to-date technology.

The Millowner's House During Le Corbusier's first visit to Ahmedabad in March 1951, Chinubhai Chimanbhai commissioned him to design both a cultural center, which included a museum, and a house, while Surottam Hutheesing, the president of the Millowners' Association, asked for a new headquarters overlooking the Sabarmati River, as well as a house for himself. The Chimanbhai house was never realized, and only the museum portion of the cultural center was built, though in greatly altered form. The Millowners' Association was built as designed, but the Hutheesing house was abandoned by its intended owner. The plans were acquired by fellow millowner Shyamubhai Shodan and built exactly as originally designed for another site. Both the Millowners' Association Building and the Shodan House fall into the category of the Maison Citrohan model: frame and flat-plate structures fitted with either a deep egg crate or *brise-soleil* façade and a separate, elevated, "parasol" roof to adapt them to the extreme climate of India. As innovative as these adaptations are, the basic type remains substantially unchanged in them, but his approach to the Sarabhai House advances the diametrical, *Monol*-type considerably. Where the Roq and Rob project had been an attempt to render indigenous pattern in a light, modular frame, and the Maisons Jaoul use a much more muscular concrete frame and brick infill rendition of the Cap Martin idea, the Sarabhai House is organized within a series of parallel bearing walls (with pieces left out to allow cross ventilation), with the vaults in line with the front and back of the house, implying circulation patterns between public and private areas.

Far from being constant, the climate in Ahmedabad has drastic swings from a monsoon season from June to August, when rainfall averages 50 inches (125 centimeters), temperatures vary between 90 and 120 degrees Fahrenheit (32 and 49 degrees Celsius), and the prevailing wind is from the southwest, to a winter season that is dry and cool with temperatures as low as 70 degrees Fahrenheit (21 degrees Celsius), and prevailing winds are from the northeast. The gaps in the parallel bearing walls allowed Le Corbusier to accommodate these extreme shifts, but also provide diagonal views, recalling the Cubist viewpoint, which Le Corbusier began to explore 30 years earlier. In Primitivism, as discussed earlier, reality is perceived as cyclical and episodic rather than teleological and predictable, just as time is understood in traditional societies, and these diagonal views encourage a similar reading of diurnal cycles. Rather than framing linear views, the staccato walls layer them, as well as create shifting patterns of light and shadow, depending on the time of day and season. In stark contrast to many of Le Corbusier's object buildings, which stand in isolated grandeur apart from or above their natural surroundings, as indeed do the Shodan house and the Millowners' Building, the Sarabhai residence is so seamlessly integrated into its lush tropical setting that it seems to be part of it, an impression strengthened by a planted sod roof and a green courtyard in the midst of the house. The earthen roof is refined as an insulative cooling device here with the addition of water channels that traverse it, perhaps inspired by the Mughal gardens that Le Corbusier had seen nearby.

Both this and the parasol introduced at the Villa Shodan (and later made the key design concept of the High Court at Chandigarh) show a concerted effort to come to terms with the lethal power of the sun in India, which is directly overheard well before midday, making the roof the main built surface most susceptible to heat again. Water troughs running across a planted vaulted roof were later the basis for the Sangath studio of Balkrishna Doshi, also in Ahmedabad, a long work in progress finally finished in 1981. Although air conditioning is used in part of the Sarabhai House, installed long before it was generally commercially available in recognition of the client's wish to be comfortable at the hottest time of the year, the house is oriented to the maximize natural ventilation and wide wooden doors that pivot 180 degrees are used to present as little of an obstacle as possible to air moving through the house. Cross ventilation then, as well as the prevalence of concrete, masonry, and stone to increase thermal mass, and the water-cooled earthen roof, are the key environmental strategies used here.

Chandigarh Named after Chandi, the Hindu goddess of power, the new capital city of the Indian side of recently partitioned Punjab region was intended by India's first Prime Minister to announce separation from the past and symbolize hope for the future. Based on his earlier position on urbanism, made manifest in his Plan Voisin for Paris (1925), Plan Obus for Algiers (1932), and a plan for war-ravaged Saint Die (1945–1946), Le Corbusier seemed to be the perfect choice as a *tabula rasa* city planner who would completely ignore history, culture, and context. With his Plan Voisin, he had almost single-handedly launched the modernist myth that by concentrating activities in tall towers, the land below could be returned to nature or parks and gardens for the people (resulting in less-enlightened hands in the desolate, wind-swept plazas in central business districts today). The "brave new world" he envisioned with his Plan Voisin towers flanking multilaned expressways has become a reality, a familiar sterile concrete landscape that is remarkably the same, whether it is encountered in Bulgaria, Buenos Aires, or Riyadh. In his previous plans, Le Corbusier had also demonstrated his eagerness to break with the past: his political views aligned with those who considered historical structures to be nothing more than a regrettable, tangible record of social divisions and class struggle. The Plan Voisin occupied and required the destruction of the entire medieval center of Paris and his plan for Saint-Die ensured the demolition of everything not leveled by Axis bombing, rather than the restoration of an ancient core that had been thoroughly documented and could have been at least partially rebuilt. But Chandigarh would be different, because it was a *tabula rasa*, in which the architect had to find parameters to anchor it to its vast, open plain. The axiom that restrictions are a blessing in design is proven by exception here: Le Corbusier chose to rely upon themes prevalent in "A Poem to the Right Angle" that he wrote at the time of this commission. In it, he describes the place of the human being in nature and the cosmos, in an attempt to make sense of the boundless parameters presented to him in the Punjab. At Chandigarh, he relied first on immutable, seasonal patterns and the sun as the most predictable of these, to establish boundaries: a "tower of shadows" remains as a shrine dedicated solely to his study of solar patterns. His opening moves in designing this city reveal an elemental strategy traceable to Stonehenge as a means of establishing a place in a trackless universe and inform his first steps in conjuring a specific vocabulary of architecture for Chandigarh. The Sarabhai House shows that he came to realize that the sun is not always an enemy in India, that it is welcome for four months during the winter, and that the sunshades that he was adapting as a critical part of his urban vocabulary, based on regional precedents, could accommodate that need. As Le Corbusier later wrote of this realization:

> besides the administrative and financial regulations there was the Law of the Sun in India: a calendar of sensational temperature, extraordinary heat, dry or humid according to the season or the location. The architectural problem consists: first of all to make shade, second to make a current of air (to ventilate), third to control hydraulics (to evacuate rain water). This necessitated a real apprenticeship and an unprecedented adaptation of modern methods.

This "law" dictated every move he made, from the choice of material with sufficient thermal mass to withstand the withering heat, to the orientation of streets in what was then still a relatively automobile-free country to avoid having to drive into the sun in the future, and burrowing into the ground for protection from it. His response to this "law" in his design for the High Court of Justice was particularly inspired, an institutional application of the parasol roof that he had introduced in the Villa Shoden on a monumental scale. At the High Court, it is supported on arches shaped to generate and accelerate the flow of air through it, so it both shades the second, closing roof below it and washes it with a steady laminar flow of air. The main entrance is also sized and oriented to catch and direct as much breeze as possible, the remainder of the interior converted into a soaring cool, dark, cave-like space in which ramps are used to reduce the amount of heat-generating, calorie-burning effort needed to reach the upper levels. Relegating the majority of the interior of the High Court of the portion not allocated as office or courtroom space, to darkness, reflects Le Corbusier's realization that cross ventilation is useless as a cooling strategy during the hottest time of the year, and that the only effective tactic was the "creation of cool interiors, as large as possible, and as amply protected from the southwest sun as ingenuity and funds permit." During this critical superheated period, he found, "the only defense is to retreat behind massive walls or their equivalent, with every aperture closed, and if possible sealed."

Le Corbusier chose concrete to provide the thermal mass necessary to create these massive walls and cool interiors, but this technological part of his tradition through science equations resulted in a high investment of human capital. A reporter observing construction described how more than 30,000 men and women, working seven days a week, poured concrete from buckets carried on their heads, climbed up bamboo scaffolding, and mixed mortar with their feet. Aggregate was made from boulders that were broken with hammers, and asphalt was poured and spread on roads individually by workers who wrapped their hands in burlap sacks to keep them from being burned.

A New Tradition The financial restrictions that made this hand labor necessary became Le Corbusier's second parameter, after "the Law of the sun" and climate. The third parameter he chose, to bracket the infinity of choices made possible by an open-ended site and ambitious nationalistic brief, was symbolism, referring back once again to his earlier, Cubist roots. At Chandigarh, Le Corbusier relied heavily on universal, primitive phenomenology, cosmological themes and iconographic references specifically drawn from regional sources, to an extent not seen in his earlier architecture or planning projects. The governmental center contains especially overt anthropological analogies, but more than being a straightforward gesture of respect to Indian heritage, they have been identified as "being in accord with Le Corbusier's definitions of 'types' that is, forms that have been refined over a long period of everyday use resulting in a careful selection based on utility, function and aesthetics."

The City as a House, the House as a City As a true rationalist Le Corbusier saw the historical city as not just a random assemblage of buildings, but rather a laboratory full of specimens waiting to be classified, with the most successful of these, as proven through evolution, fit to be selected and refined for future repetition. In his final city, he determined that traditional responses to physical as well as psychic well-being were far more effective than forms alone and that technology should be assigned a supporting rather than a leading role in providing those benefits.

As Chandigarh has matured, Le Corbusier's intentions have become clearer, as residents' satisfaction with their city continues to grow. Focus on the center in the media during and just after construction, for many of the same reasons that have already been discussed here, tended to obscure the fact that most of the master plan is given over to housing, organized along green fingers that extend out from the more megalithic and photogenic palm. These wide pathways are now filled with trees and are much appreciated by those who live and work along the shaded streets that connect the public residential parts of the capital. In a sense, Chandigarh is the urbanistic realization of the *Monol* experiment, finally proven in the Sarabhai residence in Ahmedabad, with its residential part being a model for the green city of the future.

Auguste Perret: Apartment House on Rue Franklin, Paris

Auguste Perret was born in Ixelles, Belgium, in 1874. His family, which was French, had taken refuge there as a result of the Communard Insurrection of 1871, and they returned to Paris in 1881 when the political climate was more favorable. Auguste entered the *Ecole des Beaux Arts*, but did not graduate because he, like his brother Gustave who entered with him, had always intended to join their father's construction company instead.[29] At the time he attended the *Ecole*, its curriculum was extensively based on Classical principles. The school had began before the French Revolution as a training ground for a select group of young architects who were primarily intended to serve the monarchy, which patronized their education. Several embarrassing structural failures led to the parallel establishment of an engineering branch, the *Ecole Polytechnique*, starting the schism that defines the two fields today. After the revolution, Napoleon Bonaparte was under a great deal of pressure to disband the schools because of their royalist associations, but decided instead to make the entry requirements less stringent and not based on connections to the aristocracy. While admission was easier, the requirements necessary to remain in the school were made more difficult, so attrition was high and the number of students who finally matriculated approximated the size of the earlier classes. To deliberately choose to withdraw from such a competitive and prestigious program in 1895 was courageous and demonstrates a highly focused sense of purpose.

The Rational Tradition Although his exposure to *Ecole des Beaux Arts* theory was abbreviated, Perret still managed to assimilate a great deal of the Rationalist tradition of the school, which dovetailed nicely with its emphasis on Classicism. The architecture of Classical Greece and Rome, after all, is based on harmony and proportion and the logical structural relationship of parts to the whole. Perret adopted the ideas of Abbé Laugier, who, in his *Essai sur l'Architecture*, proposed a return to basic typological elements as an antidote to the excesses of the *ancien régime*. Laugier offered a more simplified approach as an alternative to the overdecorated Baroque and Rococo styles that were favored by the court, suggesting a simple column and beam system based on natural forms. The frontpiece of his book has an engraving of a rough, wooden structure made entirely of pieces of tree trunk, cut into columns and lintels and beams that support a pitched roof, which Laugier calls "the primitive hut." The influence, of course, was that architects should return to essentials.

Perret did that by helping to arrange for his family firm, then known as Perret Fréres, to be one of the few in Paris to be licensed to use a reinforced concrete system devised and patented by Francoise Hennebique.[30] Hennebique was one of the first engineers to realize that by embedding steel bars, which were deformed to allow them to adhere, into concrete, it was possible to take advantage of both the strength of masonry in compression and the tensile strength of the steel, which make an almost perfect material when combined. The advantage of this unity is augmented by the fact that the modulus of elasticity, or expansion in hot weather and retraction in cold, is very similar in both the concrete and the steel, increasing their compatibility.

Limestone Is Prevalent Because limestone is so prevalent in the area around Paris, it has commonly been used in the past for building. But it is not strong enough for large, straight spans, and so has typically been used in either solid walls or arched arcades. As has been discussed earlier in this service, in an analysis of the evolution of the Place Royale in Paris into the Place Vosges, wood has also been popular as a construction material, and in that instance as elsewhere was often replaced by stone at a later date. Wood requires the use of a frame system, however, rather than the monolithic bearing wall system required by masonry. Reinforced concrete, however, finally allowed masonry to be used like wood, in a lightweight frame system that was much stronger and capable of much longer spans than its timber counterpart. Auguste Perret's interest then was to use reinforced concrete in a trabeated, post and lintel frame system that was much lighter and more flexible than masonry buildings in Paris had been in the past.[31] He was inspired by two books in this quest, which allowed him to join together Classical trabeation with reinforced concrete construction: the first study of Classical precedents and *Le Beton Armé*, by Paul Christophe, released three years later, which details reinforced concrete construction and the advantages of the Hennebique system.

The House on Rue Franklin In 1903 Auguste Perret, along with his brother Gustave, designed and built an apartment house on the Rue Franklin in Paris that marks an important transition point from the limestone bearing wall masonry tradition that had been used in Paris since the Middle Ages to the modern townhouse typology found there today. It is very modest in scale and is essentially six single family units, which each occupies a single floor, stacked on top of a reception and service lobby that also contains the elevator and stairs that lead up to them, with two additional units of a different configuration on top of them, making eight units in all in an equal number of floors. Each of the lower six are efficiently organized in a "U" toward the stair, elevator, and service bathroom core at the back. A bar, running parallel to one of the legs of the "U," contains a galley kitchen, which has direct access to the service core and stair to facilitate direct deliveries. The rooms in the interior of the single level flat consist of a dining area adjacent to this kitchen bar, which also has a separate entrance at street level to avoid having deliveries going through the lobby, a "drawing" or living room in the middle, and a bedroom on the other side, adjacent to the bathroom component of the service core in the rear. The lip of the kitchen/dining leg of the "U" extends out to become a "smoking room" on one side and a "boudoir" on the bedroom leg of the other, using nomenclature that is indicative of the social mores of a middle class family that would have occupied one of these flats at the turn of the twentieth century in pre–World War I Paris. In spite of their modest means, and the relatively small size of their apartments, the occupants of these units would have had domestic help and would probably have entertained frequently. Guests would first have been received in the drawing room, and then have moved into the dining room, after which men would have retreated to the smoking room for brandy and cigars, while women would have returned to the drawing room for conversation there. Sliding doors would have closed off the bedroom from view, as well as its attached boudoir, which was a dressing room for women. Each of the rooms on the sides of the "U," that is, the dining room and its adjacent smoking room, as well as the bedroom and its symmetrically projecting boudoir, has a fireplace, so that two chimneys that project up through the deck of the two idiosyncratic units at the top of the apartment tower and past them, to expel smoke at a safe distance above the roof of the penthouse flat at the top, bracket the units below. Windows at the top of each end of the "U," as well as at the end of the galley facing the street, ensure that the kitchen, smoking room, and boudoir are flooded with natural light. Angled windows next to these introduced light into the dining room and bedroom, and an Oriole window in the center lets light into the drawing room at the heart of each house. French doors, which make up the angled windows, provide access out to a reasonably large balcony, attached to both the dining room and bedroom, completing the thoughtful provision of humane amenities through these extremely well-planned flats. No room, except the hallway that joins the service core to each flat, is without light and natural ventilation. Service, and access to it, is well provided for. The public areas of each flat work as an entity, without compromising the integrity of the private zone. Access to each zone is well worked out so that entering and leaving each flat as the building itself is compartmentalized and can be managed in a way that is considerate of the privacy of others. The plan of the unit is brilliant and deceptively simple.

Style as a Function of Technology Auguste Perret, who was a professor at the *Ecole des Pants et Chaussees* in Paris, keeping with his proficiency in engineering, taught his students that style in architecture is technically determined, that is, that it is the result of the materials used and the construction method required to build with them.[32] This theory, which was also popularized by Viollet-le-Duc at the time the apartment house on Rue Franklin was built, sought to explain Classical Greek or Gothic Architecture, for example, as products of the building technology available at the time, but did so at the expense of social habits and conventions and other cultural dictates of form. The theory does not account for the Greeks' desire to transform a vernacular timber system into marble as the temple evolved, due to symbolic associations, or the commitment of the builders of the Gothic Cathedral to striking a balance between mysticism and subjectivity on the one hand, and empiricism and scholastic rationalism on the other.[33] Each style is indeed a product of the highest level of building skill possible at the time, but also of the social norms that prevailed as well, as is the apartment house on Rue Franklin.

Jean Prouvé: *Maison Tropicale*

Jean Prouvé was born in Nancy, France, in 1901. His father had helped to form an art collective there, which is now known as the School of Nancy, based on the idea of strengthening the connection between art, social awareness, and industrial production, in order to make it more accessible to everyone. This had a formative effect on his ideas about the role of design. He apprenticed with a well-known metal worker and blacksmith in Paris, and worked with many well-known architects and furniture designers throughout France at that time. His career trajectory is similar to that of Pierre Chareau, the architect of the *Maison de Verre*, discussed elsewhere here, with whom Prouvé shares the French tradition of being an engineer-architect, who got extensively involved in the design of each element of the buildings he was involved in. Following World War II, Prouvé was commissioned by the Ministry of Reconstruction to design houses for the homeless, and he built a factory in Maxeüille to mass-produce prefabricated components for this purpose in 1947.

His lack of conventional training, which is a characteristic that he shared with a surprising number of other modern architects, was, perhaps, one of the main reasons for his objectivity, and his talent in being able to point out the failure of contemporary architects to fully utilize the potential of industrialization. Ludwig Mies van der Rohe, who, like Prouvé, also came to architecture through a building trade, repeatedly said that the art of building only really existed when technology had reached complete fulfillment, and that the goal of Modernism should be to encourage building and industrialization to grow together. Prouvé sought to reach that fulfillment in metal, which was the medium that he knew best, and his unquestionable success in achieving it has been an inspiration to many others who have attempted to explore the architectural potential of technology ever since.

An Engineer-Architect Serving mostly in the capacity of engineering consultant to other architects throughout his career, Prouvé constantly looked for ways to introduce the techniques of industrial production into the profession, and to also have the building trades benefit from the efficiencies that have been realized there. He frequently noted that the construction process today has really changed little since the Middle Ages. It still depends primarily on separate trades working sequentially rather than in unison toward what should be a common goal. In that process, however, he realized that the architect no longer fulfilled the key role of the master builder of the past, being largely separated from the construction sequence once the working drawing stage had been completed. This division from the actual building phase, in his view, had also been aggravated by the cult of individuality that had been introduced as early as the Renaissance, but accelerated by the Modern Movement, which tacitly encouraged the development of distinct stylistic personalities that looked upon standardization as being anathema to individuality. As an alternative, Prouvé recommended that architects seek reunion with the building process. As a first step in that reunion, he advocated that they come to have a far better understanding of the materials that they specify, including the way in which these materials are made, in order to more fully appreciate their characteristics. By also becoming familiar with the way the machines that produce those materials operate, Prouvé also felt that architects could utilize them better. He differed from a majority of his contemporaries in his respect, rather than disdain, for the lessons of the past, and rather than considering historical monuments to be technologically primitive, as might be expected, he saw that each of the best of them was a complete expression of the most advanced physical knowledge and tectonic skill available at the time of their construction.

Techné When considered in this way, a megaron, pyramid, or Gothic cathedral begin to take on a completely new dimension, reminding us that *techné*, which is the Greek root word in "technology," represents craftsmanship and no electronic wizardry. When carried out as the combined effort of an entire culture, rather than a single individual, this craftsmanship carries a special kind of inspiration in it that Prouvé perceptively identified as being absent in the majority of the architecture built today, making it dead in a sociological sense. While similar feelings have been expressed by a few enlightened and more traditionally minded architects from the developing world in the past, Prouvé parts company with them in his belief that this lost inspiration will return only when the full potential of industry is realized in architecture. To do this, he also proposes that in addition to involving architects in the manufacturing process, they must also be educated differently. In the system he proposes, the conventional pedantic emphasis on methods of construction should be replaced with a stress upon the idea of a building as being composed of elements that each have infinite variations much like the parts of the automobile or the notes of a musical scale. While the numbers of notes on the scale are fixed, the possibilities within that system have been used to create seemingly endless combinations.

Of all his projects, his *Maison du Peuple*, designed in conjunction with Bodansky, Beaudouin, and Lods in Clichy, near Paris, is possibly the best example of his philosophy that architecture must totally harmonize with the methods of its production. Made up of entirely movable walls, floors, and ceiling panels, wrapped in stressed, spring-loaded metal panels, the building clearly defines what Prouvé meant when he spoke of the need to produce "conditioned" buildings descendant of this philosophy; its architect Norman Foster, perhaps more than any other designer today, seems to personify the new attitude toward technology that Prouvé had in mind.

In the many exhibitions of his work that he organized, Prouvé used the word "*Constructeur*" as a title rather than architect or engineer. The word is difficult to translate into English, having mixed connotations of contractor, master builder, and even mechanic in it. The title is very appropriate for him, as he was all of these, serving as an example of the multidisciplinary talents necessary to cope with today's highly complex construction industry.

The Maison Tropicale While the *Maison du Peuple* is widely regarded as Prouvé's greatest large-scale commission, his prototypical *Maison Tropicale* is generally thought to be one of his most visionary residential projects. He designed this house as a prototype to be used in the French colonial enterprise in North Africa soon after World War II, and three of them were actually produced between 1949 and 1951 and built in Brazzaville. They follow his basic principles of designing buildings and furniture that were efficiently conceived and could be logically and inexpensively fabricated for general use. He was primarily involved in developing prefabrication techniques that would make this goal possible, focusing on ease of production and assembly, primarily in aluminum.

The *Maison Tropicale* prototype was mostly built of prefabricated aluminum parts. It was raised off the ground and had a wide, covered verandah running around the entire perimeter. The cover of this verandah was part of an all-encompassing gable roof, which extended out over the enclosure surrounding the main living area, with a set of three operable louvers forming a deep cornice for the roof on all four sides of the house. This louvered cornice allowed the occupants to control the amount of sun and air coming into the house at all times of the day. A ventilator, similar to those used on barns to prevent the interior from overheating, ran the entire length of the gable ridge. Slender pipe columns spaced at regular intervals around the perimeter of the house supported the gable overhang, making it possible to break the louver assemblage in the deep cornice into shorter bays. This gave it more strength and less chance of deflection. The *Maison Tropicale*, which was a rectilinear I plan, was five modules wide and seven modules long with a wooden deck inset into a deep metal foundation frame on the verandah position of the house. The demountable floor to ceiling enclosure walls, which are also made of aluminum, were perforated with large circular holes to allow cross circulation. Some of these panels were fixed and others were intended to slide.

GERMANY

Ludwig Mies van der Rohe: Weissenhofsiedlung

Ludwig Mies van der Rohe was born in Aachen, Germany, in 1886 and apprenticed with his father as a stonemason. Aachen is particularly rich in the number of historical artifacts and meaningful associations that it has, in a nation with no shortage of them. The most important of these is the Palatine Chapel of the

Emperor Charlemagne, which was built soon after the beginning of the first millennium and marked the end of the Dark Ages in Europe. Mies van der Rohe was surrounded by masterpieces of stone construction as he grew up and as a young apprentice had many important monuments to inspire him. At the age of 19, he went to Berlin to work with architect Bruno Paul, and three years later joined the office of Peter Behrens. Behrens was one of the most influential architects in Europe at that time, having managed to divert attention away from the Arts and Crafts Movement in England by securing the commission to design a country home for the Bassett-Loewke family called "New Ways." Although this is a relatively small project, it had enormous significance because the choice of Behrens to design it pre-emoted the influence of Charles Rennie Mackintosh, who had renovated a small townhouse at Derngate for the same family and had expected to be given the chance to work on this larger house himself. It was a personal blow to Mackintosh, but in a larger sense was also a repudiation by a member of the British upper-middle class of what was then called "English-Free Architecture," or the more traditionally based version of Modernism that Mackintosh represented.

Passing the Torch The commissioning of Peter Behrens to design New Ways then marks the symbolic passing of the torch of the impetus behind Modernist architecture from Britain to Germany, and Ludwig Mies van der Rohe was perfectly positioned to become one of the leaders of the next generation to carry that torch forward. Behrens eventually became the corporate architect for the *Allemagne Electricish Geselshaft* or AEG, the national supplier of electricity, with the responsibility of designing everything related to the public image of the company, in addition to its factories and office buildings. His Turbine Works for AEG, built in Berlin just after World War I, is a masterful example of his attempt to balance historical and modern elements by using the latest industrial materials available to him, while also employing metaphysical references to both institutional and rural precedents that would both enable the workers in the factory and make them feel more at home.

Disparate Influences While he was working for Peter Behrens, Ludwig Mies van der Rohe interacted with just about everyone who was of any importance in the Modern Movement in both Germany and Europe as a whole, and yet he claimed as major influences the work of two people who were not part of that elite group. Karl Friedrich Schinkel, who was the first of these, was a Prussian architect, who practiced during the later half of the nineteenth century and whose Altes Gallery in Berlin is generally considered to be one of his best projects as well as the most important early museum after the Louvre in Paris. Mies van der Rohe was drawn to the Classical strain in Schinkel's rational language, and this would surface again and again in all of his later projects, in a wide variety of scales and contextural relationships.

The second rather surprising influence on Mies van der Rohe's architecture was Frank Lloyd Wright, who became well-known in Germany right after World War I because of the publication of a monograph on his work by the Berlin-based firm of Wasmuth. This so-called "Wasmuth Portfolio" made its way through the ateliers of Germany to Holland, France, and England as well, and had a profound impact in each country that surfaced in various ways. In the Netherlands Robert van't Hoff popularized Wright's more open approach to space planning in ways that arguably culminated in the De Stijl movement in that country later on. In Germany, however, the effect that the Portfolio had is more difficult to trace, but can be found primarily in the tendency of Ludwig Mies van der Rohe to "break the box," just as Wright prescribed. This term, which Wright used frequently, referred to his belief that conventional room divisions, separated by walls, should be eliminated in residential design and should be replaced by a free flow of space from zone to zone, in what is now more commonly referred to as an open plan.

In a house he designed early in his career, Mies van der Rohe famously expanded Wright's open plan idea by extending the peripheral walls of the residence far beyond the edge of the enclosure, like tentacles stretching out to hold onto the adjacent land. This exaggerated extension of the walls, as well as the opening up of the interior, the use of brick throughout, the flat roof and extensive use of glass, helped update the rather historicist image of Wright's Prairie School typology for a new generation of Modernists.

A Humiliating Defeat Ludwig Mies van der Rohe opened his own office in 1912, at age 26, just two years before the military conflagration that was to have such tragic social and economic consequences for his country. He, like many other Modernist architects of his generation, such as Walter Gropius, fought in that war, and the humiliation of defeat as well as the crippling reparations that followed left an indelible imprint on their collective psyches. They seemed to emerge from the experience with a fierce determination to raise their nation up again through design excellence, which they saw as the only avenue open to them. It is instructive that the German entry in the International Exhibition, held in Barcelona, Spain, in 1929, and designed by Mies van der Rohe, was a small pavilion that replicated the open plan and extended walls of his earlier brick house, but had a skeleton of chrome-wrapped steel columns, with marble space dividers instead. This "Barcelona Pavilion" is now regarded as an icon of early Modernist principles, which, along with its minimal spatial message, established a new standard for furniture design as well. Mies van der Rohe had absorbed the essential lesson preached by Adolf Loos, of the need to use the most luxurious materials possible in the interior of a house, to adequately reflect its role as a refuge from the rigors of daily life in the public realm, and proclaimed it to the world as part of a more ambitious mission in this pavilion. That mission was nothing less than the reconstruction of the international reputation of his country through the mechanism of renewed industrial production and a culture of design excellence, which would raise the gross national product and expedite economic recovery. There were no kitschy stalls with *leiderhosen* clad bartenders selling steins of German beer or any of the other more commonplace examples of national self-promotion here, just a stunningly beautiful and blissfully minimal pavilion, which was empty except for several exquisite chairs, tables, and benches that Mies van der Rohe also designed for his setting to represent his country and its present and future intentions.

The Villa Tugendhat in Brno, Czechoslovakia Shortly afterward, in 1928, Mies van der Rohe produced his first conceptual sketches for a house for Grete Weiss Low-Beer and Fritz Tugendhat, located on Cernopolni Street in Brno. The site slopes away from the street quite dramatically toward the southwest, which is also the direction of the center of Brno and Spilberk castle, which is the most visible

230

monument there.[34] The clients accepted his idea, which was radically new at the time, of using a steel frame system similar to the one he had introduced at the Barcelona Pavilion the year before, and then dividing spaces with the freestanding screens. They asked that several of these columns, which are cruciform in shape and also wrapped in chrome, be recessed into the wall, so that movement between spaces would be easier. They also asked the architect to shade the large areas of glass. But otherwise, they entirely approved his approach.[35]

Using the Slope to Best Advantage Mies van der Rohe took advantage of the steeply sloping site by locating an entrance and a garage on street level at the top of the hill. The roadside elevation is modestly long and low, with the house separated from the sidewalk and the street by a custom-designed steel mesh fence, which runs the entire length of the site except in front of the garage. The roof of the house is flat and the roof and the roofline are continuous, broken only by the vertical shaft of a chimney.

The front door at this level led into the top floor where the bedrooms and bath areas were located. Two bedrooms, for the couple's children and their nanny, as well as a shared bathroom were located on the street side, while the master bedroom and bath, as well as a dressing room, were located across from them, on the side overlooking the garden, the hill, and the grand distant view of the city beyond. From this upper level, where all the bedrooms and bathrooms are also located, a glass-enclosed spiral stair leads down to the living area, which has a dramatic view of the center of the city of Brno in the distance through floor-to-ceiling glass windows, as well as a landscaped garden in the foreground. The concept behind the use of a steel frame system was to have this level be as open as possible, with only one semicircular divider made of ebony wood, demarcating the dining area, and another short straight screen, made of onyx, used to separate the living room from a more private sitting area. The floor-to-ceiling glass used along the exterior wall facing the downhill side of the house makes the interior space seem much larger than it actually is and allows light to flood the space. Mies van der Rohe positioned the onyx wall so that it would seem to glow at sunset, making it translucent at that hour of the day. This level of attention to detail is typical of this architect's work, and he custom designed every part of the house, including furniture, door handles and hinges, heating and air conditioning ducts and pipes, carpets, and curtains. To satisfy his client's request that the amount of glare inside the living area be reduced, he used a black, beige, and white silk velvet material for the curtains along the floor-to-ceiling glass walls in certain areas to separate certain zones and make the space seem smaller, if need be.

The Essence of Opulence The floor was covered with white linoleum, and this, in combination with the chrome-covered columns and curtain rails, semicircular ebony wood dining enclosure, onyx wall and bluish white velvet silk curtains, as well as the white leather and chrome furniture that Mies van der Rohe had made for the house, must have conveyed an overwhelming impression of opulence. In critiques that appeared at the time, the house and its architect were judged to be an example of conspicuous consumption, built at the expense of the economically disadvantaged, such as the workers.

The Weissenhof Estate in Stuttgart Ludwig Mies van der Rohe was perfectly capable of designing minimalist workers' housing, however, which was an essential part of his Modernist credential. He was selected as the master planner of such a complex, or *siedlung*, by the membership of the Deutsche Werkbund at their meeting in Bremen in 1925, which was intended to provide prototypes of the kinds of houses that could be built for working class families with limited financial resources. It has 60 house units of different kinds, built of the latest materials available at the time. The housing complex was part of an exhibition called "The Dwelling" (*Die Wohnung*) that was held in Stuttgart from September 6 until October 31, 1927.[36] Mies van der Rohe himself designed the central housing block of the complex, and also commissioned 17 other prominent European Modernists to contribute to the *seidlung*. These included Walter Gropius, Le Corbusier, and J. J. P Oud, who provided schemes for single family and multifamily units as well as terrace houses and apartment blocks. Mies van der Rohe started out with the intention of providing a proper setting for what he termed "New Living" that would transcend purely rational and functional requirements, and he begin to explore the spatial possibilities that new materials and structural innovations offered.

HOLLAND

Gerrit Rietveld and Theo van Doesburg: The Schroeder House

It occasionally happens in the history of contemporary architecture that a building will emerge that perfectly reflects a new theory or, even more fortunately, a key aspect of the spirit of its time. The Schroeder house, in Utrecht, Holland, designed by Gerrit Rietveld is one such building. It is something of a miracle that it was realized at all, given its location at the end of a row of conventional brick apartment houses on Prins Henriklaan, at the edge of a middle class suburb in the southeastern part of the city. It is next to a large park and was originally conceived so that openings in the wall on that side were wider to take maximum advantage of the view. In a majority of the photographs that have appeared of the house over the years, it looks rather large in scale, because the row houses that it is connected to have been skillfully eliminated. But, it is actually diminutive when seen in its true context, since it is about half as high as they are, although equally as long. It is 9.6 meters wide and 12.5 meters long, but has 3.7 meter ceiling heights throughout, which is much higher than a conventional house. This proportion gives the interior of the house an air of spaciousness that defies its small perimeter.

The client was a single parent with three children. She had a restricted budget, but wanted the house to be as open and as free of furniture as possible to accommodate her family. She was also a painter and wanted an artist's studio with north light and a good view. This direction encouraged her architect, Gerrit Rietveld, to open the house as much as possible and to design built-in furniture to save space.

De Stijl This commission, however modest, allowed Rietveld and his partner Theo van Doesburg to test several new ideas that they had been exploring, related to what American architect Frank Lloyd Wright had described as "breaking the box." Wright's work had become well-known in Europe as a result of a monograph on him that had been published by the German firm Wasmuth just before World

War I. He had managed to open up the traditional pattern of enclosed residential spatial arrangements in which individual rooms were set aside for a living room, a dining room, and a kitchen, for example, replacing this series of contained volumes with a free flow of space in which functions were defined by custom-designed, built-in furniture arrangements.

This new approach was best expressed in Wright's Robie House, in Oak Park, near Chicago, in 1910, in which permanent wood screens help to define space and provide privacy wherever necessary, but still allow a feeling of openness throughout the lower two levels of the house. Wright's experimentation with the idea of the free flow of space stopped short of bedrooms and bathrooms.

Wright's work and ideas were promoted in Holland by such influential figures as Henrik Berlage, J. J. P. Oud, and Robert van't Hoff. Berlage, who designed the *Beurs*, in the middle of Amsterdam, as well as being the impetus behind a new master plan for that city, was the leader of a movement related to a rediscovery of traditional values in the Netherlands, and so his endorsement of Wright had considerable weight.

Other developments were then taking place throughout Europe, which, when layered over Wright's revolutionary insight, created the intellectual climate necessary to take his ideas further into an even more abstract realm. One of these local breakthroughs was Cubism, which was being advanced by French artists such as Braque, Picasso, and Duchamp, even Cézanne, starting in 1907.[37] The goal of this movement was to challenge the conventions of visualization that had been in place since the Renaissance, based on the idea of perspective, and to replace them with what these artists maintained was a more accurate rendition of the way people perceive the world. They argued that, rather than experiencing space from a fixed point, looking out to the horizon, as Renaissance masters such as Leonardo da Vinci, Brunelleschi, Michelangelo, and Raphael had proposed, people really absorb their surroundings in fragments as they move their head and eyes. This is especially true when they are seen at speed, from a train or a streetcar, which was the new factor that made the Renaissance theory redundant. These artists experimented with new ways of describing reality, involving time as well as space, as shown in the painting *Nude Descending Staircase* by Marcel Duchamp. In that instance, the artist attempts to show the entire event, depicting movement in sequence from the top of the stair to the bottom, as a series of overlapping broken images that convey the actual experience of watching the action rather than a perfect, realistic rendering of one point in time while it was taking place.

In Holland, artist Piet Mondrian began to experiment with these ideas in his paintings of landscapes, and of trees in particular. Between 1907 and 1914 his method of expression evolved in a more minimal, abstract direction until, by the end of that period, his trees were nothing more than pure linear forms, rhythmically organized on the canvas with the landscape around them shown as planes of pure color. Mondrian was also influenced by the theosophical philosophy that was then also popular with several influential architects, which promoted the idea of a higher spiritual order, based on mathematical laws that transcended reality.[38]

Elsewhere in Europe at that time, between 1912 and 1920, other architects like Le Corbusier were attempting to translate Cubist experimentation into built form, by combining its principles with the mechanistic images of industrialization and production. This attempt, which became known as Purism because of the intention to simplify the means of expression that was being used and make it more abstract, in the same way that Modernism was refining his landscapes, emerged as Constructivism in Russia, soon after the Revolution.

All of these revelations, taken together, inspired Gerrit Rietveld and Theo van Doesburg to put forward a Dutch variant, which they called simply *De Stijl* or "the Style." They, like the Purists, saw the legacy of the Arts and Crafts Movement, which had been reborn in Germany in the Deutsche Werkbund and first and second Bauhaus, as being tainted by the desire for materialism and tied too closely to the cycle of commodification. They wanted to elevate their new language to the level of antimateriality, as a spatial expression that was free of conventional restrictions, layered over with the aura of divine inevitability that had previously been adopted by the Theosophists. Their movement included artists, sculptors, and craftspeople as well as architects, and the house for Madame Schroeder was to be the first, three-dimensional evidence of their claims.

This debate, between those who favored the Arts and Crafts approach, perfected by the Scottish architect Charles Rennie Mackintosh, of marrying handicraft and assembly line production and those who wanted mechanization to reign supreme, unhindered by human intervention had been going on since the latter half of the nineteenth century. The leaders of the *De Stijl* movement wanted to resolve the issue once and for all, in favor of what historian William Curtis has described as "spiritualized, mechanized abstraction."[39]

In the Schroeder house, that translates into asymmetrical three-dimensional composition made up of a series of horizontal and vertical lines and planes, rendered in a series of primary colors, in addition to black, white, and grey.

Rietveld aimed to make these planes appear to float in space, concurrent with the *De Stijl* intention of contravening materiality. This was similar to a theme in the work of Supremacist Kasimir Malevich who advocated the ideal of weightlessness as a beginning point in the design process, with gravity factored back into it incrementally, and only in the minimal amounts necessary for structural stability. His idea was to replicate the perfect condition of the spiritual realm he aspired to. The *De Stijl* architects were equally utopian in their approach and seemed to be even more intent on conveying the impression of weightlessness than their Russian counterparts.

Changing Fields of Vision Rietveld and van Doesburg conceived of the house as a three-dimensional, habitable sculpture, to the extent of organizing the composition in such a way as to take advantage of the changing fields of vision that a viewer would experience in approaching it. They planned the intersection of horizontal and vertical lines and planes to be appreciated from three sequential zones.[40] The first of this is defined by a gate that closes off the street, Prins Hendriklaan, on which the house is located, so that a corner window, on both the ground and first floors, is detailed to look continuous and to wrap around the 90 degree angle of the edge, rather than just being purchased through each wall surface at that point. This is consistent with the approach of using solid planes and voids to imply space, rather than delimit it that is used throughout the project. A balcony covered by a deep, flat horizontal plane that acts as an eave and that is partially supported by a thin vertical member contributes to the assembly at that edge, as does a wide vertical band that designates the circulation "core" or stair. The second rapidly diminishing field of vision is defined by a gate in a fence around the property and a garden path leading to a patio in front of a study on the ground floor. The glass door, used as an entrance here is framed with glass shelves, and the study is shaded by the projecting balcony above. The third field of vision in this progressive sequence, which is now internal, is toward the southeastern corner of the house, toward a living area and a kitchen that is partially shielded from view by a high counter. Rietveld tried to use a balcony to extend the view from the interior of the house toward the park.

The first floor of the house was designed as a studio for Madame Schroeder, to give her the best light and view possible, and the bedrooms and bathrooms are also located on that level for privacy. Throughout the house there is no consistent, axial approach to space, and elements such as window frames, door frames, columns, balconies, and railings, all painted in a variety of primary colors, serve instead to make points of transition. The approach to structure is equally unconventional, since the construction system is a mixture of steel, concrete, and wood frame. Steel was necessary to provide the stiffness that was lost in places where corners have been opened up to convey the visual sense of openness and spatial freedom that Rietveld wanted. He pushed the limits of structural integrity here to do so, and the progression shown in the numerous study models he produced is toward more and more openness as time went on.

John Hejduk: The Wall House

John Hejduk was as much a philosopher as an architect, in the same way that Louis Kahn was. Each of them was concerned with the abstract meaning of elements and their relationship in architecture as well as their interaction with the people that inhabit a building. The design of the spaces was the end result of their search for this meaning, rather than being an end in itself. Hejduk, whose background was Dutch, started to explore these interests in depth in a series of houses he called "Nine Square Texas" between 1868 and 1974, and his own description of these tells the whole story:

> The problems of point-line-plane-volume, the facts of square-circle-triangle, the mysteries of central-peripheral-frontal-oblique-concavity-convexity, of right angle of perpendicular, of perspective, the comprehension of sphere-cylinder-pyramid, the questions of structure-construction-organization, the question of scale, of position, the interest in post-lintel, wall-slab, the extent of a limited field, of an unlimited field, the meaning of plan, of section, the meaning of spatial expansion-spatial compression-spatial tension, the direction of regulating lines, of grids, the forces of implied extension, the relationships of figure to ground, of number to proportion, of measurement to scale, of symmetry to asymmetry, of diamond to diagonal, the hidden forces, the ideas of configuration, the static with the dynamic, all begin to take on the form of a vocabulary.[41]

In the early 1960s a book entitled *Five Architects* appeared that featured the work of Peter Eisenman, Michael Graves, Charles Gwathmey, John Hejduk, and

235

The Wall House.   Courtesy of Robert Plaskota; Flickr

Richard Meier. Their joint allegiance to the five points of Le Corbusier at that time was the reason behind the joint publication. These points, as described in detail elsewhere here, were intended as a kind of shorthand, to describe the advantages provided by the use of a steel or reinforced concrete frame system, and the formal implications of its use. For Le Corbusier and these five disciples, among many others, the use of the frame, or "grid" in lieu of bearing walls allowed architects much more latitude and freedom in the design process. It meant that rather than being dependant for support on the location of bearing walls, which then determined the size and location of specific rooms, a column-supported slab allowed room dividers to be relieved of structural responsibility so that they could be placed anywhere. A point loaded rather than a bearing wall structure also allows external walls to be more free-form, since they only carry their own weight, rather than that of the floor slabs roof. It also allows windows to span across the entire elevation if need be, rather than being small, because of the uniformly distributed loads that typify a bearing wall system. Other than these three "points," of a free plan, free elevation, and the strip, or continuous, horizontal window, made possible by the first, generating one, which is the grid, Le Corbusier added the possibility of lifting a house up above the ground on the frame, and providing a garden on the roof as well, as the fifth and final advantage.

Each of the five participants in the *Five Architects* publication project, who utilized these ideas in one way or another, subsequently went on in either new or nuanced directions, becoming leaders of different styles of architecture that continue to prevail today. While John Hedjuk was involved in his Nine Square Texas series, Peter Eisenman was working through his own set of issues in a similar progression of houses that he simply referred to as a roman numeral that designated its place in the evolution of his exploration of what he termed "deep structure." He took the grid requirement of Le Corbusier into a more complex philosophical realm by trying to make it legible in three dimensions spatially, rather than as a rank of horizontal columns alone. After exhausting the possibilities of this line of investigation, Eisenman changed direction by aligning himself with the French philosopher Jacques Derrida in the early 1980s and trying to translate Derrida's theory of deconstruction into architecture at the Wexner Center in Ohio. Several other architects, such as Zaha Hadid, Bernard Tschumi, and the Austrian firm Coop Himmel, initiated parallel lines of inquiry at that time, but Eisenman was arguably the most literal interpreter of Derridian intentions, as a founder of this movement.

Michael Graves, on the other hand, went in an entirely opposite and equally radical direction. After feeling that he had reached the end of the possibilities inherent in the five points method in a series of houses that included the Benecerref addition in Princeton and the Hanselmann and Synderman houses after that, Graves started to examine more historically based precedents for inspiration. He determined that anthropomorphism, manifested in Classical architecture as a base, middle, and top that parallel the foot, body, and head of the human body, would provide a more promising basis for his future creative development, and he arrived at this decision soon after Robert Venturi and Denise Scott Brown had launched what is now referred to as postmodernism. As was the case with Peter Eisenman's formative role in Deconstructivism, Michael Graves's shift of direction was part of a more general trend toward a rejection of Modernist dogma. But, the remaining members of the New York Five, including John Hejduk, continued on in much the same way, simply expanding their aesthetic and creative repertoire, rather than changing it entirely. As a result, Richard Meier and Charles Gwathmey, now in the partnership Gwathmey and Siegel, are each leaders of the resurgence of interest in what is often referred to as New Modernism.

The Column as Part of the Wall As the previous list of Hedjuk's design interests indicates, he had an all-encompassing, highly complex, inquiring mind, which in addition to all of the interrelationships that he mentions in it, also included the planar source of the column, as the main component of the grid. Leon Alberti who was an architect in Late Renaissance Italy, was one of the first to make an analogy between the wall and the column, which has obvious relevance for Le Corbusier's five point system. Alberti speculated that his column could be considered a strip of a wall, or that a wall was simply a long series of columns joined together, and this is essentially the point of departure that John Hedjuk used in his Wall Houses I and II. As a result of his Nine Square series of houses in Texas, he became particularly fascinated by the relationship between a column and the planar surface of a wall, or the "phantom volume" of the column buried in the wall.[42] Unlike the other members of the Five, who focused primarily on the implications of using the grid, as a deep structure as Eisenman had employed it, or as a syntactical element as in Graves's last three Corbusian models, or as tartan arrangements in Meier's elegant houses of the late 1970s and early 1980s, or as an icon by Charles Gwathmey in the de Menil house, John Hedjuk decided to examine its origins as part of a wall.

Hedjuk started this search with the idea of a series, as he had done so successfully in Texas, in the late 1960s and 1970s. His first attempt was what he called the "Grandfather" wall house, which was only one story high, but contained the embryonic elements of the final design. These were the idea that the wall could also symbolize the present, with one side representing that past and the other the future. Once this became clear, geometric or organic forms could also be used in symbolic ways, and it seemed to him that rectilinear shapes and service functions were more appropriate to the past, since they are fixed, rigid, and relatively difficult to change, just as our part is. Organic, or what he called "biomorphic," forms, on the other hand, imply freedom of expression, unpredictability, and joy. This division between the past, on one side of a wall, and the future on the other also implied an equal division between private and public spaces and between the human made and the natural, as well as dark (memory) and light (dreams). Hedjuk intended that these multiple meanings coexist in a way that replicates the intricate layering of our consciousness, as well as the reality of our constant mental cycling between past and present, which is also possible in the Wall House.

The Wall House II The evolution of Hedjuk's idea for the Wall House culminated in a residence for landscape architect A. E. Bye, which he called Wall House II. It was finally realized in 2001, in Groningen, the Netherlands. It consists of a 14 meter high wall, and a steel framework. This grillage is filled in with a timber frame and coated with stucco, which was especially difficult to do on the curved surfaces on the "future" side of the massive line of demarcation.

ITALY

Casa Malaparte

Solid and void overlap in the most lyrical of Adalberto Libera's works, a villa realized in close collaboration with his client, Curzio Malaparte.

Sections reveal the extent of its solidity: the building is literally carved into the rock promontory on which it sits, the foundation progressively stepping upward toward the edge of its rocky site as if in an attempt to spring away. The void, which this tenacity makes possible, and the flat rectangular plane that is simultaneously a roof and viewing plane transcend the frequent associations of "terrace" to become a symbol with various levels of meaning. Following the Mediterranean tradition, in a way that is reminiscent of such buildings as the Temple of Sounion, there is no mimesis here, but a high contrast with nature, a heightening of perspective in relationship to the horizon that was transformed by the Rationalists into an emphasis on the roof terrace. This expression of endless space in the distance raises the house to a metaphysical level. The first of these, international or not, relates to Malaparte, who preferred to style himself as a champion of the poor and the oppressed; the obvious parallel of such a precarious *parti* is inevitably a metaphor of endurance and aspiration.

At another level, the increasingly wider steps up to the platform recall the seats of ancient theatres ubiquitous in the region. Capri was a focal point of official

Casa Malaparte. © Roberto Schezen / Esto

interest in archaeological studies of Imperial Rome that intensified while the house was under construction in light of the fact that Roman emperor Tiberius had chosen the island for his villa.

More contemporary cross-references to vernacular forms—from the generic flat roofs of houses on the island that serve as outdoor rooms to a more specific connection with the pinched, triangular steps of the Annunziata Church on the island of Lipari, where Malaparte was once imprisoned—bring the associations around full circle, to the client's contemporary experience. Malaparte once characterized Italian civilization as surrealist, ironic, fantastical, and unreal.

Adoption of such a position obviously put Malaparte at odds with his architect, who was one of the most doctrinaire members of the Gruppo 7, and dismissed him as a romantic. Libera's early schemes show a simple rectangular villa without a monumental staircase to the roof, and according to the client, the builder, a contractor named Amitrano, played a more critical role than the architect in the realization of the house, by working out ways to weld it to the rock.

Such claims are part of the mythology of many great works of architecture and, as is usually the case, the truth lies somewhere in between. What remains, on a promontory on Capri, is a poetic statement about the place of the built object in nature, a worthy entrant into a timeless debate. Malaparte's view of nature as deficient fantasy indicates it is a highly subjective statement in parts, with some windows placed like frames (sill heights almost touching the floor) to appreciate selected views that evoke Chinese painting.

The interior is a highly personalized environment; the private counterpart of the public persona is expressed outside. The detailing provides an interesting dichotomy that emerges in this public/private split. Beyond the formal aspect of the external polemic, the details are rough, almost casual in presentation; the stairs are uneven flagstones and the color of the walls a deep Pompeian red. The interior, by contrast, is minimal in the extreme. Giorgio Ciucci has explained this by saying, "the controlling idea was one of a unity that embraced contradictions" and in coherence, "a house like me," as Malaparte called it. Such contradictions evidently embraced a rational aesthetic, yet could not be entirely contained by it.

Mario Botta: Riva San Vitale

Mario Botta is an architect based in the Canton of Ticino in Switzerland. That district is unique in that it is equally influenced by its proximity to both Germany and Italy, which each have a strong rationalist tradition. It also has beautiful scenery with steep foothills cascading down to pristine Alpine lakes. Lake Lugano and Lake Como are two of the most famous of these, and each has small eponymous cities connected to them that each date back to before the Roman Empire.

Botta has been clearly influenced by several prominent architects in the past. One of these is Louis Kahn, who shared Botta's Rationalistic principles. Both visited Kahn's office in Philadelphia when the Swiss architect was just starting his career. Botta took away several key ideas from that experience that still remain constant in his work today. The most essential of these is Kahn's preference for Platonic forms, such as circles, squares, and equilateral triangles, because they are the purest and are easily proven by geometrical theorem. In a fable called the *Phaedo*, Plato compared the human condition to the existence of a person in a cave, whose entire understanding of the outside world is conditioned by the limited view from a narrow opening. He uses this as an analogy for the imperfection of our collective existence compared to the perfection that he believes must exist in a parallel universe. He says pure forms are also found there, which is why his name is used to refer to them. The second obvious influence that Kahn had on Botta was his promotion of common materials, such as concrete block, which was shunned by other Modernists, because they believed it was too utilitarian. For Kahn, it symbolized his allegiance to the common people as well as his Humanistic, populist stance, in addition to the obvious financial advantage that the choice of a less expensive material offered to his clients.

The Italian architect Carlo Scarpa also had a profound impact on Mario Botta, which is evident in the Swiss designer's love of history and tradition as well as his attention to detail and support for good craftsmanship.

Botta has developed a successful international practice of his own over his long career and, in the course of it, has decisively added his own personal interpretation to the Rationalist canon. He has tended to soften its stringent emphasis on empiricism, typological purity, and objective reasoning, layering over those commonalities an awareness of what he refers to as territory. This concept is related to his idea that the psychological, social, and visual repercussions of any work of architecture extend far beyond the legal boundaries or site lines it is confined to, and that a perceptive designer must take this phenomenon into account. While this may not seem to initially be connected to Rationalist idealism, it does conform to it, in a larger sense, because the corollary to the idea of territoriality is the ability to control future growth around a building by using it to establish a new order around it.

The House in Riva San Vitale Botta has been evolving this idea since the beginning of his career, to great effect. One of the best examples is also one of his earliest projects, which is a small house built for Carlo and Leontina Bianchi, which was completed in 1973. It is located at midslope of the San Giorgio mountain range facing Lake Lugano, standing gloriously alone like a sentinel on its steep, heavily forested mountainside. Botta has disturbed the site as little as possible, simply creating three subsequent levels in the slope that relate to each of the floors in the tower house he has designed. The first of these levels, at the top of the tower, has been used to anchor a bridge that leads to the top, entrance floor of the tower. The bridge is actually a trussed box beam, made of steel chords that have been painted bright red. The truss chords eliminate the need for a railing, since they enclose the entire bridge, and create a feeling of security, since the chasm the bridge spans is relatively deep. The top of the concrete block tower has been treated as a landing point, or platform with a roof above it, and openings on three sides. The entrance to the house itself is on the left-hand side of the tower, and the bridge end is attached to it. The opening facing the downhill side of the slope provides a stunning view of Lake Lugano far below and the mountains on its far shore.

The idea of entering at the top of a house and then moving down into it has been used to great effect by several other famous architects beside Mario Botta, such as Frank Lloyd Wright and Richard Meier. In the Douglas House by Meier, for example, which is discussed elsewhere in this volume, there is an equally precipitous slope in the design equation, as well as a lake below it, and the architect has also used a bridge in that case, to heighten a sense of anticipation, surprise, and delight, after arriving at the end of the bridge and seeing the view beyond. Entering at the top of the house, and arranging the floors below the entry in such a way as to allow an unobstructed view from top to bottom, is also an effective way of providing a sense of orientation for guests and visitors.

In the case of the Riva San Vitale house, Botta has made the entry space two stories high, and has located the bedrooms at the top level as well, to take advantage of the view from that floor. From that point on, a stairway in the middle of the square perimeter of the tower, which has also been placed in a square enclosure, leads down to each of the floors below to the living, dining, and kitchen spaces at the bottom of the tower.

The square footprint of the house and its cubic volumes belie its Rationalist roots, as does its assertive presence, in spite of its relatively small square footage.

It is unlikely that the land around it will ever become a residential enclave, but if it does, it will be difficult to ignore its stately presence and the order that it implies and establishes.

SPAIN

Antoni Gaudi: The Casa Batlló, Barcelona

In the middle of the nineteenth century, there was a resurgence of Catalan identity in Spain, which centered around Barcelona, in spite of attempts by the central government to eradicate it. This eventually led to calls for the secession of Catalonia, which grew stronger up through the Spanish Civil War.[43]

The architect Antoni Gaudi was a fervent advocate of Catalan individuality, and he was also a devout Catholic. He is perhaps best remembered today for his design of the as-yet unfinished Sagrada Familia Church in Barcelona, begun in 1898, which is also indicative of his stylistic principles. Gaudi sought to revitalize Gothic architecture by infusing it with a Mediterranean character overlaid with Islamic overtones, since Spain was exposed to Muslim culture for hundreds of years before the *Reconquista* or Reconquest, when many mosques were converted to churches and Christianity reestablished its preeminence. Gaudi wanted to transform Gothic architecture through the application of even more associations, including the use of color, to replicate the processes and elements of nature. The structure of the Sagrada family is almost skeletal in appearance. Antoni Gaudi was fortunate in having a patron, and this wealthy textile manufacturer, Eusebio Guell Bacigalupi, not only offered him key commissions of his own but also provided Gaudi with an introduction to other clients in the same socioeconomic class.

Of the many projects that Gaudi designed for his patron, two of the most well-known are the Park Guell and the Palau Guell, also in Barcelona, built in 1888. The Park was only one part of a much larger project for an entire community to be built for those who worked in the Guell Textile Mills, and so was based on the principle of social improvement that was consistent with the politics of both the architect and his client.

Gaudi was inspired by the legend of the Holy Grail, which, according to local tradition, was kept in Montsalvat Castle on a mountain near Barcelona called Montserrat.[44]

Like Paul Cézanne, who was nearly obsessed with images of Mont Sainte-Victoire, Gaudi replicated the jagged profile of Montserrat in many of his buildings, especially in the outline of the Park Guell as well as in an apartment house in Barcelona called the Casa Mila, built between 1906 and 1910. Also known as the *Pedrera*, this apartment block is located on a corner site in the middle of the city, with an undulating, organically geological façade that masks units organized around open central courtyards behind it. In addition to Montserrat, the Casa Mila was also intended by Gaudi as an homage to the Virgin Mary, with the undulations of the façade also replicating the waves of the Mediterranean nearby, lapping at the feet of Mary. Gaudi originally intended to create a sculpture of the Virgin holding the infant Jesus, surrounded by angels, to be inset into the front elevation of the *Pedrera*, but an antireligious riot that broke out soon after the building was completed led the client to abandon the idea. The intention to do so, however, gives a good indication of Gaudi's devotion.

In addition, to its wave-like façade, the Casa Mila also has something of a cult following because of its phantasmagorical chimney blues, which far exceed the menace of the gargoyles on French Gothic cathedrals, such as Notre Dame in Paris. These chimneys, which appear like an army of demons released from the underworld, are surmounted by cruciform spires, as if to imply that they have been vanquished or are at least under control. The exterior façade also has highly ornate metal balconies, decorated with large leaf-like railings of the same level of quality as the ironwork found in the houses he designed elsewhere.

The Palau Guell After his design of the Colonia and Park Guell on Montana Pelada with collaborators Berenquer and Jupol, and the completion of a Palau for the same client, in 1904 Gaudi started a redesign of a house for the Batlló family, who were also involved in textile manufacturing. It is similar to the Palau Guell in that it also has an elaborately eclectic façade, as well as hints of Islamic influence. These references in the Guell house are primarily related to a cleverly devised atrium covered by an intricately carved, elongated dome, which lets light and air penetrate deep into the interior of the house around and below it. A grand stairway, leading up from entry level at grade leads up around this court to what amounts to a *piano nobile* on the first floor above. The elongated dome is covered by a steeple-like spire and the chimney towers, which are miniature versions of those that populate the roof of the Casa Mila surround it. Projecting window boxes, which are reminiscent of Islamic *mushrabiyya* screens found in the medieval quarters of Muslim cities throughout the Middle East, complete the obvious reference to pre-*Reconquista* Catalonia, which is a constant theme in Gaudi's work.

The Batlló family wanted Gaudi to completely change the style of their existing house primarily as a way of keeping up appearances amidst other prominent houses on the same street in the wealthy area of Barcelona at that time. When his reconstruction was complete, the house could most certainly not be called boring, and quickly got the nickname locally of "The House of Bones."[45] The exterior columns look like *tibia*, and the balcony railings are skull-like in profile. The tiles that cover the house, which are iridescent green and beige in color, have also been compared to lizard skin. The reptilian metaphor here was as intentional as the religious reference used in the Casa Mila, for somewhat the same reason, since Gaudi intended to invoke the story of St. George and the slaying of a dragon.[46] Gaudi followed the model of early Gothic cathedrals, in which biblical stories were recounted in sculptural relief on the sides of churches and in their stained glass windows at a time when the majority of the churchgoing public was illiterate and the Bible had yet to be widely translated from Latin. But his allegories and metaphors were far less literal or obvious, while being equally powerful and meaningful to him.

Through the fusion of Spanish Gothic elements and motifs and tile and mosaic work that is reminiscent of Islamic influence, Gaudi tries to proclaim the unique identity of Catalonia in this house. The interior spaces are just as organically conceived as the exterior, full of swirling curves. Even the doorways and doors are irregular. There are no orthogonal reference points, giving the impression that the spaces are constantly moving. This feeling is augmented by the tile work of

Jujol who was without parallel in his skill and craftsmanship at the time the house was built.

Gaudi also designed a majority of the furniture in each of the interior rooms, even though the family retained some of the pieces they had used previously. The cabinets, tables, beds, and chests that the architect produced for these spaces are as fluid and organic as the house itself, as well as equally original.

THE UNITED KINGDOM

Hampstead Garden Suburb

Like Bedford Park, which is an earlier Garden City project conceived by Norman Shaw, Letchworth was speculative and self-contained, designed to project an image of exclusivity and individuality. It is larger in scale than anything Ebenezer Howard had attempted before. A competition for the new town was announced by Howard in 1900; and a plan by Barry Parker and Raymond Unwin was selected in 1904. In addition to Parker and Unwin, the competition included Richard Norman Shaw of Bedford Park fame, as well as W. R. Lethaby, Halsey Ricardo, Geoffrey Lucas, and Sidney Cranfield, who were all asked to prepare plans by the directors. The Parker and Unwin plan was selected because it most specifically conformed to the unusual topography, which is 3,800 acres of uneven land located near the Cambridge Branch of the Great Northern Railway, which bisects the site. Other existing features that greatly influenced the planning were the Hitchin and Baldock Road, the Norton and Wilbury Road, and the Icknield Way between them, running approximately parallel to the railway.

Parker and Unwin proposed individually designed houses in a "cottage" style, based on the preexisting estate village of Old Letchworth. The village, along with Letchworth Hall and St. Mary's Church, still had several blocks of seventeenth-century cottages, a town center, and a main north-south axis through the center. Parker and Unwin used this axis to full advantage, having residential areas of detached and semidetached houses fanning out from it. They had intended to use a uniform palette of materials throughout their new village, but the onset of war and the pressure for housing afterward introduced unintended features into the planned community. The planners did manage to save almost all existing trees, boasting in promotional brochures that only one was cut down during construction. They also identified a level plateau at the highest part of the site near the town center as the ideal location of the Common, with roads spreading out from the circular strand around it offering impressive vistas into the surrounding countryside as they slope down in all directions.

The Search for Paradise Letchworth was the first of what Ebenezer Howard envisioned as a series of Garden Cities, each with a population limit of 32,000, which would surround industrial cities throughout Britain. To ensure the success of his enterprise, Howard determined that Letchworth should be incorporated and that any increase in property value should be shared by the entire community. He formed a Garden Cities Association in 1899 to implement his plan. The association purchased the Letchworth estate in April 1903 from 15 different owners totaling 3,818 acres, for £155,587. The Association bought the parcels in ways that would prevent the individual owners from realizing they were contributing to a unified development so they would not raise their selling prices. On September 1, 1908, First Garden City Ltd. was registered and Howard's idea of public participation in a company in which the owners and tenants held shares and received dividends on their property was finally realized.

A Cheap Cottage in the Country Since Howard, Unwin, and Parker were among those owners with shares in Letchworth, their vision was not completely altruistic, even though Raymond Unwin was a fervent supporter of the Socialist League and a vocal advocate of affordable, working-class housing. Both Parker and Unwin built houses for themselves on Letchworth Lane in 1904 in a "Yeoman" Tudor style, and in 1907 Parker designed a thatched studio on Norton Way South in East Anglia vernacular, which now houses the First Garden City Heritage Museum. The unlikely pairing of egalitarian ideals and speculative motives is further personified by Howard's efforts to have Edward Cadbury, planner of Bournville, and W. H. Lever, who built Port Sunlight for company employees, on the Board of Directors of a public company from which he hoped to profit. It is also epitomized by the Cheap Cottage Exhibition, which was ostensibly intended to demonstrate that affordable workers' housing was a key component of the Letchworth community. The insistence on including these houses also demonstrates Howard's realization that, in spite of his dream of a return to a preindustrial paradise, manufacturing was necessary for financial success. It was vital to his goal of self-sufficiency, since employment in the community would be needed to sustain it.

A sales brochure for Garden City included a circular diagram entitled "The Three Magnets" separated into pie-shaped divisions labeled "Town," "Country," and "Town-Country." Garden Cities represent the final combination, having all of the advantages and none of the disadvantages of the first. Unlike the "Town," Garden Cities would have "Low Rents" and "High Wages," "A Field for Enterprise," and "Flow of Capital." Unlike the "Country," they would also have social and cultural activities as an attraction for prospective residents.

The press was invited to the unveiling of 114 houses built especially for the exhibition, advertised at £150, using every new construction method possible to lower costs without compromising the standards of quality or style originally established by Parker and Unwin for the rest of Letchworth. The exhibition attracted nearly 60,000 visitors, but it is unlikely that many of these had agrarian aspirations, given the location of the houses. The contrived attempt to make the cottages seem bucolic was a strategy intended to make them appeal to middle-class urbanites looking for an inexpensive retreat in the countryside.

Letchworth was administered by the Hitchin Council as a rural district until after the 1914–1918 war, when it was elevated to urban status, due to rapid growth. After the Second World War, development pressures drove property values up even higher. To protect this first example of Howard's Garden City concept from takeover, the Letchworth Urban District Council backed a private bill enacted into law in 1962, which established the Letchworth Garden City Corporation. It continued to administer profits for community benefit as before, but enforced stricter controls on development. Administration transferred to the Letchworth Garden City Heritage Foundation in 1992, again through a Private Bill in Parliament, creating an Industrial and Provident Society with charitable status.

Setting an Example The missionary zeal of Ebenezer Howard's "back to the countryside" movement was diverted into nationalistic fervor prior to the First World War and lost its impetus because of the profound social and economic consequences of that conflict. Its importance as a precedent for various aspects of the environmental sensibility that has begun to become so pervasive, however, cannot be overemphasized. This is primarily due to the emphasis placed on living and working in the same community that is now also a central tenet of New Urbanism. The reasons for the importance of the Garden City movement as a precedent may be outlined as follows.

First of all, it was unarguably the prototype for suburban growth, and the urban flight that went with it, beginning in the late 1940s and early 1950s, but it differs from those developments in having a more traditional approach to nature. Rather than the ubiquitous, finely manicured, and watered lawns with which suburb developments have now become synonymous and which, along with the sidewalks, separate each detached house from its neighbors, the Garden Cities that Howard completed were designed to fit into their environment and were respectful of existing contours, trees, and vegetation. They were compactly organized, with semidetached as well as detached houses provided.

The construction of the Garden Cities movement in America, led by Clarence Stein and Henry Wright, perpetuated Howard's ideals and planning tactics, but they could not withstand the economic forces unleashed by the baby boom that followed the Second World War and the speculative opportunists that took advantage of them. Howard's dream, carried forward by Stein and Wright, of profits from property serving the common good and providing affordable housing for all, fell victim to market forces, and architects who held to Howard's ideals withdrew from popular housing completely.

There was a short-lived rebellion in Southern California, just after the Second World War, referred to by Reyner Banham in his classic *Four Ecologies* about Los Angeles as "the Style that Nearly," because it almost prevented the defection of architects from the mass-housing market. Concentrated in an effort called the Case Study House Program, organized by John Entenza, this campaign was intended to convert people to modernism by using prefabrication to lower costs and make houses available to all. What Entenza and his chosen Case Study architects failed to appreciate, which Ebenezer Howard and Jonathan Carr before him did, was the power of image on the public consciousness: the need for people to feel that they were escaping the city to a bucolic cottage in the countryside, rather than a machine in a well-mowed garden.

The second reason why the Garden City movement is an important precedent is that while it ostensibly appears to be antiurban, many of its principles have now been adopted by the New Urbanists as part of their strategy to repopulate inner cities in a more humanistic way. Howard did not visualize his communities as refuges from the city but as alternatives to the urban conditions of the times, which is why he planned to have an outer belt of light industry surrounding each one. Mixed use, which is now one of the New Urbanists' most frequently repeated mantras, was a central idea of Garden City planning to reduce traffic and promote a closer sense of community.

The third reason why the Garden City movement is an important precedent is the idealistic legacy it has left. Howard's dream of having an egalitarian framework that would allow everyone to return to the land has endured in spite of the suburbs and the sprawl that are its more prevalent common denominators. That dream is evident in the early modernist emphasis on workers' housing and the numerous *Siedlungen* that resulted from it. It was also the basis for Frank Lloyd Wright's ambitious Broadacre City plan, which he envisioned as a prototype for American cities of the future, as well as for the groundbreaking plan for the Valleys, put forward by McHarg, Wallace, and Todd in 1962.

In spite of several impressively effective local ordinances in the United States, such as those enacted in parts of Oregon, to contain sprawl, the general tendency, abetted by population rise and economic opportunism, is toward exurban growth as well as movement back into the cities. Howard's model is relevant to each of these trends and offers valuable lessons on how to accommodate all of them.

Charles Rennie Mackintosh: Hill House

Charles Rennie Mackintosh was an extremely talented and highly influential advocate of Arts and Crafts principles, and is widely considered to be an important link between that tradition and Modernism. He sought to continue to honor the past, while utilizing all of the technological advances that the Industrial Revolution had made available to him by combining the two. He studied vernacular Scottish architecture thoroughly, as is obvious in the eclectic stylistic language in his houses. He was a pragmatist, as well as a romantic.

Windyhill Begun in 1899 and completed in 1902, Windyhill postdates a house of similar appearance by C. F. A. Voysey in South Parade, Bedford Park, London, and Perrycroft, Colwall, outside Malvern. The white stucco rendering of the former, intended to make it unmistakably different from its neighbors, and a central splay-chimneyed composition are of particular relevance to Windyhill in Kilmacolm. More particular still is the similarity between the plans of Windyhill and Blackwell, Windermere, Cumbria, by M. H. Baillie Scott built in 1898. There is an obvious concordance of enclosed entry from the court created by the L-shaped plan, and the bay window asymmetrically placed opposite a fireplace is especially noteworthy.

In direct contrast to the sophistication of the Hill House hall, which is entered on axis, rather than at a right angle, the central circulation spine of Windyhill is all on one level and narrower, which makes it seem more severe. As in the Hill House, this hall is also intended as a room in its own right. It was pressed into service as an extension of the main dining room during large family gatherings. A prominent historian relates that Davidson had known Mackintosh for about five years prior to this commission and had asked him to design several pieces of furniture for the Davidson family home at Gladsmuir. These pieces were augmented by his new design for Windyhill, and in an attempt to save money, as for Walter Blackie at the Hill House, the architect was instructed to focus his attention on the hall and drawing room. This was because they were most visible to visitors and guests and should convey a formal, unified impression as the owners' retreat.[47] The division between the use of oak in the public spaces, as an expression of durability and utility, and white enamel in the bedroom, to lift it above such associations, is also similar in each house. The rectangular dining table used in the hall, and its square extension, as well as two tapering high-backed chairs, which are Jacobean in profile and feeling, reiterate this study manorial approach, mitigated at the Hill House by the perpendicular, rather than axial, orientation of the stair and raised central portion of the hall, which lift and turn the space, making it lighter. These pieces were subsequently donated to the Glasgow School of Art, so the feeling of the hall has now completely changed.

Contrary to persistent criticism, Windyhill in Mackintosh's final expression is compelling simply because it lacks the balance and finish of the Hill House, for which it, through the Blackwell *parti* of Baillie Scott, was obviously a precedent. Its elevations are less assured, and, in the case of the projecting, axial stairway, deliberately disproportional. This does not diminish their significance as the first, independent declaration of a clean break with historical eclecticism as well as the Scottish Baronial impetus that was then so fashionable.

Hill House. Courtesy of Shutterstock

Hill House The Hill House in Helensburgh is the best known of Mackintosh's domestic buildings and is also considered his best. It is here that the insights seen in Windyhill emerge full-blown. In the early 1890s, the Glasgow publisher Walter Blackie, who specialized in popular titles for all ages, took the daring step of hiring Talwin Morris, who had established a reputation for *avant-garde* designs while with the *Black and White Journal* in London, as art director in 1893. The Glasgow School of artists and designers was tightly knit and Morris, by necessity, established strong connections within it. Five years later, Blackie established Gresham Publishing Company as an independent subsidiary to produce academic reference books to be sold by subscription, all of which were intended to have covers worthy of a classic collection. In its second year, the Gresham Library of Standard Fiction produced 18 titles, including *Jane Eyre*. Talwin Morris was recognized, in an article in *The Studio*, as a leader in promoting design motifs related to the Celtic Revival. Morris's arrival in Glasgow coincided exactly with publication in *The Studio* of illustrations such as the *Three Brides* by Jan Toorop and those by Aubrey Beardsley for *Le Morte d'Arthur* by Sir Thomas Malory. These issues have been identified by historian Andrew MacLaren Young as marking the birth of a direction later to be labeled "The Glasgow Style." [48] Because of his profile, Talwin Morris, who may be considered a leading practitioner of this movement, was able to broadcast it most effectively. It becomes increasingly difficult, after 1897, to separate his work from that of others like Mackintosh and his wife, Margaret Macdonald, who were also a part of it. An article published in *The Studio* in that year by Gleeson White, entitled "Some Glasgow Designers and Their Work," linked them together.

Despite the extent of this symbiotic influence, Mackintosh was introduced to Walter Blackie by Talwin Morris. As Blackie had decided to move from Dunblane in Stirlingshire to be closer to his business interests in Glasgow, in 1907 he purchased a spectacular site to the north of Helensburgh with distant views of the Firth of Clyde and needed an architect to design a house there. Windyhill is not far away, in Kilmacolm, and Mackintosh took the publisher to see it, since it had roughly the same orientation and situation. Mackintosh found Blackie to be a very receptive client, as averse to noncontextual historicism or eclecticism for its own sake as he was. Blackie was just as concerned that external appearance did not supersede function. Apocrypha about the design process includes a story, contested by Walter Blackie's daughter, that Mackintosh lived with the family in Dunblane for several weeks to determine their daily routines and patterns. But another account from Blackie's memory, written 36 years after the house was completed, relates that no elevations were presented until the plans were finalized, and that Mackintosh's preference was for simple massing, as opposed to ostentatious detailing. Blackie's recollections give the impression that there were no preconceived notions involved in the development of the plan, which evolved entirely from family requirements, but further inquiry indicates otherwise.

In an incisive analysis of the Hill House, which focuses primarily on sources and the exterior of the building, James Macaulay has examined the relevance of the *Haus Eines Kunstfreundes* Competition that Mackintosh had entered with Margaret Macdonald in 1900. They produced a scheme that was disqualified on technical grounds because of a lack of the required number of interior perspectives. Yet, it was the only entry that met the judges' expectations of an architecture that decisively broke with existing conventions. While the *parti* is different from that of the L-shaped plan of the Hill House in that it is completely linear, the Art Lovers House remained in Mackintosh's mind as he designed the Blackie residence. Hermann Muthesius could just as easily have been talking of the Hill House when he wrote in the Introduction to *Meister der Innen Kunst* of the Mackintosh's Art Lovers scheme:

> The exterior architecture of the building . . . exhibits an absolutely original character unlike anything else known. In it we shall not find trace of the conventional forms of architecture to which the artist, so far as present intentions were concerned, was quite indifferent. The mass of the building consists of a large plain block, without any breaking up of the walls, the effect being sought for in unbroken uniform surfaces. This produces a curious, yet distinctly ingenious impression. The windows have the appearance of accidental openings, deeply recessed in the walls . . . Ornament save in the two or

three places, is conspicuously absent, all allurements being sternly, repressed in order that the desired effect of plainness, reticence, and therewithal of mystery and height, might be revealed as strongly as possible.[49]

What obviously also remained in Mackintosh's mind was that M. H. Baillie Scott won the *Haus Eines Kunstfreundes* Competition, based on his skill in interior design, and had conquered the intricacies of the L-shaped plan in classic country houses such as Blackwell, in Windermere, Cumbria, completed in 1898. This was Baillie Scott's first major commission after his return from Darmstadt, where he had been involved in the renovation of the Palace of the Grand Duke of Hesse, and his work, particularly his furniture designs, were frequently published in *The Studio*. The similarities between the plan of Blackwell and those of the Hill House, not to mention the layout of Windyhill in 1900, are remarkable beyond coincidence. In Blackwell, as at the Hill House, formal functions are distributed along a central hall–corridor in the elongated leg of the L, where services are compartmentalized into the shorter half. The sequence and relative size of the spaces in the formal segment begin with a dining room near the service wing, placed there to be close to the pantry and kitchen. It continues with a central sitting-living room with projecting bay window and fireplace and concludes with a drawing room–library at the opposite end of the central hall. Rather than placing a main entrance in the middle of the elongated leg, however, as Baillie Scott did at Blackwell, and as he had done at Windyhill, Mackintosh decided that a less grandiose solution would be in order. In keeping with Blackie's wishes, he put the entry at the western end of the central hall. The retention of the semicircular Art Lovers House stair, also turned at right angles to the major circulation axis as in that plan, is also notable, since a similar form in a different orientation was also used at Windyhill and was later to be adopted by Gropius, Le Corbusier, and others as one symbol of progressive Modernism. Howarth has commented on the fact that the circular tower or turret, which was a familiar component of Scottish domestic architecture from the sixteenth century onward, may be the antecedent of this form, and Frank Walker has gone further, identifying it as part of

> plans developed first from generally quadrilateral or sometimes circular enclosures reinforced by square or round towers, regressed to simpler tower-house model during the war-torn 14th century, developed next to "L"-plan variant of the latter, the staircase tower tucked in the angle....[50]

Its appearance here as a sculptural component of the north elevation is more dramatic than at Windyhill, where it was buried into an end wall and was far less legible. It seems, like the industrial windows of the Glasgow School of Art, to be the harbinger of a coming age, at once part of the architect's highly advanced reading of a distinct traditional language and yet somehow beyond it.

This modernized turret is clearly visible from the entry gates at the western end of the house, but it is the architect's signature asymmetrical massing of windows of various sizes, door, and angled chimney reminiscent of Lamb's House, Leith, that are most memorable. The most obvious similarity is the bay window of the first floor dressing room projecting out over the deep stone lintel and jambs of the door, in contrast to the long and slender fenestration of the flanking library and cloak-room below. Achieving the same feeling of additive randomness found in vernacular buildings in new construction, without making the combinations seem forced or chaotic, was a skill in which Mackintosh excelled. The plain, uniform harling cementations pebble dash frequently used in Scottish farm buildings to weatherproof them is rarely alleviated with other materials as an external skin, and this makes the skill of the architects elevations even more evident. Mackintosh's choice of harling, a cement slurry mixed with crushed pebbles and traditionally used as added protection against infiltration by wind-driven rain, is important, considering that his client could conceivably have afforded other materials on the exterior. It is applied here over stone, since local codes discouraged the use of brick, which would have lowered the standard of construction in this wealthy community. It creates an impression of uniformity, joining the diverse sculptural elements of angled chimneys, towers, gables, and projecting bays together into one homogenous composition, contrasted against the consistent datum of extended, sheltering slate roofs. When viewed from the descending terraces that cascade down to the south, the house seems to increase in scale and magnificence, largely due to the same uniformity of surface ostensibly employed to avoid ostentation. The harled white skin of the house, which takes on a bluish coat on the rare occasions that the sun shines and a grey sheen when it does not, effectively separates the house from the verdant landscaped *parterres*, also laid out by the architect, below it.

In startling contrast to the rough weatherproof exterior, the interior of the house, which first becomes visible from the expanding central hall that telescopes from the black wooden door in the western gable end, is all wood and warmth, with judiciously placed openings providing filtered light to enhance the glow of fine materials. Frank Lloyd Wright, with whom Mackintosh is frequently compared, also understood the effectiveness of an entrance placed on axis with, rather than perpendicular to, the main line of circulation. Here it allows immediate orientation, as well as a comprehensive spatial impression of the house, with an inviting built-in window seat beyond, giving the feeling or image of comfortable, secure domesticity. A library immediately to the right of the entrance was intended to serve as an office in which Mr. Blackie could meet visitors to discuss business without disrupting the privacy of the family who might be in the living room beyond, as well as to provide a quiet place to work. The library is paneled in dark wood which, when combined with the leather-bound gold-lettered spines of the books for which Blackie and Son were famous and the glow of the fireplace that generates the angled chimney on the western wall, must have produced a contemplative ambience. In keeping with the paneling, a tree motif has been introduced here, with pieces of colored glass insets in blue, white, and red, a counterpoint to the darkness of the wood.

The hall that follows the library and the delightful interlude of the fireplace, which, in spite of its utilitarian purpose and position in a space too narrow for any use except circulation, is carefully designed as an integral element.

This hall is of another level entirely above what one normally envisions such a relatively utilitarian space to be. Windows along the stair allow clear north light to flood into the space. As they typically have in all of their designs, Mackintosh and Macdonald took responsibility for everything in the space, including the

251

furniture, which is all made of oak and has obvious Jacobean lineage. The walls are paneled with vertical strips of pine, which have been stained to match the darker finish of the furniture. These alternate with equally wide strips of exposed white plaster wall behind them. Macdonald prepared a free-form stencil that serves as a frieze around the entire room, with a range of purple, blue, and pink tones that were continued in the carpet that the couple also had custom-made for the hall.

This underscores the extent of Mackintosh's commitment to the total work of art, in which furnishings, textiles, carpeting, and silverware all combine with architecture, as part of the Arts and Crafts thesis of a unified built environment. At the Hill House, Blackie's finances and use of his own favorite pieces of furniture prevented complete integration, forcing the architect to select such spaces as the hall, drawing room, and master bedroom in which to focus on total design.

The drawing room in the middle of the house is accessible from the hall. It is raised up by four steps, and is divided into three identifiable zones, for listening to music at one end, conversation around a fire that backs onto and uses the same chimney as that in the hall on the other, and an extended bay window for reading and enjoying the view of the Gare Loch in the distance. The aspects of integration in this space, which serve to link the three parts together, generally begin with the significant elaboration of an idea that may be traced back through the Art Lovers House scheme and the drawing room of the Mackintoshes' flat at 120 Main Street, to a similar space in Dunglass Castle in Bowling, Dunbartonshire. It continues in the interior prepared for the Eighth Vienna Secession Exhibition in 1900 related to a tripartite division of sectional height. This division stems from one that is typically seen in Victorian drawing rooms, created by a picture rail near the ceiling and a dado about three feet above the floor, which each ran horizontally around the entire room. The picture rail at the top provided the structural strength needed to hang the heavy family portraits that were popular at the time. The dado, on the other hand, protected plaster walls from being damaged by the backs of chairs being pushed into them. Mackintosh simplified these two distinct and equally pragmatic lines that divided the drawing or living room laterally into thirds by using them as a way of integrating it vertically. They did this by having ceiling lights come down to picture rail height, and chair tops and fireplace mantels stop at dado height.

In the Hill House drawing room this device tends to visually expand vertical comprehension of the space, making it seem to open upwards and be loftier. It is also exaggerated. The effect is startling and fresh, as each alcove retains its own integrity, and yet contributes to a sense of a complex periphery, binding the space together. A built-in seat, filling the entire bay window, incorporates the architect's thoughtful touches, such as heating beneath to ensure comfort in winter, since this is the most open and extensively glazed expanse on the southern elevation. It also has book and magazine racks, providing easy access for a client whose business and pleasure involved a great deal of reading. A box chair, originally designed for the third conversation space by the fire, continued the theme of enclosure.

This device, of punching spaces into the bottom two-thirds of tripartite zoning and designing furniture to match, is extended further in the master bedroom, which also functioned as an extra morning room for Mrs. Blackie. Two large white wardrobes at the opposite end of the room from the arched alcove allocated for the fitted double beds continue at the same head height of an adjacent window. These take on an architectural capacity in the space. The lights here, like those originally designed for the drawing room, are equally sculptural, projecting down to the proscribed datum of the picture rail to retain it as an unbroken line around the room. The lights originally designed for the drawing room, which were substantial in size and suspended in each corner, were removed shortly after completion for unknown reasons, but photographs taken in 1904 show that they served as visual anchors, unifying even further the diverse parts of the drawing room. It may be argued, however, that this intentional tripartite division, which Mackintosh utilized so effectively in the hall, drawing room, and master bedroom of the Hill House, originated as an expedient in his flat at 120 Main Street to lower the high ceiling to a more human scale. This was in the tradition of many contemporary Arts and Crafts houses, such as those by Philip Webb, which reinterpreted and gave spatial purpose to the Victorian device of the picture rail. Mackintosh, however, immediately transformed it into a more authoritative line of demarcation, and this module takes on a higher level of meaning in his hands.

Edwin L. Lutyens: Deanery Gardens, Sonning, Heathcote

Edwin Lutyens is primarily regarded as an Arts and Crafts architect, in spite of the fact that he practiced a bit later than a majority of those who are generally associated with that Movement, as well as because of his love of Classical rather than Gothic stylistic sources. He is also perhaps best known for the larger public projects, completed later in his life, than for his country houses, which sustained him throughout a long career. These large projects include his plan for the British colonial section of Delhi, India, including the residence of the Viceroy, who was the representative of British authority during the Imperial Period. He became a member of the Delhi Planning Commission in 1912 and immediately set himself the task of redefining what had been, up until that time, a rather patronizing official approach to the style to be used in such projects. The raj style was an eclectic amalgamation of inappropriate elements that had little to do with the climate, history, or culture of a particular place in the far-flung reaches of the British Empire. Lutyens replaced that approach with a more sensitively rendered version that effectively blended western elements, based on his extensive knowledge of Classicism, with well-established Indian precedents, taken from its Buddhist, Hindu, and Islamic traditions, especially the Mughal examples. The majority of his design for New Delhi was completed and implemented between 1911 and 1920, and so was finished within only a few decades of independence. Once that occurred, his capital complex became a bitter reminder of British authority, in spite of the obvious cultural awareness that it demonstrates. After exploring several alternatives, the new government of India commissioned the internationally renowned Modernist architect Le Corbusier to design a new capitol at Chandigarh, which was completed in the early 1960s.

Among many other public buildings and monuments, Lutyens also designed a memorial to the British soldiers killed in World War I, which he called the Cemotaph, in White Hall, London, and is now the focal point of an annual day of remembrance that is held there.

The Country Estates Edwin Landseer Lutyens was of Dutch heritage but came to represent the perfect Victorian gentleman architect. Much less is known about the more than 30 large country estates he designed during his long career, as well as his remodeling of Lindisfarne Castle. He worked closely on many of these with the notable landscape architect Gertrude Jekyll, to an extent rarely seen in residential design, so that house and garden in each case are carefully integrated into one complete vision.

Lutyens initially worked with Sir Ernest George after graduating from what is now the Royal College of Art in 1885, and remained there until 1889, when he established his own practice. He met Gertrude Jekyll in the spring of that year and designed her house at Munstead Wood, which was completed in 1896. He married Lady Emily Lytton the following year and became heavily involved in the design of many country houses, such as Fulbrook.[51]

In 1898, Gertrude Jekyll's brother, Sir Herbert, was influential in having Lutyens chosen as the architect for the British Pavilion of the Paris Exhibition of 1900, which gave him international recognition.[52] Between 1899 and 1908, he produced Deanery Garden in Sonning and Heathcote among many other houses.

Deanery Garden in Sonning and Heathcote Sonning is an idyllic village near the River Thames, in Berkshire, with a complex layering of vernacular houses, including several that have been either designed or restored by the noted Victorian architect Henry Woodyer.

Many of these are built in a local rose-colored brick, which has an identifiably soft red tone, rather than the harsher hue found elsewhere in London. Edwin Lutyens and Gertrude Jekyll designed a house and garden for Edward Hudson near this village, which is generally considered to be one of their best collaborations. They took advantage of the fact that the property was surrounded by an old wall made of the same red brick as the majority of the houses in the village, as well as having an orchard on it. The house takes its name from a local tradition related to an ecclesiastical function for the property in the past, but no remnant of a monastic use remained when Lutyens and Jekyll began their design. They used the same rose red brick for the house as found elsewhere in the circuit wall and the village. Lutyens pulled the roof eave down over the front entrance to provide a feeling of protection and privacy. This heightens the surprise of seeing a framed view of the elegant garden, designed by Gertrude Jekyll, on the other, southwest side of the house. A two-story bay window divided into small sections, with 48 medieval scaled panes in all, is the dominant feature of this garden side elevation, which floods the great hall, sitting room, and dining room with light, and provides that view. An arched doorway leads out from these rooms onto a raised terrace, and a curved stairway in the midst of it, which echoes the arch of the door, leads down to the garden that is perpendicular to the house.

Heathcote Heathcote, on the other hand, which is in Ilkley, Yorkshire, is much more formal, demonstrating Lutyens's virtuosity with the Classical and, especially, English Renaissance languages. This elegant country house, which was completed in 1906, is sited on a four-acre property outside the village, but the estate seems much larger because of the skill that Lutyens and Jekyll have shown in its planning.

It is built of local yellow Guiseley stone, trimmed with grey stone from Morley, with a red tile roof.[53]

The two main elements that Lutyens uses in this Italianate house as a recurring structural language are the pilaster and rustication to tie it together. Lutyens and Jekyll continue the geometrical modules used by the architect out into the garden, further unifying the scheme.[54] This project demonstrates that, regardless of his proficiency in creating an Arts and Crafts, quasi-medieval gem in Sonning, Lutyens was at heart a Palladian devotee, and mastered that language better than any of his British predecessors. He admired Inigo Jones, Sir Christopher Wren, and Norman Shaw more than the Gothicists of the Arts and Crafts Movement. Unlike Deanery Gardens, the massing of Heathcote is compressed and powerful, reminiscent of Syon House, near Chiswick, but in a much more cosmopolitan and accomplished way.

A. W. N. Pugin: Ramsgate

Augustus Welby Northmore Pugin was the son of a French antiquarian. The family fled to England to escape the Revolution and subsequent terror. Father and son shared a passion for French cathedrals, and together they published *Specimens of Gothic Architecture* and *Examples of Gothic Architecture*. The younger Pugin enrolled in the Christ's Hospital School in London, but did not go on to university, collaborating instead with his father on projects of mutual interest such as the books just mentioned. After the revolution, as soon as the danger to those with royalist leanings such as himself had passed, A. W. N. Pugin started to make trips across the Channel to measure, survey, and draw Gothic cathedrals, and he was one of the first to record them in this way, serving a purpose similar to that of Brunelleschi in Renaissance Florence, who rediscovered Classical Roman ruins in the same way. By his early teens, Pugin was already recognized as an authority on Gothic architecture. At that time there was a surge of interest in it during the Gothic Revival, and many bad renditions of the tradition that were being made. Strawberry Hill in Twickenham, by Horace Walpole, which is thoroughly described in Volume 2 of this series, was one of the best of these because Walpole diligently collected every book he could find on the style. But many other less skillful attempts were also being put forward as authentic, when they were far from it.

With his unique background and interest, Pugin shone out amidst a great deal of mediocrity, and when he was only 19 years old, he was commissioned to design furniture for the Royal family.

The Victorian Age Queen Victoria ascended to the throne in 1837, to become one of the longest reigning monarchs in British history. Her tenure also coincided with the cataclysmic growth of the Industrial Revolution, the rise of an Empire that both sustained it and was spread by it, rural-urban migration on an unprecedented scale, and a host of social ills that resulted from it. Because of the concentration of labor in factories in urban centers such as London, Manchester, Birmingham, and Glasgow as a consequence of the wider utilization of steam power, cottage industries could not compete, and entire families left the countryside for the city. Following what is now seen to be a predictable pattern that is occurring again in developing nations around the world, many of those who relocated did so without any assurance of a job or a place to live once they had arrived in the city. This resulted in widespread homelessness, poverty, crime, disease, and death. Social reform to address these issues, and the growing economic rift between the rich and the poor that only served to further calcify a well-entrenched class system, was slow in coming, but it did come. It was led by intellectuals such as John Ruskin, William Carlyle, and William Morris, who adopted the idea of the regeneration of Gothic architecture as part of their campaign. The logic behind this was that Gothic architecture represented a collaborative communal effort in the past, and as such was symbolic of a time in which social classes were less stratified. There was also a spiritual agenda in promoting it, since Gothicism was seen to be part of a less secular and less materialistic age and so was a perfect antidote to the consumer mentality promoted by the industrial age.

Pugin Was Their Guide A. W. N. Pugin in both his writings and his architecture was the guide for this group of reformers. After the initial publications that he produced with his father, Pugin went on to write *The True Principles of a Pointed or Christian Architecture* in 1841, in which he praised the Gothic style for its honest use of materials and formal expression and promoted it as the one true national architecture as a palliative to social problems. This book followed close on the heels of a previous tract with the long title of *Contrasts, A Parallel Between the Nobile Edifices of the 14th and 15th Centuries and Similar Buildings of the Present Day Showing a Decay of Taste*, which appeared in 1836. A derisory poem that appeared soon afterward said, in part:

> "Oh have you seen the work just out,
> By Pugin, the great builder?
> 'Architectural Contrasts' he's made out
> Poor Protestants to bewilder
> The Catholic Church, she never knew
> Till Mr. Pugin taught her
> That orthodoxy had to do
> At all with bricks and mortar."[55]

In both his *Contrasts* and *True Principles* books, Pugin equated Gothic architecture with moral purity, and this belief carried through into his design work as well.

Pugin predated this group, but was still alive when they came to the forefront. In 1851 he was given the opportunity by the organizers of the Crystal Palace Exhibition in London to contribute a design for a "Medieval Court" pavilion in one of its bays, which probably seemed like an anachronism but was well received by the public nonetheless. At that time, William Morris, who had been a divinity student at Oxford University, had just decided to change his career course to architecture after hearing John Ruskin deliver the Slade lecture about the social ills caused by industrialization. After graduation he joined the architectural office of G. E. Street, where his friend Philip Webb was working, and Morris and Webb set up their own firm in 1857. Webb designed Red House for William Morris in Bexleyheath, Kent, in 1859, following the direction that Pugin had already established in his own house, called the Grange, in Ramsgate nearby in 1843.

The Grange, Ramsgate The 1830s were a chaotic, as well as highly productive, time for Pugin. Because of his Gothic expertise, he was approached by Charles Barry and asked to assist in the rebuilding of the Houses of Parliament in 1834 that had been damaged by fire. His contribution to the partnership was extensive, so that Parliament, as it appears today, owes much to Pugin's skill. He married in 1831 and his wife died in childbirth the following year. His father also died in 1832, and his mother followed a year later. He converted to Catholicism in 1834 and settled in Salisbury to be near the great Gothic cathedral there.[56]

He built a house in Salisbury, based on Gothic principles, with arched windows and steeply gabled roofs, as well as a bell tower. But, he had remarried, and because of his growing family and his desire to be closer to the Channel so that he could visit France more easily, he decided to move to Ramsgate, in Kent, in 1841 and build a larger version of his Salisbury house there.

Rather than using brick, as he had previously, however, he chose to use a flinty local stone instead, which gives the house a less delicate, more substantial feel. The house is located near a monastery called St. Augustine's Priory, and Pugin sited his house to take advantage of it to create a sense of enclosure.

The plan of the house literally duplicates the L-shaped configuration that would later become so popular among Arts and Crafts devotees in the decades that followed; in that it is a pair of "L"s placed back-to-back separated by a square entrance hall with a grand stairway leading up to the second floor. The first of these L-shaped portions, on the north, contains a chapel and a kitchen. The second,

The Grange, Ramsgate.   Courtesy of Kelvin Barber; Flickr

which is joined to the first by a connecting hallway, has a dining room, sitting room, and library, which are each well proportioned, and each has a fireplace. The bedrooms and bathrooms are on the second floor. Pugin had a daughter from his first marriage, and he had five additional children with his second wife, Louisa Burton, so the additional space that this house provided must have been most welcome. A second, service stair served the kitchen and chapel wing.

A Master Builder In realizing the design of the house, Pugin followed the Gothic tradition of architect as master builder, becoming involved in all aspects of its construction. It was a repository of his detailing skill in all media and an example of what would become the Arts and Crafts precept of the total work of art. Masons, carpenters, blacksmiths, and artisans were all under his supervision, and he was known to be an energetic and exacting supervisor. As opposed to other, less informed and correct attempts at Gothic Revival at this time, the Grange represents an accurate rendition of the design and detailing of a private home of the eleventh and twelfth centuries, due to Pugin's scrupulous surveys of original examples.

In a rare exhibition of his sketchbooks, held at the Victoria and Albert Museum in the early 1990s, page after page of minute, carefully drawn details of Gothic houses and cathedrals that Pugin did throughout France and England provided ample testimony of his dedication and skill. That was translated into the third

Red House. © Wayne Andrews / Esto

dimension in the few architectural commissions that he was able to carry out during his relatively short lifetime, and the Grange at Ramsgate is among the best of these.

William Morris and Philip Webb: Red House

William Morris is one of the towering intellectual figures of the Victorian Age and is closely associated with the attempts at social reform that started to coalesce in England in the middle of the nineteenth century. These eventually resulted in the formulation of the Arts and Crafts Movement there. Morris was born in 1834 in Walthamstow, of Welsh heritage on both his mother's and father's sides. After attending private school near his home, he went to Marlborough College when he was 14, and then to Exeter in Oxford five years later in 1853. His father, William Sr., died in 1847 at age 50, leaving behind a large estate accumulated through investment in the Devonshire Great Consolidated Copper Mining Company. His inheritance provided William Jr. with a monthly allowance that would be considered substantial even by today's standards.[57]

William Morris as King Arthur Morris studied history at Exeter with an emphasis on religion. He was particularly taken with *Le Mort d'Arthur* by Sir Thomas Malory, which had been popularized by Sir Walter Scott at that time. Morris seemed to internalize the chivalric code that is one of the main themes of that tragic story, and to some extent his personal life may also be seen as a reenactment of the Arthurian legend of Camelot. The ideological position that Morris started to formulate while he was at Oxford has been compared by his biographer, Fiona MacCarthy, to that of the Young England Movement started by several influential Conservative politicians in the 1840s. MacCarthy describes the goals of this group as the emulation of the "ideals of medieval England, not in a regressive way but in a creative one. They wanted to extract from medieval England those elements from which the Victorian age could learn." These lessons included equality and the elimination of a class-based society, the return to small communities and rural values, and "architecture as the measure of civilization and the means by which the people reconnected themselves with the past."[58] The monastery and the convent, which emerged as indispensable social institutions during the Middle Ages because of the uncertainty, random violence, and destitution of that historical period, are also the paradigmatic egalitarian community and appealed as a symbol to Morris because of the sense of camaraderie and self-denial that they represented.

While he was at Oxford, he married Jane Burden, who came from a far less prosperous family than his own. Her appeal to him, beside the difference in their social position, was her exotic appearance, and while she came to respect him, she later claimed never to have loved him. She said she was primarily attracted by the financial security that marriage to him offered. He painted her as Guinevere at one point early in their relationship, and then only lacked a Lancelot to make his Arthurian fantasy complete. Dante Gabriel Rossetti, who was the founder of the Pre-Raphaelite Movement and shared many of Morris's beliefs, filled that role. Rossetti's attentions quickly shifted from his own partner, Elizabeth Siddal, to Jane Burden soon after she married.

The Red House Bexleyheath, in Upton, which is close to London, was selected in 1859 as the location of Morris's new Camelot. It appealed to him because it was near Watling Street, which pilgrims used to get to Canterbury, as well as the ruins of Abbey Farm, which was once a monastery. By this time his business venture, which would finally be formalized as Morris, Marshall, Faulkner and Co. in 1861, was beginning to demand more of his time and prodigious energy. William Morris had a lasting effect on the future direction of architecture, since it can be argued, as Peter Davey has, that Arts and Crafts principles morphed almost completely into those of the Modern Movement.[59] But, Morris realized early in his postacademic career that he did not want to actually practice architecture, or painting either, given the awkwardness of his portrait of Jane Burden as Guinevere. His talent was in what is now generally called interior design, but the term does not come close to describing his explorations and contribution. Interior design today rarely runs parallel to its architectural equivalent, and the two professions are now typically viewed as being separate and distinct disciplines. Arts and Crafts advocates, however, viewed a dwelling as an entity, in which the spaces and interiors, including all of the furniture, floor coverings, fabrics, and other accoutrements were all part of a total work of art. The ideological basis of this approach was social improvement, beginning with the family, or group of people living in the house as the catalyst of change. Beauty was considered to be transformative and could be effective only if it was integral to the entire living experience. Architecture and interior design, completed at different stages by different contributors, present ideas that would have been anathema to an Arts and Crafts believer, such as Morris. This principle is one of the most essential similarities between the Arts and Crafts and Modern Movements, which is why the Red House is often mentioned as being one of the first modern houses, in spite of its medieval cast. Another reason for the designation of Red House as a modern design is its minimalism and practicality, which is also central to Morris's ideological intention. In an article entitled "Art and the Beauty of Life," he famously said, "Have nothing in your houses that you do not know to be useful or believe to be beautiful."[60] This contradicted the Victorian tendency of filling the house with furniture, portraits, decorations, potted plants, heavy drapes, carpets, and bric-a-brac. It was also a mantra intended to be an antidote to the meaningless production of things for their own sake, at the expense of the time and effort of a laborer to do so. By calling for the judicious selection of items to be placed in each house, Morris was trying to sensitize people to the human price, rather than the financial cost of each piece that was chosen, asking them to consider if it was really worth the soul-destroying, repetitive effort that the assembly line demanded. This minimalistic approach was also intended as a critique of industrial production for profit by a budding iconoclast, who was instrumental in composing the Manifesto of the Socialist League, which he also signed in 1885.[61]

Red House is close to Abbey Wood railroad station, which allowed Morris to go down to London easily when business interests required him to. The site he and his architect friend Philip Webb chose also had an apple orchard on it, which heightened the rural romance of the place for him.[62] Morris and Webb envisioned Red House, which is named after the color of the brick used to build it, as a monastery, and these typically had orchards that sustained the monks who lived in them. It was inspired by the bricks used in Tattershall Castle in Lincolnshire, built for the Lord

Treasurer of England, Ralph Cromwell, in 1440.[63] The plan of the Red House is L-shaped, but was positioned to be easily extended into a quadrangle with an open central courtyard. The allocation of spaces in the house was also unconventional, conforming to Morris's communal, utopian ideal of friends and family sharing life together. Accordingly, the zone that is usually associated with receiving guests during the Victorian age, such as the drawing room and living room, are located on the second floor of the two-story house, near the bedrooms and bathrooms. The ground floor is dominated by a large Gothic-style oak staircase at the end of a large entrance hall. It has a sharply pointed ball-capped newel post and solid rails pierced with circular cutouts that contribute to the medieval aura of the residence.

The furniture, designed primarily by Morris and Webb, was also inspired by Gothic and Medieval motifs, layered with a tendency for the romantic, such as a dresser lacquered in a color they called "Dragon's Blood Red." One of the most imposing pieces is a settle at the end of the drawing room, which is architectural in scale. It has a ladder on the side so that musicians can climb up to a "minstrels' gallery" on top, which was used on holidays, such as Christmas. The walls are filled with murals intended to relate to Morris and his wife, Jane. One of the most revealing of these, painted by family friend Edward Burne Jones, is based on a fifteenth-century romance of Sir Degrevault, and shows Morris as a king and Jane Burden as queen attending a wedding banquet.[64] Morris and his wife, as well as his close circle of friends, were also involved in the preservation and renewal of crafts of all kinds, such as embroidery, which was also displayed on the walls. Morris was obsessed with recreating medieval techniques with absolute accuracy down to the last detail, in his production of furniture, carpets, silverware, and embroidery. He researched the kinds of plants that would have been used to create the dyes and grew them in the garden of Red House. He went to Aubusson, France, which was a thriving tapestry center during the Middle Ages, to research the technique and materials used in making these wall hangings.

Kelmscott On the outside, Red House looks like an apparition, or a re-creation of a setting in a fairy tale by the brothers Grimm, complete with a circular turreted wishing well. As Morris's business expanded, he, his wife, and their close friends, including Dante Gabriel Rossetti, required a more spacious stage set in which to act out their medieval fantasy. And so Red House was sold and Morris bought a sixteenth-century house, which he renamed Kelmscott, near Oxford in 1871, when he was 37 years old.[65]

The Richard Rogers House, London

Richard Rogers is widely regarded as the archetypal Modernist and one of the chief international proponents for that aesthetic. Best known for the Pompidou Center in Paris and the Lloyd's building in London, he has been given the title Lord Rogers and has been credited with changing the direction of contemporary architecture. As part of his Modernist heritage, Rogers believes in the primacy of technology and the need to express the way that it is used to make each of the buildings he has designed in a very clear way. This has led to his having been classified as being part of the high-tech school of British Modernism, but he rejects that label. He simply agrees to relying upon the empirical tradition, which has been such a powerful force in contemporary architecture. His belief in that direction began with Team 4, a mid-1960s partnership that included fellow English architect Sir Norman Foster, whom Rogers had met while on a Fulbright scholarship at Yale. The firm produced the Reliance Controls Factory in Swindon, which would effectively redefine the Modernist approach to industrial and commercial architecture. After Team 4 broke up and a brief time collaborating with Su Rogers, he worked for several years with Italian architect Renzo Piano with whom he designed the Pompidou Center. He then formed his own practice in 1977.

The process of ongoing reinterpretation, which Rogers sees as the central issue of Modernism, is clear in his newly remodeled residence in London. It is located near Kings Road and the Thames, and overlooks the Royal Hospital gardens in Chelsea. Rogers and his wife, Ruthie, bought the house in 1983 after an extensive search for property on which to build was unsuccessful. They were seduced by the central location of this house and the orientation. They feel that the best thing about the house is the view and the fact that it faces south. This provides it with light from three sides and a cool breeze coming from the garden across the way.

The building was originally a pair of 1840s houses, each 15 feet wide, located on the corner of a small square. They were once divided by a party wall, and the interiors, including elements such as the staircase, fireplaces, and moldings, had been lost in earlier renovations. The first of Rogers's periodic efforts toward rehabilitating the structure was to seal off the entrance to one house and make the doorway to the other into a private entry to his mother-in-law's flat. He converted the old tradesman's entrance to the second house into a new front door. This involved taking out a small badly lit garden and inserting a stair. He opened up a huge living area and kitchen on the first floor by removing the common wall and part of the upper floor. He then installed a staircase to a second-floor gallery that served as the couple's bedroom. Separate spiral stairs to the third floor also lead to a library, a children's bedroom, and a playroom.

The Rogerses have two sons, Bo and Roo, and their house is also a London base for Rogers's three sons from a previous marriage: Ben, Zad, and Ab. They stay in a basement apartment when they visit.

The need for more space and for light prompted Rogers to undertake the current renovation. This resulted in having only a small study upstairs, but Rogers actually prefers reading in bed, especially in the early morning before the demands of the day start to intrude on his time.

In its latest remodeling the Rogerses extended the staircase from the gallery to the third floor, changing the mezzanine bedroom into a library and study, and made the third floor into a bedroom and bathroom zone. Rogers has also expanded a rooftop garden, which previously covered only one house, onto the roof of the second. This has created a private, quiet sanctuary for him and his wife.

Rogers's essential design idea for his residence, which is a functional mezzanine overlooking a soaring central living space, stems from the lasting impact that seeing several classic Modernist California houses had on him. While working for Skidmore, Owings and Merrill in San Francisco in 1961, Rogers became familiar with the work of Rudolph Schindler, Raphael Soriano, and Charles and Ray Eames. The Eames House had an especially strong effect, especially in the way that the mezzanine is used there to overlook the two-story-high living room below. Rogers shares the Eameses' process of design as well as his habit of beginning with the detail and then working up from there. He was also influenced by the Eameses' use of primary colors, which has its roots in the De Stijl movement, Constructivism, and Purism.

Like the Eameses, Rogers is fascinated by artifacts from the past and the sense of continuity that historical elements bring with them. In spite of the fact that Modernism is often regarded as involving the rejection of history, Rogers sees unison between the two, such as in the art of Japan where objects are old but look modern. Rogers believes that he can be a Modernist and still appreciate the past.

Rogers and his wife furnished the house with pieces they like, such as Jacobsen stacking chairs in different colors. These provide a counterpoint to the more classical modern pieces, such as a Norman Foster glass table and a Le Corbusier leather sofa and chairs, and this brings the interior alive. The bed in the master bedroom was designed by Ab Rogers, and it can also be used for storage. It is painted yellow to add to the brightness of the room.

Rogers's preference for large sealed space is evident from the size of the first floor main living area, which visually extends up the stairway from the kitchen, dining and sitting areas to the mezzanine. Rogers and his wife refer to this living area as "the piazza" because everyone gathers there. The original full-length windows are now hinged and open inward.

Good food is an important part of the Rogerses' lifestyle since they are also involved in the River Café restaurant. Despite its cleanly refined, metallic efficiency, the kitchen in the piazza is transformed when in use into a compact, ergonomically tested model of professional, foldout efficiency. Ruthie Rogers is also one of the chefs of the River Café.

Rogers, who was born in Italy and spent his childhood in Florence, has been raised on great Italian food. He designed this house so that he and his wife can socialize with their guests, rather than disappearing while cooking goes on. A counter-height island of stainless steel is all that separates the cooking and sitting areas, so that people can talk easily and everyone can enjoy the cooking experience.

A solitary totemic plated steel I beam, used vertically as a column in the kitchen, is a hint that the *Maison de Verre*, which is described elsewhere in this volume, was another important design resource for Rogers, in addition to the Eames House in Los Angeles. His quoting it here reinforces his view that Modernism need not be antiseptic and sterile but should include relevant references to time, place, and people. The Glass House, like the Rogers House, was an experiment that involved the latest innovations that industry could then produce. But this empirical approach on the part of the architect, Pierre Chareau, was tempered by his awareness of the needs of his clients to personalize their house, most specifically with a collection of Art Deco furniture that the couple had inherited from Dr. Dalsace's wife's parents. The *Maison de Verre* is perhaps a more aggressively Modern context than the Eames House because of its scale and the degree to which its architect interjected himself into the design process. But both Pierre Chareau and Charles and Ray Eames now represent a concerted effort to personalize technology and make it user friendly.

Rogers believes that his early years, including his family's move to England in the late 1930s, played an important role in the development of his deeply held architectural ideals and preferences. He had an Italian background and his mother was a potter. He recalls having Bauhaus furniture in the house and always being surrounded by good design when he was young.

The Richard Rogers house is a good example of the balance between permanence and change that he constantly looks for in his work. He has attempted to popularize modern architecture and, in contrast to the prevailing view that Modernists dislike history, has also tried to reconfigure the past. More people see the Pompidou Center every year than the total number of visitors to the Eiffel Tower and the Louvre combined. He wants to use architecture as a vehicle with which to make London a model for other cities. He has done so in his renovation of Billingsgate Market; his scheme to turn Trafalgar Square from a traffic roundabout to a pedestrian piazza; and his visionary, long-range plans to convert the Thames, which is the biggest open space in London, into a vibrant civic meeting place. It was once this way. Viewed in this context, Rogers's house is only a small part of his vision, but it reveals the consistency of his principles and their allegiance with the Humanistic tradition.

Charles F. Annesley Voysey: The Orchard at Charleywood, Hertsfordshire

Charles F. Annesley Voysey was the quintessential English Arts and Crafts architect, practicing in and around London at the end of the nineteenth century. Charles Rennie Mackintosh seems to have received a majority of attention as a leader of the Movement in the recent past, perhaps due to the recognition he received from an appreciative audience on the Continent in the late 1800s, and that support, outside of Britain, eventually led to his playing a formative influence at the beginning of the Modern Movement in Germany and then throughout Europe in general. But as a Scotsman, from a financially restricted background, who was raised in a tenement in Glasgow, Mackintosh was never fully accepted into the closed society of the British Arts and Crafts branch. He was considered to be far too plebian and provincial. William Morris and John Raskin, who provided the theoretical underpinnings of the Arts and Crafts Movement, were each independently wealthy members of the British upper-middle class, as were Webb, Ashbee, Baillie Scott, Shaw, and many of the other talented members of this elite group. While Morris, as someone of Welsh heritage, shared the passion for a Celtic Revival personified by Mackintosh and his mentor, Patrick Geddes, the clientele for his extremely lucrative practice were primarily members of the English aristocracy. This and the obvious dilemma of a confirmed Socialist being extremely wealthy were the two seemingly irreconcilable conflicts of Morris's life.

A Paragon of Arts and Crafts Principles While Charles F. Annesley Voysey was not wealthy, he arguably represents the English branch of the Arts and Crafts Movement best because of the clarity of his design principles, made legible in his work. These are most especially visible in a house he designed for himself and his family near the Charleywood station of the Metropolitan Line of the London

Underground, which he called the Orchard because of a stand of old apple trees on the site. His budget was limited to between £1,000 and £1,500, which was not much even in 1899, when the plans were drawn up.[66]

Voysey had always wanted to design a home for himself, but the demands of a successful growing practice had not allowed him the luxury of having the time to do so. His marriage to Mary Evans in 1897, however, seemed to finally offer him the perfect opportunity to realize his dream. The newlyweds first looked at land in Colwall, near Perrycraft, but were eventually unable to obtain it. They found another property near Charleywood, which is a station on the Metropolitan Line of the London Underground. This decision to build near a commuter stop is reminiscent of a similar choice by William Morris when he chose a site for Red House for himself and his wife, Jane Burden, at Baxley Heath, and it once again underscores the obvious paradox involved in wanting to live in a house that approximates a country cottage as closely as possible, while still being able to commute to an office in the city. This preference did not begin with Morris, since developers such as Jonathan Carr had gotten wealthy on the trend as early as 1875, when he bought a 45-acre parcel at Turnham Green, which is a station for both the Central and Piccadilly Lines, and commissioned architect Richard Norman Shaw to design homes on it for families with annual incomes in the £300 to £1,500 range per year. The new community was treated as a self-contained village, with its own church and inn, as well as a sports club with tennis courts and an art school. This community, named Bedford Park, started with nearly 900 houses, which was eventually expanded to 113 acres because of its popularity. Shaw chose to design in the Queen Anne style, which this project also served to popularize, in order to avoid the aesthetic war then taking place between the Gothic Revivalists, on the one hand, and the Classicists, on the other.

Although they were inaugurated much later, the Garden Cities promoted by Ebenezer Howard, such as Letchworth in 1903, Hampstead Garden Suburb in 1907, and Welwyn Garden City in 1919, and produced in partnership with Barry Parker and Raymond Unwin, were also aimed at the same audience to "return people to their last paradise."[67]

Once the rural-urban migration into London, which had started at the beginning of the Industrial Revolution in the mid-eighteenth century, started to slow down, there was a reverse migration of sorts as the workers who led the rush to the city began to prosper. They wanted to move to the suburbs once the railroad allowed them easy access to their jobs to escape the pollution, congestion, clamor, and worse that were the legacy of industrialization.

The Orchard The house that Voysey designed for himself, his wife, and their three children conforms to the ideal middle and upper-middle class image of a country cottage, even though it would be difficult to find a home of similar style in any rural district in Britain. That is the essential importance of the Orchard, in that Voysey created it to embody all of the subconscious clues of bucolic living, without literally collaging them together in one house. Construction of the house started in 1899 and the final cost was about £1,500.00.[68]

The elements that Voysey chose to include in this highly edited and carefully thought-out paragon are as telling as those he also decided to exclude. The first is the roof, which is the most elemental of all, since it has primeval connotations of shelter and security. The roof here, as elsewhere in Voysey's residential *oeuvre* is gracefully steep, with slightly curved, deeply overhanging eaves and a very thin barge board, or edge, which makes it look thin and light, like a hat. He chose slate for the Charleywood house, because he liked its gray simplicity and the slightly iridescent quality it has when it gets wet, which is quite often in London. This notion, of the potential of unexpected, hidden beauty in the most commonplace things, extends to every other aspect of the house, as well. Voysey wanted to allow as much light into the interior as possible, and so he used dormers on the roof here as elsewhere. These tended to break down the scale and potential monotone of a long horizontal slate surface but did not allow them to cut through the surface in a major way. The surface of the house is called roughcast, similar to the harling or pebbledash favored by Mackintosh for the exterior walls of Hill House and Windyhill in Helensburgh, near Glasgow. As the name implies, it consists of small pebbles that act as an aggregate in a cementations wash, which seals the structure against the worst weather. It was a favorite solution to the nearly horizontal rains in the Highlands by farmers and crafters, because it is relatively inexpensive and as easy to apply as whitewash.

In addition to a simple, long, and broad slate roof that seems to sit almost weightlessly on these roughcast walls, and the tall, slender dormers that rise up like vigilant sentinels along its perimeter, Voysey used a line of red tile that extends out slightly from the exterior wall and runs above the top of the ground floor windows around the entire perimeter of the house to serve as a horizontal datum that ties the entire elevation together. He also uses a porch here, as he frequently did elsewhere, to protect people using the front door from the weather. In other houses he has designed, such as Broadlegs, near Lake Windermere in Cumbria, a similar thoughtful gesture, around and above the entrance into the house from the service yard, is a substantial building in its own right and indicates the architect's sensitivity to detail.

Living at the Orchard This sensitivity extends to every part of the interior of the house, which is rectangular in shape. Voysey has located the main social, or public, spaces, which include the entrance hall and foyer, the study, and dining room, along its western edge to make the most of the late afternoon sun, while the service spaces, such as the kitchen and an extended pantry, are on the northern side. The study also has a view out toward a small wooded area to the north so that it takes advantage of the light from that direction as well. Voysey's attention to the prevailing direction of sunlight at certain times of the day and the need to locate the rooms that would be used at those times to take advantage of it may seem elementary, but it is remarkable how few architects are aware of this technique, which is also called diurnal zoning, let alone are able to use it skillfully. The result at the Orchard, as well as in other Voysey houses, is a warm glow in the major rooms during the early morning and at the end of the day. Voysey balanced his love of light, with a keen understanding of thermal heat loss through large expanses of glass, carefully sizing windows to the minimum necessary to satisfy both requirements. He also changed sill heights for the same reason, to frame views yet also cut down on drafts and heat loss. The warmth of natural light in his own house was matched by the color of the materials, fabrics, and paint colors that he chose for each space. The ceilings above the picture rail were white to better reflect the light, but below it were covered with richly hued wallpapers. Each room has a fireplace, each of which is a work of art with small openings for coal and peat, and a broad surface clad in thin long vivid tiles.

5

West and Southwest Asia

SAUDI ARABIA

Abdel Wahed El-Wakil: Suliaman Palace, Jeddah, K.S.A.

In his design for the Suliaman Palace, Abdel Wahed El-Wakil has not only over-come the twin challenges of a large and relatively flat site, but has also successfully turned them to his advantage. To fully understand how this has been done and the subsequent importance of these residences as a prototype for others in this region, it is first necessary to recall that until relatively recently Jeddah where the palace is located was a walled city confined to a few square miles of area along the coast of the Red Sea. For reasons of efficiency, as well as privacy, the house within this walled area was organized within a vertical tower, typically using three main divi-sions of space. Ground level, which was much more accessible to the public, was usually reserved for rooms associated with service and storage, as well as an official reception room for guests. The second and third floors of these tower houses were set aside for the family with the topmost floor being the most private of all. Because of the compact nature of these residential quarters and the proximity of the houses inside them, *mushrabiyya* screens or *roshan*, as they are called in Jeddah, were an essential addition to the windows of each house as was a central courtyard that also provided privacy.

After the city wall was demolished and Jeddah began to expand after World War II, the restraints that had faced house builders in the past became redundant as detached villas sprung up on individual lots as quickly as civic services could be extended to them. As the architect himself explained his concept for this particular residence then:

> In the Suliaman Palace I wished to make explicit a philosophy of design for the tradi-tional Arab house. An architecture that serves society is dynamic and is proof to change. The challenge of architecture is to maintain continuity within the change that occurs by referring to the constants and reinterpreting them within the new context. This interaction between what is constant and what is change brought on by newly arising situations results in new formal entities ... The Suliaman Palace is located in new

Jeddah, which is reclaimed desert area to the north of the older city and is mainly for housing. There are no narrow streets and plots are isolated by wide avenues to provide for modern traffic. The Palace differs therefore from older houses in that it is on an individual isolated plot.

As a visible symbol of these new conditions, the Suliaman Palace extends horizontally from the middle of its triangular site with long elevations toward the north and south to take maximum advantage of the best light and views toward the Red Sea. As the architect once again explains:

> The Palace is clearly and visually defined by the different functions: the public area, the semi-public and totally private sleeping quarters and service wing. The building extends on the southern elevation to over 70 meters in length. This elongation was imposed by the site an extended triangular shape and the desire to obtain a maximum view of the Red Sea. A standard square module of 6 feet, or 180 centimeters, was used throughout the design for dimensioning purposes. Planning on a module helped to bring order in what would be a confusing disposition of walls and a variety of dimensions that would be burdensome in executing an edifice as large as this one. Also, the use of a dominant axis was adopted to give order to the massing of the plan.

As originally conceived, the sequence of spaces along this axis begins with a small courtyard that acts as one part of a *magaz*, leading to the main entrance of the house itself. A large *majlis*, or *salamlik*, which is located on one side of this court upon entrance, is organized in the shape of a "U" with its open end facing the court; it has a continuous banquette running along three walls in the fashion of a traditional male reception room. Of these three walls, the one to the south facing the door is dominant and has a large ornately carved wooden panel running from the back of the banquette to the ceiling to designate a place of honor for the sheikh himself; with windows looking out to the gardens and the sea beyond flanking it on both sides. The walls of the two sides of the "U" also have smaller carved wooden panels, which alternate with solid vertical bands of brick and plaster wall. Antique Bedu rifles from the sheikh's extensive collections of weapons, hanging muzzle down in these white bands, are a vivid reminder of the bands of tribal fealty that he still commands.

Sometime after the construction of the house had already begun, the client decided that there was a need for several guest rooms and, in spite of the generous size of the site, the placement of the foundations and linear increasingly private character of the concept dictated that these be located near the entrance courtyard as well. Because of municipal setback the proximity of the site line to the guest wing dictated that it be deflected from the main axis. With characteristic optimism, the architect also looked upon this unexpected turn of events as an opportunity rather than a difficulty, using the apparent conflict between the space required and the area remaining to the advantage of the design. To some the result may be reminiscent of the kind of juxtaposition intentionally created by Robert Venturi to exaggerate the contemporary drift away from the functionalist aesthetic of the modernists in projects such as the Vanna Venturi house in Chestnut Hill or the Brant House in Bermuda; another level is also evocative of the kind of transformation that takes place in the Fatamid and Mamluk complex in Medieval Cairo, as an example in the madrasa of Al Salih Najm al Din Ayyub, the madrasa and mausoleum of Amir Sanjar al Jawli, and the khangah and mosque of Amir Shaykhu, and such examples were definitely in the architect's mind as he went about solving this problem. As he says:

> As the space for this added wing was confined within the existing internal vehicle drive-ways use was made of an old design technique; aligning the elevation walls with the streets and disposing of the rooms inside accordingly filling in spaces where necessary. This solution was often used in the old irregular street patterns and especially in Mosques where the buildings were aligned with the street whilst prayer space was directed toward Makkah.

The resulting addition, which represents one of the few such examples of complexity and contradiction in El-Wakil's residential work, serves to augment the entry court and *samalik* across the drive and to act as a visual hinge generating the extended fugal of movement of spaces that extend horizontally from it. As such, it both begins and ends the linear form of the house, paradoxically giving it more animation than it could otherwise have had.

The towering *Qa'a*, which is the highest volume in this extended elevation, is reached through a long, exquisitely tiled hallway that joins the public zones of the palace. A subtle shift in zoning, from the grouping of the *majlis* to an inner sanctum reserved for close friends, is marked by level as well as scale with three semicircular steps leading up into the high, square space. This change of level, which is repeated in an even more exaggerated way between the semiprivate and private zones, is far from accidental, as can be seen in an early rendering, in which a tripartile garden, rendered in the fashion of Hassan Fathy, pharoanically inspired gouaches, clearly indicates these horizontal break points and an increasing sense of closure where they occur. The dining room, the kitchen, and the party wing that is perpendicular to it further confirms the purpose of this zone, meant for entertaining important guests, relatives, and close friends. The family quarters located across an open courtyard from this middle zone terminates the line and is really a self-contained atrium house in its own right. A wooden cupola, inspired by one of similar formed design for the Monesterli residence in Cairo by Hassan Fathy, signifies the fragile character of this grouping as compared to the *Qa'a* across the court, casting delicate shadows on the white walls of the bedroom arcades below. This sense of playfulness continues in the central fountain of the atrium itself, which is updated here into a plunge connected by a covered passageway to the swimming pool beyond.

Through such innovation, El-Wakil has shown the possibility inherent in the typologies of the past.

Notes

CHAPTER 1: THE AMERICAS

H. H. Richardson: The Ames Gate Lodge

1. Pfeiffer, *Frank Lloyd Wright*Henry-Russell, Hitchcock, *The Architecture of H. H. Richardson and His Times* (Cambridge, MA: MIT Press, 1966), 203.

Richard Morris Hunt and Frederick Law Olmstead: Biltmore

2. Paul R. Baker, *Richard Morris Hunt* (Cambridge, MA: MIT Press, 1980), 419.

3. Ibid., 414.

4. Ibid., 414.

5. Ibid., 431.

Gwathmey Siegel Architects: The De Menil House

6. Joseph Giovanni, "An Amicable Parting of Man and Home," *New York Times*, May 26, 1988, 10.

Louis Kahn: The Esherick and Fisher Houses

7. Kerner Commission, *Report of the National Advisory Commission on Civil Disorders* (Washington, DC: United States Government Printing Office, 1969), 19.

8. Anne Tyng, *Louis Kahn and Anne Tyng: The Rome Letters 1953–1954* (New York: Rizzoli, 1997).

9. Ibid., 6.

10. Ibid., 8.

11. Ibid., 13.

12. Ibid., 14.

Mill Town Houses in Lowell, Massachusetts

13. John Coolidge, *Mill and Mansion* (New York: Columbia University Press, 1993), 128.

14. Ibid., 128.

15. Ibid., 99.

16. Ibid., 38.

17. Ibid., 74.

Michael Graves: The Benacerraf, Hanselman, and Snyderman Houses

18. Alan Colquhoun et al., *Michael Graves (Architectural Monographs, No. 5)* (Rizzoli International, 1979), 10.

19. Colin Rowe, *The Mathematics of the Ideal Villa* (Cambridge, MA: MIT Press, 1976).

20. Colquhoun et al., *Michael Graves*, 18.

21. Michael Graves, Vincent Scully, Peter Arnell, Karen V. Wheeler, and Ted Bickford, *Michael Graves: Buildings and Projects* (New York: Rizzoli, 1982), 216.

The Walter Gropius House, Lincoln, Massachusetts

22. Kenneth Frampton, *Modern Architecture; A Critical History* (London and New York: Thames and Hudson, 2007).

23. Ise Gropius, "History of the Gropius House," *GA Houses*, no. 25 (March 1989): 6–31, esp. 7.

24. Eric Kramer, "The Walter Gropius House Landscape; A Collaboration of Modernism and the Vernacular," *Journal of Architectural Education* 57, no. 3 (February 2004): 46.

25. Gropius, "History of the Gropius House," 16.

The Philip Johnson Glass House

26. James Steele, *The Eames House* (London: Phaidon, 1994), 16.

Robert Venturi: The Vanna Venturi House

27. Robert Venturi, *Complexity and Contradiction in Architecture* (New York: Museum of Modern Art; distributed by Doubleday, Garden City, NY, 1966).

28. Denise Scott Brown, "On Houses and Housing," in *Denise Scott Brown and Robert Venturi* (London: Academy Editions, 1992), 16.

29. Frederic Schwartz, ed., *Mother's House* (New York: Rizzoli, 1992), 35.

30. Ibid., 50.

31. Dimitri Porphyrios, *Classicism Is Not a Style* (London: Academy Editions, 1992), 26.

The White House

32. William Seale, *The White House: The History of an American Idea* (Washington, DC: The American Insitiute of Architects Press, 1992), 1.

33. Ibid., 5.

34. Ibid., 6.

35. Ibid., 10.

36. Ibid., 16.

37. Ibid., 12.

38. Ibid., 12.

The Shotgun House

39. Melville J. Herskovit, *The Myth of the Negro Past* (Boston: Beacon Press, 1959), xxiii.

40. Sheryl G. Tucker, "Roots: Reinnovating the African American Shotgun House," *Places* 10, no. 1 (1995): 64.

The Stretto House

41. Steven Holl, *Stretto House* (New York: Monacelli Press, Inc., 1996), 7.
42. Ibid., 7.
43. Ibid., 7.

The American Townhouse

44. Kevin D. Murphy, *The American Townhouse* (New York: Harry N. Abrams, 2005), 9.
45. Ibid., 13.
46. Ibid., 18.
47. Ibid., 22.
48. Ibid., 35.
49. Ibid., 31.

Frank Lloyd Wright: The Oak Park, Robie, Hollyhock, Jacobs, and Fallingwater Houses

50. Frank Lloyd Wright, *Frank Lloyd Wright: An Autobiography* (New York: Horizon Press, 1977), 5.
51. Ibid., 6.
52. Ibid., 57.
53. Ibid., 80.
54. Ibid., 100.
55. Ibid., 104.
56. Bruce Brooks Pfeiffer, *Frank Lloyd Wright* (Köln, Germany: Taschen, 1994), 10.
57. James Steele, *Hollyhock House* (London: Phaidon, 1995), 36.
58. Pfeiffer, *Frank Lloyd Wright*, 38.
59. Ibid., 1.
60. Ibid., 32.
61. K. Smith, "Frank Lloyd Wright, Hollyhock House, and Olive Hill, 1914–24," *Journal of the Society of Architectural Historians* XXXVIII, no. 1 (1979): 18, note 7.
62. Vincent Scully, *Frank Lloyd Wright* (New York: George Braziller, 1960), 47.
63. Wright, *Frank Lloyd Wright: An Autobiography*, 63.
64. Ibid., 106.
65. Scully, *Frank Lloyd Wright*, 52.
66. Ibid., 64.
67. Egar Tafel, *About Wright: An Album of Recollections by Those Who Knew Frank Lloyd Wright* (New York: John Wiley and Sons, 1995), 63.
68. R. Venturi, "On Frank Lloyd Wright" (unpublished paper prepared for an exhibition of Frank Lloyd Wright drawings at the Pennsylvania Academy of Fine Arts in Philadelphia, 1990).

Buff and Hensman: The Bass House

69. Donald Hensman, *Buff and Hensman*, ed. James Steele (Los Angeles, CA: The Guild Press, 2003), 16.

Morphosis: The Crawford House

70. "Crawford Residence," *GA House* (Tokyo), no. 30–55 (July 1992): 30.

Charles and Ray Eames: The Eames House

71. See Reyner Banham, *Los Angeles: The Architecture of Four Ecologies* (Berkeley, CA: University of California Press, 2000).

72. R. J. Clark and A. P. A. Belloli. *Design in America: The Cranbrook Vision 1925–1950* (New York: Metropolitan Museum of Art, 1983), 26.

Charles and Henry Greene: The Gamble House

73. Randell Makinson, *Greene and Greene: The Passion and the Legacy* (Layton, UT: Gibbs Smith Publisher, 1998), 103.

74. Ibid., 118.

75. Ibid., 113.

Julia Morgan: Hearst Castle

76. Nancy E. Loe, *Hearst Castle* (Santa Barbara, CA: Aramark Leisure Services, Inc., 1991), 7.

77. Ibid., 8.

78. Alan Magary and Kerstin Fraser Magary, *South of San Francisco* (New York: Harper and Row, 1983), 183.

79. Thomas R. Aidala, *Hearst Castle* (New York: Hudson Hills Press, 1981), 49.

80. Ibid., 40.

81. Magary and Magary, *South of San Francisco*, 185.

82. Ibid., 184.

83. Loe, *Hearst Castle*, 15.

Irving Gill: The Dodge House and Horatio West Court, Los Angeles

84. Thomas Hines, *Irving Gill and the Architecture of Reform: A Study in Modernist Architectural Culture* (New York: Monacelli Press, 2000), 38.

85. Ibid., 77.

86. Ibid., 79.

87. Ibid., 97.

88. Ibid., 80.

89. Ibid., 222 and 242.

Rudolph Schindler: The How House

90. "Bowery Greets Hobo King," *New York Times*, October 18, 1909, 16.

91. Ibid., 16.

92. James Steele, *Rudolph Schindler* (Berlin: Taschen, 1998), 53.

93. A. Sarnitz, *R. M. Schindler* (New York: Rizzoli, 1986), 48.

94. Beatriz Colomina, *M. Risselada Raumplan versus Plan Lilve* (Delft: Delft University, 1987), 46.

95. Ibid., 47.

96. Judith Sheine, *R. M. Schindler* (Barcelona: Gili SA, 1998), 20.

John Lautner: The Sheats House, Los Angeles

97. Le Corbusier, *The Athens Charter* (New York: Grossman Publishers, 1973), 30.

98. Ibid., 31.

99. Hasan-Uddin Kahn, *The International Style, Modernist Architecture from 1925 to 1965* (Köln, Germany: Taschen, 1998), 23.

100. Frank Escher, *John Lautner, Architect* (London: Artemis, 1994), 16.

Eric Moss: The Lawson-Westen House

101. James Steele, *Lawson-Weston House: Eric Owen Moss* (London: Phaidon Press Limited, 1995), 24.

102. Frederic Schwartz, ed., *Mother's House* (New York: Rizzoli, 1992), 3.

Richard Neutra: The Lovell Health, VDL Research, and Kaufmann Palm Springs Houses

103. Frederick Koeper, *The Richard and Dion Neutra VDL Research House I and II* (Pomona: California State University, 1985), 9.

104. David Hay, "A Modernist Masterpiece in the Desert Is Reborn.," *Architectural Record* (September 1999): 8.

A. Quincy Jones

105. Ester McCoy, *Case Study Houses. 1945–1962.* (Santa Monica, CA: Hennessey and Ingalls, 1977), 15

106. Ibid., 20.

107. Ibid., 34.

Oscar Niemeyer: The Canoas and Strick Houses

108. Alan Hess, *Oscar Niemeyer Houses* (New York: Rizzoli International Publications, Inc., 2006), 83.

109. Ibid., 83.

110. Greg Goldin, "Lost Then Found," *Los Angeles Magazine* (May 2007), 89.

A Contemporary Hacienda in Colombia, Casa Puente Rogelio Salmona

111. Laura Laviada-Checa, ed., *Legorreta & Legorretta* (New York: Rizzoli International Publications, Inc., 2004), 193.

112. Ibid., 193.

113. Ibid., 194.

114. Ibid., 195.

115. Simon Romero, *Obituary of Rogelino Salmona, New York Times*, October 6, 2007, 214.

CHAPTER 2: AFRICA

Abdel Wahed El-Wakil: The Halawa, Chourbaggy and Hydra Houses

1. Aga Khan Award for Architecture.

2. Abdel Wahed El-Wakil. Personal interview with author, 1986.

3. Ibid.

4. Ibid.

5. Ibid.

6. Ibid.

Charles Boccara: The Abtan House, Marrakesh

7. Brian Brace Taylor, *Tunisia, Egypt, Morocco: Contemporary House, Traditional Values* (London: Zamana Gallery Catalogue, 1985), 12.

8. Julia S. Berrall, *The Garden* (London: Thames and Hudson, 1966), 55.

9. Ibid., 56.

10. Ibid., 57.

CHAPTER 3: ASIA AND AUSTRALIA

The Great Wall Commune

1. Craig Au Yeung, *Gary Chang: Suitcase House* (Hong Kong: Map Book Publishers/ MCCM Editions, 2004), 1–168.

Tadao Ando: The Kashino, Nakayama, and 4 X 4 Houses

2. Kenneth Frampton, "Tadao Ando and the Cult of Shintai," in *Tadao Ando; The Yale Studio and Recent Works* (New York: Rizzoli, 1989), 7.

3. Ibid., 7.

4. Ibid., 7

5. Tadao Ando, "The Wall as Territorial Delineation," *Japan Architect* 254 (June 1978): 41.

6. Ibid., 41.

7. Ibid., 41.

The Ushida Findlay Partnership: Soft and Hairy House

8. "Ushida Family Partnership," *Architectural Design*, 65, no. 5–6 (May–June 1995): 68.

9. Ibid., 56.

10. James Wines, *Green Architecture* (Köln, Germany: Taschen Books, 2002), 25.

11. Ibid., 26.

12. Herve Bailey, Association Sens Espace, founded in Paris in 1969, with the mission of reconnecting people to the natural environment.

The Cheong Fatt Tze Mansion

13. Guided Tour: James Steele Interview with Eric Farn, June 2008.

14. Gregory Wittkopp, ed., *Saarinen House and Garden: A Total Work of Art* (New York: Harry N. Abrams, 1995), 51.

15. Ibid., 50.

16. Guided Tour.

17. Wittkopp, *Saarinen House and Garden*, 51.

18. Ibid., 54.

19. Ibid., 53.

Ken Yeang: Roof Roof House

20. Colin Davies, *Key House of the Twentieth Century* (New York: W. W. Norton & Company, Inc., 2006), 17.

Abdul Harris Othman: Serandah House

21. Interview with Abdul Haris Othman, Kuala Lumpur, July 2007, transcribed by Giuliana Haro.

CHAPTER 4: EUROPE AND THE WESTERN MEDITERRANEAN

Adolf Loos: The Villa Scheu, Vienna

1. Panayotis Tournikiotis, *Adolf Loos* (New York: Princeton Architectural Press, 1994), 10.

2. Ibid., 70.

Josef Hoffmann: The Palais Stoclet, Brussels

3. Edward F. Seklar, "Stocklet," *Josef Hoffman: The Architectural Work* (Princeton, NJ: Princeton University Press, 1985).

4. Ibid., 97.

5. Giuliano Gresieri, *Josef Hoffman* (Bologna, Italy: Nicola Zanichelli, S.P.A., 1981), 69.

6. Seklar, *Josef Hoffman: The Architectural Work*, 94.

7. Gresieri, *Josef Hoffman*, 14.

Hvittrask, Lindgren, Gesellius, and Saarinen

8. William Curtis, *Modern Architecture Since 1900* (London: Phaidon, 1982), 135.

9. J. M. Richards, *800 Years of Finnish Architecture* (Vancouver: David and Charles, 1978), 188.

10. Ibid., 50.

11. James Steele interview with guide, 1996.

12. Richards, *800 Years of Finnish Architecture*, 119.

13. Ibid., 54.

14. Ibid., 53.

Alvar Aalto: Villa Mairea

15. Louna Lahti, *Aalto* (Köln, Germany: Taschen, 2004), 41.

16. Peter Reed, ed., *Alvar Aalto: Between Humanism and Materialism* (New York: Museum of Modern Art, 1998), 33.

Pierre Chareau: *Maison de Verre*

17. Brian Brace Taylor, *Pierre Chareau* (Köln, Germany: Benedikt Taschen Verlag, 1998).

18. Ibid.

19. Ibid.

20. Adam Gopnick, "The Ghost of the Glass House," *The New Yorker*, May 9, 1994, 54.

21. Ibid., 61.

22. Ibid., 63.

23. Nicoli Ououssoff, "The Best House in Paris," *New York Times*, August 26, 2007, 23.

24. Gopnick, "The Ghost of the Glass House," 65.

25. Alastair Gordon. "The End of an Era," *Architectural Digest* (2007): 134.

Le Corbusier: The Villa Savoye

26. Jacques Sbiglio, *Le Corbusier: La Villa Savoye* (Basel: Birkhauser Publishers, 1999).

27. Le Corbusier, *Villa Savoye and Other Buildings and Projects, 1929–1930* (New York: Garland, 1982).

28. *Villa Savoye, Poissy, France 1929–1931* (Tokyo: A.D.A. EDITA, 1972).

Auguste Perret: Apartment House on Rue Franklin, Paris

29. Amy Gardner, "Auguste Perret: Invention in Convention, Convention in Invention," *Journal of Architectural Education* (February 1997): 140.

30. Ibid., 141.

31. Kenneth Frampton, "August Perret: The Evolution of Calssical Rationalism," *Modern Architecture; A Critical History* (New York and London: Thames and Hudson, 2007), 106.

32. Ibid., 107.

33. Erwin Panofsky, *Gothic Architecture and Scholasticism* (Cleveland, OH: Meridian Books, 1957), 15.

Ludwig Mies van der Rohe: Weissenhofsiedlung

34. Peter Lizon, "Mies Imperative: A Total Design; The Villa Tugendhat is Open to the Public," *A + U* (April 1997): 4.

35. Alexander von Vegesack and Matthias Kries, *Mies van der Rohe* (Milan: Skira Editore, 1998), 180.

36. Ibid., 136.

Gerrit Rietveld and Theo van Doesburg: The Schroeder House

37. William Curtis, *Modern Architecture Since 1900* (London: Phaidon, 1982), 151.

38. Ibid., 152.

39. Ibid., 56.

40. Paul Overy et al., *The Rietveld Schroeder House* (Cambridge, MA: MIT Press, 1988).

John Hejduk: The Wall House

41. Marijke Martin, "Hedjuk's Wall House #2," *Architecture and Urbanism* (February 2001): 83.

42. Ibid., 80.

Antoni Gaudi: The Casa Batlló, Barcelona

43. Kenneth Frampton, *Modern Architecture; A Critical History* (London and New York: Thames and Hudson, 2007), 64.

44. Ibid., 60.

45. Derek Avery, *Antonio Gaudi* (London: Chaucer Press, 2004), 135.

46. Ibid., 138.

Charles Rennie Mackintosh: Hill House

47. James Steele, *Charles Rennie Mackintosh, Synthesis in Form* (London: Academy, 1997), 16.

48. Ibid., 23.

49. Ibid., 50.

50. Ibid.

Edwin L. Lutyens: Deanery Gardens, Sonning, Heathcote

51. Margaret Richardson, *Sketches by Edwin Lutyens* (London: Academy Editions, 1994), 6.

52. "Chronology," *The Lutyens Trust*, June 15, 2008. Available at http://www.lutyenstrust.org.uk/frameset.html (Referenced on Web site from Richardson's "Sketches by Edwin Lutyens," and Amery's "The Work of English Architect, Sir Edwin Lutyens.")

53. Colin Amery and Margaret Richardson, *The Work of English Architect, Sir Edwin Lutyens 1869–1944, Exhibition Catalogue* (London: The Arts Council, 1981), 108–109.

54. Ibid., 109.

A. W. N. Pugin: Ramsgate

55. Wendy Hitchmough, *CFA Voysey* (London: Phaidon Press Limited, 1995), 146.

56. Ibid., 146.

William Morris and Philip Webb: Red House

57. Fiona MacCarty, *William Morris* (London: Faber and Faber, 1994), 23.

58. Ibid., 63.

59. Ibid., 37.

60. Peter Davey, *Arts and Crafts Architecture* (London: Phaidon Press, 1997).

61. Diane Waggoner,. *The Beauty of Life: William Morris and the Art of Design* (London: Thames & Hudson, 2003).

62. MacCarty, *William Morris*, 505.

63. Ibid., 155.

64. Ibid., 156.

65. Ibid., 158

Charles F. Annesley Voysey: The Orchard at Charleywood, Hertsfordshire

66. Wendy Hitchmough, *CFA Voysey* (London: Phaidon Press Limited, 1995), 125.

67. James Steele, *Ecological Architecture A Critical History* (London and New York: Thames and Hudson, 2005), 53.

68. Ibid., 125.

Bibliography

Chapter 1: The Americas

H. H. Richardson: The Ames Gate Lodge

"The Ames Memorial Buildings, North Easton, Mass./H.H. Richardson, Architect." *Monographs of American Architecture*, no. 3. Boston: Ticknor, 1886.

The Architecture of Henry Hobson Richardson in North Easton, Massachusetts. North Easton: Oakes Ames Memorial Hall Association and Easton Historical Society, 1969.

Brown, Robert F. "The Aesthetic Transformation of an Industrial Community." *Winterthur Portfolio 12* (1997): 35–64.

"Gate Lodge to the Estate of F. L. Ames, Esq., North Easton, Mass." *AABN 18* (December 26, 1885): 304.

Hitchcock, Henry-Russell. *The Architecture of H. H. Richardson and His Times.* Cambridge, MA: MIT Press, 1966.

Ochsner, Jeffrey Karl. "F.L. Ames Gate Lodge." *H. H. Richardson; Complete Architectural Works.* Cambridge, MA: MIT Press, 1982, 202–279.

O'Gorman, James. *Living Architecture: A Biography of H. H. Richardson.* New York: Simon and Schuster Editions, 1997.

Richard Morris Hunt and Frederick Law Olmstead: Biltmore

Baker, Paul R. *Richard Morris Hunt.* Cambridge, MA: MIT Press, 1980.

Bryan, John Morrill. *Biltmore Estate: The Most Distinguished Private Place.* New York: Rizzoli, 1994.

Messer, Pamela Lynn. *Biltmore Estate: Frederick Law Olmsted's Landscape Masterpiece.* Asheville, NC: WorldComm, 1993.

Rickman, Ellen Erwin. *Biltmore Estate.* Charleston: Arcadia Publishing, 2005.

Wesler, Cathy A., ed. *Biltmore Estate: Specialties of the House.* Birmingham: Oxmoor House, 1994.

Gwathmey Siegel Architects: The De Menil House

Breslow, Kay. *Charles Gwathmey & Robert Siegel: Residential Works, 1966–1977.* New York: Architectural Book Pub. Co., 1977.

Collins, Brad, ed. *Gwathmey Siegel.* New York: Universe Publishing, 2000.

Goldeberger, Paul. *Gwathmey Siegel*. New York: Monacelli Press, 2000.

Heyer, Paul. *American Architecture: Ideas and Ideologies in the Late Twentieth Century*. New York: Van Nostrand Reinhold, 1993.

Huls, Mary Ellen. *Charles Gwathmey and Gwathmey Siegel Associates: A Bibliography*. Monticello, IL: Vance Bibliographies, 1987.

Richard Meier: The Smith House and Douglas House

Blaser, Werner. *Richard Meier: Details*. Basel: Birkhauser Verlag, 1996.

Meier, Richard. *Richard Meier, Architect*. New York: Oxford University Press, 1976.

Meier, Richard. *Smith House, Darien, Connecticut, 1967, House in Old Westbury, Long Island, New York, 1971*. Tokyo: A. D. A. Edita Tokyo, 1976.

Rybczynski, Witold. *The Look of Architecture*. New York: Oxford University Press, 2001.

Schittich, Christian, et al. *Single Family Houses: Concepts, Planning, Construction*. Basel: Birkhauser, 2000.

Louis Kahn: The Esherick and Fisher Houses

Gast, Klaus-Peter. *Louis I. Kahn: The Idea of Order*. Basel: Birkhauser Verlag, 1998.

Latour, Alessandra, ed. *Louis I. Kahn: Writings, Lectures, and Interviews*. New York: Rizzoli International Publications, 1991.

Ronner, Heinz, Sharad Jhaveri, and Alessandro Vasella. *Louis I. Kahn: Complete Works 1935–74*. Basel; Boston: Birkhauser Verlag, 1987.

Rykwert, Joseph. *Louis Kahn*. New York: Harry N. Abrams, Inc., 2001.

Mill Town Houses in Lowell, Massachusetts

Bender, Thomas. *Toward an Uran Vision: Ideas and Institutions in Nineteenth Century America*. Baltimore: John Hopkins University Press, 1982.

Coolidge, John. *Mill and Mansion*. New York: Columbia University Press, 1993.

Lowell Historical Society. *Lowell: The Mill City*. Charleston: Arcada, 2005.

Michael Graves: The Benacerraf, Hanselman, and Snyderman Houses

Dunster, David, ed. *Michael Graves*. New York: Rizzoli International Publications, 1979.

Nichols, Karen Graves, et al. *Michael Graves: Buildings and Projects, 1982–1989*. New York: Princeton Architectural Press, 1990.

The Walter Gropius House, Lincoln, Massachusetts

Berdini, Paolo. *Walter Gropius; Works and Projects*. Bologna: Nicola Zanichelli Editore, S. P. A., 1983.

Giedion, S. *Walter Gropius: Work and Teamwork*. New York: Reinhold Publishing Corporation, 1954.

Gropius, Ise. "History of the Gropius House." In "Walter Gropius; Gropius House, Lincoln Massachusetts, U.S.A. 1937–1938." *GA House*, no. 25 (March 1989): 6–31.

Gropius, Ise. *Walter Gropius: Buildings, Plans, Projects 1906–1969*. Cambridge: MIT Press, 1972.

Isaacs, Reginald. *Gropius: An Illustrated Biography of the Creator of the Bauhaus*. Boston: Bulfinch Press, 1991.

Kramer, Eric F. "The Walter Gropius House Landscape: A Collaboration of Modernism and the Vernacular." *Joural of Architectural Education* 57, no. 3 (Feburary 2004): 39–47.

Lupfer, Gilbert, and Paul Sigel, *Walter Gropius, 1883-1969, The Promoter of a New Form*, Taschen, Germany, 2004.

The Philip Johnson Glass House

Earls, William D. *The Harvard Five in New Canaan: Mid-century Modern Houses by Marcel Breuer, Landis Gores, John Johansen, Philip Johnson, Eliot Noyes & others*. New York: W. W. Norton, 2006.

Fox, Stephen. *The Architecture of Philip Johnson*. Boston: Bulfinch Press, 2002.

Hitchcock, Henry-Russell, and Philip Johnson. *The International Style*. New York: W. W. Norton, 1996.

Whitney, David, and Jeffrey Kipnis, eds. *Philip Johnson: The Glass House*. New York: Pantheon Books, 1993.

Robert Venturi: The Vanna Venturi House

Cook, John W., and Heinrich Klotz. *Conversations with Architects*. London: Lund Humphries, 1973.

Curtis, William. *Modern Architecture Since 1900*. Oxford, U.K.: Phaidon Press Ltd., 1982.

Diamonstein, Barbarelee. *American Architecture Now*. New York: Rizzoli; Vol. 1, 1980; Vol. 2, 1985.

Drew, Philip. *The Third Generation: Changing Meaning in Architecture*. London: Praeger, 1972.

Frampton, Kenneth. "America 1960–1970. Notes on Urban Images and Theory." *Casabella* 389/390, XXV (1971): 24–38.

Handlin, David P. *American Architecture*. London: Thames and Hudson, 1985.

Jencks, Charles. *Current Architecture*. London: Academy Editions, 1982.

Jencks, Charles. *The Language of Post-Modern Architecture*. London: Academy Editions, 1977.

Jencks, Charles. *Modern Movements in Architecture*. Harmondsworth: Penguin Books, 1973.

Jencks, Charles (ed.). *Post-Modern Classicism*. London: Academy Editions, 1980.

Klotz, Heinrich. *Die Revision der Moderne. Postmoderne Architektur 1960–1980*. (Katalog Deutsches Architektur-museum, Frankfurt am Main). Munich: Prestel, 1984.

Klotz, Heinrich (ed.). *Moderne and postmoderne Architektur der Gegenwart, 1960–1980*. Brunswick-Wiesbaden: Vieweg, 1984.

McCoy, Esther. "Buildings in the United States." *Lotus* 4 (1967–1968): 15–123.

Mead, Christopher, ed. *The Architecture of Robert Venturi*. Albuquerque: University of New Mexico Press, 1989.

Muller, Michael. *Architektur und Avantgarde*. Frankfurt: Syndikat, 1984.

Portoghesi, Paolo. *Dopo l'architettura moderna*. Bari: Laterza, 1980.

Portoghesi, Paolo, et al. *The Presence of the Past: First International Exhibition of Architecture—Venice Biennale 1980*. London: La Biennale di Venezia, Venice and Academy Editions, 1980.

Scully, Vincent. *American Architecture and Urbanism*. New York: Praeger, 1969.

Scully, Vincent. *The Shingle Style Today or The Historian's Revenge*. New York: Braziller, 1974.

Schwartz, Frederick, ed. *Mother's House*. New York: Rizzoli International Publications, 1992.

Simity, C. Ray. *Supermannerism: New Attitudes in Post Modern Architecture*. New York: Dutton, 1977.

Stern, Robert A. M. *New Directions in American Architecture*. New York: Braziller, 1969.

Tafuri, Manfredo, and Dal Co, Francesco. *Architettura Contemporanea*. Milan: Electa Editrice, 1976.

Venturi, Robert. "The Campidoglio: A Case Study." *Architectural Review* (May 1953): 333–34.

Venturi, Robert. "A Justification for a Pop Architecture." *Art and Architecture* (April 1965).

Venturi, Robert. "Three Projects: Architecture and Landscape, Architecture and Sculpture, Architecture and City Planning." *Perspecta* 11 (1967): 103–6.

Venturi, Robert. "A Bill-Ding Board Involving Movies, Relics and Space." *Architectural Forum* (April 1968): 74–76.

Bibliography

Venturi, Robert. "Complexity and Contradiction in the Work of Furness." *Pennsylvania Academy of the Fine Arts Newsletter* (Spring 1976), 5.

Venturi, Robert. "Alvar Aalto." *Arkkitehti* (July–August 1976): 66–67.

Venturi, Robert. "A Definition of Architecture as Shelter with Decoration on It, Another Plea for a Symbolism of the Ordinary in Architecture." *A+U* (January 1978): 3–14.

Venturi, Robert. "Leaning from Right Lessons from the Beaux Arts." *Architectural Design* (January 1979): 23–31.

Venturi, Robert. "RIBA Discourse July 1981." Transactions 1. *RIBA Journal* (May 1981): 47–56.

Venturi, Robert. "Diversity, Relevance and Representation in Historicism, or Plus ça Change... plus A Plea for Pattern all over Architecture with a Postscript on my Mother's House." *Architectural Record* (June 1981): 114–19.

Venturi, Robert. "Il Proprio Vocabolario. Four Houses." *Gran Bazaar* (January–February 1982): 152–57.

Venturi, Robert. "On Aalto." *Quaderns* 157 (April–May–June 1983): 55.

Venturi, Robert. "Proposal for the Iraq State Mosque, Baghdad." *L'Architecture d'aujourd'-hui* (September 1983): 28–35.

Venturi, Robert. "A Bureau in William and Mary Style." In *Le Agginita' Elettive. Ventuno progettisti ricercano le proprie affinita*, edited by Carlo Guenzi. Milan, Italy: Triennale di Milano, 1985, 153–58.

Vogt, Adolf M. Stathaus, Ulrike Jehle-Schulte, and Bruno Reichlin. *Architektur 1940–1980*. Frankfurt am Main, Vienna, Berlin: Propylaen, 1980.

Wolfe, Tom. *From Bauhaus to Our House*. New York: Farrar, Staus & Giroux, 1981.

The White House

Caroll, Betty Boyd. *Inside the White House: America's Most Famous Home, the First 200 Years*. Garden City, NY: Doubleday Book & Music Clubs, 1992.

Fazio, Michael W., and Patrick A. Snadon. *The Domestic Architecture of Benjamin Henry Latrobe*. Baltimore: Johns Hopkins Universtiy Press, 2006.

Seale, William. *The White House: The History of an American Idea*. Washington DC: The American Institute of Architects Press, 1992.

Truman, Margaret. *The President's House: 1800 to the Present: the Secrets and History of the World's Most Famous Home*. New York: Ballantine Books, 2005.

White House Historical Association. *The White House: an Historic Guide*. Washington DC: White House Historical Association, 2003.

The Shotgun House

Bullard, Robert D. *Invisible Houston*. College Station, TX: Texas A&M University Press, 1987.

Herskovitz, Melville J. *The Myth of the Negro Past*. Boston: Beacon Press, 1959.

Tucker, Sheryl G. "Roots; Reinnovating the African American Shotgun House." *Places* 10, no. 1 (1995): 64–71.

Vlach, John Michael. "Sources of the Shotgun House: Antecedents for Afro-American Architecture." Doctoral Dissertation, Indiana University, March 1975.

The Stretto House

Holl, Steven. *Intertwining*. New York: Princeton Architectural Press, 1996.

Holl, Steven. *Stretto House*. New York: Monacelli Press Inc., 1996.

"Steven Holl; Compressed Planar Library, Dallas, Texas, USA." *GA Houses* 66 (2001): 64–69.

"Steven Holl, Stretto House." *Architectural Design* 1–165 (1995): 41–43.

The American Townhouse

Ames, Kenneth. "Robert Mills and the Philadelphia Row House." *Journal of the Society of Architectural Historians* 27, no. 2 (1968): 140–46; Murtagh, William John. "The Philadelphia Row House." *Journal of the Society of Architectural Historians* 16, no. 4 (1957): 8–13.

Ballon, Hilary. *The Paris of Henri IV: Architecture and Urbanism.* Cambridge, MA: MIT Press, 1991.

Braudel, Fernand. "Pre-modern Towns." In *The Early Modern Town*, edited by Peter Clark. New York: Longman, 1976.

Bunting, Bainbridge. *Houses of Boston's Back Bay: An Architectural History, 1840–1917.* Cambridge, MA, and London: The Belknap Press of Harvard University, 1967, 69.

Cohen, Jeffrey Alan. "The Queen Anne and the Late Victorian Townhouse in Philadelphia, 1878–1895." Ph.D. Diss., University of Pennsylvania, 1991.

Gorlin, Alexander. *The New American Town House.* New York: Rizzoli, 1999, 10.

Hamlin, Talbot. *Greek Revival Architecture in America.* New York: Dover Publications, Inc., 1964, Reprinted from 1944, 171.

Herman, Bernard. *Town House Architecture and Material Life in the Early American City, 1780–1830.* Chapel Hill: University of North Carolina Press for the Ohmohundro Institute for Early American History and Culture, 2005.

Heuer, Ann Ronney. *Town Houses.* New York: Friedman/Fairfax, 2000, 17.

Hoskins, W. G. "English Provincial Towns in the Early Sixteenth Century." In *The Early Modern Town*, edited by Peter Clark. New York: Longman, 1976.

Lockwood, Charles. *Bricks and Brownstone: The New York Row House, 1783–1929*, 2nd ed. New York: Rizzoli, 2003, 70.

Murphy, Kevin D. *The American Townhouse.* New York,: Harry N. Abrams, 2005.

Sennett, Richard. *The Conscience of the Eye.* New York: Knopf, 1990, 93.

Summerson, Sir John. *Georgian London*, new ed. London: Barrie Jenkins, 1988, 18–19.

Wright, Gwendolyn. *Building the Dream: A Social History of Housing in America.* Cambridge, MA, and London: MIT Press, 1983, 24, 40.

Zierden, Martha A., and Bernard L. Herman. "Charleston Townhouses: Archaeology, Architecture, and the Urban Landscape, 1750–1850." In *Landscape Archaeology: Reading and Interpreting the American Historical Landscape*, edited by Rebecca Tamin and Karen Bescherer Metheny. Knoxville: University of Tennessee Press, 1996, 204–7.

Bruce Goff: The Bavinger House

Anderson, G. M. L. *Bruce Goff: The Luminous Environment.* Ph.D. thesis, Texas Tech University, 1985.

Cook, Jeffrey. *The Architecture of Bruce Goff.* New York: Harper and Row Publishers, 1978.

DeLong, D. G. *The Architecture of Bruce Goff.* New York: Garland, 1977.

Frank Lloyd Wright: The Oak Park, Robie, Hollyhock, Jacobs, and Fallingwater Houses

Connors, Joseph. *The Robie House of Frank Lloyd Wright.* Chicago: University of Chicago Press, 1984.

Gill, Brendan. *Many Masks.* New York: Putnam, 1987.

Jencks, Charles. *Kings of Infinite Space.* New York: St. Martins. 1983.

Johnson, Donald Leslie. *Frank Lloyd Wright versus America: 1930s.* Cambridge, MA: The MIT Press, 1990.

Kaufmann, E. *Fallingwater.* New York: Abbeville Press, 1986.

Laseau, Paul, and James Tice. *Frank Lloyd Wright Between Principle and Form.* New York: Van Nostrand Reinhold, 1992.

McCarter, Robert. *Fallingwater: Frank Lloyd Wright.* London: Phaidon Press Limited, 1994.

McCarter, Robert. *Frank Lloyd Wright.* London: Phaidon Press Ltd., 1997.

Meehan, Patrick J. *Frank Lloyd Wright Remembered.* Washington, DC: The National Trust for Historic Preservation, 1991.

Sergeant, John. *Frank Lloyd Wright's Usonian Houses.* New York: Watson-Guptill Publications, 1976.

Smith, Katryn. *Frank Lloyd Wright's Taliesin and Taliesin West.* New York: Harry N. Abrams Inc., Publishers, 1997.

Tafel, Edgar. *Apprentice to Genius.* New York: McGraw-Hill, 1979.

Toker, Franklin. *Fallingwater Rising.* New York: Alfred A. Knopf, 2003.

Zevil, Bruno. *La Casa Sulla Cascata.* Milano: ETAS, 1965.

Buff and Hensman: The Bass House

Buisson, Ethel, and Thomas Billard. *The Presence of the Case Study Houses.* Basel: Birkhauser Publishers for Architecture, 2004.

Hensman, Don, and James Steele. *Buff & Hensman.* Los Angeles: Balcony Press, 2004.

Morphosis: The Crawford House

"Morphosis Crawford Residence." *GA Houses* (July 1992): 30–55.

Murphy, James. "Literal Abstractions." *Progressive Architecture* (November 1991): 53–63.

Phillips, Patricia. *Morphosis: The Crawford House.* New York: Rizzolli International Publications, Inc., 1998.

Charles and Ray Eames: The Eames House

Carpenter, Edward. *Industrial Design 25th Annual Design in Review.* New York: Whitney Library of Design, 1979.

Collins, Michael. *Towards Post-Modernism: Design since 1851.* London: British Museum Publications, 1987.

Drexler, Arthur. *Charles Eames: Furniture from the Design Collection.* New York: The Museum of Modern Art, 1973.

Dunster, David, ed. *Key Buildings in the Twentieth Century, vol. 2, Houses 1945–1989.* London: Butterworth, 1990.

Emery, Marc. *Furniture by Architects: 500 international masterpieces of twentieth-century deisgn and where to buy them.* New York: Abrams, 1983.

Fehrman, Cherie, and Kenneth Fehrman. *Post-War Interior Design 1945–1960.* New York: Van Nostrand Reinhold, 1980.

Gill, Brendan. *The Dream Come True: Great Houses of Los Angeles.* New York: Lippincott and Crowell, 1980.

Harris, Frank, and Weston Bonenberger, eds. *A Guide to Contemporary Architecture in Southern California.* Los Angeles: Watling and Co., 1951.

McCoy, Esther. *Modern California Houses: Case Study Houses 1945–1962.* New York: Reinhold Publishing Corporation, 1962.

McCoy, Esther et al. *Blueprints for Modern Living: History and Legacy of the Case Study Houses.* Los Angeles: Museum of Contemporary Art, 1990. Published on the occasion of an exhibition held at the Museum of Contemporary Art, October 17, 1988–February 13, 1990.

Morrison, Philip and Phyllis, and the Office of Charles and Ray Eames. *Powers of Ten: About the Relative Size of Things in the Universe.* Scientific American Library, Vol. 1. New York: W. H. Freeman and Co., 1982.

Naylor, Coling, ed. *Contemporary Masterworks.* Chicago, London: St. James Press, 1991.

Neuhart, John, and Marilyn Connections. *The Work of Charles and Ray Eames, Exhibition Catalogue.* Los Angeles, CA: Los Angeles Art Council, 1976.

Neuhart, John, Marilyn Neuhart, and Ray Eames, *Eames Design: The Work of the Office of Charles and Ray Eames.* London: Thames and Hudson, 1989.

Page, Marian. *Furniture Designed by Architects.* New York: Whitney Library of Design, 1980.

Charles and Henry Greene: The Gamble House

Bosley, Edward R. *Gamble House: Greene and Greene.* London: Phaidon Press Ltd., 1992.

Bosley, Edward R. "Greene and Greene, Gamble House." *Architecture in Detail Series.* London: Phaidon, 1992.

Current, Karen. *Greene and Greene: Architect in the Residential Styles.* Fort Worth, TX: Amon Carter Museum of Western Art, 1974.

Ford, Edward R. "The Arts and Crafts Movement: The Greene Brothers and Their English Contemporaries, David B. Gamble House." *The Details of Modern Architecture.* Cambridge, Massachusetts/London, England: The MIT Press, 1990.

Greene, Charles Sumner. "Bungalows," *The Western Architect* (July 1908).

Jordy, William H. "Progressive and Academic Ideals at the Turn of the Twentieth Century." *American Buildings and Their Architects,* Vol. 3. Garden City, New York: Doubleday, 1972.

Makinson, Randell L. *Greene and Greene: Architecture as a Fine Art.* Salt Lake City: Peregrine Smith Inc., 1977.

Makinson, Randell L. *Greene and Greene: Creating a Style.* Salt Lake City: Gibbs Smith, 2004.

Makinson, Randell L. *Greene and Greene: The Passion and the Legacy.* Salt Lake City: Gibbs Smith, 1998.

Makinson, Randell L. "Trip to Epoch-Making Greene and Greene, Blacker House—Gamble House." *Global Architecture GA Houses 2.* Japan: A. D. A. EDITA Tokyo Co., Ltd., 1977.

Makinson, Randell L. "Greene and Greene David B. Gable House." *Global Architecture GA Houses 2.* Japan: A. D. A. EDITA Tokyo Co., Ltd., 1984.

Stickley, Gustav. *Craftsman Homes.* New York: Dover Publications, 1979.

Thomas, Jeanette A. *Images of the Gamble House, Masterworks of Greene and Greene.* University of Southern California: The Gamble House, Pasadena, California, 1989.

Wolfe, Tobias Arthur. "The Integration of Architecture and Landscape in Greene and Greene's Gamble House." Master's thesis, Cornell University, 1993.

Julia Morgan: Hearst Castle

Aidala, Thomas. *Hearst Castle: San Simeon.* New York: Hudson Hills Press, 1981.

Brown, Joseph A. "Hearst's Amazing Castle." *Historic Preservation* 40, no. 2 (March 1988): 66–68.

Loe, Nancy E. *Hearst Castle: The Official Pictoral Guide.* Santa Barbara, CA: Aramark Leisure Services, Inc., Companion Press, 1991.

Magary, Alan, and Kerstin Fraser Margary. *South of San Francisco, A Guide to California's Central Coast.* New York: Harper and Row, 1983.

Irving Gill: The Dodge House and Horatio West Court, Los Angeles

Hines, Thomas. *Irving Gill and the Architecture of Reform: A Study in Modernist Architectural Culture.* New York: Manacelli Press, 2000.

Kamerling, Bruce. *Irving J. Gill, Architect.* San Diego: San Diego Historical Society, 1993.

McCoy, Ester. *Five California Architects.* New York: Praeger, 1975.

Rudolph Schindler: The How House

March, Lionel, and Judith Sheine, eds. *RM Schindler: Composition and Construction.* London: Academy Editions, 1993.

Noever, Peter. *MAK Center for Art and Architecture R.M. Schindler.* Munich: Prestel-Verlag, 1995.

Sheine, Judith. *R.M. Schindler.* Barcelona: Editorial Gustavo Gili, SA, 1998.

Steele, James. *How House: RM Schindler.* London: Academy Group Ltd., 1996.

Bibliography

Pierre Koenig Case Study Houses No. 21 and No. 22

Goldstein, Barbara. "The History and Legacy of the Case Study House." *Architecture: The AIA Journal* 78, no. 12 (1977): 19–22.

Hines, Thomas S. "Case Study Gem in Los Angeles." *Architectural Digest* 56, no. 7 (2005): 104–111.

Jackson, Neil. *The Modern Steel House.* New York: John Wiley. Sons, Inc., 1996.

McCoy, Esther. *Case Study Houses 1945–1962.* 2nd ed. Los Angeles: Hennessey and Ingalls, Inc., 1977.

Smith, Elizabeth. *Case Study Houses.* New York, Köln: Taschen, 2002.

Steele, James, and David Jenkins. *Pierre Koenig.* London: Phaidon Press, 1998.

John Lautner: The Sheats House, Los Angeles

Campbell Lange, Barbara-Ann. *John Lautner.* Köln: Taschen, Benedkt Verlag, 1999.

Escher, Frank. *John Lautner, Architect.* London: Artemis, 1994.

Escher, Frank, ed. *John Lautner, Architect.* New York: Princeton Architectural Press, 1998.

Gossel, Peter, ed. *John Lautner.* Köln: Taschen Verlag, 1999.

Hess, Alan. *The Architecture of John Lautner.* New York: Rizzoli International Publications, Inc., 1999.

Eric Moss: The Lawson-Westen House

Giaconia, Paola. *Eric Owen Moss. The Uncertainty of Doing.* Milan: Skira, 2006.

Ojeda, Oscar Riera. *The New American House: Innovations in Residential Design and Construction: 30 Case Studies.* New York: Whitney Library of Design, 1995.

Steele, James. *Contemporary California Houses: Frank Gehry, Schnabel House; Eric Owen Moss, Lawson-Westen House; Franklin D. Israel, Drager House.* London: Phaidon Press, 1999.

Steele, James. *Lawson-Westen House: Eric Owen Moss.* London: Phaidon Press Limited, 1995.

Bernard Maybeck: Wyntoon

Cardwell, Kenneth H. *Bernard Maybeck: Artisan, Architect, Artist.* Santa Barbara, CA: Peregrine Smith, 1976.

Cardwell, Kenneth H. *Bernard Maybeck: Artisan, Architect, Artist.* Santa Barbara: Peregrine Smith, 1977.

Marvin, Betty. *Maybeck and His Legacy: Houses by Bernard Maybeck and in the Maybeck Tradition.* The Association, 1986.

Woodbridge, Sally B. *Bernard Maybeck: Visionare Architect.* New York: Abbeville Press, 1992.

Richard Neutra: The Lovell Health, VDL Research, and Kaufmann Palm Springs Houses

Boutin, Marc Joseph. *Richard Neutra: The Idealization of Technology in America.* Calgary: University of Calgary, 2001.

Farrel, Tery. "Building Favorites." *Architects Journal (Steel Design)* 210, no. 22 (December 1999): 54–55.

Hay, David. "A Modernist Masterpeice in the Desert is Reborn." *Architectural Record* (September 1999): 92–98.

Koeper, Frederick. *The Richard and Dion Neutra VDL Research House I and II.* Pomona: California State University, 1985.

Lamprecht, Barbara. *Richard Neutra: Complete Works.* New York: Taschen, 2000.

Lavin, Sylvia. *Form Follows Libido.* Cambridge, MA: MIT Press, 2004.

McCoy, Esther. *Richard Neutra.* New York: George Braziller, Inc., 1960.

Ouroussoff, Nicolai. "Reflecting on Neutra's Genius." *Los Angeles Times,* January 30, 1997, Sect. F.

Sack, Manfred. *Richard Neutra.* Zurich: Artemis, 1994.

Steele, James. *Los Angeles Architecture: The Contemporary Condition*. London: Phaidon Press, 1993.

Webb, Michael. "Pal Springs Eternal: Marmol and Radziner Reclaim Richard Neutra's Kaufmann House from Decay and Encroaching Civilization." *Interiors* (October 1999): 70–75.

The Pugh Scarpa Residence, Venice, California

Beltramini, Guido, and Italo Zannier, eds. *Carlos Scarpa: Architecture and Design*. New York: Rizzoli International Publications, 2006.

Los, Sergio. *Carlos Scarpa*. Köln: Taschen, 2002.

McLeod, Virginia. *Detail in Contemporary Residential Archtecture*. London: Laurence King Publisher, 2007.

Williams, Daniel E. *Sustainable Design: Ecology, Architecture and Planning*. Hoboken, NJ: Wiley, 2007.

A. Quincy Jones

Buckner, Cory. *A. Quincy Jones*. London: Phaidon, 2002.

Jones, Quincy. *Q: The Autobiography of Quincy Jones*. New York: Doubleday, 2001.

Frank Gehry: The Schnabel Residence

Co, Francesco Dal, and Kurt W. Forster. *Frank O. Gehry: The Complete Works*. New York: The Monacelli Press, Inc., 1998.

Glancey, Jonathan. *The Story of Architecture*. London & New York: Dorling Kindersle, 2000.

Mathewson, Casey C. M. *Frank O. Gehry: Selected Works: 1969 to Today*. Buffalo, NY: Firefly Books, 2007.

Steele, James. *Frank Gehry: Schnabel House*. London: Phaidon Press Limited, 1999.

Oscar Niemeyer: The Canoas and Strick Houses

Hess, Alan. *Oscar Niemeyer Houses*. New York: Rizzoli International Publications, Inc., 2006.

Philippou, Styliane. *Oscar Niemeyer: Curves of Irreverence*. New Haven: Yale University Press, 2008.

Salvaing, Matthieu. *Oscar Niemeyer*. Paris: Assouline, 2001.

Underwood, David. *Oscar Niemeyer and the Architecture of Brazil*. New York: Rizzoli International Publications, Inc., 1994.

Chapter 2: Africa

Hassan Fathy

Richards, J. M. *Hassan Fathy*. London: Concept Media Pte. Ltd., 1985.

Steele, James. *Hassan Fathy*. New York: St. Martin's Press, 1988.

Charles Boccara: The Abtan House, Marrakesh

Canizaro, Vincent B., ed. *Architectural Regionalism: Collected Writings on Place, Identity, Modernity and Tradition*. New York: Princeton Architectural Press, 2007.

Chapter 3: Asia and Australia

Glenn Murcutt: The Magney House

Beck, Haig, and Jackie Cooper. *Glenn Murcutt*. Victoria, Australia: The Images Publishing Group, Inc., 2002.

Bibliography

Davies, Colin. *Key Houses of the Twentieth Century*. New York: W. W. Norton & Company, Inc., 2006.

Fromonot, Francoise. *Glenn Murcutt Buildings and Projects 1962–2007*. London: Thames and Hudson Ltd., 2003.

Jahn, Graham. *Contemporary Australian Architecture*. Roseville East, NSW: Craftsman House, 1994.

The Great Wall Commune

Chang, Gary. *Suitcase House*. Hong Kong: MCCM Creations, 2004.

Ruan, Xing. *New China Architecture*. Singapore: Periplus Editions, 2006.

Tadao Ando: The Kashino, Nakayama, and 4 X 4 Houses

Frampton, Kenneth. "Tadao Ando and the Cult of Shintai." *Tadao Ando: The Yale Studio and Recent Works*. New York: Rizzolli International Publications, 1989.

Hozumi, Kazuo, and Nishi Kazuo. *What is Japanese Architecture?: A Survey of Traditional Japanese Architecture*. New York: Kodansha America, 1983.

Jodidio, Philip. *Tadao Ando*. New York: Taschen, 1997.

Jodidio, Philip. *Tadao Ando: The Complete Works*. New York: Taschen, 2007.

Matsuba, Kazukiyo. *Ando: Architect*. New York: Kodansha America, 1998.

Tadao Ando: Architecture and Spirit. Barcelona: Editorial Gustavo Gili, SA, 1998.

The Ushida Findlay Partnership: Soft and Hairy House

Gill, Monica, ed. *Ushida Findlay*. Barcelona: Editorial Gustavo Gili, S.A., 1997.

Oswald, Michael J. *Ushida Findlay*. Barcelona: G. Gili, 1998.

"Soft and Hairy House." *Japan Architect* No. 17 (Spring 1995): 198–199.

Ushida Findlay Partnership. "Soft and Hairy House." *Kenchiku Bunka* 49, no. 576 (October 1994): 121–130.

"Ushida Findlay Partnership." *Architectural Design* 65, no. 5–6 (May–June 1995): 68–69.

Wines, James. *Green Architecture*. Köln: Taschen, 2002.

Shigeru Ban: The Picture Window House

Buck, D. N. *Shigeru Ban*. Barcelona, Spain: GG Editorial Gustavo Gili, 1997.

McQuaid, Matilda. *Shigeru Ban*. New York: Phaidon, 2003.

Pollock, Naomi. "Amid rice paddies, Shigeru Ban creates Naked House, a luminous translucent shed with moving rooms." *Architectural Record* 189, no. 4 (2001): 148–153.

Stocchi, Attilio. "Shigeru Ban a Tokio: Naked House." *Arbitare* 412 (2001): 126–133.

Tiry, Corinne. "Naked House, Case Study #10, Kawagoe (Saitama), Japon: Shigero Ban Architects." *Architecture d'Aujourd'hui* 334 (2001): 77–79.

Ken Yeang: Roof Roof House

Powell, Robert. *Rethinking the Skyscraper: The Complete Architecture of Ken Yeang*. New York: Whitney Library of Design, 1999.

Yeang, Ken. *Ecodesign: A Manual for Ecological Design*. London: Wiley-Academy, 2006.

Yeang, Ken. *Eco Skyscrapers*. Mulgrave, Victoria: Images Publishing, 2007.

Jimmy C. S. Lim: The Salinger House

Beal, Gillian. *Tropical Style: Contemporary Dream Houses in Malaysia*. Singapore: Periplus, 2003.

Goad, Philip, et al. *New Directions in Tropical Asian Architecture*. Singapore: Periplus, 2005.

Roaf, Sue, et al. *Ecohouse: A Design Guide*. Burlington, MA: Oxford Architectural Press, 2007.

SCDA: Heeren Street House, Malaka

Powell, Robert. *The New Singapore House*. Singapore: Select Pub., 2001.

Powell, Robert. *SCDA Architects: Selected and Current Works*. Mulgrave, Victoria: Images Publishing Group, 2004.

Chapter 4: Europe and the Western Mediterranean

Adolf Loos: The Villa Scheu, Vienna
The Architecture of Adolf Loos. London: Arts Council of Great Britain, 1985.
Schezen, Roberto. *Adolf Loos, Architecture 1903–1932*. New York: The Monacelli Press, 1996.
Tournikiotis, Panayotis. *Adolf Loos*. New York: Princeton Architectural Press, 2002.

Josef Hoffmann: The Palais Stoclet, Brussels
Eduard, F. Sekler. "Stoclet." *Josef Hoffman: The Architectural Work*. Princeton: Princeton University Press, 1985.
Franco, Borsi, and Alessandra Perizzi. *Josef Hoffman, tempo e Geometria*. Rome: Officing Edizioni, 1982.
Giuliano, Gresieri. *Josef Hoffmann*. Bologna: Nicola Zanichelli, S.P.A., 1981.

Hvittrask, Lindgren, Gesellius, and Saarinen
Wittkopp, Gregory, ed. *Saarinen House and Garden: A Total Work of Art*. New York: Cranbrook Academy of Art Museum, 1995.

Alvar Aalto: Villa Mairea
Gutheim, Frederick. *Alvar Aalto*. New York: George Braziller, Inc., 1960.
Poole, Scott. *The New Finnish Architecture*. New York: Rizzoli International Publications, 1992.
Quantrill, Malcolm. *Finnish Architecture and the Modernist Tradition*. London: E & FM Spon, 1995.
Ray, Nicholas. *Alvar Aalto*. New Haven, CT: Yale University Press, 2005.
Schildt, Goran. *Alvar Aalto: The Decisive Years*. New York: Rizzoli International Publications, 1986.
Schildt, Goran. *Alvar Aalto Masterworks*. New York: Rizzoli International Publications, 1998.
Weston, Richard. *Villa Mairea: Alvar Aalto*. London: Phaidon Press Limited, 1992.

Pierre Chareau: *Maison de Verre*
Frampton, Kenneth. "*Maison de Verre. Perspecta*." *Yale Architectural Journal* 12 (1969): 77–126.
Gopnik, Adam. "The Ghost of the Glass House." *The New Yorker*, May 9, 1994.
Gordon, Alastair. "The End of an Era." *Architectural Digest* (2007): 134–140.
Grillet, T., ed. *Pierre Chareau: Architecte, un art interieur*. Paris: Centre Georges Pompidou, 1993.
Lampugnani, V. *Encyclopedia of Twentieth Century Architecture*. New York: Harry N. Abrams, Inc., 1985.
Ouroussoff, Nicolai. "The Best House in Paris." *The New York Times*, August 26, 2007, 23–25.
Taylor, Brian Brace. *Pierre Chareau*. Koln: Benedikt Taschen Verlag, 1998.

Bibliography

Le Corbusier: The Villa Savoye

Le Corbusier. *Villa Savoye and Other Buildings and Projects, 1929–1930*. New York: Garland, 1982.

Curtis, William J. R. *Le Corbusier: Ideas and Forms*. New York: Rizzoli International Publications, Inc., 1986.

Frampton, Kenneth. *Le Corbusier*. New York: Thames and Hudson, 2001.

Sbiglio, Jacques. *Le Corbusier: La Villa Savoye*. Basel: Birkhauser Publishers, 1999.

Villa Savoye, Poissy, France 1929–1931. Tokyo: A. D. A. EDITA, 1972.

Auguste Perret: Apartment House on Rue Franklin, Paris

Collins, Peter. *Concrete: The Vision of a New Architecture*. London: Faber and Faber, 1959.

Frampton, Kenneth. "Auguste Perret: The Evolution of Classical Rationalism." *Modern Architecture: A Critical History*. London: Thames and Hudson, 2007, 105–108.

Gardner, Amy. "Auguste Perret: Invention in Convention, Convention in Invention." *Journal of Architectural Education* (February 1997).

Gargiani, Roberto. *Auguste Perret*. Milan: Gallimard / Electa, 1994.

Jean Prouvé: *Maison Tropicale*

Chaslin, Francois. "The Great Tinsmith, Jean Prouvé." *Rassegna* (Milan; June 1982).

Mellor, C. J. *Jean Prouvé; Aspects of Innovation*, Thesis, University of Liverpool, 1978.

Motro, Rene. "Robert Le Ricolais: The Father of Spatial Structures." *International Journal of Space Structures* 22, no. 4 (December 2007): 233–238.

Newton, Nigel. "Jean Prouvé, Modern Movement Pioneer." *Building Design* (March 30, 1984).

Nils, Peter. *Prouve*. Köln: Taschen GmbH, 2006.

Verrei, Michael. "Jean Prouvé; Architect Mechanic." *Architectural Review* (July 1983).

Ludwig Mies van der Rohe: Weissenhofsiedlung

Blaser, Werner. *Mies van der Rohe*. Basel: Birkhauser Verlag, 1997.

Cohen, Jean-Louis. *Mies van der Rohe*. London: E & FN Spon., 1996.

Cremonino, Lorenzino, and Marino Moretti. *Casa Tugendhat*. Florence: Alinea Editrice S.R.L., 1997.

Hammer-Tugendhat, Daniela, and Wolf Tegethoff. *Ludwig Mies van der Rohe: The Tugendhat House*. Vienna: Springer Verlag, 2000.

Iovine, Julie V. "The Art of Living: A Visit to Mies' Great, Controversial Tugendhat House in Czechoslovakia." *Connoisseur* (September 1997): 114–119.

Rusell, Frank. *Mies van der Rohe: European Works*. London: Academy Editions, 1986.

Schulze, Franz. *Mies van der Rohe: A Critical Biography*. Chicago and London: The University of Chicago Press, 1985.

Von Vegesack, Alexander, and Matthias Kries, ed. *Mies van der Rohe*. Milan: Skira Editore, 1998.

Gerrit Rietveld and Theo van Doesburg: The Schroeder House

Curtis, William. *Modern Architecture Since 1900*. Phaidon, London, 1982.

Mulder, Bertus. *Rietveld Schroder House*. Princeton Architectural Press, New York, 1999.

Overy, Paul. *The Rietveld Schroder House*. Cambridge: MIT Press, 1988.

Szenassy, Istvan L. *G. Rietveld, Architect*. Amsterdam: Stedelijk Museum, 1972.

John Hedjuk: The Wall House

Frampton, Kenneth. "John Hedjuk and the Cult of Humanism." *Architecture and Urbanism* (December 2001): 102–109.

"John Hedjuk." *Architectural Record* (November 2001): 150–153.

Martin, Marijke. "Hedjuk's Wall House #2 Realized in Groningen." *Architecture and Urbanism.* (February 2001): 65–84.

Shkapich, Kim, ed. *Mask of Medusa: John Hejduk.* New York: Rizzoli International Publications, Inc., 1985.

Casa Malaparte
McDonough, Michael. *Malaparte: A House Like Me.* New York: Clarkson Potla, 1997.

Mario Botta: Riva San Vitale
Clark, Roger H., and Michael Pause. *Precedents in Architecture.* New York: Van Nostrand Reinhold, 1985.

Pizzi, Emilio, et al. *Mario Botta: Architecture 1980–1990.* Barcelona: Editorial Gustavo Gili, S.A., 1991.

Sacchi, Luisa, ed. *Mario Botta, Architectural Poetics.* New York: Universe Publishing, 2000.

Wrede, Stuart. *Mario Botta.* New York: The Museum of Modern Art, 1986.

Antoni Gaudi: The Casa Batlló, Barcelona
Avery, Derek. *Antonio Gaudí.* London: Chaucer Press, 2004.

Bergos, Joan. *Gaudí: The Man and His Works.* Spain: Bulfinch Press, 1999.

Crippa, Maria Antonietta. *Living Gaudí: the Architect's Complete Vision.* New York: Rizzoli International Publications, Inc., 2002.

Domench I Girau, Lluis. "Modernista Architects." *Modernismo Architecture and Design in Catalonia.* New York: Monacelli Press, 2003.

Frampton, Kenneth. *Modern Architecture: A Critical History.* London and New York: Thames and Hudson, 2007, 64–73.

Gill, John. *Essential Gaudi.* Bath, UK: Parragon, 2001.

Güell, Xavier. *Gaudí Guide.* Barcelona: Editorial Gustavo Gili, S.A., 1991.

Nonell, Juan Bassegoda. *Antonio Gaudí, Master Architect.* New York: Abbeville Publishing Group, 2000.

Tapie, Michel. *Gaudí: La Pedrera.* Barcelona: Ediciones Poligrafa, 1971.

Thiebaut, Phillipe. *Gaudí: Visionary Architect.* New York: Harry N. Abrams, Inc. Publishers, 2001.

Van Henbergen, Giss. *Gaudí.* New York: Harpers Collins, 2001.

Zerbst, Rainer. *Antonio Gaudí: The Complete Buildings.* Italy: Taschen GmbH, 2002.

Zerbst, Rainer. *Gaudi.* Köln: Benedikt Taschen Verlag GmbH, 1991.

Zerbst, Rainer. *Gaudí: A Life Devoted to Architecture.* Köln: Taschen, 1988.

Hampstead Garden Suburb
The Hampstead Garden Suburb Trust Gazette. Hampstead U.K. Issue No. 1. December 2005.

Charles Rennie Mackintosh: Hill House
Swinglehurst, Edmund. *Charles Rennie Mackintosh.* San Diego: Thunder Bay Press, 2001.

Macaulay, James. *Hill House: Charles Rennie Mackintosh.* London: Phaidon, 1994.

Edwin L. Lutyens: Deanery Gardens, Sonning, Heathcote
Barker, Michael. *Sir Edwin Lutyens.* London: Shire Publications, 2005.

Brown, Jane. *Gardens of a Golden Afternoon: The Story of a Partnership; Edwin Lutyens and Gertrude Jekyll.* London: Allen Lane, 1982.

Brown, Jane. *Lutyens and the Edwardians.* New York: Viking Press, 1997.

Emry, Colin, and Margaret Richardson, eds. *Lutyens: The Work of English Architect, Sir Edwin Lutyens, 1869–1944.* London: Exhibition Catalogue, The Arts Council, 1981.

Richardson, Margaret. *Sketches by Edwin Lutyens: Monograph #1.* London: Academy Editions, 1994.

Stamp, Gavin. *Lutyens Country Houses.* London: Aurum Press, 2001.

Weaver, Lawrence. *Houses and Gardens by E. L. Lutyens.* Woodbridge, England: Antique Collectors' Club, Ltd., 1987.

Wilhide, Elizabeth. *Sir Edwin Lutyens; Designing in the English Tradition.* London: Pavillion, 2000.

A. W. N. Pugin: Ramsgate

Aldrich, Megan. *Gothic Revival.* London: Phaidon Press Limited, 1994.

Aldrich, Megan, et al. *A. W. N. Pugin: Master of Gothic Revival.* New Haven, CT: Published for the Bard Graduate Center for Studies in the Decorative Arts, New York, by Yale University Press, 1995.

William Morris and Philip Webb: Red House

Burdick, John. *William Morris: Redesigning the World.* New York: Todtri, 1997.

Coleman, Brian D. *Historic Arts and Crafts Homes of Great Britain.* Salt Lake City, UT: Gibbs Smith, 2005.

Hollamby, Edward. *Red House, Philip Webb.* London: Phaidon Press, 1999.

MacCarty, Fiona. *William Morris.* London: Faber and Faber, 1994.

Massey, James, and Shirley Maxwell. *Arts and Crafts.* New York: Abbeville Press, 2000.

Todd, Pamela. *William Morris and the Arts and Crafts Home.* San Francisco: Chronicle Books, 2005.

Waggoner, Diane. *The Beauty of Life: William Morris and the Art of Design.* London: Thames and Hudson, 2003.

The Richard Rogers House, London

Powell, Kenneth. *Richard Rogers: Architecture of the Future.* Basel: Birkhauser, 2005.

Sudjic, Deyan. *New Directions in British Architecture: Norman Foster, Richard Rogers, James Stirling.* New York: Thames and Hudson, Inc., 1986.

Charles F. Annesley Voysey: The Orchard at Charleywood, Hertsfordshire

Hitchmough, Wendy. *CFA Voysey.* London: Phaidon Press Limited, 1995.

Index

Index

About the Author

JAMES STEELE received a Bachelor of Arts degree, as an English Major, from Lafayette College in Easton, Pennsylvania, and both a Bachelor's and Master's Degree in Architecture from the University of Pennsylvania. He practiced architecture in and around the Philadelphia area for twelve years and became registered in Pennsylvania before relocating to Saudi Arabia where he taught for eight years at King Faisal University in Dammam. He then moved to London and served as Senior Editor of *Architectural Design* magazine, while also teaching at the Prince of Wales's Institute for Architecture. Since 1991, he has taught at the University of Southern California, where he has also received a Doctorate in Urban Planning and is now a tenured Professor there. He has written extensively about both traditional and contemporary architecture and has had several books published.